A POLITICAL CHRONOLOGY
OF THE MIDDLE EAST

A POLITICAL CHRONOLOGY OF THE MIDDLE EAST

FIRST EDITION

EUROPA PUBLICATIONS · Taylor & Francis Group ·

First Edition 2001

© **Europa Publications Limited 2001**
11 New Fetter Lane, London EC4P 4EE, United Kingdom
(A member of the Taylor & Francis Group)

ISBN   1-85743-115-4

Editor: David Lea
Assistant Editor: Annamarie Rowe
Contributor: Dr Isabel Miller

Data manipulation and database design: Mark Wilson, Bibliocraft Ltd

Typeset by Bibliocraft Ltd, Dundee
Printed and bound by TJ International Limited, Trecerus Industrial Estate, Padstow, Cornwall

Foreword

This is the third title in a new six-volume series of Political Chronologies of the World. The first volume was A Political Chronology of Europe, the second covered Central, South and East Asia and forthcoming titles will deal with Africa, South-East Asia and Oceania, and the Americas.

Although the book includes greater coverage of more-recent events—particularly in countries with a recent history of political upheaval—it also provides invaluable detail on the early history of each nation. The importance of the Middle East in the first millennium AD and earlier entails a greater number of entries from this period in certain countries than in other volumes in this series. Each chronology begins at least as early as the emergence of an entity resembling the modern nation, and in many cases considerably earlier.

The territorial disputes on the island of Cyprus and in the Israeli Occupied Territories present a difficulty for the Editors of a book such as this. In order to avoid the repetition of much of the Cyprus chapter, inter-community relations on that island are covered only once: the chapter on the 'Turkish Republic of Northern Cyprus' deals chiefly with that entity's internal politics. Regarding Israel and the Palestinian Autonomous Areas, it is intended that these two chapters should complement each other to form a Chronology of the geographical area concerned. It is inevitable that some duplication will occur when the respective political histories are so largely dominated by bilateral relations; however, it is intended that the Palestinian Autonomous Areas chapter should concentrate principally on the development of the Palestinian political entities, with some earlier information, while events relating to Palestinians in other countries will appear in those countries' chapters.

In addition to coverage of purely political events, each title in the series also includes details of the principal economic, cultural and social landmarks in the history of each nation. Examples might include the adoption of new languages, alphabets, calendars or religions.

This series aims to be the first point of reference for concise information on the history of each nation in the world. It is hoped that the volumes in the series will enable readers easily to locate self-contained entries on the period and area in which their interest lies.

August 2001

Contents

Abbreviations

AD	*anno Domini*
Adm.	Admiral
a.m.	*ante meridiem* (before noon)
BC	before Christ
Brig.	Brigadier
c.	*circa*
Cdre	Commodore
CIS	Commonwealth of Independent States
Col	Colonel
Dr	Doctor
EC	European Communities
EEC	European Economic Community
EU	European Union
etc.	et cetera
f.	founded
Gen.	General
HM	His (or Her) Majesty
kg	kilogram(s)
km	kilometre(s)
kW	kilowatt(s)
Lt	Lieutenant
m.	million
Maj.	Major
Mgr	Monsignor
MP	Member of Parliament
NATO	North American Treaty Organization
OIC	Organization of the Islamic Conference
Prof.	Professor
SSR	Soviet Socialist Republic
St	Saint
UN	United Nations
UNHCR	United Nations High Commissioner for Refugees
US	United States
USA	United States of America
USS	United States Ship
USSR	Union of Soviet Socialist Republics

Armenia

c. **850 BC:** Indo-European tribes, Chaldeans, occupied territory to the south of the Caucasus, destroying the ancient kingdom of Urartu (Ararat); these two peoples were the ancestors of the Armenians.

64 BC: The Roman Empire secured its pre-eminence in the region with the final defeat of the Kingdom of Pontus, to which the Armenians had been allied; parts of Armenia eventually became a Roman province.

AD 117: The Emperor Hadrian retracted the borders of the Roman Empire back to the River Euphrates (i.e. still including what was known as Lesser Armenia), despite his predecessor Trajan's conquest of much territory to the east (Greater Armenia).

c. **300:** St Gregory the Illuminator began the conversion of Armenia, which became the first Christian state at a time of renewed struggle for dominance in the region, between the Empires of Rome and Persia.

451: The Fourth Council of Chalcedon condemned Monophysitism, isolating the Armenians from the rest of the Christian Church.

639: The first Arab raids on Armenia marked the beginning of Muslim influence in the area.

1071: The Seljuq Turk victory at the Battle of Manzikert (now Malazgirt, Turkey) confirmed the Eastern Roman ('Byzantine') expulsion from Armenia and its environs and the dominance of the Sultanate of Iconium (Konya) or Rum.

1375: Mamelukes of Egypt conquered the Armenian capital of Sis and ended the country's nominal independence.

1639: After many years of dispute, Armenia was partitioned between the Turkish Ottoman Empire (which secured the larger, western part) and the Persian Empire, by the Treaty of Zuhab.

1828: Persia (now Iran) ceded Eastern (Persian) Armenia to the Russian Empire by the Treaty of Turkmanchai.

1878: Russia gained the province of Kars from the Ottomans by the Congress of Berlin.

1915: The Ottoman massacres and persecution of Armenians, increasing since the 1890s, were at their most severe, rapidly depopulating Anatolian Armenia.

April 1918: Proclamation of a Transcaucasian federation (Armenia, Azerbaijan and Georgia), following the collapse of tsarist rule and the Soviet signing of the Treaty of Brest-Litovsk.

28 May 1918: Turkish menaces caused the collapse of Transcaucasia and the proclamation of an independent Armenia, which was governed by the Armenian Revolutionary Federation (ARF—Dashnaktsutiun); Armenia was forced to cede territory around Kars to the Turks.

10 August 1920: The Treaty of Sèvres, between the Allied Powers and the Ottoman authorities, recognized an independent Armenia, but the Treaty was rejected by the new Turkish leader, Mustafa Kemal (Atatürk).

September 1920: Turkish troops invaded Armenia after the ARF Government intervened in Anatolia, concerned at the savage persecution of ethnic Armenians there.

29 November 1920: Proclamation of the Soviet Republic of Armenia, following the invasion of Bolshevik troops.

1921: A series of treaties led to the establishment of Nagornyi Karabakh (Artsakh) as a mainly ethnic Armenian enclave within, and part of, Azerbaijan; Turkey recognized its borders with Soviet Transcaucasia.

December 1922: Armenia became a member of the Transcaucasian Soviet Federative Socialist Republic (TSFSR), which itself joined the Union of Soviet Socialist Republics (USSR).

December 1936: The new Soviet Constitution dissolved the TSFSR and Armenia became a full Union Republic in its own name.

September 1987: As a result of the policies of *glasnost* (openness) of the new leader of the USSR, Mikhail Gorbachev, Soviet Armenia experienced its first public demonstrations against ecological degradation and corruption in the local Communist Party of Armenia (CPA).

February 1988: The Nagornyi Karabakh Soviet passed a resolution demanding a transfer to Armenian jurisdiction. Armenians, led by a group of Yerevan intellectuals known as the Karabakh Committee, demonstrated in support. The demands led to anti-Armenian violence in Sumgait, Azerbaijan.

December 1988: Northern Armenia, particularly the city of Leninakan (now Gyumri), was devastated by an earthquake.

May 1989: Large-scale demonstrations secured the release of the leaders of the so-called Karabakh Committee, who had been in prison since December 1988.

1 December 1989: The Armenian Supreme Soviet (republican legislature) declared Nagornyi Karabakh to be part of a unified Armenian Republic, following the end of direct rule in the enclave by the all-Union Government (since January) and the restoration of Azerbaijani authority.

January 1990: The all-Union Supreme Soviet declared that Armenia's December declaration was unconstitutional, whereupon the Armenian Supreme Soviet resolved that it had the power to veto central legislation.

May 1990: In the elections to the Armenian Supreme Soviet, the Armenian Pan-National Movement (APNM), the successor to the opposition Karabakh Committee, became the largest single party, gaining some 35% of the votes cast; the APNM leader, Levon Ter-Petrossian, was elected Chairman of the Supreme Soviet (republican Head of State).

23 August 1990: The Armenian SSR declared its sovereignty and changed its name to the Republic of Armenia.

March 1991: Armenia refused to participate in the referendum on the Union, having declined to join negotiations since late 1990.

August 1991: Vazgen Manukian resigned as premier, to be replaced by Khosrov Haroutunian.

21 September 1991: Armenia held a referendum on secession from the USSR; the new Soviet law on secession, involving a five-year transitional period, was expected to govern the process.

23 September 1991: The results of the referendum (94.4% of the electorate participated and, of them, 99.3% voted in favour of secession) prompted the republican Supreme Soviet (Supreme Council) to declare Armenia an independent state, immediately.

16 October 1991: Ter-Petrossian remained Head of State after national elections for the post of President of the Republic.

21 December 1991: Armenia signed the Almaty (Alma-Ata) Declaration, by which it became a member of the Commonwealth of Independent States (CIS), the formation of which, effectively, dissolved the USSR.

February 1992: Armenia was admitted to the Conference on Security and Co-operation in Europe (CSCE or, from December 1994, the Organization on Security and Co-operation in Europe—OSCE).

March 1992: Armenia became a member of the UN.

May 1992: Following months of full-scale conflict, Armenia and Azerbaijan negotiated a short-lived cease-fire, although Armenia claimed to have no control over the Nagornyi Karabakh militia, which had secured the whole enclave and a 'corridor' to Armenia.

August 1992: Supporters of the National Union, a grouping of opposition legislators, held mass rallies in Yerevan, to protest against President Ter-Petrossian's policies on the Nagornyi Karabakh crisis and on economic reform.

December 1992: President Ter-Petrossian declared a national emergency in Armenia.

February 1993: Following the resignation of Khosrov Haroutunian, Hrant Bagratian was appointed as Prime Minister.

30 April 1993: The UN Security Council, under Resolution 822, demanded that all Armenian forces immediately withdraw from Azerbaijani territory and that a cease-fire be observed. Further motions were adopted on 29 July (Resolution 853) and 14 October (Resolution 874).

24 May 1993: The Armenian Government agreed to a CSCE-negotiated peace plan for Nagornyi Karabakh. Azerbaijan also signed the plan, but it was not accepted by the Nagornyi Karabakh leadership until June.

August 1993: Armenia, the Russian Federation and four other member states of the CIS signed a resolution on military co-operation, reinforcing the Five-Year Collective Security Agreement signed in Tashkent, Uzbekistan, in May 1992.

22 November 1993: An Armenian currency, the dram, was introduced, despite previous agreements to participate in a rouble zone.

9–11 May 1994: Following protracted mediation by the CSCE and the Russian Federation, a new cease-fire agreement was signed by the Ministers of Defence of Armenia and Azerbaijan, and representatives of Nagornyi Karabakh. The agreement was formalized on 27 July.

July 1994: Up to 50,000 people attended a series of anti-Government protests organized by opposition parties.

October 1994: Armenia joined the North Atlantic Treaty Organization (NATO)'s Partnership for Peace programme.

17 December 1994: The former mayor of Yerevan, Ambartsum Galstian, was assassinated, leading to the introduction of anti-terrorist measures, including the suspension, on 29 December, of the opposition ARF, which was accused of engaging in terrorism.

19 June 1995: The Medzamor nuclear power-station, closed since 1989, following the earthquake, was reopened, owing to severe energy shortages.

5 July 1995: In legislative elections the Republican (Hanrapetutiun) bloc, a coalition led by the APNM, won 119 of the 190 seats in the legislature. At the same time, a referendum on the Armenian Constitution was held: some 68% of those voting approved amendments to the Constitution, which gave wider executive power to the President and reduced the number of seats in the National Assembly to 131, effective from the next general election.

24 July 1995: Hrant Bagratian was confirmed as premier by the new parliament.

1 March 1996: The parliaments of Armenia and Nagornyi Karabakh signed a co-operation agreement.

20 March 1996: The National Assembly approved a two-year privatization programme, aimed at improving the economic situation.

22 April 1996: Armenia, Azerbaijan and Georgia signed an agreement on co-operation and partnership with the European Union (EU).

22 September 1996: Presidential elections were held, with Ter-Petrossian, gaining 51.8% of the votes cast; there were protests in Yerevan over alleged electoral irregularities. In November the Constitutional Court rejected opposition appeals that the election results be declared invalid.

4 November 1996: Hrant Bagratian resigned as Prime Minister, allegedly because of opposition to his programme of economic reforms; Armen Sarkissian was appointed in his place on the same day.

6 March 1997: Sarkissian resigned as Prime Minister, to be replaced by Robert Kocharian (hitherto the President of Nagornyi Karabakh) on 20 March.

April 1997: The National Assembly ratified a treaty allowing the Russian Federation to maintain military bases in Armenia for a period of 25 years. In August Armenia and the Russian Federation signed a Treaty of 'Friendship, Co-operation and Mutual Understanding', signifying continuing close relations.

3 February 1998: Ter-Petrossian resigned as President, following disputes within the Government over his support of an OSCE peace settlement of the conflict in Nagornyi Karabakh, which entailed some withdrawal of Armenian forces. The Chairman of the National Assembly, Babken Ararktsian, resigned the following day.

16 March 1998: Robert Kocharian, who, as Prime Minister, had been acting President since Ter-Petrossian's resignation, gained 38.8% of the votes cast during the first ballot of the presidential elections.

30 March 1998: Kocharian was confirmed as President in a second round of voting, with 59.5% of the votes cast. Of the registered electorate, 68.1% voted; despite some electoral irregularities, the results were considered valid.

10 April 1998: Armen Darbinian was appointed Prime Minister. In the same month President Kocharian met with President Aliyev in Moscow (Russia), and agreed to recommence negotiations over the issue of Nagornyi Karabakh.

6 August 1998: Genrikh Khachatrian, the Procurator-General, was shot dead by a fellow prosecutor, following a disagreement.

8 September 1998: Darbinian attended a summit meeting in Baku, Azerbaijan, in which Armenia, together with 11 other nations of Central Asia, the Caucasus and the Black Sea region, signed an agreement to recreate the 'Silk Road' trade route to Europe. This was the first high-level governmental visit between Armenia and Azerbaijan for four years.

January 1999: A new judicial system came into force.

5 February 1999: A controversial new law on electoral procedure, which provided for a 131-member legislature composed of 80 deputies elected by majority vote through single-mandate constituencies, with the remainder chosen under a system of proportional representation on the basis of party lists, was fully adopted. Also in February the Deputy Minister of the Interior and National Security, and Commander of Armenia's internal troops, Maj.-Gen. Artsrun Makarian, was found murdered. The victim's bodyguards were subsequently charged with the murder.

May 1999: Vano Siradeghian, the Chairman of the APNM and a former Minister of the Interior, was arrested for his alleged participation in a number of political murders in the mid-1990s; his trial commenced in September.

30 May 1999: Legislative elections were held; of the registered electorate, 33.59% voted. The Unity bloc (Miasnutiun), an alliance of the Republican Party of Armenia (RPA) and the People's Party of Armenia (PPA), proved highly successful, winning a total of 55 seats in the 131-seat National Assembly.

11 June 1999: Armen Darbinian was replaced as Prime Minister by Vazgen Sarkissian, the unofficial leader of the RPA and, hitherto, the Minister of Defence. At the first session of the new National Assembly, Karen Demirchian, a former communist leader but now head of the PPA, was elected Chairman.

29 June 1999: Karekin II, the Catholicos of all Armenians, elected in 1995, died. Archbishop Garegin Narsissian was inaugurated as Garegin II on 4 November.

27 October 1999: Five gunmen, led by a radical nationalist, Nairi Unanian, besieged the National Assembly, in protest at the 'corrupt political élite'. Eight people were killed during the attack, including Prime Minister Sarkissian and Karen Demirchian. Some 50 hostages were held for several hours until their release was negotiated by President Robert Kocharian; the President then assumed control of the Government until a new Prime Minister could be assigned. The assailants were subsequently charged with terrorist offences and murder.

2 November 1999: The National Assembly held an extraordinary sitting at which Armen Khachatrian, a member of the PPA, was elected Chairman of the National Assembly. On the following day, President Kocharian appointed Aram Sarkissian, the younger brother of the murdered premier, as the new Prime Minister.

25 April 2000: The majority Unity bloc initiated impeachment proceedings against President Kocharian, prompted by his decision not to allow the Military-Prosecutor General, Gagik Jahangirian, to testify in a parliamentary hearing concerning the shootings of October 1999. Three days later, however, a majority in the National Assembly voted to cancel the proceedings, on the grounds that the President's actions had not contravened the Constitution.

2 May 2000: President Kocharian relieved Aram Sarkissian of the post of Prime Minister and Lt-Gen. Varshak Haroutunian of the post of Minister of Defence. Andranik Markarian was appointed Prime Minister on 12 May and a cabinet reshuffle took place eight days later.

4 May 2000: A number of right-wing parties, including the Armenian National Democratic Party (21st Century), Azatutyun (Freedom) and the Liberal Democratic Party, signed a declaration to form a Union of Right Forces; on 12 May the Union organized an opposition rally, attended by some 2500 people. A Union of Social Democratic Forces was established in the same month, including the Hunchakian Social Democratic Party.

28 June 2000: The Parliamentary Assembly of the Council of Europe (PACE) voted to admit both Armenia and Azerbaijan to the Council of Europe.

25 September 2000: President Kocharian visited Russia to discuss security issues with President Vladimir Putin.

30 October 2000: Several thousand people attended a rally in Yerevan organized by the 21st Century Party, to demand the resignation of President Kocharian.

15 February 2001: The trial began of 13 men accused of involvement in the assassination of the former Prime Minister, Sarkissian, and seven others in the National Assembly in October 1999.

27 February 2001: The Chairman of the OSCE visited to discuss with the Government a solution to the Nagornyi Karabakh issue.

5 March 2001: The Presidents of Armenia and Azerbaijan met in France to discuss the issue of Nagornyi Karabakh; both Presidents reported that the discussions had been tense.

27 March 2001: The Anrapetutun (Republic) Party was formed by members of the Union of Volunteers, which had been set up in 1993 by the former defence minister, Vazgen Sarkisyan, the former Mayor of Yerevan, Albert Bazeyan, and other former government officials.

3–6 April 2001: Further discussions on the subject of Nagornyi Karabakh, attended by the Presidents of Armenia and Azerbaijan, were held in Florida, USA. The discussions were mediated by the delegates of the OSCE Minsk Group from France, Russia and the USA.

28 April 2001: The Government signed a protocol on military co-operation with Turkey.

4 May 2001: Armenia was one of 14 new member countries elected to the UN Human Rights Commission by the UN Economic and Social Council.

18 May 2001: At a meeting of the CIS defence ministers, the Azerbaijani Minister of Defence, Lt-Gen. Safar Abiyev, demanded the unconditional withdrawal of Armenian forces from his country's territories and demanded that Armenia be suspended from the CIS Collective Security Treaty.

25 May 2001: At a meeting of the CIS Collective Security Treaty countries, President Kocharian agreed to the formation of a Rapid Reaction Force by Russia, Kyrgyzstan, Kazakhstan and Tajikistan to combat terrorism in the region.

6 June 2001: President Kocharian travelled to Brussels, Belgium, for talks with the President of the European Commission, Romano Prodi, and the Secretary-General of NATO, George Robertson, regarding a solution to the Nagornyi Karabakh dispute. Kocharian expressed his support for proposals to create an independent state of Karabakh.

22 June 2001: Azerbaijan alleged that Armenian troops had opened fire on its positions in Babek Raion and terrorized Azerbaijani villages near Nakhichevan; Armenia denied the accusations.

9 July 2001: Senior government officials reached an agreement with their Turkish counterparts providing for the establishment of a Reconciliation Commission to improve relations between the two countries.

10 July 2001: The trial of 27 people charged with causing damage to public property and resisting arrest during anti-government demonstrations the previous November was concluded; 18 of the defendants were sentenced to between four and six years' imprisonment and a further nine were put on probation for nine years.

Azerbaijan

625 BC–585 BC: The Medes, under their ruler Cyaxares, with his capital at Ecbatana (now Hamadan, Iran), became a major power in the territories west of the River Tigris.

550 BC: Cyrus II ('the Great') of Persia (Iran) conquered the kingdom of Media (Mada) and united the Medes and the Persians.

323 BC: After the death of Alexander III ('the Great') of Macedon, who had conquered the Persian Empire, the satrap Atropates established an independent state in northern Media.

AD 637: The Persian Empire of the Sassanids (Sassanians), which had ruled Atropatene Media (from which is derived the name of Azerbaijan) since the third century ad, was conquered by the Arabs, under the Caliph 'Umar (Omar); the islamicization of the area began.

11th century: The assimilation of Turkic settlers by the previous population was to produce the Azeri people, distinct from the Persic people of modern Iran.

1502: The Safavids, an Azeri dynasty, assumed control of the Persian Empire.

1728: After two centuries of rivalry between the Ottoman and Persian Empires, the Treaty of Constantinople affirmed Ottoman control; continued disputes and the decline of the two powers enabled the rise of increasingly independent khanates in Azerbaijan.

1828: By the Treaty of Turkmanchai, following years of increasing Russian influence, Persia conceded the partition of Azerbaijan; territory to the north of the River Araks (Araxes) became part of the Russian Empire.

c. **1900:** The province of Azerbaijan was a major producer of petroleum, attracting increasing Slav immigration.

1911: The 'Equality' (Musavat) Muslim Democratic Party was founded; it was a left-wing, nationalist movement, similar to the 'Young Turks' of the Ottoman Empire.

1917: The Russian Revolution impelled Musavat and the Bolsheviks to assume control in Baku, although Musavat withdrew from this administration in the following month and established the Transcaucasian Commissariat.

April 1918: A Bolshevik and left-Menshevik soviet (council) was established in Baku; a Democratic Federal Republic of Transcaucasia (Azerbaijan with Armenia and Georgia) was proclaimed, following the Soviet signing of the Treaty of Brest-Litovsk.

28 May 1918: The collapse of Transcaucasia forced Azerbaijan to establish its own government. Subsequently, Musavat began negotiations with the Turks; the Red Army was prevented from attempting to occupy Baku by a British military presence.

September 1918: The British left Baku, leaving anti-Bolshevik forces in charge, but were implicated in the execution of the Bolshevik leaders involved in the previous governments; this was accompanied by a massacre of Armenians.

November 1918: The British reoccupied Baku, but did not favour an independent Musavat regime's close links with Turkey (an ally of the Central Powers in the First World War); the United Kingdom did recognize a coalition Government in the following month.

August 1919: British forces left Baku, withdrawing to Persia.

28 April 1920: Following the occupation of Baku by the Red Army, on the previous day, a Soviet Republic of Azerbaijan was proclaimed.

March 1921: In a friendship treaty, the Turks and Soviet Russia agreed to guarantee that the enclave of Nakhichevan should fall under the jurisdiction of Azerbaijan.

June 1921: The arbitrating Soviet Bureau of Transcaucasian Affairs (Kavburo) voted to recommend the union of Nagornyi Karabakh (a predominantly ethnic Armenian enclave within Azerbaijan) with the Soviet Republic of Armenia, but the Soviet leader, Stalin (Iosif V. Dzhugashvili), enforced the reversal of this decision; in 1923 Nagornyi Karabakh was granted special status within Azerbaijan, as an autonomous oblast (region).

October 1921: The Treaty of Kars agreed the borders of the Soviet Republics of Azerbaijan, Armenia and Georgia with Turkey, and the status of Nagornyi Karabakh and Nakhichevan as territories of Azerbaijan.

December 1922: The Soviet Socialist Republic (SSR) of Azerbaijan became a member of the Transcaucasian Soviet Federative Socialist Republic (TSFSR), which itself became a constituent member of the Union of Soviet Socialist Republics (USSR).

December 1936: The TSFSR was dissolved and the Azerbaijan SSR became a full Union Republic.

1937–38: Purges of the local Communists included Azerbaijan's leader, Sultan Mejit Efendiyev.

1946: Following a protest to the UN by Iran, Allied pressure forced the USSR to end its attempts to integrate Iranian Azerbaijan with Soviet Azerbaijan.

1969: Heydar Aliyev became First Secretary of the Communist Party of Azerbaijan (CPA) and the republic's leader.

October 1987: Aliyev was dismissed, owing to corruption in government and in the Party.

February 1988: Nagornyi Karabakh's attempts to be transferred to Armenian jurisdiction caused increased inter-ethnic tension, culminating in anti-Armenian riots in Sumgait, in which 32 people were killed.

12 January 1989: The local authorities in Nagornyi Karabakh were suspended and the oblast was placed under the administration of a Special Administrative Committee (SAC), responsible to the all-Union Council of Ministers.

September 1989: A general strike secured the official recognition of the nationalist opposition movement, the Popular Front of Azerbaijan (PFA), established earlier in the year.

23 September 1989: Under increasing popular pressure, the Supreme Soviet, the legislature, of Azerbaijan effectively declared the republic's sovereignty and imposed an economic blockade on Armenia (Soviet troops maintained the Baku-Yerevan rail link).

November 1989: The SAC for Nagornyi Karabakh was replaced by a republican Organizing Committee, dominated by ethnic Azerbaijanis.

1 December 1989: The Armenian Supreme Soviet declared Nagornyi Karabakh to be part of a 'unified Armenian republic', a claim that was termed unconstitutional by the all-Union Supreme Soviet the following month.

January 1990: The PFA were prominent in attacks on government and Party buildings, on Armenians and on the border posts with Iranian Azerbaijan; PFA demonstrators also attempted to declare the secession of Nakhichevan from the USSR; Soviet troops evacuated non-Azeris from Baku and enforced a state of emergency, amid some violence. On 20 January Abdul Vezirov was replaced by Ayaz Niyaz ogly Mutalibov as First Secretary of the CPA.

18 May 1990: Mutalibov was appointed Chairman of the Supreme Soviet (republican Head of State).

September 1990: In the elections to the Azerbaijan Supreme Soviet (postponed from February), the CPA, now resolved on the Nagornyi Karabakh issue, won some 80% of the seats; the opposition PFA, which had campaigned with other groups as the Democratic Alliance, alleged irregularities in the conduct of the elections and criticized the state of emergency.

5 February 1991: The Supreme Soviet convened, with the opposition deputies grouped as the Democratic Bloc of Azerbaijan.

March 1991: Azerbaijan participated in the Soviet referendum on the renewal of the Union; official results were that 93.3% of those who had voted (75.1% of the electorate) favoured remaining in the USSR, although in Nakhichevan only 20% supported this; the opposition claimed that only some 20% of the electorate had voted.

30 August 1991: Following the failure of a coup attempt in the Soviet capital, Moscow (Russia), and large anti-Government demonstrations, the Supreme Soviet of Azerbaijan voted in favour of claiming independence.

2 September 1991: Nagornyi Karabakh declared itself a republic.

8 September 1991: Mutalibov won 84% of the votes cast at elections to an executive presidency, which were boycotted by the opposition.

18 October 1991: The Supreme Soviet enacted legislation effecting the declaration of independence of 30 August. Later that month the PFA persuaded the Government and the Supreme Soviet to delegate some legislative powers to a smaller body, the Milli Majlis (National Assembly).

10 December 1991: In a referendum, residents of Nagornyi Karabakh voted overwhelmingly for independence; the Azerbaijani authorities considered the poll irregular, and the Karabakh Armenians gained no international recognition.

21 December 1991: President Mutalibov signed the Almaty (Alma-Ata) Declaration, by which Azerbaijan became a founding member of the Commonwealth of Independent States (CIS).

6 January 1992: The new 'parliament' of Nagornyi Karabakh, elected on 28 December 1991, proclaimed the region's independence. In the same month President Mutalibov declared Nagornyi Karabakh to be under direct presidential rule.

February 1992: Azerbaijan was admitted to the Conference on Security and Co-operation in Europe (CSCE, from December 1994 the Organization for Security and Co-operation in Europe—OSCE) and signed, with eight other countries, the Black Sea Co-operation Accord.

March 1992: President Mutalibov resigned, owing to military reversals in Nagornyi Karabakh. (He was replaced on an interim basis by Yagub Mamedov.) In the same month CIS troops were withdrawn from the area as Armenian forces began to achieve some success against Azerbaijan. Azerbaijan became a member of the UN.

May 1992: By the time Armenia and Azerbaijan negotiated a short-lived cease-fire, the Nagornyi Karabakh militia had secured control over the whole enclave and a 'corridor' along the Lachin valley to Armenia. The Supreme Soviet voted to reinstate Mutalibov as President, but he was deposed after one day in office; this effective coup by the PFA was reinforced by the suspension of the Supreme Soviet and the transfer of its powers to the Milli Majlis.

7 June 1992: Abulfaz Elchibey (*né* Aliyev), leader of the PFA, was elected President of Azerbaijan by direct vote. Azerbaijan launched a counter-offensive in Nagornyi Karabakh.

August 1992: The Nagornyi Karabakh legislature declared a state of martial law; a State Defence Committee replaced the enclave's government.

October 1992: Azerbaijan and the Russian Federation signed a Treaty of Friendship, Co-operation and Mutual Security. In the same month the Milli Majlis voted overwhelmingly to withdraw Azerbaijan from the CIS.

February 1993: Col Surat Husseinov, who had successfully commanded Azerbaijani forces in the conflict over Nagornyi Karabakh, withdrew to Gyanja, prompting allegations by President Elchibey that he was planning a military coup against the Government. Husseinov was subsequently dismissed from his posts and expelled from the PFA.

April 1993: President Elchibey declared a three-month state of emergency. Azerbaijan withdrew from CSCE-sponsored negotiations, in protest at a large-scale Armenian offensive.

30 April 1993: The UN Security Council adopted Resolution 822, demanding an immediate cease-fire and the withdrawal of all Armenian units from Azerbaijani territory.

May 1993: Azerbaijan approved a peace plan formulated by the Russian Federation, Turkey and the USA, and negotiated by the CSCE; it was not accepted by the Nagornyi Karabakh leadership until June.

4 June 1993: President Elchibey ordered a punitive attack in Gyanja by the Azerbaijani army on the 709th Brigade, a unit still loyal to their rebel leader, Col Surat Husseinov. Over 60 people were killed. Husseinov assumed control of the town.

15 June 1993: Heydar Aliyev, the former Communist Party leader, was elected Chairman of the Milli Majlis.

17–18 June 1993: President Elchibey fled to Nakhichevan.

25 June 1993: The Milli Majlis voted to transfer, on an acting basis, the majority of President Elchibey's powers to Aliyev and to impeach Elchibey.

28 June 1993: Husseinov's troops, having marched to Baku, pledged allegiance to acting President Aliyev.

1 July 1993: Aliyev nominated Husseinov Prime Minister and Supreme Commander.

29 July 1993: The UN Security Council adopted Resolution 853, demanding the immediate withdrawal of the Nagornyi Karabakh militia from Agdam, which had been seized to the detriment of the CSCE peace proposals.

23 August 1993: Alikram Gumbatov, leader of the so-called 'Talysh-Mugan Autonomous Republic' (proclaimed during the Husseinov revolt of June), based in Lenkoran, fled the city after his headquarters were attacked by PFA supporters.

1 September 1993: The Milli Majlis endorsed the results of a referendum, in which 97.5% of participants voted in favour of President Elchibey's impeachment.

20 September 1993: A resolution for Azerbaijan to rejoin the CIS was adopted by the Milli Majlis; the country was officially admitted on 24 September and parliament ratified the Almaty Declaration, the Commonwealth Charter and the Tashkent Agreement on Collective Security on 29 September, despite PFA protests.

3 October 1993: Heydar Aliyev was elected President of Azerbaijan, against two other candidates, with 98.8% of the votes cast.

14 October 1993: Resolution 874, adopted by the UN Security Council, endorsed the CSCE's schedule for implementing Resolutions 822 and 853.

27 October 1993: In reaction to CSCE cease-fire proposals, Armenia and Nagornyi Karabakh agreed to the schedule for the withdrawal of ethnic Armenian militia from Azerbaijani territory, but Azerbaijan rejected it as the CSCE plan did not envisage Armenian withdrawal from the Lachin corridor.

November 1993: The 'Minsk Group', established by the CSCE, organized a peace conference in Minsk, Belarus, on the issues concerning Nagornyi Karabakh.

May 1994: Azerbaijan joined the North Atlantic Treaty Organization (NATO's) Partnership for Peace programme of military co-operation.

9–11 May 1994: Following protracted mediation by the CSCE and the Russian Federation, a new cease-fire agreement was finally signed by the Ministers of Defence of Azerbaijan and Armenia and representatives of Nagornyi Karabakh. The agreement was formalized on 27 July.

20 September 1994: Azerbaijan's state petroleum company and an international consortium signed an agreement establishing the Azerbaijan International Operating Company (AIOC), which was to develop Azerbaijani petroleum reserves.

29 September 1994: The Deputy Chairman of the Milli Majlis and the presidential security chief were assassinated, allegedly by members of special militia forces attached to the Ministry of Internal Affairs (known as OPON).

2 October 1994: In protest at the arrests of his men, the OPON military chief, Rovshan Javadov, attacked the offices of the Procurator-General, prompting President Aliyev to declare a state of emergency in Baku and Gyanja.

5 October 1994: Husseinov was dismissed as Prime Minister following allegations of a coup attempt, in Gyanja, reportedly led by a relative; he was replaced as premier by the First Deputy Prime Minister, Fuad Kuliyev.

13–14 March 1995: A decree disbanding the special militia forces prompted violent OPON protests; in the ensuing clashes with government troops on 17 March, at least 70 people, including Javadov, were killed. The PFA was accused of involvement in the insurrection and its activities temporarily suspended.

12 November 1995: Elections to the new 125-member Milli Majlis were held. Only eight of the country's official parties were permitted to participate and, of these, only two, the PFA and the National Independence Party (NIP), were opposition parties. At the same time a reported 91.9% of the electorate approved a new state Constitution in a nation-wide referendum; the country became the Azerbaijan Republic. Further rounds of voting for seats to the Milli Majlis were held on 26 November, 4 February 1996 and 18 February—the overwhelming majority of deputies elected were supporters of President Aliyev and his New Azerbaijan Party (NAP).

14 April 1996: The former defence minister, Rahim Gaziyev, and former President Mutalibov were arrested in Moscow, accused of plotting to overthrow the Azerbaijani Government (Mutalibov escaped extradition owing to ill health).

22 April 1996: Azerbaijan, Armenia and Georgia signed a co-operation agreement with the European Union.

19 July 1996: Following accusations of economic mismanagement by President Aliyev, Fuad Kuliyev resigned as premier. Three other ministers were dismissed on charges of corruption. The First Deputy Prime Minister, Artur Rasizade, was appointed to head the Government; his appointment was confirmed in November.

September 1996: The Chairman of the Milli Majlis, Rasul Kuliyev, resigned. He was replaced by Murtuz Aleskerov. In April 1998 Kuliyev was charged with alleged abuses of power while in office.

24 November 1996: A presidential election in Nagornyi Karabakh was won by Robert Kocharian, already the *de facto* republican Head of State, with some 86% of the votes cast; the election was condemned by Azerbaijan and the OSCE as a hindrance to the peace process.

January 1997: Many opponents of Aliyev's regime were arrested, following allegations of foiled coup attempts, usually involving the former President, Mutalibov, and the former premier, Husseinov (the latter was extradited from Russia, where he had fled following his dismissal as premier, in March).

20 March 1997: Kocharian resigned the presidency of Nagornyi Karabakh upon his appointment as Prime Minister of Armenia; he was succeeded, on an acting basis, by Artur Tovmassian, the speaker of the legislature.

11 April 1997: Aliyev established a Security Council, as stipulated in the 1995 Constitution. Azerbaijan accused Russia of violating the Conventional Forces in Europe (CFE) Treaty, by providing weapons to Armenia.

1 September 1997: Arkadii Gukassian gained some 90% of the votes cast in the Nagornyi Karabakh presidential election (he was inaugurated on 8 September).

16 October 1997: President Aliyev and President Ter-Petrossian of Armenia agreed to an OSCE proposal for a gradual, or staged, resolution of the conflict in Nagornyi Karabakh. President Ter-Petrossian resigned in February 1998 following criticism of his moderate approach to the crisis.

12 November 1997: Despite security concerns, the AIOC officially began the first export of petroleum from the Caspian Sea, along the pipeline running from Baku to Novorossiisk, Russia, via Chechnya (the Chechen Republic of Ichkeriya). (As a result of conflict in Chechnya from late 1999, a new section of the pipeline, avoiding the republic, was completed in March 2000.).

February 1998: Hassan Hassanov, the foreign minister, was dismissed, following allegations of corruption.

29 April 1998: President Aliyev met the new Armenian President, Kocharian, at the CIS summit in Moscow, where it was agreed to resume negotiations on Nagornyi Karabakh.

6 August 1998: President Aliyev abolished press censorship, one of the conditions for opposition participation in the presidential elections.

15 August 1998: The leaders of the main opposition parties held a rally in Baku, reportedly attended by some 50,000 people, in protest at the perceived undemocratic nature of the presidential contest; major activists and some of the demonstrators were later arrested. In September police used violence to disperse protesters during another rally organized by the opposition parties.

8 September 1998: At meeting held in Baku, Azerbaijan signed an agreement with 11 Asian and European countries, including Armenia, to recreate the 'Silk Road' trade route to Europe.

1 October 1998: The Government passed a draft law increasing the restrictions on the holding of demonstrations.

11 October 1998: President Aliyev was re-elected as head of state with 77.6% of total votes cast; the opposition protested the legitimacy of the elections and international observers noted a number of irregularities. Unrest continued as a result of this and criminal proceedings were instigated, in November, against a number of opposition leaders, accused of making seditious speeches at protest rallies.

18 October 1998: Aliyev was again inaugurated as President of Azerbaijan. The Prime Minister, Rasizade, was confirmed as premier on 23 October.

December 1998: The opposition alliance, the Round Table bloc, announced its dissolution and the intention of its erstwhile constituent parties to co-operate with a new opposition coalition, the Movement for Democratic Elections and Electoral Reform, founded on 9 November and composed of 23 opposition groups. Also in December, the Milli Majlis approved a revised Constitution for Nakhichevan, endorsed by the Nakhichevan legislature, which defined the enclave as 'an autonomous state' within Azerbaijan.

10 February 1999: A criminal case against the former President, Abulfaz Elchibey, was closed at the instigation of President Heydar Aliyev; Elchibey had been accused of 'insulting the honour and dignity' of the President by claiming in November 1998 that Aliyev had participated in the creation of the Kurdistan Workers Party (PKK) in Turkey.

16 February 1999: The Supreme Court sentenced Husseinov, the former Prime Minister, to life imprisonment, for his involvement in the October 1994 coup attempt. Also in February, it was reported that Azerbaijan was not to renew its membership of the CIS Collective Security Agreement for a second five-year period (subsequently signed in April by six countries), owing to the continued occupation of Nagornyi Karabakh by Armenian troops, and in protest at Russia's continuing supply of armaments to Armenia.

17 April 1999: A new pipeline, transporting crude petroleum from Baku to Supsa, Georgia, was inaugurated. The same day, a newly founded opposition grouping, the Democratic bloc, comprising the PFA and the Civic Solidarity Party, began a boycott of the Milli Majlis, on the grounds that the Government had violated the rights of opposition deputies by refusing to discuss draft laws on municipal elections; the boycott ended in late June, following negotiations.

30 June 1999: Anushavan Danielian was appointed Prime Minister of Nagornyi Karabakh by President Arkadii Gukassian. The previous Government had been dismissed by Gukassian on 24 June, as a result of the serious economic situation in the region.

July 1999: After having been awarded observer status at NATO the previous month, Azerbaijan sent 30 troops to the Serbian province of Kosovo and Metohija, Yugoslavia, as part of a NATO peace-keeping force.

18 November 1999: At a summit meeting of the OSCE, held in İstanbul, Turkey, an agreement was signed by the Presidents of Azerbaijan, Georgia, Kazakhstan, Turkey and Turkmenistan, on the construction of a pipeline to transport petroleum from Baku, via Tbilisi, Georgia, to the Turkish port of Ceyhan.

22 March 2000: Arkadii Gukassian, the President of Nagornyi Karabakh, was seriously wounded by gunmen in the territory's capital, Stepanakert. Over 20 people were arrested in connection with the incident, including Nagornyi Karabakh's former Minister of Defence, Samuel Babaian.

28 June 2000: The Parliamentary Assembly of the Council of Europe (PACE) voted to admit both Armenia and Azerbaijan to the Council of Europe.

9 October 2000: Kazakhstan signed a co-operation agreement with Russia on resolving the legal status of the Caspian Sea; the two governments urged Azerbaijan, Iran and Turkmenistan to hold a 'summit' meeting to discuss the issue.

5 November 2000: Parliamentary elections were scheduled to be held.

15 December 2000: The Chairman of the Liberal Democrat Party, Zakir Mammadov, was killed when the party's building in Baku collapsed.

29 December 2000: President Aliyev pardoned 54 criminals, including 30 who had been found guilty of participating in coup attempts throughout the previous decade.

6 January 2001: Elections were held in 11 districts where the results of the November polls had been annulled owing to discrepancies.

25 January 2001: Azerbaijan was formally admitted to the Council of Europe.

5 March 2001: The Presidents of Armenia and Azerbaijan met in France to discuss the issue of Nagornyi Karabakh; both Presidents reported that the discussions had been tense.

3–6 April 2001: Further discussions on the subject of Nagornyi Karabakh, attended by the Presidents of Armenia and Azerbaijan, were held in Florida, USA. The discussions were mediated by the delegates of the OSCE Minsk Group from France, Russia and the USA.

5 April 2001: A UN human rights investigator reported that there was evidence to suggest that torture was used on a regular basis on anyone detained by Azerbaijani law enforcement officials.

26–27 April 2001: At a meeting of leaders of the Turkic-speaking countries, the Presidents of Azerbaijan, Kazakhstan, Kyrgyzstan, Turkey and Turkmenistan, and the Chairman of Uzbekistan's Oly Majlis (Supreme Assembly) signed an agreement on regional co-operation to combat terrorism and drug trafficking, the revival of the old 'Silk Road' trade route between China and Europe, and protection of the environment.

3 May 2001: The foreign ministers of Azerbaijan and Kyrgyzstan met with President Imamali Rahmonov of Tajikistan to discuss co-operation and regional security.

4 May 2001: Azerbaijan and Kazakhstan signed an agreement on the demarcation of borders in the Caspian Sea.

18 May 2001: At a meeting of the CIS defence ministers, the Azerbaijani Minister of Defence, Lt-Gen. Safar Abiyev, demanded the unconditional withdrawal of Armenian forces from his country's territories and demanded that Armenia be suspended from the CIS Collective Security Treaty.

4 June 2001: The Turkmen Ministry of Foreign Affairs closed its embassy in Baku, ostensibly owing to financial difficulties; the two countries were at the time in dispute over ownership of the Caspian oilfields.

19 June 2001: President Aliyev decreed that from 1 August 2001, the Azerbaijani language would use the Roman alphabet rather than the Cyrillic script.

10 July 2001: A court sentenced 18 men to between four and six years' imprisonment for attending protests against apparent irregularities in the conduct of the legislative election held in November 2000. Among those convicted were four heads of local opposition party branches.

23 July 2001: An Iranian navy ship and military aircraft threatened a research vessel exploring potential crude petroleum fields in the southern Caspian Sea. The Iranian Government claimed that, since the maritime borders had not yet been agreed by all the nations surrounding the Caspian Sea, no country had the right to conduct petroleum-exploration operations.

Bahrain

c. **190 AD:** Arab tribes migrated to Bahrain from the Hedjaz and Yemen.

early 4th century: Shapur II of Persia invaded Bahrain and it became a part of the Persian province of Fars.

622: Al-Ala was sent by the Prophet Muhammad to Mundhir Sheikh, of the Abd al-Qais, a lieutenant of the Sassanid Shah of Persia, to convert him and his people to Islam.

639: Al-Ala attempted to conquer Fars.

676: A Nestorian Christian synod was held at Darin.

680s: The Kharijites, an extremist Shi'a sect, established themselves in Bahrain and extended their influence to Oman and elsewhere in Arabia.

894–95: The Abbasid governor of Bahrain led an expedition against the Ibadites in Oman.

930: The Karmatians, a radical Shi'ite sect allied to the Isma'ilis, removed the Black Stone (a relic significant in Islamic pilgrimage) from the Ka'aba in Mecca (the Islamic holy city, now in Saudi Arabia) and took it to Bahrain where it was kept for some 20 years until the Fatimids persuaded them to return it.

1077–78: The Karmatians were overthrown by a new dynasty, the Ujunids of Abd al-Qais, with help from the Seljuks in Iraq.

1235: The Atabeg of Fars, the Salghurid Abu Bakr ibn Sa'id, occupied Bahrain.

1253: Bahrain regained its independence and was ruled by the Usfurids.

1330: Bahrain was annexed by Tahamtam II of Hormuz.

mid-15th century: Ajwad ibn Zamil of the Jabrid dynasty annexed Bahrain and asserted the Maliki Sunni School of Islam over the mainly Shi'a population.

1521: Bahrain was colonized by the Portuguese.

1528: The Portuguese took advantage of a rebellion against the rule of the King of Hormuz to mount an expedition to Bahrain; however, the invasion was unsuccessful.

1556: An Ottoman commander, Mustafa Pasha, acting independently of the Ottoman leadership, attacked Bahrain; his troops were repelled by the Portuguese.

1602: Bahrain was conquered by Shah Abbas I ('the Great') of Persia, and the Portuguese expelled; the archipelago was subsequently governed by the Matarish, an Omani family based in Bushehr (now in Iran).

1717: Sultan ibn Saif of Oman briefly took control of Bahrain.

1736: Forces sent by Nadir Shah, the ruler of Persia, occupied Bahrain.

1782: The Governor of Bahrain and Bushehr, Sheikh Nasr al-Maskur, attacked ships sailing to and from al-Zubara.

1783: The Persians were expelled by the Utub tribe whose leading family, the al-Khalifa (hitherto based in Zubarah), became the Sheikhs of Bahrain.

1801: The Ibadite ruler of Muscat attacked Bahrain in an attempt to challenge the sheikhdom's domination of the transit trade in the Persian (Arabian) Gulf; The al-Sa'ud of Najd, leaders of the Muslim Wahhabi sect, assisted Bahrain against the Ibadite invasion.

1810–11: Abdallah bin Ufaysan, a Wahhabi, governed Qatif, Qatar and Bahrain.

1811: After a successful expedition by Sultan Sa'id of Muscat, the Wahhabis withdrew and the al-Khalifa returned to power.

1820: The al-Khalifa signed the first treaty with the British, in which they agreed to suppress piracy in the Persian (Arabian) Gulf.

1835: Bahrain and the British Government signed the First Maritime Truce.

1840–1849: Two sheikhs, Abd Allah and Muhammad disputed the governorship of the sheikdom; Muhammad's campaign was supported by Qatar.

1843: Sheikh Muhammad established his rule at Muharrak.

1847: The Government signed an international treaty, in which it agreed to suppress the slave trade.

1851: The Government concluded a peace treaty with the Sa'udi Amir, Faisal bin Turki, by which the Sheikh agreed to pay an annual tax to ensure the safety of Bahrain from attack by tribesmen under Sa'udi control.

1854: Muhammad al-Khalifa attempted to remove Wahhabi influence on Bahrain; the Wahhabis responded by attacking the sheikdom. Sheikh Muhammad sought the help of British forces, who subsequently established a degree of control over Bahrain.

31 May 1861: The Sheikh and the British representatives signed a treaty of perpetual maritime truce, by which the Government agreed to abstain from the prosecution of war, piracy and slavery by sea, in return for British support in case of foreign aggression.

1867: Bahrain and Abu Dhabi made a joint expedition against the cities of Doha and Wakrah on the east coast of Qatar.

1869: Sheikh Isa bin Ali al-Khalifa became ruler of Bahrain.

1880: The Sheikh agreed with the British Government not to cede, mortgage or otherwise dispose of parts of his territories to any country or entity except the United Kingdom, nor to enter into a relationship with any other government without British consent.

1895: A rival family to the al-Khalifas, the Al bin Ali, attempted to invade Bahrain with the support of Qatar and the local Ottoman governor. However, the British forces intervened, destroying large numbers of the invaders' ships.

July 1913: The British and Ottoman governments signed a convention acknowledging Bahrain's independence, although the islands remained under British administration.

1919: The Bahrain Order-in-Council was instituted; conduct of Bahrain's affairs was subject to control by a British Political Agent, as well as the Sheikh. The Council gave the Agent powers of extra-territorial jurisdiction over British subjects and dependents, foreign nationals entitled to British jurisdiction and Bahrainis.

1919: The first election to the Municipal Council took place.

June 1923: Sheikh Isa bin Ali was forced to abdicate by the British Political Agent; he was succeeded by his son, Sheikh Hamad. Bahrainis refused to acknowledge the abdication, however, and Sheikh Hamad was widely regarded as a deputy for his father. A series of institutional reforms were introduced, including a universal land tax, the reorganization of customs and of the state courts.

26 October 1923: Tribal groups opposed to reform and British control organized a Congress.

1924: A Land Registry Office was opened.

1927: A department of Waqf (charitable and religious endowments), both Sunni and Shi'a, was established.

1931: Petroleum was discovered in Bahrain; production began the following year.

1935–58: Bahrain was appointed the principal British naval base in the Persian Gulf.

1938: There was public disaffection with Government and demands for reform of the judicial system; the unrest was exacerbated by a increase in the price of basic commodities and the decline of the pearling industry (historically of great significance to the Bahraini economy), owing to competition from Japan.

July 1939: The dispute between Bahrain and Qatar over sovereignty of the Hawar islands was settled in favour of Bahrain by the United Kingdom.

1942: Sheikh Sulman bin Hamad al-Khalifa became ruler of Bahrain.

1946: The British Political Residency in the Persian Gulf was moved from Bushehr to Bahrain.

1954: The first locally founded political party was established in Bahrain.

1956: An election to the Education and Health Council took place. Shortly after the elections, there was a strike at the petroleum refinery in protest against the percieved paternalism of the British advisor towards the Sheikh.

1957: Sir Charles Belgrave, the British Advisor to the Sheikh since 1926, retired.

1957: The Government took over legal jurisdiction for many issues from British control.

1958: The Government concluded an agreement with Saudi Arabia delineating the international boundary in the waters between the two countries.

31 May 1962: Port Sulman, a new deep-water port, was opened.

21 February 1966: The United Kingdom announced that the troops from its base at Aden would be relocated to Bahrain upon that base's closure in 1968.

January 1968: The United Kingdom announced its intention to withdraw its military presence in the region by 1971.

March 1968: Bahrain joined Qatar and the Trucial States (now the United Arab Emirates) in the Federation of Arab Emirates.

30 March 1968: The Federation of Arab Emirates formally came into existence in the Persian Gulf. Iran reiterated its claim to Bahrain.

January 1970: A 12-member Council of State was established as an executive body; Sheikh Khalifa bin Sulman al-Khalifa, the ruler's brother, was appointed President of the Council.

2–14 May 1970: A UN report on Bahrain's future was published; it concluded that Bahrain preferred independence to association with Iran; Iran subsequently agreed to renounce its territorial claim.

15 August 1971: Bahrain seceded from the Federation of Arab Emirates, becoming a fully independent state; Sheikh Isa assumed the title of Amir, while the Council of State was restyled the Cabinet, with Sheikh Khalifa as Prime Minister.

December 1972: A Constituent Assembly was convened; it formulated a new Constitution, providing for a National Assembly, to comprise 14 cabinet ministers and 30 elected members.

6 December 1973: The new Constitution came into force.

7 December 1973: Elections to the National Assembly were held.

1974: There was industrial unrest provoked by the delay in establishing trade unions and the sharp rise in the cost of living.

March 1974: Abu Dhabi, Algeria, Bahrain, Egypt, Kuwait and Saudi Arabia agreed to lift the embargo on petroleum supplies to the USA imposed following US support for Israel the previous year; shipments to the Netherlands were resumed in July.

December 1974: The Amir issued a new national security law; pro-Marxist and pro-Shi'a opposition parties demanded it be put to the National Assembly.

1975: The Shah of Iran formally renounced all Iranian claims to Bahrain.

1975: The Government renewed the US Navy Middle East Force's lease, which had been suspended a few years earlier.

August 1975: The Prime Minister submitted his resignation; he complained that the National Assembly was preventing the Government from carrying out its functions. The Amir invited him to form a new administration, dissolved the National Assembly and suspended the Constitution.

1977: As a result of complaints from other Arab States, the Government requested that the USA reduce its military activities in Bahrain. The USA subsequently closed its military bases in the country.

March 1979: Bahrain joined other Arab states in condemning the peace treaty signed by Israel and Egypt and suspended diplomatic relations with Egypt.

September 1979: Iranian Shi'ite elements urged Bahraini Shi'ites to demonstrate against the Sunni Amir of Bahrain; there was a series of demonstrations in support of the Islamic Revolution in Iran.

April 1980: There were demonstrations by Shi'a against the Government's support for Iraq in its conflict with Iran.

25 March 1981: Bahrain joined five other Gulf states in forming the Cooperation Council for the Arab States of the Gulf (Gulf Cooperation Council—GCC).

May 1981: Bahrain, Kuwait, Oman, Qatar, Saudi Arabia and the United Arab Emirates founded the Co-operation Council for Arab states of the Gulf (Gulf Co-operation Council—GCC) to promote economic and military co-operation in the region.

December 1981: Some 60 people were arrested on charges of conspiring to overthrow the Government. The Minister of the Interior claimed that an Iranian cleric, Hojatoleslam Hadi al-Mudarasi, and other members of the Islamic Front for the Liberation of Bahrain, were implicated in the conspiracy.

1984: Following the discovery of a cache of weapons in a Bahraini village, there were renewed fears of Iranian attempts to destabilize the country.

June 1985: A further conspiracy to overthrow the Government was discovered.

26 April 1986: Qatari military forces raided the island of Fasht al-Dibal, a coral reef situated between Bahrain and Qatar, over which both countries claimed sovereignty. Qatar seized 29 foreign nationals, who were constructing a Bahraini coastguard station on the island, but later released them.

December 1986: A causeway linking Bahrain to Saudi Arabia was opened.

January 1987: The USA agreed to sell 112 F-18 fighter aircraft to Bahrain as part of a contract, valued at US $400m, to provide military equipment.

July 1987–December 1988: The Government allowed the US Navy to use Bahrain as the base for its operations to protect international shipping in the Persian (Arabian) Gulf; vessels in the Gulf had been attacked by both Iranian and Iraqi forces in the conflict between the two countries.

July 1991: Qatar instigated proceedings at the International Court of Justice (ICJ) regarding the disputed Hawar islands, awarded to Bahrain by the British in 1939.

16 December 1992: Political reforms were announced in Bahrain—a 30-member Consultative Council was appointed by the Government, and met for the first time in January 1993.

March–April 1995: Amid serious political disturbances, an influential Shi'ite cleric and critic of the Government, Sheikh Abd al-Amir al-Jamri, was arrested and subsequently imprisoned.

June 1995: The first major reorganization of the Cabinet for some 20 years took place; however, the principal portfolios remained unchanged.

26 June 1995: A new Cabinet was announced.

August 1995: Some 150 people detained in the disturbances in March and April were released. Sheikh al-Jamri was released the following month.

January 1996: Amid renewed political unrest, Sheikh al-Jamri was again arrested on charges of inciting disturbances; a prominent Sunni lawyer was arrested in connection with the disturbances in February.

28 September 1996: A new Consultative Council was appointed, its membership expanded to 40.

7–12 December 1996: The 17th GCC annual summit was convened in Doha, Qatar; Bahrain boycotted the meeting, owing to its ongoing territorial dispute with Qatar regarding the Hawar islands.

6 March 1999: The Amir died; Sheikh Hamad bin Isa al-Khalifa, hitherto Crown Prince, succeeded him.

31 May 1999: The Amir announced the appointment of a new Cabinet.

7 July 1999: Sheikh al-Jamri, who had been detained since 1996, was sentenced to 10 years' imprisonment on charges of inciting violence; however, he was pardoned by the Amir the following day, after he agreed to read a statement of apology to the Amir on national television.

30 September 2000: Four women, a Jewish businessman and a businessman of Indian descent were sworn in as members of the Consultative Council; it was the first time that women and non-Muslims were permitted to become members of the body.

December 2000: The Amir announced that he intended to restore a democratically elected Assembly.

30–31 December 2000: At a meeting of the GCC in Manama, the members discussed the introduction of a single currency and signed a defence pact which committed all the member states to take joint action if any members became subject to external aggression.

23 January 2001: The Amir announced that a referendum would be held in February on proposals for a new constitution and the restoration of a democratically elected Assembly. Men and women over the age of 20 were eligible to take part in the vote.

5 February 2001: The Amir announced an amnesty for political prisoners held under security laws and opposition figures in exile.

5 February 2001: Some 900 exiles and prisoners were pardoned.

15 February 2001: A referendum was held on the Amir's proposal to establish Bahrain as a constitutional monarchy with an elected assembly and an independent judiciary by 2004; some 90% of those eligible to vote participated in the referendum, with some 98% of those supporting the proposal.

17 February 2001: The State Security Court was abolished and the State Security Law, which was enacted in 1975 and was widely criticized as anti-democratic, was repealed.

16 March 2001: The ICJ confirmed Bahrain's sovereignty over the Hawar Islands, and Qatar's over Zubarah and the Fasht ad-Dibal reefs. Both Bahrain and Qatar agreed to abide by the verdict; the Amir of Bahrain claimed that the judgement was a significant victory for his country. The two countries subsequently agreed to resume the activities of the Bahrain-Qatar Supreme Joint Committee, and the construction of a causeway linking Bahrain with the Arabian mainland in Qatar was scheduled to commence later in 2001.

17 April 2001: The Cabinet was reorganized; the principal posts remaining with their incumbents.

4 June 2001: The Prime Minister received the Qatari Minister of State for the Interior, Sheikh Hamad Bin Nasser Bin Jasim ath-Thani, for discussions on strengthening bilateral relations.

12 June 2001: The state of military alert in the Hawar islands was revoked.

Cyprus

11th century BC: Significant numbers of Greek migrants settled on Cyprus and established several city-states.

750 BC–333 BC: Cyprus was successively conquered by the Assyrians, Egyptians and Persians.

333 BC: Cyprus was conquered by the Macedon king and Greek military leader, Alexander III ('the Great'), thus restoring Hellenic dominance over the island. Cyprus eventually came to be ruled by the Ptolemies, a Hellenistic dynasty based in Egypt.

58 BC: The Roman Empire annexed Cyprus.

46 AD: The Proconsul of Cyprus, Sergius Paulus, converted to Christianity at Paphos.

330: Upon the division of the Roman Empire, Cyprus became part of the Eastern (Byzantine) Empire.

647: The Muslim governor of Syria, Mu'awiya, organised an expedition to Cyprus and the capital Constantia (Salamis) was sacked.

653–54: Following a second Muslim raid on the island, an occupying force of 12000 was stationed there.

685: Emperor Constantine IV and the Muslim Caliph, Abd al-Malik, signed a treaty providing for a division of the revenues from Cyprus.

747: A fleet from Alexandria was destroyed by a Byzantine force.

965: The Byzantine Emperor, Nicephoros Phocas, expelled the Arabs from Cyprus and Asia Minor.

1042–43: There was a revolt on the island against the rule of Emperor Alexius Comnenus.

1155: Renaud de Châtillon and King Thoros II of Lesser Armenia (Cilicia) launched an expedition against Cyprus.

1185–91: Isaac Ducas Comnenus ruled the island as the self-styled Emperor of Cyprus.

1191: King Richard I of England, leading the Third Crusade, was shipwrecked on Cyprus and came into conflict with Emperor Isaac Comnenus. Richard's forces took control of the island.

1192: Richard sold Cyprus to the Knights Templar; later that year they sold it for the same sum to Guy de Lusignan, the deposed Frankish King of Jerusalem. The Lusignans created a feudal monarchy in Cyprus.

1365: King Peter I of Cyprus captured the Egyptian city of Alexandria; however, he was soon forced to abandon his conquest.

1372: Famagusta, which had developed into a wealthy and important centre of international trade, was seized by forces from the Italian city-state of Genoa.

1426: An expedition from Egypt invaded Cyprus. At the Battle of Khoirakoitia, the Cypriot King, Janus, was defeated and captured by the invaders.

1464: The Genoese were expelled from Famagusta, with Egyptian assistance.

1489: Venice annexed Cyprus with the agreement of the Queen (the widow of the last Lusignan king), who was herself Venetian.

September 1570: Nicosia fell to the Ottoman army.

August 1571: Famagusta was captured by the Ottomans, and Cyprus became part of the Ottoman Empire. The Orthodox religion was restored to the island, in place of the Lusignans' Latin rite. Many of the conquering soldiers settled on the island—this was subsequently augmented by immigration of Muslims from Anatolia.

1665: There was a revolt of the Greek Orthodox peasantry against Ottoman rule; a further major revolt took place in 1690.

1699: Cyprus was incorporated into the province of the kapudan pasha (Admiral of the Ottoman fleet) following the Ottomans' conquest of Crete.

1703: The governorship of the island was sold for a period of a year in return for the right to collect tax revenues; this process was repeated annually throughout the early 18th century.

1745: Cyprus became an independent province of the Ottoman Empire, with its own pasha (governor).

1764: Land tax was doubled—popular unrest escalated into a revolt, suppressed by Ottoman forces.

1770–74: Cyprus was repeatedly raided by the Russian fleet after the Ottoman fleet was destroyed at the Battle of Cesme in July 1770.

1808–39: Various reforms were introduced in Cyprus as part of the wider reforms of the Ottoman Empire, including reform of the tax system and the creation of an administrative body with equal numbers of Muslims and Christians.

1821: The Greek population of the island was supportive of the rebellion against Ottoman rule in Greece, although most manifestations of such support were suppressed by Ottoman forces; the Orthodox Archbishop was executed for fomenting unrest.

1831: The Ottomans granted Greek independence, but rejected claims that Cyprus should become part of the new state.

1833: The Ottomans granted the administration of Cyprus to Muhammad Ali Pasha, the ruler of Egypt.

1840: By the terms of the London Convention, the major European powers forced Muhammad Ali to return Cyprus to direct Ottoman possession.

1878: At the Congress of Berlin the British and Ottoman delegations agreed that Cyprus should remain an Ottoman possession, but should be administered by the United Kingdom. A legislative council was established.

1914: Upon the entry of the Ottoman forces into the First World War, the United Kingdom annexed Cyprus.

1923: By the terms of the Treaty of Lausanne, Turkey agreed to recognize British rule of Cyprus.

1925: Cyprus was declared a British crown colony.

1931: Protests among Greek Cypriots in opposition to British rule and in support of *enosis* (union) with Greece escalated into violent unrest. The Turkish community on the island opposed any such union. Military government was instituted, remaining in place until after the Second World War.

1941: During the Second World War Cypriot troops fought in the Greek campaign under British command.

1950: In response to British plans for greater autonomy for Cyprus, the Greek Cypriot nationalist movement organized a plebiscite—some 96% of those participating among the Greek Cypriot community voted for *enosis*.

July 1954: The British Government proposed a restricted form of constitutional government for the island—the Greek Cypriots rejected the proposals.

1955: Amid continued protests by Greek Cypriots seeking unification with Greece, a political and military movement emerged—the National Organization of Cypriot Combatants (EOKA) was led politically by Archbishop Makarios III, head of the Greek Orthodox Church in Cyprus, and militarily by Col Georgios Grivas.

August 1955: A conference was held in the British capital, London, to discuss the British proposals for Cypriot autonomy.

27 November 1955: A state of emergency was declared, following a succession of guerilla attacks by EOKA activists.

March 1956: Archbishop Makarios and three other leaders of the *enosis* movement were deported; Makarios was detained in the Seychelles.

March 1957: Makarios was released from the Seychelles and based his campaign for *enosis* in Athens.

10 June 1958: The British Government announced a new, seven-year 'partnership' plan for Cyprus.

7–11 July 1958: The British Prime Minister, Harold MacMillan, visited the capitals of Cyprus, Greece and Turkey in an attempt to gain support for British peace proposals.

15 August 1958: Greece requested the inclusion of the Cyprus issue in the agenda of the next session of the General Assembly of the United Nations.

25 October 1958: Greece rejected a NATO proposal for a 'round-table' conference on Cyprus.

5 December 1958: The General Assembly of the UN expressed confidence in the efforts being made for the solution of the Cyprus question.

5–11 February 1959: Greek and Turkish Ministers discussed the future of Cyprus in Zürich (Switzerland).

19 February 1959: An agreement was signed in London providing for the creation of an independent, sovereign Republic of Cyprus. The new country's Constitution (which provided for a President from the Greek Cypriot community and a Vice-President from the Turkish Cypriot community) was to enter into force not later than 19 February 1960.

2 April 1959: Six Greek Cypriots and four Turkish Cypriots were nominated to fill Ministerial posts on the Cyprus transitional committee.

14 December 1959: Archbishop Makarios and Dr Fazil Kücük were elected President and Vice-President of Cyprus, respectively.

16 August 1960: The Republic of Cyprus attained independence.

13 March 1961: Cyprus became a member of the British Commonwealth.

22 December 1963: Following clashes between Greeks and Turks in Cyprus, Turkish members withdrew from active government.

26 December 1963: A British peace-keeping force was flown to Cyprus.

23 January 1964: Conflict between Greek and Turkish communities in Cyprus resumed.

25 March 1964: Sakari Tuomioja was appointed as a UN Mediator in Cyprus; a UN peace-keeping force was established, which replaced the British force in April.

16 August 1964: Galo Plaza appointed UN Mediator in Cyprus, following the death of Tuomioja.

25 August 1964: The mandate of the UN Cyprus Force was renewed for a further three months; in December it was extended until March 1965.

15–30 November 1967: Amid heavy fighting between the Greek and Turkish communities, Turkey prepared to invade Cyprus. However, mediation by the UN and the USA achieved Graeco-Turkish agreement and reduced tension.

25 February 1968: Archbishop Makarios was elected President of Cyprus for a further five-year term.

8 March 1970: President Makarios survived an assassination attempt.

15 March 1970: Polycarpos Georghadjis, a former Minister of the Interior, was found dead, the victim of gunshots.

5 July 1970: In the first general election in Cyprus since 1960, no party won an overall majority.

30 August 1971: Gen. Grivas disappeared from his home in Athens; he was thought to have returned to Cyprus, and this suspicion was subsequently confirmed. Gen. Grivas revived EOKA (the organization became known as EOKA-B), and began a terrorist campaign (allegedly supported by the Greek military regime) against the Makarios regime and in favour of *enosis*.

9 February 1972: The Greek Government alleged that President Makarios had imported large quantities of Czechoslovak arms for use against Gen. Grivas.

2 March 1972: Three Bishops of the Orthodox Church of Cyprus demanded the resignation of President Makarios.

16 June 1972: A new Council of Ministers was appointed, only three ministers retained their posts.

6 December 1972: Cyprus and the European Economic Community (EEC—the precursor of the European Union, EU) signed an association agreement.

8 February 1973: President Makarios was re-elected unopposed for a third five-year term of office.

16 February 1973: Rauf Denktaş was elected Vice-President, in succession to Kücük.

8 March 1973: The Bishops of Kitium, Paphos and Kyrenia announced that they intended to unfrock Archbishop Makarios in view of his refusal to relinquish the presidency.

15 July 1973: A synod of the Eastern Orthodox Churches in the Middle East deposed and unfrocked the three Bishops who had previously demanded that similar action be taken against President Makarios if he did not resign.

January 1974: Gen. Grivas died.

June 1974: President Makarios ordered a purge of EOKA-B sympathizers from the police, National Guard and civil service, accusing the Greek regime of subversion.

15 July 1974: Makarios was ousted in a *coup d'état*, led by Greek officers of the National Guard, who appointed Nikos Sampson, a former EOKA-B activist, to the presidency.

20 July 1974: At the invitation of Denktaş, the Turkish army intervened to protect the Turkish community and to prevent Greece from using its control of the National Guard to take over the island. The Turkish military seized the port of Kyrenia and established a corridor connecting it to the Turkish quarter of Nicosia; Turkish forces eventually occupied the northern third of the island, which was divided along the so-called 'Attila Line', from Morphou through Nicosia to Famagusta.

23 July 1974: Following the resignation of the military government in Greece, President Sampson resigned; and Glavkos Klerides, the President of the House of Representatives, became acting head of state. Peace talks began between representatives of the two communities were unsuccessful.

December 1974: Makarios returned to Cyprus and resumed the presidency.

January 1975: Talks began in Vienna (Austria) between Denktaş and Klerides, under the chairmanship of Dr Kurt Waldheim, the UN Secretary-General.

13 February 1975: The Turkish Government declared the establishment of the Turkish Federated State of Cyprus ('TFSC') in the north of the island, with Denktaş as President.

June 1976: Presidential and legislative elections were held in the 'TFSC'. Denktaş was elected President and the Ulusal Birlık Partisi (UBP—National Unity Party) held a majority in the legislative assembly.

September 1976: In legislative elections the Dimokratico Komma (DIKO—Democratic Front) won 21 of the 35 seats.

January 1977: President Denktaş met President Makarios to establish the basis for inter-communal talks. Makarios stated that his administration was prepared to accept a federation of a Greek and a Turkish entity only if the Turkish authorities made territorial concessions and a central government was established.

3 August 1977: President Makarios died.

January 1978: Spyros Kyprianou, previously the President of the House of Representatives, was elected President.

April 1978: Despite having announced its dissolution in January, a plot by members of EOKA-B was discovered; 22 members of the organization were arrested.

19 May 1979: Presidents Kyprianou and Denktaş created a 10-point agenda for megotiations, based on the earlier agreement between Denktaş and President Makarios.

June 1979: Further negotiations on the island's future failed.

9 September 1980: A ministerial reshuffle by President Kyprianou caused the communist party Anorthotiko Komma Ergazomenou Laou (AKEL—Progressive Party of the Working People) to withdraw its support from the DIKO. Consequently, the President lost his overall majority in the House of Representatives.

16 September 1980: The inter-communal peace talks resumed. The principal obstacle to a settlement was perceived as the differing views on the representation of the Turkish community—the Turkish Cypriots continued to demand equal status for the two communities, the Greeks insisting that the communities' representation should reflect the composition of the island's population (of which the Turkish community formed less than 20%).

24 May 1981: A general election was held in the Greek sector; the AKEL and Glavos Klerides' right-wing Dimokratikos Synagermos (DISY—Democratic Rally) each won 12 seats, the DIKO secured eight.

November 1981: A proposal for a federation, with a federal council and a presidency alternating between the two communities was presented by the UN; the plan provided for the allocation of 70% of the island to the Greek community.

February 1982: The UN-sponsored negotiations faltered when the Greek Prime Minister, Andreas Papandreou, proposed the withdrawal of all Greek and Turkish troops and the convening of an international conference.

May 1982: The UN General Assembly voted in favour of the withdrawal of Turkish troops from the island.

15 November 1983: The 'TFSC' made a unilateral declaration of independence as the Turkish Republic of Northern Cyprus ('TRNC') with Denktaşcontinuing as President. The declaration was recognized only by Turkey.

April 1984: Diplomatic links were established between the 'TRNC' and Turkey; the 'TRNC' rejected UN proposals for a suspension of its declaration of independence prior to further talks.

8 December 1985: In a general election (organized after Parliament was dissolved following a debate on President Kyprianou's leadership) the DISY won 19 seats, DIKO won 16 seats and the AKEL 15. The election result (which denied the AKEL and the DISY the two-thirds majority required to amend the Constitution and thus potentially remove the President) was regarded as a vindication of President Kyprianou's policies.

April 1986: Settlement plans proposed by the UN Secretary-General were rejected by the Greek Cypriots.

14 February 1988: A presidential election was held in the Greek Cypriot zone. It was won by Georgios Vassiliou, an independent, who attracted the support of the AKEL. Upon taking office, President Vassiliou promised to re-establish the National Council, a body including representatives of all the principal Greek Cypriot political parties, to discuss the resolution of the inter-community dispute.

28 February 1988: President Vassiliou proposed a meeting with the Turkish Prime Minister, Turgut Özal, to discuss the withdrawal of Turkish troops from Cyprus. This was rejected by Özal who said that Mr Vassiliou should meet with Denktaş.

March 1988: President Vassiliou rejected various proposals submitted via the UN by Denktaş, including a plan to form committees to study the possibilities of inter-communal cooperation.

August 1988: Inter-communal talks were resumed between the two Presidents as leaders of their respective communities at a 'summit' meeting under UN auspices in Geneva (Switzerland).

2 March 1990: Further negotiations between leaders of the Greek and Turkish Cypriot communities, aimed at ending the division of the island, collapsed.

July 1990: Cyprus formally applied for membership of the European Community; Denktaş condemned the application, claiming that the Turkish Cypriots had not been consulted.

19 May 1991: In elections to the House of Representatives, the DISY, in alliance with the Komma Phileleftherion (Liberal Party), received 35.8% of the votes cast, securing 20 seats. The AKEL otained 30.6% of the ballot, equating to 18 seats.

2 August 1991: The US President, George Bush, announced that the Greek and Turkish Prime Ministers would attend a US-sponsored conference aiming to resolve the Cyprus question.

12–14 August 1992: The Presidents of Cyprus and the 'TRNC' held direct talks.

14 February 1993: Glavkos Klerides was elected President; he appointed a new Government later in the month.

4–6 March 1993: President Klerides held talks with Greek leaders in Athens.

31 May 1994: A report by the UN Secretary-General claimed that Turkish Cypriot recalcitrance impeded the conclusion of a peace agreement between Greek and Turkish Cypriots.

22–23 May 1995: 'Proximity' discussions were held between Greek Cypriot and Turkish Cypriot officials in London.

26 May 1996: In elections to the House of Representatives, the DISY obtained 34.5% of the votes cast, retaining its 20 seats. The AKEL, with 33.0% of the ballot, won 19 seats, an increase of one, while the DIKO won 10 seats.

25 June 1996: UN-sponsored negotiations on peace in Cyprus resumed in Nicosia, prior to a visit by the UN Secretary-General's newly appointed Special Representative, Han Sung-Joo.

8 April 1997: The Council of Ministers was reshuffled.

11–15 August 1997: An unsuccessful second round of UN-sponsored talks between the Greek Cypriot and Turkish Cypriot leaders was held in Montreux, Switzerland.

5 November 1997: President Klerides accepted the resignations of five DIKO party cabinet members new ministers were appointed to serve until elections scheduled for February 1998.

13 December 1997: Following an announcement that Cyprus was to begin EU accession negotiations in March 1998, the Government of the 'TRNC' announced the suspension of its participation in intercommunal talks.

8 February 1998: The first round of the presidential election led to the progress to the second round of President Klerides and Georgios Iacovou, an independent candidate supported by both the AKEL and the DIKO.

15 February 1998: In the second round of the presidential election, Klerides narrowly defeated Iacovou, and was re-elected.

28 February 1998: A new coalition Government, formed by the DISY, several smaller parties and some independents, was inaugurated.

June 1998: Greek military aircraft landed at an airfield in southern Cyprus; Turkish aircraft made landings in the 'TRNC' shorty afterwards. The following month the Greek Cypriot Government condemned the arrival of Turkish naval vessels and aircraft in the 'TRNC' for the celebrations of the anniversary of the Turkish invasion in 1974.

October 1998: The Greek Cypriot Government, which had accused Turkish aircraft of violating its airspace on a number of occasions throughout the year, alleged that Turkish fighter planes had harassed Greek aircraft participating in joint Greek-Greek Cypriot exercises.

29 December 1998: In response to international disapproval, the Government announced that Russian-supplied missiles were not to be deployed on Cyprus; the.

4 January 1999: The Ministers of Defence and of Education and Culture resigned, following the withdrawal of their party from the ruling coalition.

18 March 1999: The Minister of the Interior, Dios Michaelides, resigned following allegations of corruption, which he strenuously denied.

25 August 1999: The Council of Ministers was again reorganized.

3–14 December 1999: Presidents Klerides and Denktaş attended UN-sponsored 'proximity' discussions in New York (USA).

31 January–8 February 2000: UN-sponsored proximity talks on Cyprus took place in Geneva.

June 2000: The UN Security Council passed a resolution extending the mandate of UNFICYP for a further six months; this reslution was notable for the lack of reference to the authority of the Government of the 'TRNC'; the 'TRNC' subsequently instituted a number of retaliatory measures against UNFICYP.

5–12 July 2000: Further proximity talks on Cyprus were held in Geneva.

24 July–4 August 2000: The Geneva round of proximity talks on Cyprus resumed; a further round of negotiations took place in New York in September.

October 2000: At the request of the International Criminal Tribunal for the former Yugoslavia, Cyprus impounded bank accounts linked to the regime of the former President of the Federal Republic of Yugoslavia, Slobodan Milošević.

November 2000: The 'Progress Towards Accession' report, published by the European Commission, assessed Cyprus as among the candidate countries best equipped to join the EU, and urged the Turkish Cypriot community to participate in accession negotiations.

November 2000: A fifth round of UN-sponsored talks was held in Geneva. The UN Secretary-General, Kofi Annan, said that in his view the negotiations had moved beyond procedure into substance. However Denktaş said that he would not resume the talks until the 'TRNC' was given international recognition.

21 November 2000: President Klerides claimed that new radar equipment had detected six Turkish military aircraft flying over the 'TRNC'; he alleged that they had been taking part in joint, three-day military manouevres with the forces of the 'TRNC'.

December 2000: The UN Security Council extended the mandate of the UN force on the island for a further six-month period. However, it was reported that Turkey had increased its military presence in the 'TRNC' to 36000 troops.

10 May 2001: The European Court of Human Rights found Turkey guilty of abusing Greek Cypriots' rights to life, liberty and security during its occupation of northern Cyprus; Turkey criticized the ruling.

23 May 2001: The European Court of Human Rights condemned Cyprus for the inhumane treatment of a group of nine Turkish Cypriots who had been expelled from the south of the island, where they had been seeking work, in 1994.

27 May 2001: In the legislative election, the AKEL won 34.7% of the votes cast and 20 seats, compared to the 34.0% (19 seats) gained by the DISY; the DIKO, which obtained 14.8% of the ballot, secured nine seats. A coalition Government formed by DISY, the Enomeni Dimokrates (United Democrats, who held four seats) and several independents, subsequently took office.

4 June 2001: The UN Secretary-General, Kofi Annan, recommended that the UN peace-keeping forces' mandate in Northern Cyprus be extended for a further six months.

4 July 2001: Following the arrest of an member of the House of Representatives who had been protesting at the British forces' plans to erect a radio mast near Akraviti, rioting occurred outside a British military base, during which some 40 police-officers were injured.

'Turkish Republic of Northern Cyprus'

20 July 1974: At the invitation of the Turkish Cypriot leader, Rauf Denktaş, the Turkish army intervened to protect the Turkish community in Cyprus and to prevent Greece from using its control of the National Guard to take over the island. The Turkish military seized the port of Kyrenia and established a corridor connecting it to the Turkish quarter of Nicosia; Turkish forces eventually occupied the northern third of the island, which was divided along the so-called 'Attila Line', from Morphou through Nicosia to Famagusta.

13 February 1975: The Turkish Government declared the establishment of the Turkish Federated State of Cyprus ('TFSC') in the north of the island, with Denktaş as President.

June 1976: Presidential and legislative elections were held in the 'TFSC'. Denktaş was elected President and the Ulusal Birlık Partisi (UBP—National Unity Party) held a majority in the legislative assembly.

June 1981: Denktaş was returned as President of the 'TFSC', but his party, the UBP, lost its overall majority in the concurrent election to the entity's legislature.

March 1982: In the 'TFSC' a coalition government was formed comprising the UBP, the Demokratik Halk Partisi (Democratic People's Party) and the T'rkiye Birlık Partisi (Turkish Unity Party) was formed by the incumbent Prime Minister, Mustafa Çağatay.

15 November 1983: The 'TFSC' made a unilateral declaration of independence as the Turkish Republic of Northern Cyprus ('TRNC') with Denktaşcontinuing as President. The declaration was recognized only by Turkey.

April 1984: Diplomatic links were established between the 'TRNC' and Turkey; the 'TRNC' rejected UN proposals for a suspension of its declaration of independence prior to further talks.

May 1985: In a referendum, the population of the 'TRNC' approved the draft consitution.

9 June 1985: Denktaş was returned as president of the 'TRNC' with over 70% of the votes cast.

23 June 1985: A general election was held in the 'TRNC'. The UPB, led by Dr Derviş Eroğlu, won 24 of the 50 seats in the Legislative Assembly.

July 1985: Dr Eroğlu became Prime Minister of the 'TRNC', leading a coalition government.

July 1985: Proposals for a settlement made by the UN Secretary-General were rejected by the Turkish Cypriots.

April 1988: Dr Eroğlu and other members of the Council of Ministers of the 'TRNC' resigned following a disagreement between the UBP and the Yeni Doğuş Partisi (New Dawn Party), its coalition partner since September 1986.

May 1988: Dr Eroğlu resumed the office of Prime Minister at the request of President Denktaş.

2 March 1990: Further negotiations between leaders of the Greek and Turkish Cypriot communities, aimed at ending the division of the island, collapsed.

22 April 1990: Denktaş was re-elected President of the 'TRNC', receiving some 67% of the votes cast.

6 May 1990: A general election in the 'TRNC' was won by the UBP, which secured 34 of the 50 seats. Dr Eroğlu remained Prime Minister.

12–14 August 1992: The Presidents of Cyprus and the 'TRNC' held direct talks.

31 December 1993: A new coalition Government was formed in the 'TRNC'.

31 May 1994: A report by the UN Secretary-General claimed that Turkish Cypriot recalcitrance impeded the conclusion of a peace agreement between Greek and Turkish Cypriots.

16 April 1995: Denktaş defeated Eroğlu in the second round of voting in the presidential election in the 'TRNC'.

3 June 1995: A new coalition Government, formed by the DP and the CTP, took office.

10 November 1995: The Government resigned, following Denktaş' refusal to accept Atun's prposed changes to the administation.

27 November 1995: Atun was invited to form new Government; the administration was appointed on 11 December.

13 December 1997: Following an announcement that Cyprus was to begin EU accession negotiations in March 1998, the Government of the 'TRNC' announced the suspension of its participation in intercommunal talks.

6 December 1998: Elections for the Legislative Assembly were held; the UBP won 24 of the 50 seats, the DP 13, the TKP seven and the CTP six. A UBP-TKP coalition Government, led by Eroğlu, took office later in the month.

15 April 2000: In the presidential election, Denktaş failed to secure an overall majority at a first round of voting; he was subsequently declared re-elected following the withdrawal of his second-round challenger, Eroğlu.

December 2000: The UN Security Council extended the mandate of the UN force on the island for a further six-month period. However, it was reported that Turkey had increased its military presence in the 'TRNC' to 36000 troops.

7 December 2000: Denktaş declared that UN peace-keepers would no longer be welcome in the 'TRNC' unless the UN recognised it as an independent state. Three days previously, he had announced that he would not be attending peace talks mediated by the UN special envoy, Alvaro de Soto.

12 January 2001: The Government received a loan of $350m. from Turkey to fund a new economic programme.

12 January 2001: Turkey agreed to a new loan for the 'TRNC', amounting to US $350m.

11 May 2001: Turkey criticized a ruling by the European Court of Human Rights that it was guilty of human rights violations in northern Cyprus following the invasion of 1974.

24 May 2001: The UBP-TKP coalition collapsed owing to unresolved disputes regarding the participation of the 'TRNC' in peace talks; Eroglu resigned the following day; the UBP was able to form a new coalition with the DP in June, Eroglu again assuming the premiership.

4 June 2001: The UN Secretary-General, Kofi Annan, recommended that the UN peace-keeping forces' mandate in Northern Cyprus be extended for a further six months.

Georgia

c. **299 BC–234 BC:** Parnavaz (Farnavazi, Pharnabazus), traditionally the first king of an identifiably 'Georgian' state, reigned over eastern Georgia (anciently known as Iberia); his realm was centred on the province of Kartli, but he also came to dominate the kingdom in western Georgia (Egrisi—the area known as Colchis by the ancient Greeks).

64 BC: The Roman general, Pompei, incorporated Colchis, part of the just-defeated kingdom of Pontus, into the Empire and secured hegemony in Kartli-Iberia and Armenia; the Persian (Parthian) Empire soon disputed this.

c. **AD 328:** The 'Apostle of the Georgians', St Nino (according to tradition a Cappadocian slave woman), began the evangelization of the Georgians; the king of Kartli-Iberia, Mirian III (Meribanes, 284–361), adopted Christianity in 334.

5th century: The first known inscriptions in the Georgian alphabet (*mrglovani*) were created, at a time when the Georgian Church was attempting to resist Persian cultural dominance and the advance of Zoroastrianism.

523: Tsete, the ruler of Lazica (established in Egrisi, Roman Colchis, in the previous century), accepted Orthodox Christianity; the territory soon returned to dependence on the Eastern Roman ('Byzantine') Empire.

580: The Persians abolished the Kartli-Iberian monarchy, upon the death of Bakur III; the Georgian aristocracy acquiesced in the effective partition of the kingdom, between the Byzantines (based at the old capital of Mtskheta) and the Sasanian Persians (located at the new capital a short distance away, Tbilisi).

645: Tbilisi fell to the Arabs; the presiding prince of Kartli-Iberia was forced to acknowledge the Muslim Caliph as overlord.

888: The monarchy of Kartli-Iberia was restored by the Armenians, both kingdoms being ruled by branches of the Bagration family; there was also a kingdom in western Georgia (Egrisi), known as Abasgia (Abkhazia) or Abkhazeti.

1008: Bagrat III, King of Abkhazia, inherited the kingdom of Kartli-Iberia upon the death of his father, uniting Egrisi and Kartli into a single Georgian kingdom ('Sakartvelo', the land of the Kartvelians or Georgians), with his capital at Kutaisi.

1089–1125: Reign of King David IV (the 'Restorer' or 'Builder'), who created a powerful kingdom and gained control of the remaining Georgian lands: the process began when he renounced the tribute to the Seljuq Turkish sultanate (1096); it was secured by the defeat of the Muslims at the Battle of Didgori (12 August 1121); and was symbolized by the final capture of Muslim Tbilisi, which became the royal capital (1122).

1184–1212: Reign of Queen Tamar; this marked the apogee of the independent, medieval Georgian kingdom, which witnessed the work of the 'national bard', Shota Rustaveli, repulsed the Muslims and helped establish the Byzantine 'Empire' of Trebizond.

1223–45: Reign of Queen Rusudan, under whom Georgia was devastated by Mongol and Khwarazem raiders; the power of the monarchy was destroyed, the kingdom was fractured and the Georgians became tributary to the Mongol rulers of the Persian Empire.

1314: Georgia was briefly reunited by Giorgi V (the 'Brilliant'), until the invasion of the Mongol leader, Timur 'the Lame' (Tamerlane, 1370-1405).

1554: The Russians captured the Caspian port of Astrakhan; the Georgians, divided into several kingdoms and principalities (the main ones being Imereti, in the west, and Kartli and Kakheti, in the east) disputed by the rival Persian and Turkish Ottoman Empires, could begin to expect help from these Orthodox co-religionists.

1783: King Irakli II, of a reunited Kartli-Kakheti (1762-98), concluded the Treaty of Georgievski with Russia, whereby his eastern Georgian kingdom surrendered responsibility for defence and foreign affairs, but retained internal autonomy.

18 December 1800: Tsar Paul I of Russia declared Kartli-Kakheti annexed outright to the Russian Empire, although the question of the continuance of the Bagration dynasty was left in abeyance—however, Giorgi XII, the last king of eastern Georgia, died before tsarist troops entered Tbilisi (henceforth known as Tiflis, until 1936).

12 September 1801: The new Tsar, Alexander I, decreed the abolition of the kingdom of Kartli-Kakheti.

December 1803: Moving westwards, the Russians placed Samgrelo (Mingrelia) under the formal protection of the Empire.

1804: The last reigning Bagration, King Solomon II of Imereti (the main principality of western Georgia, based at Kutaisi), was forced to accept Russian sovereignty; he, and his title, died in 1810.

1809: Safar bey Sharvashedze placed his principality of Abkhazia under Russian protection.

1811: Mamia Gurieli placed the principality of Guria (western Georgia, on the Black Sea coast) under the protection of the Tsar; the Russians had also seized Sukhum-Kale and other cities from the Turks.

1812: The autocephaly of the eastern Georgian Orthodox Church was ended; a new hierarchy was imposed on the western Georgian Church three years later.

1828: The Treaty of Turkmanchai concluded the war between Russia and Persia, confirming Russian rule over the Georgians.

1864–65: Emancipation of the serfs, first in Tiflis province, then in Guria and Imereti (Kutaisi province).

1892: The first radical Marxist group, Mesami Dasi (Third Generation), was formed; Iosif Dzhugashvili (Ioseb Jugashvili, when transliterated from the Georgian—later known as Stalin) became a member.

1899: The first Tiflis committee of the All-Russian Social Democratic Labour Party (RSDLP) was formed, dominated by the Menshevik wing—the Bolsheviks of the main, Russian RSDLP were to include many prominent Georgians, notably Stalin and 'Sergo' Ordzhonikidze (Orjonikidze).

1 August 1914: Russia entered the First World War against Austria-Hungary, Germany and Ottoman Turkey.

2 March (New Style: 15 March) 1917: Following the abdication of Tsar Nicholas II, the Provisional Government nominated an executive in Transcaucasia, although its power was dependent upon the soviets (councils) established in Tiflis and Baku (Azerbaijan).

November 1917: The Georgian Mensheviks and the Armenian leaderships in Georgia and Armenia denied the legitimacy of the new, Bolshevik, central Government and established a Transcaucasian Commissariat to assume temporary authority (an assembly, or Seim, convened in January 1918).

14 February (Old Style: 1 February) 1918: First day upon which the Gregorian Calendar took effect in Soviet Russia.

22 April 1918: The Transcaucasian Seim declared the independence of the Democratic Federative Republic of Transcaucasia.

26 May 1918: The Georgian leadership, realizing that the new Transcaucasian state was untenable, declared an independent Georgian state, allied to Germany.

July 1920: The British withdrew the last of their forces from Batumi, refusing to aid the Transcaucasian states militarily against Russia.

25 February 1921: The Menshevik Government fled Tiflis, which was occupied by the Red Army, under Ordzhonikidze; Georgia, the last of the Transcaucasian states to fall to the Bolsheviks, was declared a Soviet Socialist Republic (SSR).

10 December 1922: The Federal Union of SSRs of Transcaucasia (formed 12 March) was transformed into a single republic, the Transcaucasian Soviet Federative Socialist Republic (TSFSR); the TSFSR, became a founder member of the Union of Soviet Socialist Republics (USSR) on 22 December.

28 August 1924: A widespread revolt, led by the Mensheviks, commenced; it failed and was followed by severe repression.

5 December 1936: Under the second Constitution of the USSR, the TSFSR was dissolved and the Georgian, Armenian and Azerbaijani SSRs became full Union Republics.

1937: The leader of Georgia, Lavrenti Beria, assured Stalin, the Soviet leader, of his loyalty by conducting among the most severe of the Stalinist purges.

1938: A new Abkhazian alphabet, based on the Georgian script (33 characters the same and six unique ones), was introduced.

1941–45: The German-Soviet struggle during the Second World War had a severe effect on Georgia, although there was no fighting on its territory; the population declined from 3.5m. in 1939 to 3.2m. by 1945.

March 1953: Death of Stalin; most members of the Georgian leadership were subsequently dismissed.

March 1956: The anniversary of the death of Stalin (whose memory remained popular in Georgia) occasioned the first 'nationalist' demonstration since the 1920s; there was great opposition in this year to perceived 'russification'.

29 September 1972: Eduard Shevardnadze became head of the Communist Party of Georgia (serving until 1985 when he became Soviet Minister of Foreign Affairs), as part of an anti-corruption policy by the central authorities.

9 April 1989: A number of people were killed in Tbilisi when soldiers dispersed a demonstration opposing Abkhazian secessionism and supporting Georgian independence.

July 1989: Several people were killed at Sukhumi University during fighting between students; a state of emergency and curfew were imposed in the Abkhazian capital.

November 1989: The Supreme Soviet of Georgia declared the supremacy of Georgian over all-Union (USSR) laws; the article in the Constitution safeguarding the Communist Party of Georgia's monopoly on power was abolished.

December 1989: There were violent confrontations in South Ossetia, between Ossetians and Georgians, after demands that South Ossetia be made an autonomous republic and, eventually, be reunified with North Ossetia (part of the Russian Federation) were refused.

February 1990: The Georgian Supreme Soviet declared Georgia an 'annexed and occupied country'.

March 1990: The Supreme Soviet revoked the Communist ban on opposition parties, at the behest of which the republican parliamentary elections were postponed.

25 August 1990: The Abkhazian Supreme Soviet voted to declare independence from Georgia and adopt the status of a full union republic; this declaration was pronounced invalid by the Georgian Supreme Soviet and Georgian deputies in the Abkhazian legislature succeeded in reversing the declaration.

20 September 1990: The South Ossetian Supreme Soviet proclaimed the region's independence and state sovereignty within the USSR; this was declared unconstitutional by the Georgian Supreme Soviet.

30 September 1990: The more radical opposition parties rejected all Soviet institutions and conducted elections to a National Congress, in which only 51% of the electorate participated.

28 October 1990: In the first round of elections to the Georgian Supreme Soviet the Round Table-Free Georgia coalition of pro-independence parties won some 64% of the votes cast (after the second round of voting, on 11 November, the coalition had 155 seats).

14 November 1990: Zviad Gamsakhurdia, leader of the Georgian Helsinki Union and of the victorious coalition, was elected Chairman of the Supreme Soviet; the state was renamed the Republic of Georgia.

11 December 1990: The Georgian parliament abolished South Ossetia's autonomous status, resulting in renewed violence in the region. The Soviet leadership annulled this decision in the following month.

31 March 1991: Having boycotted the all-Union referendum on continued federation (although polling stations were opened in South Ossetia and Abkhazia) and the negotiations on a new union treaty, the Georgian authorities conducted a republican referendum on independence, which was overwhelmingly supported.

9 April 1991: Georgia became the first republic to secede from the USSR, when the Supreme Soviet (Supreme Council) approved a decree formally restoring Georgian independence; six days later Gamsakhurdia was appointed to the new post of executive President of the Republic.

26 May 1991: Gamsakhurdia was directly elected to the presidency, with 85.6% of the votes cast.

September 1991: Following criticism of his reaction to the failed Soviet coup of August, and accusations of authoritarian rule, opposition parties united to demand Gamsakhurdia's resignation.

December 1991: The South Ossetian Supreme Soviet declared a state of emergency, following the dispatch of Georgian troops to the region; a second declaration of independence was adopted, as was a resolution, endorsed by a referendum held in January 1992, in favour of integration into the Russian Federation.

21 December 1991: Georgia sent observers to a meeting in Almaty, Kazakhstan, where the leaders of 11 former Union Republics of the USSR signed a protocol on the formation of the new Commonwealth of Independent States (CIS).

2 January 1992: President Gamsakhurdia was declared deposed by the opposition; he fled to Chechnya, Russia, four days later. A Military Council was formed, headed by Tengiz Kitovani and Jaba Ioseliani; this subsequently appointed Tengiz Sigua as premier.

10 March 1992: Shevardnadze was appointed Chairman of the State Council, which had recently replaced the Military Council.

24 June 1992: Shevardnadze and President Boris Yeltsin of the Russian Federation reached an agreement for the cessation of hostilities in South Ossetia; however, no political settlement was reached.

July 1992: Civil disturbance increased in violence, following repeated attempts by Gamsakhurdia and his supporters ('Zviadists') to regain control. In South Ossetia, where conflict was continuing, a cease-fire agreement was signed and peace-keeping monitors deployed. The Abkhazian legislature proclaimed the region's sovereignty as the 'Republic of Abkhazia'.

31 July 1992: Georgia became the last former Soviet Republic to be admitted into the UN.

11 August 1992: Zviadists kidnapped the Georgian Minister of Internal Affairs and other senior officials, who had been sent to western Georgia (Mingrelia) to negotiate the release of a deputy premier, taken hostage the previous month.

14 August 1992: Three thousand National Guard members arrived in Abkhazia, allegedly in an attempt to release the hostages; Abkhazian troops responded with a series of attacks, but the Georgian forces succeeded in capturing Sukhumi.

September 1992: Abkhazian forces launched a counter-offensive and gained control of all of northern Georgia; Shevardnadze claimed that secessionist forces were receiving military aid from Russia.

11 October 1992: Elections to the Supreme Council were participated in by an estimated 75% of the electorate; Shevardnadze was elected Chairman, in direct elections held simultaneously, with 96% of the votes cast. The new parliament convened for the first time on 6 November.

6 August 1993: Sigua and the Council of Ministers resigned, after parliament rejected their proposed budget.

10 September 1993: A two-month state of emergency was declared (it ended on 20 February 1994) and a new, smaller Cabinet of Ministers, under Otar Patsatsia, was appointed. Shevardnadze forced parliament to accept these measures after offering his resignation (which was refused). The state of emergency ended on 20 February 1994.

15 September 1993: Forces loyal to deposed President Gamsakhurdia began an offensive to the west of Samtredia.

16 September 1993: Abkhazian forces launched numerous surprise attacks, breaking the UN cease-fire agreement of 27 July; Sukhumi was taken and government troops defeated after 11 days of fighting.

30 September 1993: The last government troops were driven from Abkhazia and the region was officially declared liberated from Georgia; there were reports of ethnic Georgians being expelled and killed by victorious troops.

2 October 1993: Zviadist forces captured the port of Poti and gained control of the railway line to Tbilisi, thereby blocking all rail traffic to the capital.

20 October 1993: The Supreme Council agreed that Georgia should join the CIS, which Shevardnadze had proposed a few days earlier. The next day Russian troops and supplies arrived in Georgia and government forces were able to reopen supply lines, while Poti and other towns were soon recaptured. Georgia was formally admitted to the CIS on 3 December.

8 November 1993: Gamsakhurdia and his supporters fled to Abkhazia, after being defeated at their main base, the town of Zugdidi, by Georgian troops.

1 December 1993: Georgian officials and Abkhazian separatists signed a UN-mediated eight-point peace 'memorandum'.

23 December 1993: South Ossetia adopted a new Constitution.

31 December 1993: Gamsakhurdia was killed, reportedly by his own hand, after being surrounded by government troops in western Georgia.

March 1994: Georgia joined the Partnership for Peace programme of the North Atlantic Treaty Organization (NATO).

14 May 1994: The Georgian and Abkhazian Governments declared a full cease-fire agreement, under which a contingent of some 3,000 CIS (mainly Russian) peace-keepers were deployed in the region from June; this was in addition to the UN observer forces already in place. Nevertheless, hostilities recommenced.

26 November 1994: The Abkhazian legislature adopted a new Constitution, which declared the region to be a sovereign state; the speaker of the legislature, Vladislav Ardzinba, was appointed President—the Georgian Government suspended peace negotiations.

December 1994: The leader of the National Democratic Party of Georgia, Giorgi Chanturia, was assassinated.

March 1995: Georgia and Russia signed an agreement on the establishment of four Russian military bases in Georgia, for a period of 25 years.

July 1995: Discussions on a political settlement in South Ossetia began, under the supervision of the Organization for Security and Co-operation in Europe (OSCE).

24 August 1995: The Supreme Council finally adopted Georgia's new Constitution, the drafting of which had been prepared by a special commission appointed in 1992; the new Constitution provided for a strong executive presidency and a 235-member, unicameral Georgian Parliament (Sakartvelos Parlamenti).

29 August 1995: Shevardnadze survived an assassination attempt, sustaining only minor injuries. In early October the Minister of State Security, Igor Giorgadze, was named as the chief instigator of the plot, and warrants were issued for his arrest. In May 1996 Ioseliani, leader of the Rescue Corps (as the paramilitary Mkhedrioni, or Horsemen, had been renamed in February 1994), was convicted of complicity in the assassination attempt.

25 September 1995: The Government introduced a new currency, the lari, which replaced the interim currency coupons introduced in April 1993. The lari became the sole legal tender on 2 October.

5 November 1995: In the election to the restored post of President, Shevardnadze won 74.9% of the votes cast. In the parliamentary election, held simultaneously, Shevardnadze's Citizens' Union of Georgia (CUG) won 90 of the 150 seats filled by proportional representation and 17 of the 85 seats filled on a single-mandate basis.

11 December 1995: A new Council of Ministers was announced; Nikoloz Lekishvili was appointed Minister of State, which replaced the post of Prime Minister.

19 January 1996: At a meeting of CIS leaders in Moscow, Russia, it was agreed to impose an economic blockade of Abkhazia until it agreed to accept Georgian sovereignty.

10 November 1996: South Ossetia having introduced a presidential system of government, an election to the post was won by Ludvig Chibirov, who gained some 65% of the votes cast; the election was criticized by Shevardnadze.

23 November 1996: Elections to the Abkhazian People's Assembly were held, despite condemnation by the UN and the OSCE; the Georgian legislature declared them invalid.

9 July 1997: Violent clashes occurred in the Kodori Gorge region of Abkhazia, with 20 people reportedly killed.

14 August 1997: The President of Abkhazia, Vladislav Ardzinba, visited Georgia proper for the first time since 1992.

11 November 1997: Parliament formally abolished capital punishment.

17–19 November 1997: In UN-sponsored talks, it was decided to establish a joint co-ordinating council, comprising representatives of Georgia and Abkhazia, as well as delegates from Russia, the UN and the European Union (EU), to resolve the issues in Abkhazia.

December 1997: The South Ossetian parliament voted in favour of an independent South Ossetian republic within the CIS; negotiations scheduled to take place under Russian and OSCE supervision were cancelled.

9 February 1998: Shevardnadze survived a second assassination attempt when grenades were fired at his motorcade; Zviadists were blamed for the attack and in March Guram Absandze, a former finance minister, was extradited from Russia to stand trial; in May 1999 13 people, including Absandze, were charged with state treason.

29 April 1998: A document proposing a settlement of the conflict in Abkhazia was signed by certain CIS countries at a summit meeting in Moscow. Abkhazia, which had wanted to attend the talks, refused to accept the resolutions.

25 May 1998: A cease-fire agreement was signed, following violent clashes in the Gali district of Abkhazia, a supposedly neutral zone, where many refugees had been resettled; some 30,000 refugees left the region once more.

16 July 1998: With the removal of Russian patrols, Georgia began independently to patrol its territorial waters (Abkhazia began patrols of its waters on 7 September); a phased withdrawal of Russian troops from the land borders was also planned.

26 July 1998: Following criticism of the Government over the economy and the issue of Abkhazia, Lekishvili resigned as Minister of State. The entire cabinet subsequently resigned, with one exception; Vazha Lortkipanidze was confirmed as Minister of State the following month.

8 September 1998: Together with 11 other countries of Central Asia, the Caucasus and the Black Sea region, Georgia signed an agreement to re-create the ancient 'Silk Road' trade route between the People's Republic of China and Europe.

27 April 1999: Georgia was admitted to the Council of Europe.

May 1999: Seventeen people were arrested following the discovery of a new conspiracy to overthrow the President. All were reported to have connections with Igor Giorgadze, who was accused of involvement in the attempted assassination of Shevardnadze in 1995. Also in May, Georgia refused to sign the Collective Security Treaty of the CIS on its expiry, claiming that it was not relevant to its particular problems.

12 May 1999: Legislative elections were held in South Ossetia, in which the Communist Party secured some 39% of the votes cast. The results were not recognized by the Georgian Government and the OSCE.

3 October 1999: Vladislav Ardzinba was re-elected as President of the Republic of Abkhazia, with 99% of the votes cast; the participation rate was 87.7%. A simultaneous referendum upheld the 1994 Constitution, and a State Independence Act was passed by the legislature shortly afterwards.

14 November 1999: A second round of legislative elections was held (the first had taken place on 31 October), in which the ruling CUG secured 41.9% of the votes cast and 130 seats (85 were filled by proportional representation and 45 were filled on a single-mandate basis). The Union for the Revival of Georgia bloc, comprising parties loyal to former President Gamsakhurdia, and the Industry will Save Georgia bloc won 58 seats (51 proportional, 7 single-mandate) and 15 seats (14 proportional, 1 single-mandate), respectively. Of the remaining seats, 17 were obtained by independents and two by the Georgian Labour Party. One seat remained unfilled, and the mandates of 12 Abkhazian candidates were renewed, following the region's boycott of the election.

18–19 November 1999: At a summit meeting of the OSCE held in İstanbul, Turkey, it was agreed that Russia was to vacate two of its four military bases in Georgia by 1 July 2001. Agreement was also reached by the Presidents of Azerbaijan, Georgia, Kazakhstan, Turkey and Turkmenistan on the construction of a pipeline to carry petroleum from Baku, Azerbaijan, to Ceyhan, Turkey, via Tbilisi.

29 November 1999: Vazha Lortkipanidze was awarded presidential powers for the settlement of conflicts in Georgia; these powers were further extended on 22 December.

9 April 2000: Eduard Shevardnadze was re-elected as President for a further five-year term, with 79.8% of the votes cast; he was sworn in on 30 April. The OSCE expressed concern over violations in voting procedures and called for an investigation; the Parliamentary Assembly of the Council of Europe, however, witnessed no major violations.

11 May 2000: Parliament endorsed the appointment of Gia Arsenishvili as the new Minister of State, replacing Vazha Lortkipanidze.

18 May 2000: Representatives of six Black Sea countries (Bulgaria, Georgia, Romania, Russia, Turkey and Ukraine) agreed to create an international naval unit, Blackseafor.

1–5 June 2000: Four UN military observers were taken hostage in the Kodor Gorge in Abkhazia; this followed a similar incident in the area in October 1999.

14 June 2000: Georgia joined the World Trade Organization (WTO).

9 July 2000: Col Akaki Eliava, the leader of an armed revolt in October 1998, was killed, along with one other, in the western village of Zestafoni, following a confrontation with police; unrest followed.

4 August 2000: Three workers with the International Committee of the Red Cross (ICRC) were kidnapped in the Pankisi Gorge, close to the border with the Russian separatist republic of Chechnya (the Chechen Republic of Ichkeriya). They were released 9 days later.

6 September 2000: The EU announced that it would provide special equipment to Georgian military units protecting Chechnya and the Dagestan border.

29 January 2001: Turkey and Georgia signed an agreement to clear anti-personnel mines from their common border and prohibited the use of landmines in the area in the future.

February 2001: The CUG began a campaign for the removal of the Communist Party from politics; members were to collect signatures for a petition to be delivered to the Supreme Court.

1 February 2001: The UN Security Council announced that it was to extend the mandate of the UN military observers' regional mission in Georgia to the end of July 2001.

23 February 2001: The Chairman of the Supreme Council of the self-proclaimed Autonomous Republic of Ajaria, Aslan Abashidze, announced that he was categorically opposed to the holding of NATO's Co-operation Partner 2001 exercises in June, saying he feared that it might provoke a *coup d'état*.

1 March 2001: The OSCE announced that it was to extend the mandate of its border patrols between Georgia and Chechnya for a further eight months.

1 March 2001: The Constitutional Court annulled the results of the 1999 parliamentary elections in three districts, following allegations of irregularities made by the CUG.

2 March 2001: Parliament issued a statement condemning the proposed elections to be held in Abkhazia on 10 March as illegal; Russia, the OSCE and the UN subsequently expressed their support for the resolution.

7 March 2001: Demonstrators in Tbilisi called for the resignation of Shevardnadze, holding him responsible for loss of government control over the regions of Abkhazia and South Ossetia.

16 March 2001: At the conclusion of a UN-sponsored meeting in Yalta (Ukraine) delegations from Georgia and Abkhazia signed an agreement renouncing violence and permitting the safe return of refugees.

22 March 2001: The Minister for the Control of State Property, Mikheil Ukleba, was dismissed by the President; it was climed that he had failed to eradicate corruption in the ministry or attract sufficient foreign investment.

2 April 2001: Bulgaria, Georgia, Romania, Russia, Turkey and Ukraine formally established Blackseafor, a multi-national naval unit with a humanitarian and environmental role.

8 April 2001: The new Ossetian Constitution, which designated Russian and Ossetian as the state languages, was approved in a referendum; the Georgian community in Ossetia boycotted the poll.

22 April 2001: The Main Council of the CUG passed a resolution advocating the introduction of a cabinet of ministers led by a premier.

25 May 2001: A battalion of the National Guard siezed a military base near Tbilisi in protest at conditions and pay in the army.

26 May 2001: Demonstrations by the supporters of the late President Gamsakhurdia in Tbilisi degenerated into violence; 25 policemen were injured and three demonstrators arrested.

30 May 2001: The Prime Minister of the Republic of Abkhazia, Vyacheslaz Tsugba, resigned.

6 June 2001: Merab Chigoev resigned as premier of South Ossetia; the region's President, Ludvig Chibirov, subsequently nominated Dima Sanakoev, who previously held the defence portfolio, to succeed him.

12 June 2001: Opposition deputies left the paliamentary chamber during discussions regarding the President's proposed amendments to the Constitution, including the introduction of a cabinet of ministers led by a prime minister.

15 June 2001: The Russian Government unilaterally imposed a ban on flights between Russia and Georgia.

25 June 2001: President Shevardnadze admitted that there could be as many as 300 Chechen militants among refugees in the Pankisi Gorge who had fled the conflict between Chechnya and Russia. Shevardnadze refused Russia's demand for its troops to be allowed into the area.

3 July 2001: The Government complained to Russia regarding the failure of its troops to comply with the agreement to evacuate the Gudauta military base in Abkhazia by 1 July; Russia claimed that the troops' presence remained necessary, as Georgia was unable to guarantee the security of the base. Shevardnadze subsequently protested to the OSCE.

13 July 2001: Following media reports that a Georgian border guard had been abducted by Chechen rebels in the Kakhtei region, local Georgian residents took seven Chechens hostage; the Government declared a state of emergency in the area.

Iran

***c*. 3000 BC:** The Elamite civilization was established in Khuzestan, in the west of modern Iran, with a federal capital at Susa. The Elamites conducted trade with the nearby Sumerian, Babylonian and Assyrian civilizations.

1764 BC: The Elamite kingdom was occupied by the Babylonians under King Hammurabi.

1749 BC–1712 BC: During the reign of King Kutir Nahhunte I, the Elamites attacked the Babylonian King Samsuiluna and drove the Babylonians out of Elam.

1244 BC–1208 BC: King Tukulti-Ninurta I of Assyria led campaigns against the Elamites in the north of the region.

1124 BC–1103 BC: The Elamites repulsed a Babylonian attack led by Nebuchadnezzar I.

***c*. 1000 BC:** The Scythians, Medes and Persians—nomadic, horse-riding peoples from Central Asia—began to migrate to the region.

728 BC–675 BC: Deioces is traditionally thought to have founded the Median kingdom in the Zagros mountains, with a capital at Ectbana—present-day Hamadan.

7th century BC: A group of Persians, led by Hakamanish (Achaemenes) are believed to have founded the Achaemenid dynasty in Fars, south-western Iran.

692 BC–639 BC: King Ashurbanipal led the Assyrian army to victory against the Elamites and destroyed Susa.

539 BC–538 BC: The Achaemenids, led by Cyrus II ('the Great'), captured Babylon.

533 BC: Cyrus II defeated the Medians and founded the first Persian Empire, known as the Achaemenid Empire.

529 BC: Cyrus extended his kingdom eastwards as far as the Hindu Kush in present-day Afghanistan.

525 BC: Following his accession to the throne, Cambyses added Egypt to the Achaemenid territories. He was subsequently deposed by a priest, Gaumata, who led a successful revolt against his rule.

522 BC: Gaumata was overthrown by a member of the Achaemenid family, Darius. Darius I ('the Great') divided the empire into geographical administrative units called satrapies and introduced a legal code called the *data*; gold and silver coinage was also introduced.

516 BC: Darius began to extend his empire northwards towards the Black Sea and the Caucasus mountains, leading to frequent conflict with the Greek Empire.

490 BC: The Persian army was heavily defeated by the Greeks at Marathon.

480 BC: Under the leadership of King Xerxes, the Persian army was again defeated by the Greeks.

333 BC: Alexander III ('the Great') of Macedon led the Greek army to victory against the Persians at the Battle of Issus in Asia Minor. He defeated the Persians again at Arbela in 331 BC and set fire to the Achaemenid capital, Persepolis. The last Achaemenid emperor fled the region and Alexander took control of the Persian territories.

323 BC: Following the death of Alexander, one of his generals, Seleucus Nicator, took control of the Greek colonies in the East, including the Persian lands.

175 BC: The Parthians (Arsacids), orignally a nomadic tribe from Turkestan, began to rebel against Greek rule in the region.

126 BC: The Parthians captured the Tigris-Euphrates river valley in present-day Iraq.

_c._ AD 209: The Parthian Empire was divided between Volgases V, who governed the a region approximately equivalent to modern Iraq from Ctesiphon, and Artabanus V, who ruled Iran from Susa.

212: Another group of Persians, the Sassanids (Sassanians), led by Ardashir Babak, launched a series of rebellions against Parthian rule.

224: The Parthians were defeated and Artabanus killed at the Battle of Hormizdagan.

227: Ardashir embarked on a conquest of the former Achaemenid lands; the Sassanids captured Seiston (Sakastan), Gorgan (Hyrcania), Marv (Margiana), Balkh (Bactria) and Khwarezm (Chorasmia) and crowned himself *shahanshah* ('king of kings') of the Iranians at Ctesiphon. Similar efforts to extend the Empire by Ardashir's successors brought the Sassanids into frequent conflict with the Roman Empire.

531–79: During the reign of Khosrow I (Anurshirvan the Just), a new tax system was introduced, the army and bureaucracy were reorganized and new towns were built; the King also introduced literature from India to the region.

591–628: Khosrow II led a campaign against the Byzantine Romans in the west and captured Damascus and the Holy Cross from Jerusalem; however, the campaign was considered responsible for domestic economic decline and social unrest.

636–37: The Sassanids were defeated by a Muslim Arab army led by Saad ibn Abi Waqqas at the Battle of Qadiysia and their leader, Rustam, was killed.

651: The last Sassanid king, Yazdegerd III, was assassinated near Marv; Persia ceased to be a political entity and was incorporated into the Muslim Arab territory which, during the Umayyad caliphate, was centred at Damascus.

661: The Shi'at Ali ('party of Ali') was established in Iraq in support of one of the claimants to the caliphate on the death of Uthman; the movement found many sympathisers in Iran and was later to become the official religous sect of the region.

696: Arabic was proclaimed the official language of the caliphate, although Persian continued to be widely spoken.

747: The Abbasids, a branch of the family of the Prophet Muhammad distantly related to Ali and his descendants, began to challenge Umayyad rule. The Abbasid army included a large number of Khorasians and was led by Abu Muslim.

749: The first Abbasid caliph, As-Saffah, was proclaimed at a mosque in Kufa; Umayyad rule in Iran came to an end the following year.

1055: A group of Ghuzz (Oghuz) Turks known as the Seljuqs conquered Khorasan from the Ghaznavids; their leader, Tughril Beg, was proclaimed King of the East by the Caliph at Baghdad.

1072–92: During the reign of Tughril Beg's successor, Malik Shah, religious schools were built and learned theologians from all over the Islamic empire were invited to the Baghdad court. Following the death of Malik Shah, however, the Seljuq empire disintegrated into a number of small states.

1258: Hülökü, the grandson of the Mongol leader Temujin (Chinghiz or Genghis Khan) captured Baghdad and ended the Abbasid caliphate. The Mongol invasion led to a decay in civil government, serious damage to the irrigation system essential for agriculture and frequent bedouin raids.

1295–1304: The Mongol ruler, Ghazan Khan, lowered taxes for artisans, encouraged agriculture, reconstructed irrigation works and extended trade routes, precipitating a brief economic revival in Iran.

1335: Following the death of the last Mongol Khan, Abu Said ('Bahadur the Brave'), Iran again became a succession of small states, ruled by Salghurid, Muzaffarid, Inju and Jalayrid dynasties.

1381–87: Timur ('the Lame'—Tamerlane), a Turkmen emir from Transoxania began a series of military campaigns against Persia, destroying Shiraz and Esfahan.

1410: A confederation of Turkmen tribes from Lake Van (present-day Turkey), known as the Kara Koyunlu (Black Sheep), defeated the last Jalayirid ruler, Ahmed; they proceeded to create a new state which extended from Tabriz to the Shatt al-Arab waterway.

1447–68: The Kara Koyunlu state was the subject of challenges by a rival confederation, the Ak Koyunlu (White Sheep), who eventually succeded in taking control of the state.

1499–1508: The Safavid leader, Ismail, led an army of Turkoman tribesmen into Iran and captured Tabriz; he proclaimed himself Shah of Iran and declared Shi'a Islam to be the state religion.

1524: The Ottoman Sultan, Selim I, defeated the Safavid forces at Chaldiran and occupied Tabriz.

1534–1535: Sultan Suleyman ('the Magnificent') captured Baghdad.

1587–1629: During the reign of Shah Abbas, the Safavid Empire reached its zenith. Georgia, Iraq and parts of the Caucasus were recaptured from the Ottomans; the Government also established a monopoly over the silk trade, thereby increasing revenues.

1628: The Ottomans successfully reconquered Baghdad; the following year they and the Safavids signed the Treaty of Qasr-i Shirin (Treaty of Zuhab) which concluded 150 years of intermittent conflict.

1725: Following repeated incursions into Safavid territory, the Turks captured Tabriz.

1736: The chief of the Afshar tribe, Nadir Shah, expelled the Ottomans from Georgia and Armenia, drove the Russians from the Persian coast of the Caspian Sea and re-established Persian sovereignty over Afghanistan.

1750–1779: Under the rule of Karim Khan Zand, Persia, with the exception of Kurasan, was once again unified.

1794: Following several years of political chaos, Agha Mohammad Qajar established his rule over Iran and founded the Qajar dynasty.

1800: The British and French competed for mercantile and political influence in the Persian Gulf. The Persian ruler, Fath Ali Shah, made an agreement with the British not to receive French agents and to prevent any French forces from entering Persia. Nevertheless, by the 1807 Treaty of Finkenstein, the French were permitted to station troops in the country, under the command of Gen. Gardanne.

1801: Russia annexed Georgia; Persia subsequently began a campaign for its recovery.

1809: The British and Persians negoitiated the Treaty of Tilsit, by which the French were prohibited from aiding the Shah against Russia; the French troops left and Gardanne was dismissed.

1813: Persia surrendered to the Russians and in the agreement of Gulistan ceded Georgia, Qara Bagh (Karabakh) and seven other provinces.

1814: In an agreement made at Tehran, the United Kingdom agreed to provide troops and a subsidy to Persia in the event of an unprovoked attack on the country.

1821: Frontier disputes with the Ottoman Empire escalated into war.

1823: The conflict with the Ottoman Empire was ended by the Treaty of Erzerum, which fixed the mutual border.

1825: Russia occupied the disputed territory of Gokcheh; the following year Persia declared war in an attempt to recover Gokcheh and other territories lost by the Treaty of Gulistan.

1828: A series of Persian defeats forced the signing of the Treaty of Turkmanchai, by which the territories of Eirvan (Yerevan) and Nakhjivan (Nakichevan) were ceded to Russia. In addition, Persian armed vessels were prohibited from the Caspian Sea and an indemnity was paid.

1834: Muhammad Shah launched an offensive against Herat (Afghanistan). In 1837 the Persian forces beseiged the city; the seige came to an end when the British threatened to intervene.

1848: The Prime Minister, Mirza Taqi Khan Amir Kabir, reformed the tax system, centralized control over the bureaucracy and provincial governors and sought to encourage trade and industry. He also established a new school, Dar ol Fonin, to create an educated elite.

1854: The Russians captured Marv and subsequently came to influence the province of Khorasan.

1856: The Persians succeeded in capturing Herat, which in turn led to the Anglo-Persian war. The hostilities were concluded the following year in the Treaty of Paris, in which Persia surrendered all claims to Herat and territories in Afghanistan.

1871: The Prime Minister, Mirza Hosain Moshir od Dowleh, created a European-style cabinet with administrative responsibilities and a consultative council of senior princes and officials.

1872: The Shah granted a naturalized British national, Baron de Reuter, a monopoly over all railways and tramways in Persia, all minerals (except gold, silver and precious stones), irrigation, roads, factory and telegraph enterprises and the right to farm customs dues for 25 years. The concession was eventually rescinded following protests by court officials.

1889: Baron de Reuter established the first bank in Persia with British capital.

1890: A monopoly on the sale of tobacco was granted to a British national—the award provoked civil unrest.

1891: Persia and Russia made an agreement on favourable trade tariffs; trade between the two countries increased and the agreement was amended in 1901 and 1903.

1896: The Shah was assassinated by a political activist. Muzaffar-ud-Din succeeded to the throne.

January 1906: Intellectual leaders and clerics led popular protests against the granting of concessions to foreign companies and called for a reduction in the powers of the Shah; fearing arrest, merchants and clerical leaders took refuge in mosques in Tehran.

June 1906: Following the Shah's failure to fulfil his promise to permit political reform some 10,000 protesters took refuge in the compound of the British legation in Tehran.

October 1906: An elected assembly was convened to draft a constitution, which provided for strict limits on royal power, a *majlis* (consultative assembly) and a cabinet.

30 December 1906: Muzaffar-ud-Din Shah signed the Constitution; he died five days later and was succeeded by Muhammad Ali Shah.

1907: The Majlis approved Supplementary Fundamental Laws, which guaranteed relative freedom speech and of the press and the security of life and property.

1907: The British and Russian governments signed a convention declaring mutual respect for the sovereignty and independence of Persia. The country was divided into zones of influence, the Russians overseeing the northern region and the British the southern and eastern areas.

June 1908: Muhammad Ali Shah commanded the Persian Cossacks Brigade to attack the Majlis building; the assembly was closed and many deputies arrested; several months of civil unrest ensued.

July 1909: Supporters of constitutional governance deposed Muhammad Ali Shah and re-established the Constitution; the Shah abdicated in favour of his son, Ahmad Mirza, and fled to Russia.

December 1911: Owing to the Majlis' refusal to dismiss the American Administrator-General of the Finances, Shuster, the Russians mobilized troops to occupy Tehran. The Majlis was closed and the Constitution suspended.

1914–1918: At the outbreak of the First World War, Persia declared itself to be neutral, although many British and Russian offensives against the Ottomans were fought on Persian soil. A group of nobles led by Nezam os Saltaneh Mafi established a pro-German provisional government at Kermanshah, which was dissolved at the end of the war.

1919: The British Government attempted to gain influence in Persia by offering to provide assistance in reforming the army and the Ministry of Finance, in addition to a loan of £2m. France and the USA opposed the proposals and the Majlis refused to ratify the agreement.

1921: An officer of the Persian Cossack Brigade, Reza Khan, and a journalist, Said Zia ad Din Tabatabai, led a *coup d'état*; Tabatabai was appointed Prime Minister and Reza Khan Minister of War.

February 1921: The USSR declared all Persia's treaties and conventions made with the Russian Tsarist Government to be null and void in a Soviet-Persian Treaty; however, Article VI of the new agreement did provide for the entry of Soviet troops into Persia in the event of aggressive action toward either country by a third party.

1923: Ahmad Shah dismissed Tabatabai and appointed Reza Khan as Prime Minister.

October 1925: The Majlis deposed the Qajar dynasty and in December conferred the crown on Reza Khan and his heirs.

April 1926: Reza Khan was crowned as Reza Shah Pahlavi. Among his first acts as Shah was to increase the size of the army by the introduction of universal military conscription; the troops were used to restore public order.

1928: The Majlis approved legislation terminating all extra-territorial agreements.

1930: The rights to collect shipping duties on the Persian littoral of the Persian (Arabian) Gulf were transferred from the British to the Persian Government.

1932: The Government cancelled the Anglo-Persian Oil Company's concession, prompting the British Government to refer the matter to the League of Nations. The following year, a new arrangement was agreed, whereby the concession area was reduced and royalties to the Persian Goverment increased.

1935: The name of the state was changed to Iran.

1936: Women were no longer required to wear a veil in public.

1937: Afghanistan, Iran, Iraq and Turkey agreed to the Sa'dabad Pact, which provided for mutual consultation in all disputes that might affect the common interests of the four states.

1941: Iran declared its neutrality in the Second World War. In the period prior to the war, however, the Government had sought to strengthen economic links with Germany and there remained a large number of German nationals in the country.

26 August 1941: Following the Government's refusal to expel German citizens from the country, the Allied troops invaded and two days of conflict ensued.

16 September 1941: Reza Shah abdicated in favour of his son, Muhammad Reza.

1942–43: American advisers were appointed by the Persian Government in an attempt to reorganize the administration.

January 1942: Iran concluded the Tripartite agreement with the United Kingdom and the USSR. The Allies agreed to respect the sovereignty and territorial integrity of Iran in return for the unrestricted right to use, maintain, guard and, if necessary, control all communication in Persia. The Allied forces were to be withdrawn not later than six months after the end of the war.

September 1943: Iran declared war on Germany.

November 1943: At the Tehran Conference, the Allies reaffirmed their commitment to Persia's territorial integrity and reiterated their willingness to extend economic assistance.

December 1945: The Azerbaijan Democratic Party, which had close links with the communist Tudeh Party, proclaimed an autonomous republic in the region; the Kurdish Republic of Mahabad was similarly established in Kurdistan. The movements collapsed the following year, however, following the evacuation of Soviet troops from the regions.

March 1946: The Tripartite agreement expired and British and US armed forces evacuated Persia; the Soviet forces remained in the country until May.

October 1947: A US military mission was set up to assist the Minister of War in improving the efficiency of the army.

February 1949: The Shah was the subject of an unsuccessful assassination attempt; the Government blamed Tudeh for the incident.

July 1949: A Supplemental Oil Agreement was signed with the Anglo-Iranian Oil Company; amid demands for the nationalization of the petroleum industry, the Oil Commissioning Department of the National Assembly recommended the agreement's rejection.

1950: The Shah began the distribution of his land among peasants; the process was completed in 1963.

March 1951: The Prime Minister, Ali Razmara, who had advised against the nationalization of the petroleum industry, was assassinated by Khalil Tahmasebi, a member of the nationalist group Fadayan-e Islam.

April 1951: The National Assembly approved legislation for the nationalization of the petroleum industry.

May 1951: Dr Muhammad Musaddeq, who had led the campaign for the nationalization of petroleum, was appointed Prime Minister. The Anglo-Iranian Oil Company and all its British technicians left the country.

July 1951: The British Prime Minister and the US President offered to negotiate with the Government proposals for the compensation of the Anglo-Iranian Oil Company; the parties failed to reach an acceptable agreement.

September 1951: Having already imposed a worldwide embargo on the purchase of Iranian petroleum the United Kingdom impounded Iran's sterling assets and banned the export of goods to Iran. The Anglo-Iranian Oil Company was unsuccessful in an appeal to the International Court of Justice.

October 1951: The Government terminated diplomatic relations with the United Kingdom.

mid-1952: Mussadeq resigned, owing to the Shah's refusal to grant him the power to appoint a Minister of War; this precipitated pro-Musaddeq rioting and the Shah was forced to reappoint him.

June 1953: Suspicious of Tudeh's support for Musaddeq and fearing Soviet influence, the British and US governments, with the support of the Shah and the Iranian army, began an operation to remove him from power.

3 August 1953: In accordance with the results of a plebiscite organized by Musaddeq, the Majlis was dissolved.

13 August 1953: The Shah appointed the head of the Iranian army, Gen. Fazlollah Zahedi, as Prime Minister; however, Mussadeq refused to accept his dismissal and the Shah and Zahedi were forced to flee the country.

19 August 1953: Following serious unrest, pro-Shah army units and street crowds defeated Musaddeq's forces and martial law was imposed; Musaddeq was subsequently sentenced to three years' imprisonment for illegally dissolving the Majlis and hundreds of other political activists were arrested.

December 1953: The new Government, led by Zahedi, resumed relations with the United Kingdom and began negotiations for a resolution to the dispute regarding the petroleum industry.

September 1954: An agreement was signed with the British Government, which granted petroleum concessions to a consortium of eight companies. The Anglo-Iranian Oil Company was to receive compensation and profits were to be shared equally between the Government and the consortium.

December 1954: The Government signed an agreement with the USSR providing for the repayment of the latter country's war debts to Persia.

April 1955: Zahedi resigned and was succeeded as Prime Minister by Hussein Ala.

October 1955: Iran joined the Baghdad Pact, a defence alliance formed several months previously by Iraq, Pakistan and the United Kingdom.

17 November 1955: The Prime Minister survived an assassination attempt by Mozaffar Ali Zulghader, a member of the Fadayan-e Islam movement.

April 1957: Hussein Ala resigned; he was replaced by Dr Manoutchehr Egbal, who formed a new administration, ended martial law and declared his intention of forming a democratic two-party system.

1958: The Pahlavi Foundation was established by the Shah with the aim of improving education, health and social welfare.

February 1958: The pro-Government Nation Party was formed.

March 1959: Iran and the USA signed a bilateral defence agreement.

29 May 1959: The World Bank and four US banks granted loans to the value of US $72m. to Iran.

24 July 1960: The Shah announced Iran's *de facto* recognition of Israel. The United Arab Republic (UAR—formed by the union of Egypt and Syria) suspended diplomatic relations with Iran in response.

1 September 1960: The results of legislatve elections held in August were annulled by the Shah; a new Government was formed.

12 March 1961: A new Government was formed, led by Sherif-Emami.

5 May 1961: Sherif-Emami resigned; the Shah named Dr Ali Amini as the new Prime Minister; the National Assembly was subsequently suspended and the Prime Minister granted powers to rule by decree in certain circumstances.

24 January 1962: The Shah signed the Land Reform Act.

18 July 1962: Ali Amini resigned as Prime Minister; Assadolah Alam was appointed to succeed him.

2 September 1962: An earthquake in Iran killed an estimated 11,000 people.

5 June 1963: Martial law was imposed in Tehran following rioting directed against the Shah.

March 1964: Assadolah Alam resigned; Hassan ali Mansour was appointed to succeed him.

3–4 July 1964: The Regional Co-operation for Development, a tripartite arrangement between Iran, Pakistan and Turkey that aimed to promote economic co-operation, was established.

26 January 1965: Hassan Ali Mansour was assassinated in Tehran. He was succeeded as Prime Minister by Amir Abbas Hoveida.

19 February 1967: Iran agreed to purchase Soviet arms valued at US $110 million.

31 August 1968: A series of earthquakes in the Khorasan province resulted in the deaths of an estimated 20,000 people.

24 October 1968: Iran and Saudi Arabia signed an agreement delineating territorial claims in the Persian (Arabian) Gulf.

21 April 1969: An Iranian vessel sailed along the Shatt al-Arab waterway flying its national flag, thus abrogating a 1937 treaty granting Iraq sovereignty over the waterway.

20 January 1970: Following an attempted *coup d'état* in the Iraqi capital, Baghdad, Iran was accused of collusion.

14 February 1971: A new, five-year agreement was signed by 23 international petroleum companies and the governments of Abu Dhabi, Iran, Iraq, Kuwait, Qatar and Saudi Arabia.

12–19 October 1971: The 2,500th anniversary of the foundation of Persian monarchy was marked by celebrations in the ancient city of Persepolis.

30 November 1971: Iran occupied the Greater and Lesser Tunbs islands, expelling Arab inhabitants; Iraq suspended relations with Iran in retaliation, and began to expel some 60,000 resident Iranians.

24 May 1973: Iran and the consortium of Western petroleum companies signed an agreement in Tehran whereby the National Iranian Oil Company assumed operations in the Consortium area; in return the companies were granted a 20-year supply of crude petroleum as privileged buyers.

1974: Sporadic fighting occurred throughout the year on the Iran-Iraq border, despite UN efforts to mediate between the two countries.

March 1975: At a meeting of the Organization of Petroleum Exporting Countries (OPEC), it was announced that the Shah and Saddam Hussain Takriti, Vice-President of the Revolutionary Command Council of Iraq, had signed an agreement to eliminate conflict between 'two brotherly countries'.

March 1975: The Shah announced the creation of a single-party system – the Iran National Resurgence Party (Rastakhiz) was designated the sole legal party, with the Prime Minister, Amir Abbas Hoveida, as its Secretary-General.

June 1975: A formal peace agreement was signed between Iran and Iraq, which defined their frontiers according to the 1913 Protocol of Constantinople. The division of the waters of the Shatt al-Arab was defined according to the 'Thalweg line', which ran along the middle of the deepest shipping lane.

1977: Muhammad Reza Shah released a number of political prisoners and announced a number of new regulations to protect the legal rights of civilians tried by military courts.

August 1977: Following the resignation of Hoveida, Jamshid Amouzegar, formerly the Minister of the Interior, was appointed Prime Minister.

January 1978: A pro-Government article in a leading national newspaper questioned the piety of the Ayatollah Ruhollah Khomeini (a Shi'a Muslim religious leader who had been exiled in 1964) and suggested that he was a British agent. While in exile, Khomeini had conducted a campaign opposing the Shah's reforms and advocating stricter observance of the principles of Islam.

August 1978: More than 400 people died in a fire at a cinema in Abadan. The opposition accused agents of the secret police (SAVAK) of instigating the fire; the Shah consequently dismissed Amuzegar and Jafar Sharif Emami was appointed Prime Minister. Upon taking office, Emami promised that his Government would respect Islamic tenets.

September 1978: A prayer ceremony to mark the beginning of Ramadan (the Islamic holy month) precipitated anti-government demonstrations; martial law was subsequently declared.

November 1978: Muhammad Reza Shah established a military Government led by the army Chief of Staff, Gen. Gholamreza Azhari, and ordered the arrest of Hoveida; petroleum and public-service workers began industrial action.

9–10 December 1978: Thousands of protesters participated in anti-government demonstrations.

January 1979: Khomeini formed an Islamic Revolutionary Council in the French capital, Paris.

3 January 1979: Dr Shapour Bakhtiar, the former deputy leader of the National Front, was appointed as the new Prime Minister; his Government dissolved SAVAK and terminated the export of petroleum to Israel and South Africa.

16 January 1979: Muhammad Reza Shah left the country, ostensibly for a short holiday; he never returned.

1 February 1979: Khomeini arrived in Tehran; he declared the Bakhtiar Government to be illegal and urged the continuation of the anti-government strikes and demonstrations.

6 February 1979: Khomeini named Mehdi Bazargan as Prime Minister of new provisional government.

8–11 February 1979: Amid serious unrest, anti-government forces captured several strategic areas of the capital. The army refused to support Bakhtiar and he was forced to resign.

March 1979: Khomeini organised a referendum on the question 'Do you favour an Islamic Republic?'; the results of the ballot were almost unanimously in favour of the proposal.

1 April 1979: The Islamic Republic of Iran was formally declared. A constitution was drafted, which proposed that the country should be governed by a President, a Prime Minister and a single-chamber Islamic Consultative Assembly (Majlis-e Shura e Islam) of 270 deputies.

May 1979: Khomeini terminated diplomatic relations with Israel and allowed the Palestinian Liberation Organization (PLO) to open an office in Tehran.

3 August 1979: The draft constitution was submitted to a 'Council of Experts' for revision; among several amendments, the Council added a provision for a *wali faqih* (religious leader) as the most important executive position in Iran. The document was subsequently approved by national referendum in December.

4 November 1979: Students, demanding the return of the Shah from the USA, seized 53 hostages from the US embassy in Tehran; Khomeini supported the action; the USA introduced economic sanctions in response.

5 November 1979: Mehdi Bazargan and his entire Government resigned, as a result of disagreements with Khomeini regarding the distribution of executive power. The Islamic Republican Party (IRP) assumed the task of governing the nation.

25 January 1980: Abolhasan Bani-Sadr won 75% of the votes cast in a presidential election.

14 March 1980: Elections to the Majlis began; voting was disrupted by violence in areas chiefly populated by Arabs, Kurds and Turkomans.

May 1980: The Chief Justice of the Islamic Revolutionary Courts, Ayatollah Khalkhali, claimed that he had ordered more than 300 executions as part of his campaign against 'un-Islamic' behaviour.

9 May 1980: The final round of voting in the legislative election was held; the results gave the IRP a large majority in the Majlis. In some Kurdish areas there were allegations of fraud and delay in the appointment of deputies.

18 July 1980: The IRC was dissolved and Muhammad Ali Rajai was appointed Prime Minister. There was a delay in the formation of a new government, however, since many of the candidates proposed by the Majlis were deemed unacceptable by President Bani-Sadr.

27 July 1980: The Shah died in exile in Egypt.

17 September 1980: President Saddam Hussain of Iraq announced that he was to abrogate the 1975 frontier agreements with Iran, owing to alleged Iranian border incursions.

22 September 1980: Iraqi aircraft attacked Iranian air bases; the Iranian air force retaliated with raids on Iraqi military installations.

28 September 1980: President Mohammed Zia ul-Haq of Pakistan led a delegation from the Islamic Conference to exchange views on the conflict between Iran and Iraq.

20 January 1981: The US hostages were released; during an unsuccessful attempt by the US Air Force to release the hostages in April 1980, eight US servicemen died when a helicopter collided with a transport aircraft.

June 1981: Khomeini dismissed Bani-Sadr from his post as head of the armed forces and subsequently from the presidency; Bani-Sadr fled to France and formed the National Council of Resistance with Massoud Rajavi, the former leader of the opposition guerrilla group, Mujahidin-e Khalq. Pending a presidential election, a Presidential Council comprising three senior officials was appointed.

28 June 1981: A bomb exploded at the headquarters of the IRP; the party's leader, Ayatollah Beheshti, four ministers, six deputy ministers and 20 parliamentary deputies were killed.

24 July 1981: Rajai won the presidential election; he was succedeed as Prime Minister by Muhammad Javar Bahunar.

29 August 1981: A further bomb attack killed both the President and the Prime Minister. The following month, Ayatollah Muhammad Reza Mahdavi Kani was appointed Prime Minister.

2 October 1981: Hojatoleslam Ali Khameini won 95.0% of the votes cast in the presidential election occasioned by the death of Rajai, and was duly elected to the post.

28 October 1981: Mahdavi Kani resigned as Prime Minister and was replaced by Mir Hussein Moussavi.

February 1982: The leader of the principal anti-government guerrilla group Mujahidin-e Khalq, Musa Khiabani, was killed.

March 1982: The Iranians launched successful counter-offensives against Iraq; they made further territorial gains the following month.

April 1982: An anti-government plot was revealed the Minister of Foreign Affairs, Sadeq Ghotbzabeh, was accused of involvement, as was Ayatollah Shariatmadari (the spiritual leader of the Azeri minority).

September 1982: Ghotbzabeh was convicted of anti-government activities and executed.

1983: Islamic codes of punishment for criminal activity were introduced.

February 1983: Iran began an offensive into the Iraqi province of Misan but failed to make any significant progress.

February 1983: The Secretary-General of the Tudeh Party, Nour ed-Din Kianuri, was arrested on charges of spying for the USSR; the party was banned in April.

July 1983: Iranian forces were able to advance 15 km into northern Iraq.

October 1983: Iran instigated a series of attacks and gained a large area of Iraqi territory, threatening the Kirkuk petroleum pipeline. Iraq retaliated by threatening to destroy Iran's petroleum installations with French-built fighters and missiles.

February 1984: Iran began an offensive in the marshlands around Majnoon Island, as part of a strategy to capture the Iraqi city of Basra.

15 April 1984: The first round of elections to the Majlis took place; Bazargan's Liberation Movement, the only opposition party recognized by the IRP, boycotted the poll.

December 1984: Iraq began a series of attacks on shipping in the Gulf, particularly on tankers using the Iranian Kharg Island terminal.

March 1985: Some 50,000 Iranian troops participated in an offensive in the Hawizah marshes, east of the River Tigris, and blocked the main road from Basra to Baghdad. Saddam Hussain was accused of ordering his troops to use chemical weapons to repel this offensive; Iraqi aircraft also raided 30 Iranian towns, despite having agreed with the UN to suspend attacks on civilians the previous June.

April 1985: In an attempt to persuade Iran to begin peace negotiations, Saddam Hussain announced the suspension of air raids on Iranian cities; the gesture was ignored—a further such attempt in June similarly failed.

April 1985: The UN Secretary-General, Javier Pérez de Cuéllar, held separate talks in Tehran and Baghdad in an attempt to begin peace negotitations. Iran continued to demand US $350,000 in reparations from Iraq, an admission of responsibility for initiating hostilities and the withdrawal of Iraqi troops from Iranian territory, before such negotiations could begin.

August 1985: Iraq began a series of concentrated raids on the Iranian petroleum plant on Kharg Island, occasioning a severe reduction in Iranian petroleum exports—shipments virtually ceased by the end of the year.

16 August 1985: Ali Khameini was re-elected President, recieving 85.7% of the votes cast.

13 October 1985: Hussein Moussavi was appointed Prime Minister, despite the fact that 99 Majlis deputies had either abstained or voted against him. The composition of the new Council of Ministers was also announced and included only two changes to the previous administration.

1986: Attacks by both Iran and Iraq on tankers and other commercial vessels in the Gulf intensified.

9–11 February 1986: Iran embarked on the Wal-Fajr (Dawn) offensive and captured the Iraqi port of Faw.

April 1986: Iran began the Karbala-8 offensive and, by the following month, claimed to have advanced within 1 km of of Basra.

May 1986: Iraqi forces began a land offensive into Iranian territory and carried out airborne attacks on Tehran.

October 1986–April 1987: It was estimated that 15 ships travelling to/from Kuwait were attacked by Iran in the Gulf and several Kuwaiti cargoes seized. Kuwaiti commercial tankers were subsequently re-registered under US and other foreign flags.

November 1986: Contrary to its official policy of neutrality, it became apparent that the USA had made three shipments of weapons and other items of military equipment to Iran since September 1985.

December 1986: It was reported in the *Washington Post* that the US Central Intelligence Agency (CIA), had been supplying Iraq with detailed information for two years, in particular regarding planned raids on Iranian oil and power plants. In January 1987 it further emerged that the US had deliberately provided both countries with inaccurate information in an attempt to cause an impasse in the conflict.

24 December 1986: Iranian troops carried out a further assault on the Basra region.

1987: Tunisia accused Iran of fomenting Islamic fundamentalist opposition to its Government and suspended diplomatic relations.

8 January 1987: The Iranian forces established a bridgehead inside Iraq, between the Shatt al-Arab in the west and Fish Lake to the east.

13 January 1987: Saddam Hussein offered Iran a cease-fire and peace negotiations; Iran declined and began the Karbala-6 offensive into north-eastern Iraq.

February 1987: The UN Commission on Human Rights estimated that at least 7,000 executions had taken place in Iran in 1979–85.

18 February 1987: In response to Iraq's declaration of a two-week moratorium on the bombing of Iranian towns, Iran agreed to suspend attacks on Iraqi cities.

June 1987: Iran refused to allow French authorities to interview Wahid Gordji, a translator working at the Iranian embassy in Paris, in connection with a bombing campaign in 1986. A cordon of armed police was subsequently stationed around the embassy—the Iranians responded with a similar deployment around the French embassy in Tehran. The blockades were lifted in November and Gordji returned to Iran.

June 1987: Ayatollah Khomeini approved a proposal by Hashemi Rafsanjani, the Speaker of the Majlis, to disband the IRP.

20 July 1987: The UN Security Council unanimously approved Resolution 598, urging Iran and Iraq to negotiate a cease-fire and proposing the establishment of an 'impartial body' to determine responsibility for starting the war.

24 July 1987: The USS *Bridgeton*, formerly a Kuwaiti oil tanker, struck a mine, believed to be Iranian, near the island of Farsi. France and the United Kingdom subsequently sent minesweepers to the region.

31 July 1987: Saudi Arabia accused Iranian pilgrims of instigating a stampede at Mecca which caused the death of 402 people as they performed the *Hajj*. The Government in turn claimed that the Saudi police had caused the incident by opening fire on the Iranians—Rafsanjani proclaimed a day of hatred on 2 August.

August 1987: Hojateslam Mehdi Hashemi, an aide to Khomeini's designated successor, Ayatollah Ali Hossein Montazeri, was tried by an Islamic court and convicted of murder, the abduction of a Syrian diplomat in Tehran, forming a private army in opposition to the Government and planning to carry out bomb attacks during the *Hajj*; he was executed the following month.

29 August 1987: Iraq resumed attacks on Iranian petroleum installations and industrial sites.

September 1987: Iran fired three missiles into Kuwaiti territory; the Kuwaiti Government subsequently expelled five Iranian diplomats.

8–11 September 1987: At the conclusion of a meeting in Amman (Jordan), the Arab League unanimously condemned Iran for prolonging the war with Iraq and urged the Iranian Government to implement UN Resolution 598 without pre-conditions.

11–15 September 1987: UN Secretary-General Javier Pérez de Cuéllar visited both warring countries with the aim of implementing Resolution 598. The Iranian Government announced that it would only agree to a cease-fire if Iraq's culpability for the conflict was established; Iraq was only prepared to negotiate a cease-fire on the terms of Resolution 598.

25 September 1987: The Government proposed the imposition of a *de facto* cease-fire while the UN appointed a commission of inquiry to determine responsibility for starting the war. Iraq rejected the proposals as being a deviation from Resolution 598.

19 October 1987: Four US naval vessels destroyed the Rostam and Rakhsh petroleum-extraction platforms, which lay some 100 km east of Qatar; the USA claimed that they had been used as a base for military operations against neutral shipping.

3 November 1987: The Iranian Deputy Minister of Foreign Affairs, Muhammad Javad Larijani, reiterated Iran's earlier statement that it would only observe a cease-fire if the UN Security Council were to identify Iraq as the agressor.

22 December 1987: The USSR proposed discussions in the UN Security Council regarding the prohibition of the sale of arms to Iran, in addition to the establishment of an international naval force in the Gulf, under the direction of the UN.

Early 1988: Iraq launched a series of counter-offensives, in which it regained much of the territory it had lost to Iran.

January 1988: The Syrian Government's offer to mediate between Iran and Iraq was rejected by both countries.

February 1988: Reciprocal attacks on civil and economic targets were resumed by Iran and Iraq. At the same time, Kurdish guerrillas advanced into government-controlled territory in Iraqi Kurdistan and established bridgeheads in the Mawat region along the Iranian border.

March 1988: At a meeting of the Organization of the Islamic Conference (OIC), the members agreed to Saudi Arabia's proposal to establish quotas for the number of pilgrims from each Muslim nation who would be permitted to undertake the *Hajj*. Khomeini denounced the resolution and no Iranian pilgrims participated in the *Hajj* that year.

March 1988: With the support of Iraq, the National Liberation Army (NLA), which was linked to the Iranian resistance group, Mujahidin-e-Khalq, began a major offensive in the province of Khuzestan.

April 1988: Saudi Arabia severed diplomatic ties with Iran, following several Iranian attacks on its shipping.

April 1988: The first round of elections to the Majlis took place; for the first time since the proclamation of the Islamic Republic the IRP did not take part, candidates standing as individuals.

April 1988: Iraqi forces recaptured the Faw peninsula.

May 1988: The second round of voting took place in the elections to the Majlis—an unprecedented 68% of the electorate voted, The composition of the new chamber was considered to reflect increasing support for reformist elements within the Government.

Mid-June 1988: Iraq recaputred Majnoun Island and the al-Hawizah marshes; Iranian forces were also expelled from Iraqi territory in Kurdistan.

June 1988: Rafsanjani was re-elected as Speaker of the Majlis and Hussein Moussavi was endorsed as Prime Minister.

2 June 1988: Rafsanjani was appointed acting Commander-in-Chief of the armed forces and given the task of eradicating inefficiencies in the army.

July 1988: A US Navy vessel in the Strait of Hormuz shot down an Iran Air passenger aircraft, killing all 290 passengers and crew; the US Navy claimed the ship's crew had mistakenly believed the aircraft to be an attacking fighter-bomber. The US Government agreed to pay compensation for each of the vicitms in July 1989.

16 July 1988: Iraqi forces captured the Iranian border town of Dehloran.

18 July 1988: Iran agreed to accept Resolution 598.

24 July 1988: Iraqi troops withdrew from Iran.

25 July 1988: In a three-day offensive, NLA forces advanced 150 km into Iranian territory.

6 August 1988: The Governments of Iran and Iraq agreed to begin peace negotiations.

20 August 1988: A cease-fire was officially implemented; it was monitored by the UN Iran-Iraq Military Oserver Group (UNIIMOG).

25 August 1988: Peace negotiations began in Geneva (Switzerland); progress was, however, impeded by the continuing dispute over responsibility for starting the war. Iran claimed that Iraq had initiated hostilities by invading Iran on 22 September 1980; Iraq maintained that the war had begun with the Iranian bombardment of border posts on 4 September 1980.

26 August 1988: The UN Security Council unanimously adopted Resolution 620, condemning the use of chemical weapons in the conflict between Iran and Iraq.

February 1989: Ayatollah Khomeini issued a *fatwa* (edict) ordering that a British author, Salman Rushdie, be killed for writing material offensive to Islam in his novel, *The Satanic Verses*; relations with the United Kingdom and other Western countries deteriorated sharply.

7 March 1989: Iran announced the termination of diplomatic relations with the United Kingdom; all staff at the British mission in Tehran had previously been withdrawn, as had Iranian diplomatic staff in the countries of the EEC.

3 June 1989: Ayatollah Khomeini died.

4 June 1989: Sitting in emergency session, the Council of Experts elected President Khameini to succeed Khomeini as the country's spiritual leader (Wali Faqih); the presidential election scheduled to be held in August was brought forward to 28 July.

8 June 1989: Rafsanjani was re-elected Speaker of the Majlis; during the course of the month, however, it became apparent that he would seek election to the presidency, and enjoyed the support of both 'conservatives' and 'liberals' wthin the country's leadership.

28 July 1989: Rafsanjani received 95.9% of the votes cast in the presidential election; in a concurrent referendum, a series of amendments to the Constitution (the most notable of which provided for the abolition of the post of Prime Minister and the installation of the President as head of government) was approved by some 95% of those voting.

17 August 1989: Rafsanjani took office as President, having resigned as Speaker of the Majlis, to be succeeded in that post by Ayatollah Mahdi Karrubi.

29 August 1989: The Majlis approved the Council of Ministers nominated by President Rafsanjani.

4 October 1989: A Committee to Determine the Expediency of the Islamic Order was appointed.

14–15 October 1989: An international conference on the 'Kurdish question' was held in Paris.

2–3 November 1989: The USA agreed to release US $567m. (of a reported total of $810m.) of the Iranian assets 'frozen' in 1979.

9 February 1990: Ayatollah Khamenei confirmed the death sentence on Salman Rushdie.

3 June 1990: The first anniversary of the death of Ayatollah Khomeini was commemorated by mass rally in Tehran.

21 June 1990: An earthquake struck Iran's north-western provinces of Gilan and Zanjan.

3 July 1990: The Ministers of Foreign Affairs of Iran and Iraq met in Geneva for direct talks.

15 August 1990: Iraq accepted Iranian terms for a final settlement of the conflict between the two countries.

10 September 1990: Iraq's Minister of Foreign Affairs, Tareq Aziz, visited Iran to discuss a peace treaty.

22–24 September 1990: President Hafiz al-Assad of Syria visited Tehran for talks with Iranian leaders.

24 September 1990: Iran and Tunisia restored diplomatic relations.

27 September 1990: Iran and the United Kingdom agreed to restore diplomatic relations, after the British Government acknowledged that *The Satanic Verses* had caused offence to Muslims, and stated that it had no wish to insult Islam.

14 October 1990: Iran and Iraq formally resumed diplomatic relations.

28 October 1990: The British Embassy in Tehran was reopened.

14 January 1991: Iran and Jordan restored diplomatic relations; the respective embassies reopened in March.

26 March 1991: Iran and Saudi Arabia restored diplomatic relations.

10 December 1991: A UN report on the conflict between Iran and Iraq found that Iraq's invasion of Iran in September 1980 contravened international law.

10 April 1992: The first round of voting in the legislative election took place; the second round was held on 8 May.

10 February 1993: It was reported that an assassination attempt directed at President Rafsanjani had failed.

11 June 1993: In the presidential election, President Rafsanjani received 63.2% of the votes cast; the low participation rate (some 56%) and the decline in support for Rafsanjani since the election of 1989 appeared to indicate increasing dissatisfaction with his style of Government among both 'conservatives' and 'liberals'.

8 August 1993: The Council of Ministers was reorganized.

1 December 1993: Iran and Turkey signed a security co-operation agreement.

1 February 1994: A further unsuccessful attempt on the life of President Rafsanjani was reported.

5 February 1994: The Ministers of Foreign Affairs of Iran, Syria and Turkey met in Istanbul for talks on the implications of events in Iraqi Kurdistan. Turkey urged Iraq to prevent the Kurdistan Workers' Party (PKK, a proscribed party in Turkey) from maintaining bases on its territory.

14 February 1994: The Council of Ministers was reorganized, with several new appointments made.

1 January 1995: The Majlis approved legislation prohibiting the import, distribution and use of satellite dishes.

8 January 1995: Iran signed an agreement with Russia on the completion of work at the Bushehr nuclear-power plant.

8 February 1995: The Speaker of US House of Representatives recommended the development of a long-term programme to overthrow the Iranian Government.

30 April 1995: The USA imposed an embargo on trade with and investment in Iran by US companies and individuals.

9 June 1995: Japan refused to enforce the US-led trade embargo against Iran.

8 March 1996: The first round of elections to the 270-seat Majlis took place.

19 April 1996: A second round of voting, to allocate the 125 seats in which no conclusive result was obtained in the first round, was held.

1 June 1996: The fifth Iranian Majlis was inaugurated.

19 June 1996: The US House of Representatives approved secondary sanctions against Iran and Libya.

8 October 1996: President Rafsanjani excluded the possibilty of his serving a third term of office.

23 May 1997: In the presidential election, Sayed Muhammad Khatami, considered a 'liberal' candidate, received 69.1% of the votes cast, and was elected President; the Speaker of the Majlis, Ali Akbar Nateq Nouri, obtained 24.9% of the ballot.

3 August 1997: Sayed Muhammad Khatami was inaugurated as President.

13 November 1997: Diplomats from European Union (EU) countries were permitted to return to Iran, following a compromise agreement.

19–26 November 1997: Numerous demonstrations, frequently violent, were organized by supporters of Ayatollah Khamenei in protest at the pronouncements of Ayatollah Montazeri, who had been Ayatollah Khomeini's designated successor prior to March 1989, and was now a prominent dissident.

29 November 1997: President Khatami appointed a new Committee for Ensuring and Supervising the Implementation of the Constitution.

9–11 December 1997: The eighth summit meeting of the OIC was convened in Tehran.

21–24 February 1998: Former President Rafsanjani became the first senior Iranian to visit Saudi Arabia since the 1979 Revolution.

23 February 1998: The EU ended a ban on high-level ministerial contacts between member states and Iran.

4 April 1998: The Mayor of Tehran, Gholamhossein Karbaschi, was arrested on corruption charges.

27 April 1998: Iran and Saudi Arabia signed a comprehensive co-operation agreement.

21 June 1998: The Iranian Minister of the Interior, Abdollah Nuri, who had opposed the prosecution of Karbaschi, was impeached and dismissed by the Majlis—he was subsequently appointed Vice-President in charge of Development and Social Affairs by President Khatami.

23 July 1998: Sayed Abdolvahed Musavi-Lari, the former Vice-President in charge of Legal and Parliamentary Affairs, was appointed Minister of the Interior.

23 July 1998: The former Mayor of Tehran, Karbaschi, was sentenced to five years' imprisonment and 60 lashes, having been found guilty on charges of corruption; he was also fined and banned from holding public office for 20 years. Upon appeal, heard in December, the length of the custodial sentence was reduced to two years, the lashes replaced by an additional fine, and the prohibition from public office reduced to 10 years.

8 August 1998: Eleven Iranian diplomats and more than 30 other Iranian nationals were reported missing in Afghanistan, following the capture of Mazar-i-Sharif by forces loyal to the Taliban movement.

2 September 1998: Iranian Revolutionary Guards organized large-scale military exercises along the border with Afghanistan.

10 September 1998: The bodies of several of the missing Iranian diplomats were discovered in Afghanistan.

15 September 1998: Iran vowed to avenge the deaths of the diplomats murdered in Afghanistan, and placed its armed forces on full alert.

24 September 1998: The Iranian Government pledged formally to dissociate itself from the *fatwa* imposed on the author Salman Rushdie in 1989.

23 October 1998: Elections to Iranian Assembly of Experts produced an overwhelming victory for 'conservative' candidates.

9 February 1999: The Minister of Information, Qorbanali Dorri Najafabadi, resigned, following revelations of involvement of intelligence offcials of the ministry in the killings of dissident intellectuals in late 1998.

26 February 1999: Iran's first local-council elections since the Revolution resulted in considerable success for 'centrist' and 'liberal' candidates.

7 July 1999: Following the approval by the Majlis of stringent new press laws, the closure of the pro-reform newspaper *Salaam* prompted demonstrations at Tehran University, the suppression of which by security forces and right-wing vigilantes precipitated demonstrations and rioting in Tehran and other cities in mid-July. The security forces' actions attracted domestic and international condemnation. Four people were subsequently sentenced to death for their part in the protests.

17 August 1999: Ayatollah Mahmoud Hashemi-Shahrudi was installed as the head of the Iranian judiciary, succeeding Muhammad Yazdi.

27–29 October 1999: President Khatami made an official visit to France.

21 November 1999: The border with Afghanistan, which had been closed since September 1998, was reopened for trade purposes.

27 November 1999: Nuri was sentenced to five years' imprisonment, after having been convicted on charges including insulting (in his capacity as Editor of a pro-reform newspaper) Islamic sanctities and refuting the values of the late Ayatollah Khomeini.

18 February 2000: First-round voting in Iranian legislative elections resulted in overwhelming successes for 'liberal' and 'moderate' candidates.

17 March 2000: The USA announced an end to the ban on imports of certain non-energy products from Iran.

5 May 2000: A second round of legislative voting in Iran confirmed that supporters of President Khatami were likely to command a substantial majority in the sixth Majlis.

1 July 2000: A court in Shiraz convicted 10 Iranian Jews and two Muslims of spying on behalf of Israel.

28 September 2000: Two leading Iranian human rights lawyers were given suspended prison sentences and banned from working for five years following their conviction on charges of producing a defamatory video tape which inferred that leading 'conservative' figures had supported the activities of violent right-wing groups.

3 October 2000: The Minister of Culture and Islamic Guidance, Ayatollah Mohajerani, resigned; right-wing factions had accused him of excessive liberalism and pro-Western views.

9 October 2000: Kazakhstan signed a co-operation agreement with Russia on resolving the legal status of the Caspian Sea; the two governments urged Azerbaijan, Iran and Turkmenistan to hold a 'summit' meeting to discuss the issue.

14–15 October 2000: The Minister of Foreign Affairs, Kamal Kharrazi, visited Iraq for talks with Saddam Hussain and other Iraqi government officials. The two countries decided to revive the border agreement signed in June 1975, which had been suspended since 1980.

November 2000: President Khatami warned that he lacked the necessary powers to implement the Constitution, stating that extreme right-wing groups were creating a government within the Goverment.

2 November 2000: The trial began of 15 'reformists' accused of acting against national security and disseminating anti-government propaganda by attending a conference on political reform in Iran held in Berlin, Germany, the previous year. Among the accused were a leading investigative journalist, Akbar Ganji, a 'reformist' politician, Jamileh Kadivar, and Hassan Yousefi Eshkevari, a dissident cleric.

5 December 2000: The Government rejected a UN resolution denouncing Iran's human-rights record.

13 December 2000: Algeria, Egypt, Iran, Kuwait, Morocco, Saudi Arabia, Syria and Tunisia signed the UN Convention Against Organized Crime, which provided for co-ordination between national crime-fighting bodies, the protection of witnesses, measures to combat money-laundering and the acceleration of extradition proceedings.

13 January 2001: The trial of the 15 'reformists' accused of acting against the Government, which had begun in November 2000, was concluded; Akbar Ganji received a prison sentence of 10 years, followed by five years' internal exile; seven other defendants were sentenced to between four and ten years' imprisonment.

2 February 2001: The Governments of Iran and Kuwait announced plans to construct a 540-km pipeline to supply Kuwait with drinking water.

18 March 2001: The Revolutionary Courts banned the Iran Freedom Movement (IFM) and closed three reformist newspapers; 21 associates of the IFM had already been arrested on charges of collaboration with counter-revolutionary and terrorist groups.

19 April 2001: The Iraqi armed forces claimed that they had shot down an unmanned Iranian surveillance aircraft near Mendali, 400 km north-east of Baghdad.

20 April 2001: A senior Iranian Commander alleged that Mujahidin-e Khalq had attacked Iranian targets from inside the Iraqi border. Iraq claimed that two days earlier, Iran had fired more than 50 missiles into Iraqi territory, injuring and killing several civilians; this was later confirmed by the Iranian Government.

5 May 2001: The Government withdrew its diplomatic staff from the Iranian consulate in Herat, Afghanistan, following an explosion at the building the previous day. The Taliban miltary leadership of Afghanistan blamed dissident Iranian groups, which aimed to undermine the improved relations between the two countries, for the attack.

8 May 2001: The Cuban leader, Dr Fidel Castro Ruz, visited Iran to discuss bilateral relations with senior government officials; Castro praised Iran's anti-US policies.

9 May 2001: The USA vetoed Iran's application for membership of the World Trade Organization, claiming that Iran was a 'terrorist nation'.

4 June 2001: At a meeting of the Gulf Co-operation Council, the members urged Iran to submit its territorial dispute with the United Arab Emirates over three islands, Abu Mussa and the Greater and Lesser Tunbs, and access to the Strait of Hormuz, to the International Court of Justice.

8 June 2001: Khatami was re-elected as President, receiving 76% of the votes cast in the election.

19 June 2001: Ayatollah Khameini ruled that the Majlis could monitor the activities of the 'pro-conservative' national radio and television networks.

28 June 2001: The Council of Guardians rejected draft legislation which aimed to define political crimes and determine conditions for political prisoners.

Iraq

6000 BC: Migrants from Asia Minor and southern Transcaucasia settled an area between the Tigris and Euphrates rivers, which became known as Mesopotamia and constituted an area approximate to that of modern-day Iraq.

3000 BC: The Sumerians (Southern Mesopotamians) established a complex, agriculturally based society. They are considered to be the first people to have developed a written form of communication, known as cuneiform, and are also credited with developing the spoked chariot wheel.

***c.* 2500 BC:** The Sumerian city-state of Lagash formed a short-lived union with four of its rival cities and extended its authority as far as Elam in south-western Persia.

2334 BC: King Sargon I of the Semitic city of Akkad conquered the Sumerian civilization and founded the Akkadian Empire.

1900 BC: The Akkadian Empire fell under the pressure of attacks from the Semitic Amorites from the West and the Caucasian Elamites from the east. The Amorites subsequently established cities on the Tigris and Euphrates and made Babylon, in southern Mesopotamia, their capital.

***c.* 1792 BC–*c.* 1750 BC:** During the reign of King Hammurabi, the Babylonian Empire reached its apogee. A sophisticated administrative structure was created and a code of law established.

1600 BC: The Babylonian Empire began to weaken under attacks from the Kassites and Hurrites; a group of Hurrites migrated to southern Iraq and established themselves as rulers.

1500 BC: Following their invasion of northern Mesopotamia at the end of the 15th century BC, the Mitanni asserted their authority over much of the region.

1350 BC: The Hittites began to launch incursions from Asia Minor into Mitanni territory.

1295 BC–1197 BC: The Assyrians, whose civilization was based around the city of Ashur, in northern Mespotamia, carried out offensives on the Mitanni Empire.

729 BC: The Assyrian leader, Tiglath-Pileser III, asserted himself as the new ruler of Babylon.

671 BC: The Assyrian Empire reached its zenith under King Esarhaddon, who conquered Egypt.

626 BC–605 BC: The Babylonian state was briefly re-established under the reign of King Nabopolassar, who founded the Chaldean (Neo-Babylonian) dynasty.

609 BC: The Assyrian empire fell, following offensives by the Babylonians, Medes and Scythians.

539 BC–538 BC: Cyrus II ('the Great') of Persia conquered the Chaldean Empire and Mesopotamia became one of the many provinces of the Achaemenid Empire, which came to extend from Asia Minor in the west to the Punjab in the east and from southern Russia in the north to Egypt in the south.

520 BC–485 BC: During the reign of Darius I ('the Great'), a programme of road-building was instituted and trade in the region prospered.

482 BC: Popular unrest, which had begun in response to increased taxation and poverty following the death of Darius, culminated in a major rebellion by the Babylonians against Assyrian rule.

334 BC–327 BC: Alexander III ('the Great'), the King of Macedon and Greek military leader, ended Assyrian rule. During his period of governance, he respected Babylonian institutions and allowed native religious practices to be observed.

323 BC: Alexander died; one of his generals, Seleucus Nicator, took control of much of his Asiatic Empire, including Mesopotamia. Under his rule, trade routes to the Greek Empire were established, the economy revived and western art forms and deities introduced.

126 BC: The Parthians (Arsacids), a nomadic people from Turkestan, captured the Tigris-Euphrates river valley and proceeded to control Mesopotamia.

AD 113: The Roman Emperor Trajan conquered a large area of Mesopotamia, although the territory was abandoned during the rule of his successor, Hadrian.

193–211: Emperor Septimus Severus led a further brief Roman occupation of the region.

227: Following a popular revolt against Parthian rule in 224, another group of Persians, the Sassanids (Sassanians), conquered the region.

260: The Sassanid King, Sapor I, defeated a Roman offensive near Edessa (modern-day Sanliurfa, Turkey) and captured Emperor Valerian.

488–579: Under the reigns of Kobad I and Anushirvan, the Sassanid state enjoyed a period of peace and stablilty.

6th–7th centuries: Continual conflict with the Romans devastated the Babylonian civilization and ravaged the land.

634: The Sassanids defeated a Bedouin incursion at the Battle of the Bridge; Bedouin attacks on the Empire continued, however.

637: Saad ibn Abi Waqqas led the Muslims to victory at the Battle of Qadisiya and subsequently captured the Sassanid capital, Ctesiphon.

638: The Muslims conqered the greater part of modern Iraq—there remained only small areas of resistance in the north. The last Sassanid king, Yazdegerd III, fled to Persia where he was assassinated in 651.

641: The Arabs subdued the last centre of Sassanid resistance, Mosul. The garrison cities of Kufa and Basra were established, largely populated by immigrants from eastern Arabia and Oman.

656: Upon the death of Caliph Uthman, a dispute between two of his potential successors, Ali and Mu'awiya, arose and escalated into conflict. Ali's campaign was based in Iraq, Mu'awiya's in Syria.

late 661: The Shi'at Ali (party of Ali) was established in opposition to Umayyad rule.

January 661: Ali was killed; Mu'awiya succeeded as Caliph and Syria became the centre of the Umayyad Caliphate and, consequently, the Muslim world.

October 680: At the Battle of Karbala, Husain, the son of Ali, was killed in battle against the Umayyads; he became an important Shi'a martyr.

685–687: A major Shi'a rebellion occurred at Kufa.

685–705: Al-Hajjaj ibn Yusuf was appointed Umayyad Governor in Iraq. He encouraged the development of agriculture and education, while instituting strict controls to contain Iraqi resistance.

701: A further insurrection took place, led by Muhammad ibn al-Ash'ath; Syrian soldiers were used to suppress the resistance.

705–15: Recently converted Iraqi Muslims were encouraged to join Arab expeditions into Central Asia; however, Muslims remained the minority in Iraq.

747: The Abbasids, a branch of the family of the Prophet Muhammad, distantly related to Ali and his descendants, began to challenge Umayyad rule.

749: The first Abbasid Caliph, as-Saffah, was proclaimed at a mosque in Kufa; the following year, Umayyad rule in Iraq was ended.

762: The second Abbasid Caliph, al-Mansur, made Baghdad the capital of the Empire; he created an autocracy based on divine authority, the armed forces, a paid bureaucracy, the *Ulema*—an influential group of religious scholars—and a cosmopolitan ruling class composed of officials, landowners, merchants and bankers.

789: Trade and agriculture flourished during the reign of Harun ar-Rashid.

809–813: Following the death of ar-Rashid, a dispute over the succession between his two sons, Mam'm and Amin, developed into civil war. After laying siege to Baghdad for almost a year, Mam'm defeated Amin with the assistance of Persian soldiers.

869–883: East African slaves in the state of Zanj, in southern Iraq, rebelled against their owners. The slaves brought a large part of southern Iraq and south-western Iran under their control and enslaved many of their former masters; in 871, the slaves sacked the city of Basra.

10th century: Qarmatians from Bahrain made frequent attacks on Iraq.

945–1055: Shi'a Buwahids, led by chief Mu'izz ad-Dawlah, occupied Baghdad.

1055: Sunni Muslim Seljuq Turks, the ruling clan of the Oghuz Turks from north of the Oxus River, invaded the region and captured Baghdad.

1092: Following the death of their ruler, Malik Shah, the Turks rebelled and a succession of states governed by Seljuq princes or military leaders emerged.

1194: The last Seljuq governor of Iraq, Tughril, was defeated in battle by the Turkish ruler of Khwarzim.

1258: Hüläkü, the grandson of the Mongol leader Temujin (Chinghiz or Genghis Khan) captured Baghdad and ended the Abbasid caliphate. The Mongol invasion led to a decay in civil government, serious damage to the irrigation system essential for agriculture and frequent Bedouin incursions. Iraq became subordinate to the Mongol Khan of Persia.

1335: The last Mongol Khan, Abu Said ('Bahadur the Brave') died; a period of political instability ensued, allowing a local dynasty, the Jalayirids, to seize power.

1393: Timur ('the lame'—Tamerlane), a Turkmen emir from Central Asia, sacked Baghdad and caused further damage to the irrigation system.

1410: A confederation of Turkmen tribes from Lake Van (modern Turkey), known as the Kara Koyunlu (Black Sheep), defeated the last Jalayirid ruler, Ahmed; they proceeded to create a new state which extended from Tabriz to the Shatt al-Arab waterway.

1447–68: The Kara Koyunlu state was the subject of challenges by a rival confederation, the Ak Koyunlu (White Sheep). The Ak Koyunlu eventually succeded in taking control of the state.

1514: The Ottoman Sultan Selim I ('the Grim') declared war on the Safavids, thus precipitating over a century of conflict.

1534–35: Sultan Suleyman ('the Magnificent') captured Baghdad.

1623: The Safavids recaptured Baghdad under the leadership of Shah Abbas.

1628: The Ottomans successfully reconquered Baghdad.

1629: The Safavids and Ottomans signed the Treaty of Qasr-i-Shirin (Treaty of Zuhab), concluding the period of conflict.

1694–1701: Tribal dynasties ruled Basra and the delta marshlands in southern Iraq independently of the Ottoman administration at Bagdhad. These local governors encouraged British, Dutch and Portuguese merchants active in the Red Sea to establish trading posts in Basra.

1704: Hasan Pasha, an Ottoman ruler of Georgian origin, was appointed Governor of Iraq.

1723: The Ottomans became involved in a new war against the Persians.

1729: The Persian ruler, Nadir Shah, invaded and Iraq descended into a state of anarchy; Baghdad was besieged in 1733 and 1743.

1746: Ahmed Pasha, the son of Hasan Pasha, made peace with Persia in an agreement similar to the Treaty of Qasr-i-Shirin.

1750: Suleyman Agha, a Mameluke (Caucasian Christian former slaves who had been forced to convert to Islam), became Governor of Baghdad and Basra.

1763: The British East India Company was permitted to establish an agency in Basra.

1764: Umr Agha, also a Mameluke, succeeded Suleyman as Governor.

1776–79: The Persians exploited internal political unrest within Iraq and occupied Basra.

1780: Suleyman 'the Great', assumed the Governorship of Baghdad. He appointed large numbers of Mamelukes to strengthen the administration and sought to develop trade and agriculture.

1790s: Muslim Wahhabi warriors from central Arabia made frequent incursions into Iraq.

1798: Suleyman gave permission for a permanent British agent to be appointed to Baghdad.

1801: Wahhabi forces raided the Shi'a holy city of Karbala.

1803–04: Further Wahhabi incursions took place in the areas surrounding Najaf and Basra.

1817: The last Mameluke Ottoman ruler, Da'ud Pasha, regained control of the territory lost to the Wahhabis and embarked on punitive campaigns against the Kurds in the north and the nomadic tribes of the desert lands to the south.

1831: The Ottoman Emperor, Mahmud II, acted to regain direct Ottoman rule of Iraq by appointing Ali Ridha Pasha as Governor. Mameluke resistance was undermined by an epidemic of plague and the Ottoman forces deposed Da'ud Pasha.

1858: A new land law was enacted, aimed to encourage tribal leaders to become landowners and tribesmen to settle as their tenants.

1860s: A telegraph system was established, linking Baghdad with Istanbul (the Ottoman capital, in modern Turkey). Christian and Jewish missionary organizations also opened schools and colleges.

1869: Iraqi trade benefited from the opening of the Suez Canal, which linked the Mediterranean with the Red Sea.

1869: Midha Pasha was appointed Ottoman ruler of Baghdad. He ordered the demolition of a section of the old city wall to allow for urban expansion; he also established municipal and administrative councils, military factories, a hospital, almshouses, schools, a tramway, conscription for the army and Baghdad's first newspaper.

1910–13: The Hindiya Barrage on the Euphrates was rebuilt.

1912: A group of British, Dutch and German companies formed the Turkish Petroleum Company, which was given a concession to explore for petroleum deposits in the areas surrounding the cities of Mosul and Baghdad.

1914: A railway linking Baghdad with Samarra was completed.

22 November 1914: Following the Ottoman Empire's entry into the First World War on the side of the central powers, a British expeditionary force landed at the head of the Persian Gulf and occupied Basra.

1915: British forces failed in an attempt to capture Baghdad and were instead forced to retreat to Kut, where they were besieged for 140 days and forced to surrender unconditionally in 1916.

March 1917: A further Allied attempt to capture Baghdad was successful.

1918: The Allies took Kirkuk.

30 October 1918: The Armistice of Mudros brought the war in the Middle East to an end. The British armed forces and a civil commission took responsibility for the administration of the region between Basra and Baghdad.

25 April 1920: At the San Remo conference in Italy, Iraq was made a mandate of the United Kingdom. The decision provoked violent insurrection; the British High Commissioner, Col Talbot Wilson, met a pro-independence grouping, but rejected their demands.

July 1920: Continuing civil unrest escalated into a revolt against British rule, which subsequently became known as The Great Iraqi Revolution; the British used aerial bombardment to restore order.

October 1920: Military rule in Iraq was formally terminated; a provisional Arab Council of State, advised by British officials, was established.

March 1921: The former King of Syria, the Amir Faisal ibn Husain was offered the crown of Iraq by the British Government; following the approval of the proposals in a plebiscite, Faisal was crowned on 23 August.

May 1922: The border between Iraq and Saudi Arabia was defined in the Treaty of Mohammara; subsequent Saudi concerns over the loss of traditional grazing rights led to the establishment of 7,000 sq km of neutral territory near Kuwait.

May 1922: An Electoral Law was passed, providing for the election of a National Constituent Assembly.

10 October 1922: A new agreement on the country's governance was signed by the British and Iraqis; it maintained many of the conditions of the United Kingdom's mandate, including the advisory role in Iraq's foreign and military affairs and the obligations of Iraq to protect the judicial rights of foreign nationals.

March 1924: The newly-elected Constituent Assembly met and, despite opposition from nationalists, ratified the Treaty signed in 1922. The Assembly also approved the Organic Law, which proclaimed Iraq to be a sovereign state with a constitutional hereditary monarchy and a representative system of government.

1926: Turkey relinquished its claim to the northern district of Mosul, which was duly incorporated into Iraq.

June 1930: A further agreement with the United Kingdom was signed, providing for full Iraqi independence; the British retained the right to use certain air bases and to move troops across the country; the Assyrian and Kurdish minorities claimed the agreement failed to guarantee their status.

1932: Sectarian conflict broke out between Sunni and Shi'a Muslim communities; the Government also faced rebellions from Assyrian and Kurdish minority groups.

13 October 1932: In accordance with the agreement signed in June 1930, Iraq became independent and was admitted to the League of Nations. The country's first Government was led by Gen. Nuri as-Said.

August 1933: An uprising among Christian Assyrians was violently suppressed by Iraqi forces—several hundred Assyrians were reported to have been killed.

September 1933: King Faisal died while undergoing medical treatment in Switzerland; he was succeeded by his son, Ghazi.

1934: The Iraq Petroleum Company (IPC), began exporting petroleum through two pipelines to Tripoli (Lebanon) and Haifa (now in Israel).

1935–36: A tribal revolt along the Euphrates was brutally suppressed by the army.

October 1936: Gen. Bakr Sidqi, a Kurd operating in alliance with political reformers, carried out a *coup d'état*. The Premier, Rashid Ali, was exiled; Hikmat Sulayman formed a new administration.

1937: Afghanistan, Iran, Iraq and Turkey agreed to the Sa'dabad Pact, which provided for mutual consultation in all disputes that might affect the common interests of the four states.

August 1937: Following the failure of the new regime to fulfil its promises of political reform and amid increasing government isolation of tribal chieftains and nationalists, Gen. Sidqi was assassinated by a military group.

1939: At the outbreak of the Second World War, Iraq was obliged to terminate relations with Germany under the conditions of the agreement signed with the United Kingdom in 1930.

April 1939: King Ghazi was killed in a car accident; he was succeeded by his infant son, Faisal II, his cousin Amir Abd Allah being appointed Regent.

1941: A *coup d'état* was carried out by army officers, under the leadership of the pro-German Rashid Ali al-Gaylani. Despite the new Government's declaration of neutrality, British forces occupied Baghdad and Basra.

January 1943: Iraq declared war on Germany.

March 1945: Egypt, Iraq, Lebanon, Saudi Arabia, Syria, Transjordan and Yemen founded the League of Arab States (Arab League), which aimed to promote political, cultural, economic and social co-operation between its members and act as mediator in regional disputes.

January 1948: Iraq and the United Kingdom signed new accord; the British agreed to evacuate the air bases at Shuaiba and Habbaniya and a joint board for the co-ordination of mutual defence interests was created. However, amid ensuing popular unrest, the Government repudiated the agreement.

15 May 1948: The Government despatched sent an estimated 9,000 troops to assist the Palestinians in the Arab-Israeli war.

1952: A new petroleum pipeline to Banias (Syria), was built; a second pipeline to the Lebanese port of Tripoli had been constructed in 1949.

February 1952: The Government and petroleum companies reached an agreement whereby the Government received 50% of the companies' pre-tax profits.

November 1952: Amid tensions arising from the cost of the war against Israel and following a poor harvest, severe rioting occurred in Baghdad; the Government imposed martial law.

October 1953: The state of martial law was ended.

February 1955: Iraq and Turkey formed a defence alliance.

February 1955: Iraq, Pakistan and the United Kingdom made a defence agreement, which became known as the Baghdad Pact.

April 1956: Flood-control and irrigation works came into operation at Ramadi and Samarra.

31 October 1956: Popular unrest related to the military intervention by France and the United Kingdom in protest at the Egyptian Government's nationalization of the Suez Canal (the so-called 'Suez Crisis') led to the imposition of martial law.

November 1956: IPC installations in Syria were sabotaged.

9 November 1956: Iraq severed diplomatic relations with France, as a result of the Suez Crisis.

May 1957: Martial law was lifted.

14 February 1958: King Faisal and his cousin, King Hussein of Jordan, proclaimed the unification of their kingdoms in a new Arab Federation, formed in reponse to the creation of the United Arab Republic (UAR) by Egypt and Syria at the beginning of the month.

5 May 1958: A general election resulted in victories for pro-Government, pro-Federation candidates.

14 July 1958: A republic was established in Iraq, following a military revolt in which King Faisal and the Prime Minister, Nuri es-Said, were assassinated. Power was assumed by Brig. (later Gen.) Abd al-Karim Kassem, as Prime Minister.

19 July 1958: A defence pact between Iraq and the UAR was announced.

1 August 1958: The Arab Federation was formally suspended.

11 October 1958: Iraq and Russia signed an agreement on trade.

6 February 1959: Six ministers resigned in protest against the death sentence imposed on the former Deputy Premier and revolutionary leader, Col Abdel Aref, who had been charged with attempting to assassinate Gen. Kassem (the sentence was later commuted to life imprisonment).

8 February 1959: A new Iraqi Cabinet was formed, with the exclusion of the nationalist Istiqlal Party.

8–9 March 1959: An uprising in Mosul, led by Col Abdul Wahab Shawwaf, was quelled by the Iraqi Government.

10 March 1959: The staff of the Embassy of the UAR in Baghdad were expelled from Iraq.

16 March 1959: The USSR signed an agreement with Iraq promising economic and technical aid.

24 March 1959: Iraq withdrew from the Baghdad Pact.

29 March 1959: The Iraqi Ambassador to the UAR resigned in protest against his Government's policies.

14 July 1959: Severe rioting occurred in Kirkuk on the first anniversary of the Iraqi Revolution; an estimated 80 people were killed.

15 August 1959: Work began on the improvement of the Baghdad-Basra railway line—the programme was estimated to cost US $18m.

7 October 1959: Gen. Kassem was seriously wounded in an assassination attempt.

26 November 1959: The Iraqi Government announced four-year Defence and Development Plan, with a budget of 400m. dinars.

9 February 1960: The National Democratic Party (NDP), the Democratic Party of Kurdistan (DPK) and the Iraq Communist Party (ICP) were legalized.

10 September 1960: Following discussions among officials from petroleum-producing countries, held in Baghdad, the Organization of Petroleum Exporting Companies (OPEC) was formed.

1 October 1960: Jordan recognized the republican regime in Iraq.

1961: Gen. Kassem pardoned Col Aref.

25 June 1961: Gen. Kassem laid claim to Kuwait, stating that the Sheikhdom was an integral part of Iraq.

8 February 1963: Gen. Kassem was killed in a *coup d'état*. Col Aref was installed as President, Brig. Ahmed Bakr as Prime Minister. The Baath Party, an Arab nationalist socialist movement, gained political pre-eminence within the new Government.

17 April 1963: A proposal to create a federation of Iraq, Syria and the UAR was announced—the plans were abandoned in August.

13 May 1963: A new cabinet was formed.

8 October 1963: Iraq and Syria announced a union of their military forces.

18 November 1963: With the support of the armed forces, Aref suppressed a number of movements to displace him, and reasserted his leadership. A Revolutionary Command Council (RCC) was established. The proposed federation with Syria was abandoned.

29 April 1964: A new Constitution was enacted, vesting executive power in the President, who was to be elected, in part, by the Revolutionary Command Council (RCC).

26 May 1964: An agreement was signed establishing a Joint Presidency Council of Iraq and the UAR.

13 August 1964: A Common Market of Iraq, Jordan, Kuwait and Syria was established, under the aegis of the Arab League.

16 October 1964: An agreement was signed by Iraq and the UAR to form a Unified Political Command; the body was established in December.

1 January 1965: The provisions of the Arab Common Market entered into force.

18 July 1965: Several Pro-Egyptian ministers resigned from the Government, necessitating a major reorganization of the cabinet in which more Baathists wre appointed.

6 September 1965: A new civilian Government was formed in Iraq, led by Arif Abdel Razzak.

17 September 1965: The Prime Minister, Arif Abdel Razzak, fled to the Egyptian capital, Cairo, following his participation in an unsuccessful *coup d'état* against President Aref. Dr Abd ar-Rahman al-Bazzaz was appointed to replace him.

13 April 1966: President Aref was killed in an air accident, and was succeeded by his brother, Maj.-Gen. Abd ar-Rahman Muhammad Aref.

29 May 1966: The Iraqi Premier, Bazzaz, proposed a cease-fire agreement to the Kurds.

12 June 1966: An unsuccessful attempt to overthrow the Government was led by Arif Abdel Razzak.

9 August 1966: A new Government was formed, led by Naji Talib.

10 May 1967: President Aref formed a new Government; he assumed the office of Premier himself.

6 June 1967: The United Kingdom and the USA were accused by President Nasser of the UAR and King Hussein of Jordan of military collusion with Israel; 10 Arab states imposed an embargo on petroleum supplies to the two countries. Diplomatic relations with the USA were suspended by Algeria, Iraq, Sudan, Syria, the UAR and Yemen; Iraq and Syria terminated relations with the United Kingdom.

1 May 1968: Iraq resumed diplomatic relations with the United Kingdom.

20 July 1968: President Aref was deposed; Ahmed al-Bakr assumed the presidency and formed a Government.

30 July 1968: President al-Bakr dismissed the new Prime Minister and cabinet and appointed himself Prime Minister and Commander-in-Chief of the armed forces.

27 January 1969: Fourteen men (nine of whom were Jewish) were executed in Iraq amid much publicity, after being convicted of spying for Israel.

21 April 1969: An Iranian vessel sailed along the Shatt al-Arab waterway flying its national flag, thus abrogating a 1937 treaty granting Iraq sovereignty over the waterway.

20 January 1970: Iraq accused Iran of involvement in a failed *coup d'état*.

11 March 1970: The Kurds accepted the Government's 15-point peace proposal and ended their armed struggle.

5–6 August 1970: The foreign and defence ministers of Jordan, Libya, Sudan, Syria and the UAR met in Tripoli (Libya); Algeria and Iraq refused to send delegations.

15 October 1970: Air Marshal Hardan Takriti was dismissed from his post as Vice-President.

14 February 1971: A new, five-year agreement was signed by 23 international petroleum companies and the governments of Abu Dhabi, Iran, Iraq, Kuwait, Qatar and Saudi Arabia.

2 April 1971: An agreement was reached in Tripoli between international petroleum companies and the Libyan Government (which was also acting on behalf of Algeria, Iraq and Saudi Arabia); the posted price for Libyan crude petroleum was increased by US $0.90.

June 1971: Iraq closed its border with Jordan, in protest at Jordanian attacks on positions held by Palestinian guerrilla groups.

30 November 1971: Iran occupied the Greater and Lesser Tunbs islands, expelling Arab inhabitants; Iraq suspended relations with Iran in retaliation, and began to expel some 60,000 resident Iranians.

9 April 1972: Iraq signed a 15-year friendship treaty with the USSR.

1 June 1972: The IPC was nationalized.

27 July 1972: The USA announced that a US-interests section was to be opened in a third country's embassy in Iraq in September.

1 August 1972: Iraq and Sudan resumed diplomatic relations, which had been suspended following the July 1971 coup attempt.

5 October 1972: Agreement was reached between Abu Dhabi, Iraq, Kuwait, Qatar and Saudi Arabia for one part, and representatives of various petroleum companies for the other, on the eventual 51% participation of the producing countries in the various concessions.

30 June 1973: Lieut.-Gen. Hamad Shehab, the Minister of Defence, was killed during an unsuccessful attempt to seize power by Col Nazem Kazzar, the Director of Public Security.

October 1973: At the renewal of hostilities between Israel and the Palestinians, Iraq renewed diplomatic relations with Iran and sent forces to the Syrian front.

1974: Sporadic fighting occurred throughout the year on the Iran-Iraq border, despite UN efforts to mediate between the two countries.

16 August 1974: Iraq and Japan signed an agreement providing for the supply of Iraqi crude petroleum and derived products, in exchange for Japanese credits to finance industrialization projects in Iraq.

January 1975: The Minister of Foreign Affairs held negotiations with his Iranian counterpart; hostilities ended in February.

March 1975: At a meeting of OPEC, it was announced that Saddam Hussain Takriti, Vice-President of the RCC, and the Shah of Iran had signed an agreement to eliminate conflict between 'two brotherly countries'.

June 1975: A formal peace agreement was signed between Iran and Iraq, which defined their frontiers according to the 1913 Protocol of Constantinople. The division of the waters of the Shatt al-Arab was defined according to the 'Thalweg line', which ran along the middle of the deepest shipping lane.

February 1976: It was reported that Iraq was diverting much of its petroleum from pipelines to the Mediterranean, which used Syrian ports, to Basra, thus depriving Syria of valuable carriage revenues.

February 1977: The Government angered Shi'a pilgrims by closing Karbala during a religious ceremony amid security concerns; violence later spread to the citiy of Najaf.

November–December 1977: At the conference on the Arab-Israeli conflict in Tripoli (Libya), Iraq refused to endorse UN Security Council Resolution 242, which advocated a negotiated end to the conflict, and announced its refusal to participate in the next conference, to be held in the Algerian capital, Algiers.

October 1978: During a visit by President Hafiz al-Assad of Syria, plans for an economic and political union between Iraq and Syria were approved.

March 1979: The Communists withdrew from the National Progressive Front.

4–6 March 1979: Iraq, Jordan and Syria attended negotiations in Kuwait to mediate a cease-fire between the People's Democratic Republic of Yemen and the Yemen Arab Republic.

July 1979: Further rioting occurred among Shi'a in Karbala and Najaf, following the Government's refusal to allow Ayatollah Muhammad Baqir as-Sadr, a leading cleric, to travel with a Shi'a delegation to congratulate Ayatollah Ruhollah Khomeini on the Islamic Revolution in Iran.

12 July 1979: The Secretary of the RCC, Muhyi Abd al-Hussein al-Mashhadi, publicly confessed that he and other Baath leaders had conspired to overthrow the regime. The suspects were tried in a special court and, following their convictions, 22 were executed.

16 July 1979: Al-Bakr announced his resignation as Chairman of the RCC, Baath Party leader and President; he was succeeded by Saddam Hussain.

February 1980: Saddam Hussain announced a new National Charter and advocated greater solidarity among the Arab nations.

16 March 1980: Legislation providing for the creation of a National Assembly of 250 deputies was enacted; a Kurdish Legislative Council was also established.

20 June 1980: Elections to the National Assembly were held; although candidates were not permitted to identify themselves with political parties, it was estimated that supporters of the Baath party had gained a significant majority in the Assembly.

30 June 1980: The first session of the National Assembly took place; Naim Haddad was elected Chairman and Speaker.

17 September 1980: Saddam Hussain announced that he was to abrogate the 1975 frontier agreements with Iran, owing to alleged border incursions.

22 September 1980: Iraqi aircraft attacked Iranian air bases; the Iranian air force retaliated with raids on Iraqi military installations.

1981: The Iraqi Front of Revolutionary, Islamic and National Forces was founded by a group of Kurds, exiled Shi'a and disaffected Baath party members, with the support of Syria.

October 1981: Iraq and Jordan established a joint Committee for Economic and Technical Co-operation.

March 1982: The Iranians launched successful counter-offensives against Iraq; they made further territorial gains the following month.

June 1982: Saddam Hussain admitted that the campaign to invade Iran had failed.

July 1982: Saddam Hussain was re-elected Chairman of the RCC and regional secretary of the Baath Party.

August 1982: Iraq declared the area extending from the mouth of the Shatt al-Arab waterway to the Iranian port of Bushehr to be a maritime exclusion zone.

November 1982: The Supreme Council of Iraqi Opposition Group, led by an exiled Shi'a leader, Hojatoleslam Muhammad Baqir Hakim, was founded in Iran.

July 1983: Iranian forces were able to advance 15 km into northern Iraq.

October 1983: Following rumours of an attempted *coup d'état* in Baghdad, a number of senior army officers were reported to have been executed.

October 1983: Iran instigated a series of attacks and gained a large area of Iraqi territory, threatening the Kirkuk petroleum pipeline. Iraq retaliated by threatening to destroy Iran's petroleum installations with French-built fighters and missiles.

December 1983: The Government agreed to a suspension of hostilities with the leader of the proscribed Patriotic Union of Kurdistan (PUK).

February 1984: Iran began an offensive in the marshlands around Majnoon Island, as part of a strategy to capture the Iraqi city of Basra.

March 1984: The USSR increased its aid to Iraq, having previously sold the Government SS-12 missiles; the USA also provided Iraq with heavy military equipment, including helicopters.

26 November 1984: Iraq and the USA re-established full diplomatic relations; Iraq had terminated relations in 1967, owing to US support for Israel during the Arab-Israeli conflict.

December 1984: Iraq began a series of attacks on shipping in the Gulf, particularly on tankers using the Iranian Kharg Island terminal.

January 1985: Negotiations between the Government and Kurdish separatists regarding Kurdish autonomy failed; fighting between PUK guerrillas and government troops ensued.

January 1985: Petroleum exports were reported to be at their lowest level since the development of the industry.

March 1985: Some 50,000 Iranian troops participated in an offensive in the Hawizah marshes, east of the River Tigris, and blocked the main road from Basra to Baghdad. Saddam Hussain was accused of ordering his troops to use chemical weapons to repel this offensive; Iraqi aircraft also raided 30 Iranian towns, despite having agreed with the UN to suspend attacks on civilians the previous June.

18 March 1985: King Hussein of Jordan and President Muhammad Hosni Mubarak of Egypt visited Baghdad to demonstrate their support for the Iraqi cause.

April 1985: In an attempt to persuade Iran to begin peace negotiations, Saddam Hussain announced the suspension of air raids on Iranian cities; the gesture was ignored—a further such attempt in June similarly failed.

April 1985: The UN Secretary-General, Javier Pérez de Cuéllar, held separate talks in Tehran and Baghdad in an attempt to begin peace negotitations. Iran continued to demand US $350,000 in reparations from Iraq, an admission of responsibility for initiating hostilities and the withdrawal of Iraqi troops from Iranian territory, before such negotiations could begin.

August 1985: Iraq began a series of concentrated raids on the Iranian petroleum plant on Kharg Island, occasioning a severe reduction in Iranian petroleum exports—shipments virtually ceased by the end of the year.

1986: Attacks by both Iran and Iraq on tankers and other commercial vessels in the Gulf intensified.

9–11 February 1986: Iran embarked on the Wal-Fajr (Dawn) offensive and captured the Iraqi port of Faw.

April 1986: Iran began the Karbala-8 offensive and, by the following month, claimed to have advanced within 1 km of of Basra.

May 1986: Iraqi forces began a land offensive into Iranian territory and carried out airborne attacks on Tehran.

June 1986: A proposed meeting between the foreign ministers of Iraq and Syria, regarding a restoration of relations between the two countries, was cancelled by Syria shortly before it had been scheduled to take place.

July 1986: The Baath Party held an extraordinary regional conference; Naim Haddad was dismissed from the Regional Command and replaced by Sa'adoun Hammadi, who had succeeded him as Chairman and Speaker of the National Assembly the previous year.

November 1986: Contrary to its official policy of neutrality, it became apparent that the USA had made three shipments of weapons and other items of military equipment to Iran since September 1985.

December 1986: It was reported in the *Washington Post* that the US Central Intelligence Agency (CIA), had been supplying Iraq with detailed information for two years, in particular regarding planned raids on Iranian oil and power plants. In January 1987 it further emerged that the US had deliberately provided both countries with inaccurate information in an attempt to cause an impasse in the conflict.

24 December 1986: Iranian troops carried out a further assault on the Basra region.

8 January 1987: The Iranian forces established a bridgehead inside Iraq, between the Shatt al-Arab in the west and Fish Lake to the east.

13 January 1987: Saddam Hussain offered Iran a cease-fire and peace negotiations; Iran declined and began the Karbala-6 offensive into north-eastern Iraq.

18 February 1987: In response to Iraq's declaration of a two-week moratorium on the bombing of Iranian towns, Iran agreed to suspend attacks on Iraqi cities.

April 1987: It was reported that the Presidents of Syria and Iraq had held secret conciliatory meetings in Jordan, although no public statements were made to confirm this.

17 May 1987: An Iraqi fighter aircraft dropped a missile on a US naval vessel, the USS *Stark*, which had been protecting shipping in the Gulf; Hussain claimed that this had been an error and apologized to the US Government.

20 July 1987: The UN Security Council unanimously approved Resolution 598, urging Iran and Iraq to negotiate a cease-fire and proposing the establishment of an 'impartial body' to determine responsibility for starting the war.

29 August 1987: Iraq resumed attacks on Iranian petroleum installations and industrial sites.

8–11 September 1987: At the conclusion of a meeting in Amman (Jordan), the Arab League unanimously condemned Iran for prolonging the war with Iraq and urged the Iranian Government to implement UN Resolution 598 without pre-conditions.

11–15 September 1987: UN Secretary-General Javier Pérez de Cuéllar visited both warring countries with the aim of implementing Resolution 598. The Iranian Government announced that it would only agree to a cease-fire if Iraq's culpability for the conflict was established; Iraq was only prepared to negotiate a cease-fire on the terms of Resolution 598.

3 November 1987: The Iranian Deputy Minister of Foreign Affairs, Muhammad Javad Larijani, reiterated Iran's earlier statement that it would only observe a cease-fire if the UN Security Council were to identify Iraq as the agressor.

22 December 1987: The USSR proposed discussions in the UN Security Council regarding the prohibition of the sale of arms to Iran, in addition to the establishment of an international naval force in the Gulf, under the direction of the UN.

early 1988: Owing to the Kurds' perceived support for Iran, the Government carried out a systematic depopulation of Kurdish areas.

early 1988: Iraq launched a series of counter-offensives, in which it regained much of the territory it had lost to Iran.

January 1988: The Syrian Government's offer to mediate between Iran and Iraq was rejected by both countries.

February 1988: Reciprocal attacks on civil and economic targets were resumed by Iran and Iraq. At the same time, Kurdish guerrillas advanced into government-controlled territory in Iraqi Kurdistan and established bridgeheads in the Mawat region along the Iranian border.

March 1988: It was alleged that Iraqi troops had used chemical weapons in their attempt to recapture the Kurdish-held town of Halabjah.

April 1988: Iraqi forces recaptured the Faw peninsula.

May 1988: The DPK and the PUK announced that they were to form a pro-Iranian coalition with the Socialist Party of Kurdistan (SPK), the People's Democratic Party of Kurdistan (PDPK), the United Socialist Party of Kurdistan (USPK) and the Kurdish ICP in pursuit of Kurdish self-determination.

mid-June 1988: Iraq recaputred Majnoun Island and the al-Hawizah marshes; Iranian forces were also expelled from Iraqi territory in Kurdistan.

16 July 1988: Iraqi forces captured the Iranian border town of Dehloran.

18 July 1988: Iran agreed to accept Resolution 598.

24 July 1988: Iraqi troops withdrew from Iran.

25 July 1988: Saddam Hussain postponed the general election for six months, owing to attacks on Iraq by the NLA.

6 August 1988: The Governments of Iran and Iraq agreed to begin peace negotiations.

20 August 1988: A cease-fire was officially implemented; it was monitored by the UN Iran-Iraq Military Oserver Group (UNIIMOG).

25 August 1988: Peace negotiations began in Geneva (Switzerland); progress was, however, impeded by the continuing dispute over responsibility for starting the war. Iran claimed that Iraq had initiated hostilities by invading Iran on 22 September 1980; Iraq maintained that the war had begun with the Iranian bombardment of border posts on 4 September 1980.

26 August 1988: The UN Security Council unanimously adopted Resolution 620, condemning the use of chemical weapons in the conflict between Iran and Iraq.

September 1988: Following the cease-fire with Iran, the military began new offensives against the Kurds, in which chemical weapons were reportedly used; more than 100,000 Kurdish refugees fled to Turkey.

6 September 1988: The Government offered full amnesty to all Iraqi Kurds inside and outside the country, with the exception of the leader of the PUK, Jabal Talibani.

9 September 1988: The US Senate approved proposals for the imposition of economic sanctions on Iraq, including an embargo on imports of Iraqi petroleum and on loans to the country; an estimated 150,000 Iraqis subsequently took part in an anti-US demonstration.

17 September 1988: The Government began to evacuate all inhabitants of the Kurdish Autonomous Region to enable the creation of a 30 km-wide uninhabited 'security zone' along the length of the country's borders with Iran and Turkey.

9 September 1989: Elections held to the Legislative Council of the Kurdish Autonomous Area were held.

14–15 October 1989: An international conference on the 'Kurdish question' was held in Paris.

15 March 1990: A British journalist, Farzad Bazoft, was executed in Iraq, having been convicted of espionage.

2 April 1990: With reference to Israel's nuclear capability; Saddam Hussain emphasized Iraq's right to defend itself.

3 April 1990: The US President, George Bush, urged Iraq to abandon the production of chemical weapons.

10 April 1990: The British Government alleged that Iraq was attempting to construct a 'supergun', capable of firing missiles over long distances, using parts imported from the United Kingdom.

3 July 1990: The Ministers of Foreign Affairs of Iran and Iraq met in Geneva for direct talks.

15 July 1990: Iraq accused Kuwait, via the Arab League, of unlawfully exploiting Iraqi petroleum resources by conducting exploration in a disputed border area.

17 July 1990: Saddam Hussain threatened to take 'effective action' against those states which had persistently flouted their petroleum-production quotas.

24 July 1990: President Mubarak of Egypt visited Iraq, Kuwait and Saudi Arabia in pursuit of a solution to the dispute developing between Iraq and Kuwait.

31 July 1990: Iraqi and Kuwaiti delegations met in Jeddah (Saudi Arabia) to seek a solution to the dispute between the two countries; the meeting ended without resolution within two hours.

2 August 1990: Iraq invaded Kuwait; the UN Security Council adopted Resolution 660, demanding Iraq's immediate and unconditional withdrawal.

3 August 1990: Fourteen Arab League member states condemned the Iraqi invasion of Kuwait and demanded the immediate withdrawal of Iraqi armed forces; the United Kingdom and the USA announced their decision to send naval forces to the Gulf.

4 August 1990: Member states of the European Economic Community (EEC, the precursor of the European Union—EU) agreed to impose economic sanctions on Iraq.

6 August 1990: The UN Security Council adopted Resolution 661, imposing economic sanctions on Iraq and Kuwait.

7 August 1990: The USA announced its decision to send ground forces to Saudi Arabia as part of a multi-national force (requested by King Fahd) to deter Iraqi aggression against that country.

8 August 1990: Iraq announced the formal annexation of Kuwait.

9 August 1990: Iraq closed its own and Kuwait's borders to foreigners. The UN Security Council adopted Resolution 662, rejecting Iraq's annexation of Kuwait.

10 August 1990: Iraq ordered the closure of foreign embassies in Kuwait by 24 August.

15 August 1990: Iraq accepted Iranian terms for a final settlement of the conflict between the two countries.

18 August 1990: The UN Security Council adopted Resolution 664, urging Iraq to allow all foreign nationals to leave Iraq and Kuwait.

25 August 1990: In order to enforce the economic sanctions against Iraq, the UN Security Council adopted Resolution 665, permitting member states' naval forces to ensure their strict implementation.

28 August 1990: Iraq declared northern Kuwait to be part of Basra province, and the remainder to be the 19th province of Iraq.

30 August 1990: The UN Secretary-General, Pérez de Cuéllar met the Iraqi Minister of Foreign Affairs Tareq Aziz in Jordan.

9 September 1990: The USA and the USSR issued a joint statement stating their determination to enforce economic sanctions against Iraq.

10 September 1990: Iraq's Minister of Foreign Affairs, Tareq Aziz, visited Iran to discuss a peace treaty.

13 September 1990: The Muslim World League condemned Iraq's invasion of Kuwait.

24 September 1990: French proposals to resolve the crisis were unsuccessful.

25 September 1990: The UN Security Council agreed to impose an air blockade on Iraq.

3 October 1990: Saddam Hussain visited Kuwait for the first time since the Iraqi invasion.

14 October 1990: Iran and Iraq formally resumed diplomatic relations.

9 November 1990: The USA announced the deployment in the Persian (Arabian) Gulf of sufficient armed forces to create an offensive capability against Iraq.

27 November 1990: Tareq Aziz, held talks with the Soviet President, Mikhail Gorbachev, in he Soviet capital, Moscow.

29 November 1990: UN Security Council Resolution 678 authorized member governments to employ 'all necessary means' to ensure Iraq's withdrawal from Kuwait if it had not removed its forces from the country by 15 January 1991.

6 December 1990: Saddam Hussain ordered the release of all hostages being held in Iraq and Kuwait.

27 December 1990: Opposition groups belonging to the Iraqi National Joint Action Committee drafted a common programme, aiming to overthrow Saddam Hussain and establish democracy in Iraq.

9 January 1991: Tareq Aziz met the US Secretary of State, James Baker, in Geneva.

12 January 1991: The US House of Representatives and Senate approved the use of force against Iraq.

13 January 1991: The UN Secretary-General, Pérez de Cuéllar, visited Iraq for talks with Saddam Hussain.

16–17 January 1991: The US-led multinational force commenced an air offensive against Iraqi forces and installations in Iraq and Kuwait, known as 'Operation Desert Storm'.

17 January 1991: Iraq commenced attacks with *Scud* missiles against Israeli and Saudi Arabian targets.

6 February 1991: Iraq severed diplomatic relations with Egypt, France, Italy, Saudi Arabia, the United Kingdom and the USA.

15 February 1991: Iraq made a conditional offer to withdraw from Kuwait.

18 February 1991: President Gorbachev of the USSR proposed an eight-point peace plan to resolve the conflict.

24 February 1991: The multi-national force commenced a ground offensive against Iraqi forces in Kuwait and southern Iraq.

27 February 1991: Iraq agreed to observe all UN Security Council Resolutions adopted from August 1990 in respect of its occupation of Kuwait.

27 February 1991: The US President, George Bush, declared the defeat of the Iraqi army and the liberation of Kuwait.

28 February 1991: Hostilities between Iraq and the multi-national force were suspended.

1 March 1991: Popular revolt was reported in the southern Iraqi city of Basra.

2 March 1991: The UN Security Council adopted Resolution 686, which announced a cease-fire in the conflict over Kuwait; Iraq accepted its terms the following day.

11–13 March 1991: A Conference of Iraqi political and religious groups opposed to Saddam Hussain was held in the Lebanese capital, Beirut.

16 March 1991: Saddam Hussain promised to introduce significant political reforms.

23 March 1991: A new Council of Ministers was appointed.

26 March 1991: Kurdish guerrillas were reported to have taken control of the northern city of Kirkuk; Iraqi state media reported that the city had been recaptured on 31 March.

1 April 1991: The leader of the DPK accused the Iraqi Government of conducting a campaign of genocide against Iraqi Kurds.

3 April 1991: The detailed terms of the cease-fire were stipulated in UN Security Council Resolution 687.

4 April 1991: The Iraqi Government claimed to have suppressed the Kurdish rebellion, and that in the south of the country.

8 April 1991: The leaders of member states of the EC approved a proposal by the British Prime Minister, John Major, to create a UN-enforced Kurdish enclave in northern Iraq. An exclusion zone for Iraqi aircraft, to be monitored by British and US forces, was established north of 36°N.

9 April 1991: By the terms of UN Security Council Resolution 689, a demilitarized zone (DMZ) was created between Iraq and Kuwait.

24 April 1991: Saddam Hussain was reported to have agreed 'in principle' to grant a degree of autonomy to Iraqi Kurds.

29 April 1991: Kurdish refugees were reported to be returning to Iraq from Iran and Turkey.

2 July 1991: The UN-supervised destruction of Iraqi ballistic missiles commenced.

9 July 1991: The UN revealed evidence of an extensive Iraqi nuclear-weapons programme.

12 July 1991: The UN Security Council ordered Iraq to produce a list of its nuclear installations and materials by 25 July 1991.

19 August 1991: The Government and Kurdish leaders drafted an agreement on Kurdish autonomy.

24 August 1991: The National Assembly approved an amendment to the law governing the formation of political parties.

18 September 1991: The US Government stated its willingness to use force to compel Iraq to comply with UN Security Council Resolutions.

10 December 1991: A UN report on the conflict between Iran and Iraq found that Iraq's invasion of Iran in September 1980 contravened international law.

19 May 1992: Elections were held to a Kurdish National Assembly in Iraqi Kurdistan.

4 July 1992: The Kurdish National Assembly elected a cabinet for Iraqi Kurdistan.

30 July 1992: The Council of Ministers was reorganized.

27 August 1992: An air-exclusion zone was established by the USA in southern Iraq, south of 32°N.

24 November 1992: The UN Security Council refused to remove the economic sanctions in force against Iraq.

27 December 1992: An Iraqi fighter aircraft was shot down by US fighters in the southern Iraqi air-exclusion zone.

17–18 January 1993: US warships launched missiles against a nuclear-weapons facility near Baghdad.

29 March 1993: The economic sanctions on Iraq were again renewed by the UN Security Council.

26 June 1993: The USA launched a missile attack on Iraq's Intelligence Headquarters in Baghdad, in retaliation for an alleged attempt to assassinate the former US President, Bush, in Kuwait in April.

21 July 1993: The UN sanctions against Iraq were further renewed.

1 September 1993: The Iraqi Deputy Prime Minister met the UN Secretary-General, Boutros Boutros-Ghali, in Geneva to discuss the resumption of sales of Iraqi petroleum and the removal of economic sanctions in force against Iraq.

5 September 1993: A further reorganization of the Council of Ministers was effected.

26 November 1993: Iraq accepted long-term international monitoring of its defence industries in accordance with UN Security Council Resolution 715.

5 February 1994: The Ministers of Foreign Affairs of Iran, Syria and Turkey met in Istanbul for talks on the implications of events in Iraqi Kurdistan. Turkey urged Iraq to prevent the Kurdistan Workers' Party (PKK, a proscribed party in Turkey) from maintaining bases on its territory.

29 May 1994: Ahmad Hussein Khudayer was dismissed as Iraqi Prime Minister—Saddam Hussain assumed the post himself.

14 June 1994: The destruction of Iraq's chemical weapons was completed.

6 October 1994: Iraqi armed forces advanced southward towards the Iraq-Kuwait border; they withdrew the following week.

10 November 1994: Iraq gave formal recognition to the demarcation of its border with Kuwait.

20 March–5 May 1995: The Turkish armed forces conducted an offensive against bases of the PKK in northern Iraq.

30 June 1995: The Council of Ministers was again reorganized.

7 August 1995: Lt-Gen. Hussein Kamil al-Majid, the Minister of Industry, Minerals and Military Industrialization, defected to Jordan.

15 October 1995: In a referendum, Saddam Hussain was endorsed as President of Iraq for a further seven years.

22 October 1995: It was announced that legislative elections would be held in 1996.

6 November 1995: The Council of Ministers was reshuffled; further reorganizations were effected in December and in January 1996.

24 March 1996: The first legislative elections since 1989 were held.

8 April 1996: The first session of the new Iraqi National Assembly commenced.

20 May 1996: The Iraqi Government signed a memorandum of understanding with the UN, allowing limited sales of Iraqi petroleum; the programme was confirmed by UN Security Council Resolution 986.

31 August 1996: Iraqi infantry forces commenced a military operation in a Kurdish area of northern Iraq.

1 September 1996: The UN Security Council announced the suspension of Resolution 986, which permitted limited sales of Iraqi petroleum.

13 November 1996: A second round of peace talks were held by the Iraqi DPK and the PUK in Ankara, Turkey.

9 December 1996: The UN Secretary-General, Boutros Boutros-Ghali, approved an 'oil-for-food' arrangement, by which Iraq was permitted to sell petroleum in exchange for humanitarian supplies.

19 March 1997: Iraq received its first delivery of supplies under the 'oil-for-food' programme.

14 May 1997: Turkish forces attacked guerrilla bases of the PKK in northern Iraq.

2 June 1997: The border with Syria, which had been closed for 18 years, was reopened.

12 September 1997: The UN Security Council extended the 'oil-for-food' agreement with Iraq for 60 days, the period deemed to have begun on 5 September.

12 November 1997: The UN Security Council approved Resolution 1137, imposing a travel ban on senior Iraqi officials.

13 November 1997: US nationals in the weapons-inspection team operated by the UN Special Commission on Iraq (UNSCOM) were expelled from Iraq.

21 November 1997: The UNSCOM inspectors were allowed to return to Iraq, but were prevented from inspecting presidential sites.

4 December 1997: The 'oil-for-food' agreement was extended for a further six months.

8 December 1997: Four Jordanians were executed in Iraq, following smuggling convictions, despite appeals by the Jordanian Government for the sentences to be commuted.

10 December 1997: King Hussein of Jordan expelled several Iraqi diplomats from the country and recalled the Jordanian chargé d'affaires from Baghdad, in protest at the executions.

13–14 January 1998: Iraq prevented UNSCOM from carrying out weapons inspections, claiming that the group's leader, former US marine officer Scott Ritter, was engaged in espionage for the CIA.

17 January 1998: Saddam Hussain announced an end to all co-operation with UNSCOM until UN sanctions were ended.

17 January 1998: Iraq's chargé d'affaires in Jordan was killed; despite speculation that Iraqi government agents were responsible the Jordanian interior ministry announced the arrest of several Jordanians in connection with the incident, and claimed that the crime was not politically motivated.

24 February 1998: Following intensive negotiations, Tareq Aziz and the UN Secretary-General, Kofi Annan, signed a 'memorandum of understanding' concerning the return of UNSCOM to Iraq.

2 March 1998: The UN Security Council adopted Resolution 1154, which threatened Iraq with the 'severest consequences' if it breached the terms of the 'memorandum of understanding' signed in February. UNSCOM inspectors were permitted to return three days later.

5 March 1998: UNSCOM inspectors returned to Iraq.

27 April 1998: A motion at the UN Security Council, requiring the body to review the sanctions regime against Iraq, was defeated.

11 May 1998: The Minister of Labour and Social Affairs, Abd al-Hamid Aziz Muhammad Salih as-Sayigh, was dismissed; Saadi Tuma-Abbas was appointed to the post in June.

5 August 1998: The Iraqi Council of Ministers suspended co-operation with UN weapons-inspection teams; Saddam Hussain insisted that new terms and conditions should be negotiated.

9 August 1998: The UN Security Council endorsed a Resolution to suspend periodic reviews of the sanctions regime against Iraq.

14 September 1998: The National Assembly voted to end all co-operation with UNSCOM unless the UN Security Council annulled its decision of 9 August.

17 September 1998: An agreement signed in Washington, DC, USA, by the DPK and the PUK, formalized the aim of establishing a regional parliament in northern Iraq.

31 October 1998: Iraq announced the end of co-operation with weapons inspections by UNSCOM.

15 November 1998: Amid US-led threats of military action should Iraq not comply with inspections, Iraq agreed to permit resumption of work by UNSCOM.

7 December 1998: UNSCOM inspectors were prevented from entering a site termed as 'sensitive' in Baghdad.

16 December 1998: A report written by the head of UNSCOM, Richard Butler, was severely critical of Iraq's non-compliance with inspections obligations; in response, the air forces of the United Kingdom and USA initiated 'Operation Desert Fox', targeting strategic sites in Iraq for bombardment.

20 December 1998: 'Operation Desert Fox' ended.

25 January 1999: Following three weeks of tensions in Iraq's air-exclusion zones, US aircraft bombed targets in Basra; Iraq claimed that some missiles had hit civilian targets. Operations by US and British aircraft in the 'no-fly' zones continued in subsequent months.

19 February 1999: A senior Shi'a cleric, Grand Ayatollah Muhammad Sadeq as-Sadr, was assassinated in Najaf.

30 June 1999: Butler's mandate as chief of UNSCOM expired; efforts to agree on a new inspections regime continued.

17 December 1999: The UN Security Council adopted Resolution 1284, establishing the UN Monitoring, Verification and Inspection Commission (UNMOVIC) to conduct weapons inspections in Iraq; Iraq announced that it would not co-operate with the new body.

27 March 2000: The ruling Baath party won an overwhelming majority of seats at elections to the National Assembly.

early September 2000: Following the Government's statement that it would never allow UNMOVIC inspectors to enter the country, the UN Security Council sought to reassure Saddam Hussain that the team would only seek to conduct preliminary tasks.

September 2000: Iraq renewed its allegations that Kuwait was unlawfully exploiting Iraqi petroleum reserves by drilling in the border area.

late September 2000: The UN Security Council agreed to reduce the level of Iraq's petroleum revenue requisitioned as war reparations under the 'oil-for food' programme from 30% to 25%.

October 2000: Kuwait accused Iraq of 78 violations of the DMZ and increased the strength of its security force in the border region.

October 2000: Commercial flights between Russia and Iraq were resumed; by the following month, commercial air-links had also been established with Ireland, Jordan, Morocco, Tunisia and the United Arab Emirates.

14–15 October 2000: Two Saudi men hijacked a Saudi passenger aircraft on a flight to London (United Kingdom), forcing it to land in Baghdad, where the Iraqi authorities were able to resolve the situation without casualties. The Saudi Goverment requested the extradition of the suspects, but abandoned their attempt in December.

late October 2000: A member of the RCC, Izzat Ibrahim ad-Duri, became the first senior Iraqi official to attend an Arab League summit since 1990.

late October 2000: The Minster of Foreign Affairs, Muhammad Saeed as-Sahaf, undertook a tour of Egypt, Jordan, Libya, Qatar and Yemen in an effort to strengthen diplomatic relations.

November 2000: The Government contravened UN sanctions by delivering crude petroleum to Syria; the pipeline used was not one of the two designated for the carriage of Iraqi exports under the 'oil-for-food' agreement.

23 November 2000: Iraq lodged a complaint with the Secretary-General of the Arab League, concerning alleged aggressive behaviour by a Kuwaiti patrol boat against an Iraqi vessel in Iraqi territorial waters; the allegation was later denied by Kuwait.

29 November 2000: Vice-President Taha Yassin Ramadan visited India; he reached an agreement with senior Indian officials on the improvement of bilateral relations, particlarly with regard to petroleum.

Mid-December 2000: A Russian envoy, Nikolai Kartuzov, expressed his country's support for an end to UN sanctions on Iraq during meetings in Baghdad with Vice-President Taha Yassin Ramadan and the Minister of Foreign Affairs, Muhammad Saeed as-Sahaf.

17 January 2001: The Government asked the UN Secretary-General to order an inquiry into the effects on the Iraqi population of the remnants of ammunition containing depleted uranium used during the 'Operation Desert Storm'; it claimed that there had been a high incidence of cancers and birth deformities since the conflict.

20 January 2001: State-owned media reported that British and US aircraft had dropped bombs on civilian targets in southern Iraq, killing three people; the allegations were denied by the British and US authorities.

7 February 2001: The Government announced plans to create a free-trade zone with Jordan; similar accords had been signed with Egypt and Syria in January.

16 February 2001: British and US aircraft bombarded Iraqi air-defence and control systems with the intention of disabling any Iraqi attempts to detect and intercept international aircraft patrolling the no-fly zones. The assaults received little support from the international community, and were condemned by many countries.

20 February 2001: Iraq and Egypt signed an agreeement on the transport of passengers and goods between the two countries by railway via Jordan.

22 February 2001: US aircraft carried out further attacks on military targets in Iraq.

22 February 2001: Iraq and Tunisia agreed to form a free-trade zone.

2 March 2001: A UN weapons inspectors' assessment suggested that Iraq was in possession of chemical and biological weapons and the means to propel them to targets in other countries; a report by US intelligence services had previously claimed that Iraq had rebuilt armament factories destroyed in the 1998 'Operation Desert Fox'.

13 March 2001: The Iraqi embassy in Beirut was reopened; it had been closed since 1994.

6 April 2001: The Government refused to grant visas to some 300 UN aid workers; officials claimed that their presence was unnecessary since Iraqis could be recruited to do the work.

13 April 2001: US fighter aircraft carried out further bombing of targets in southern Iraq; the US Government claimed that the attacks were in response to anti-aircraft fire directed at Western aeroplanes patrolling the air exclusion zone.

18 April 2001: A government reorganization was effected; Tareq Ali became temporary Minister of Foreign Affairs, in succession to Muhammad Said as-Sahaf, who was appointed Minister of Culture and Information, that post's incumbent, Humam Abd al-Khaliq Abd al-Ghafur becoming Minister of Higher Education and Scientific Research.

19 April 2001: The Iraqi armed forces claimed that they had shot down an unmanned Iranian surveillance aircraft near Mendali, 400 km north-east of Baghdad.

20 April 2001: A senior Iranian Commander alleged that Mujahidin-e Khalq had attacked Iranian targets from inside the Iraqi border. Iraq claimed that two days earlier, Iran had fired more than 50 missiles into Iraqi territory, injuring and killing several civilians; this was later confirmed by the Iranian Government.

21 April 2001: UN security forces announced that they had intercepted a Honduran-registered vessel suspected of carrying Iraqi petroleum products, in contravention of UN sanctions, in the Gulf; the vessel was detained at Abu Dhabi in the United Arab Emirates.

26 April 2001: The British authorities announced that they were investigating allegations of war crimes against Saddam Hussain, specifically regarding his involvement in the detention of some 4,500 British citizens in Iraq and Kuwait in 1990–91.

28 April 2001: Iraq alleged that one civilian had died, and two others been wounded, following raids by British and US aircraft. The British Government denied the allegations, stating that its aircraft had come under fire, but had not retaliated.

1 May 2001: The Government signed an accord with Belarus concerning economic co-operation and the development of air links.

6 May 2001: A train travelled from Turkey to Iraq; the rail link had been closed in 1981 following regional disagreements. The passenger service resumed in July.

19 May 2001: At the Baath Party Congress in Baghdad, Saddam Hussain was reappointed to the post of party Secretary-General; his younger son, Qusay, who was already head of the Republican Guard and the Special Security Organisation, was elected to the RCC.

22 May 2001: Delegations from the Iraqi and Syrian Governments began discussions in Baghdad on ways to improve economic co-operation and trade between the two countries.

29 May 2001: Muhammad Ziman Abd ar-Razzaq was dismissed from the post of Minister of the Interior; the former irrigation minister, Mahmoud Diyab al-Ahmad, was appointed to the post on a temporary basis. On the same day, Muhammad Hamzah az-Zubaydi was dismissed from the office of Deputy Prime Minister.

5 June 2001: The UN Security Council began discussions on a new regime of sanctions directed at preventing Iraq from manufacturing weapons rather than prohibiting the import of basic commodities; the Council's members unanimously agreed to extend the 'oil-for-food' agreement by another month. The Government suspended deliveries of petroleum made in connection with the scheme in protest.

5 June 2001: The Deputy Premier, Tareq Aziz, alleged that, on 18 May, US fighter jets had harassed an Iraqi Airways passenger aircraft.

6 June 2001: Saudi Arabia accused Iraq of an unprovoked attack on Saudi territory, killing at least one Saudi national and wounding several others.

10 June 2001: South Africa announced that it would send an aircraft loaded with humanitarian aid to Iraq; this followed a similar relief package sent by Pakistan in February and several consignments of food and medicines sent by Egypt and France in 2000.

12 June 2001: The Ministry of Health, Labour and Social Affairs claimed that some 1.5m Iraqi citizens had died from diarrhoea, pneumonia, respiratory problems and malnutrition since the imposition of the UN sanctions.

18 June 2001: A US-based non-governmental organization alleged that Iraq had exported petroleum to several former Communist countries in Europe, in exchange for weapons components, in contravention of the 'oil-for-food' programme.

21 June 2001: Iraq alleged that bombing raids by British and US aircraft were responsible for the deaths of 23 people in northern Iraq. The US Secretary of Defense, Donald Rumsfeld, confirmed that aircraft had been patrolling the area concerned, but claimed that mis-directed Iraqi ground fire was responsible for the deaths and that the patrol had not released any bombs.

Israel

3760 BC: This date, as expressed in the modern Christian calendar, marks the beginning of the Hebrew calendar.

c. **2000 BC:** Abraham, the first of the Patriarchs of Judaism, departed from Ur (considered to have been in modern Iraq).

c. **1600 BC:** The Hebrews, the tribe formed by Abraham's descendents, migrated to Egypt; there they were subsequently enslaved.

c. **15th century BC:** Moses led the 'Exodus' (flight) from Egypt into Canaan.

1220 BC–1190 BC: Canaan was conqered by Israelite tribes; the Philistines—seafaring peoples from the Peloponnese—also attacked Canaan and came into confrontation with the Israelites.

c. **1020 BC–1000 BC:** King Saul, the first King of Israel, reigned.

c. **1000 BC–970 BC:** During the reign of King David, Jerusalem was established as the Israeli capital.

c. **990 BC:** The Philistines were defeated by King David.

965 BC–928 BC: During the reign of King Solomon, the Israelite lands were extended from the upper Euphrates to the Gulf of Aqaba; the territory was eventually divded into two Jewish kingdoms: Israel in the north and Judah in the south.

c. **957 BC:** The construction of the First Temple was completed.

722 BC: Israel was conquered by Assyrian forces led by King Shalmaneser and the Israelites were deported. The Assyrians made Judea a tributary kingdom and divided the remainder of the region into provinces for administrative purposes.

612 BC: The Assyrian Empire fell and the region was absorbed into the Chaldean (Neo-Babylonian) Empire. While under Chaldean rule the Jordan valley was the subject of incursions by several neighbouring civilizations.

586 BC: Jerusalem (al-Quds in Arabic) was destroyed by the Babylonian forces of King Nebuchadnezzar; most of the Jewish population were captured and taken to Babylon.

586 BC: Jerusalem and the First Temple were destroyed by Nebuchadnezzar. The Jews' Babylonian captivity, or exile, began.

539 BC: The Chaldean Empire was seized by Cyrus II ('the Great') of Persia who allowed the Jews to return to the Jordan valley.

520 BC–515 BC: The Second Temple was constructed in Jerusalem.

333 BC: Alexander III ('the Great') of Macedon, the Greek warrior, conquered the region. Following his death in 323 BC, the region came under the rule of one of his generals, Seleucus Nicator.

175 BC: The Seleucid ruler Antiochus IV took control of Palestine and prohibited Judaism.

167 BC: The Second Temple was desecrated by Antiochus IV, giving rise to the Maccabaean revolt.

December 164 BC: The Second Temple was reconsecrated by Judas Maccabaeus.

140 BC: The Hasmonean dynasty commenced, under the leadership of Simon Maccabaeus.

63 BC: The Romans incorporated Judah (Judea) into their empire, beginning the period of Roman domination.

54 BC: The Second Temple was plundered by Crassus.

37 BC: The Romans installed Herod as King of Judea; with their support, he was able to extend his rule over both sides of the Jordan valley.

20 BC: Work to reconstruct the Second Temple was begun under Herod the Great; the work was completed in AD 63.

6 BC: Palestine was annexed by Rome as Syria Palestina.

AD 132–135: The Second Jewish Revolt, also known as the Bar-Kochba rebellion, was unsuccessful.

140: A Jewish national movement, the Zealots, revolted against Roman rule, in what became known as the First Jewish Revolt; the revolt was defeated in 70 when the Romans captured Jerusalem and destroyed the Second Temple.

c. **200:** Jerusalem was renamed Aelia Capitolina by the Romans; Jews were prohibited from entering the city.

691: The Dome of the Rock was erected in Jerusalem on the site of the Temple of Solomon.

969: The Shi'a Muslim Fatimids of Egypt, who had seized the Caliphate from the Abbasids, took control of the region.

1071: The Fatimids were supplanted in control of the Caliphate by the Seljuq Turks.

1099: Jerusalem was captured by Western Christian forces during the Crusades, who established the principality of Oultre Jordain, with a capital at Al-Karak.

1174: Salah ad-Din Yusuf ibn Ayyub (Saladin), deposed the Fatimids and established himself as the sultan of Egypt.

1182: The Jews were expelled from France.

1187: The Crusaders were defeated by Salah ad-Din (Saladin) at the Battle of Hattin.

1251: The Crusaders' expulsion from Acre marked their removal from Palestine.

1260: The Ayyub dynasty was deposed by the Mamelukes—former Christian slaves of Kurdish and Circassian origin who had converted to Islam; the region became a province of Mameluke territory, which extended from the Nile to the Euphrates.

1290: The Jews were expelled from England.

1492: The Spanish Inquisition forced Iberian Jews either to convert to Christianity or be expelled from Spain.

1516: The Mamelukes were defeated by the Ottoman Turks; the Ottoman domination of Palestine began.

1791: The French Jewry was emancipated by Napoleon Bonaparte.

1825: Mordecai Manuel Noah invited world Jewry to create a Jewish state on Grand Island in the river Niagara, USA.

1840: The European powers forced Muhammad Ali to return Palestine to direct Ottoman rule.

1881: Following the death of Tsar Alexander II of Russia a series of *pogroms* (purges) were undertaken against Jewish communities in that country, provoking large-scale Jewish emigration to Western Europe and to the USA and emigration on a smaller scale to Palestine.

1882: The *Hovevei Ziyyon* ('Lovers of Zion') group was formed in Russia; the group promoted the settlement of Jews in Palestine.

1887–88: Palestine was organized into administrative divisions of Acre and Nablus.

1896: An Austrian journalist, Theodor Herzl, published a pamphlet, *Der Judenstaat* (*The Jewish State*), which proposed the creation of a state for the world's Jews.

August 1897: The first Zionist Congress was held at Basel (Switzerland), where Herzl defined the aims of Zionism.

1905: The failure of the Russian Revolution resulted in renewed series of *pogroms* against Jews in Russia; further such purges occurred after the successful Revolution in 1917.

1905: The Jewish Territorial Organization was founded, with the aim of finding autonomous territory for the Jewish people.

1905: The seventh Zionist Congress rejected colonization of any territory other than Palestine.

24 October 1915: Sir Henry McMahon, on behalf of the British Government, declared support for Arab independence in an area possibly including Palestine at the end of the First World War.

February 1916: France, Russia and the United Kingdom signed the Asia Minor Agreement (also known as the 'Sykes-Picot Treaty'), under which Palestine was to be administered as a British, French and Russian condominium.

November 1917: The 'Balfour Declaration', a statement made by the British Foreign Secretary, Arthur Balfour, to Baron Rothschild, leader of the British Jewry, proclaimed the Jordanian Mandate to be within the area to be allocated as a Jewish 'national home' in Palestine.

9 December 1917: Jerusalem was captured from Ottoman forces by the British.

31 October 1918: The entirety of Palestine was taken under British military rule.

1919: David Ben-Gurion founded the United Labour Zionist Party.

3 January 1919: The Faisal-Weizmann Agreement pledged Arab and Zionist communities in Palestine to cordial relations.

June 1919: The World Zionist Organization (WZO) presented a memorandum to the Paris Peace Conference (held in the French capital to create stable governance in the territories affected by the First World War) expounding its concept of a Jewish home in Palestine.

1920: A clandestine Jewish army, the *Haganah*, was formed.

1920: The Asefat Hanivharim (Elected Assembly) and the Vaad Leumi (National Council) were created by Jews in Palestine.

March 1920: The General Syrian Congress elected Amir Faisal, son of the Sharif Hussain of Mecca, King of United Syria, which included Palestine.

July 1920: Palestine became a British Mandated Territory.

30 June 1922: A joint resolution of the US Congress approved the concept of a Jewish national home.

24 July 1922: The Council of the League of Nations approved the terms of the British Mandate for Palestine.

September 1922: The British Government promulgated a Constitution providing for a legislative council and the creation of a joint Arab-Jewish Palestinian State. Arab opposition, however, meant that the Constitution did not supersede British direct rule.

22 September 1922: The British Government announced that the Balfour Declaration would not be applied to the area east of the river Jordan, which would be closed to Jewish immigration.

1929: The Mapai political party was formed.

August 1929: The WZO established the Jewish Agency, a body which strove for the partition of Palestine and the creation of a Jewish state.

August 1929: Disputes over Jewish access to the holy site of the Wailing Wall in the Old City of Jerusalem led to serious disturbances between Muslims and Jews; British military forces intervened.

30 March 1930: The Shaw Commission published its report on the causes of 1929 riots. The offer of a legislative council, to form the basis of constitutional government, was consequently renewed, but Arab leaders declined the opportunity to discuss it with Jewish counterparts.

October 1930: Legislation in the British Parliament, known as the 'Passfield White Paper', recommended a halt to Jewish immigration into Palestine and the curtailment of Jewish land purchases.

1936: A general strike was observed by the Arab population of Palestine.

April 1936: The Palestinian revolt commenced. An Arab High Committee (AHC) was formed to co-ordinate Palestinian opposition to Jews.

November 1936: A British investigatory commission, the Peel Commission, was despatched to Palestine to study the situation there.

1937: The Palestinian revolt was suppressed by the British, both by use of force and by negotiation with the AHC.

July 1937: The Peel Commission's report declared that co-operation between Arabs and Jews in a Palestinian state would be impossible, and recommended partition.

September 1937: Unofficial representatives of various Arab states, meeting in Bludan, Syria, rejected the recommendations of the Peel Commission.

October 1937: The Palestinian revolt resumed.

November 1938: The report of a further British inquiry recommended a reduction in the Jewish share of Palestinian territory.

February 1939: A Conference between Jews and Arabs was convened in the British capital, London.

May 1939: British Government legislation ('The White Paper') stated that there would be no partition in Palestine, that Jewish immigration and land purchase should cease, and that the British Government did not support the establishment of either an Arab or a Jewish state in the region. Instead, the establishment of an independent Palestinian State, within 10 years, was envisaged. Jewish groups in Palestine opposed the White Paper policy, but abandoned the opposition at the start of the Second World War, in order to present a 'united front' against Germany.

September 1939–May 1945: During the Second World War British forces prevented a German invasion of Palestine—during the course of the War (and, previously, during the chancellorship of Adolf Hitler in Germany from 1933), an estimated 6m. Jews were killed in Europe, and others displaced.

11 May 1942: The Biltmore Programme, a new policy for Palestine, urged unrestricted Jewish immigration into Palestine and the establishment there of a Jewish commonwealth.

1946–47: Arab forces made continual attacks on Jewish organizations and populations in Palestine; Jewish forces responded with violence and expelled many Arabs from the Mandate territory.

April 1946: Following the end of the Second World War, an Anglo-American Committee of Inquiry recommended the admission into Palestine of some 100,000 European Jewish refugees, the lifting of restrictions on Jewish purchases of land and the eventual creation of a binational state with the UN (the successor organization to the League of Nations) as guarantor.

1947: The British intercepted the *Exodus*, a ship carrying European Jewish refugees to Palestine.

2 April 1947: The United Kingdom referred its Palestinian Mandate to the UN.

15 May 1947: The UN General Assembly voted to create a Special Committee on Palestine (UNSCOP); which subsequently recommended the partition of Palestine.

31 August 1947: The UN General Assembly proposed two plans concerning the future of Palestine: a majority plan for the partition of the territory into two states, one Jewish and one Arab, with economic union; and a minority plan for a federal state.

29 November 1947: The UN General Assembly adopted the majority plan for Palestine.

13 May 1948: A Provisional Israeli Government was formed in Tel-Aviv, with David Ben-Gurion as Prime Minister.

14 May 1948: The British Mandate for Palestine was terminated. The State of Israel was officially declared in Palestine by the Jewish authorities; it was granted immediate recognition by the USA and the USSR.

15 May 1948: Troops of the Transjordanian army, the Arab Legion, Egypt, Iraq, Lebanon and Syria attacked Israel.

20 May 1948: The UN appointed Count Folke Bernadotte of Wisborg to mediate between Israel and the Arab states.

28 May 1948: The Israeli Defence Force (IDF) was created.

June 1948: A brief cease-fire between Israel and the Arab states was brokered by Bernadotte; a second such truce was arranged the following month.

17 September 1948: Bernadotte was assassinated by Jewish agents.

14 October 1948: Egyptian and Israeli armed forces renewed hostilities in the Negev desert.

22 October 1948: Egypt and Israel agreed to observe a cease-fire ordered by the UN Security Council in the Negev desert area. By this time the Israeli Army had made considerable territorial gains in the Negev and adjacent areas.

29 November 1948: The Provisional Government of Israel formally applied for membership of the UN.

13 January 1949: Egypt and Israel concluded an armistice agreement.

25 January 1949: The first legislative elections were held in Israel. Mapai gained the largest number of seats—but not an absolute majority—in the elected chamber and emerged as the dominant force in the coalition government subsequently formed.

February–July 1949: Bernadotte's successor, Ralph J. Bunche, brokered separate armistice agreements between Israel and Lebanon, Transjordan and Syria.

14 February 1949: *Knesset Israel*, the first Jewish legislative assembly for more than 2,000 years, held its inaugural session in the Jewish area of Jerusalem. Among other things, the Knesset adopted a Constitution at its opening session, providing for a parliamentary system of government, with a President elected by the Knesset.

17 February 1949: Dr Chaim Weizmann was elected as the first President of the State of Israel. Prime Minister David Ben-Gurion presented the resignation of his Government and was immediately charged by the President with forming a new administration (the resignation of the incumbent government upon the inauguration of a new President subsequently became a tradition).

24 February 1949: Egypt and Israel signed another armistice agreement.

3 March 1949: A new coalition administration was announced, including Mapai, the United Religious Party, the Progressive Party and the Sephardic Party.

20 July 1949: Israel and Syria signed an armistice agreement.

5 December 1949: The Knesset unanimously adopted a resolution which declared Jerusalem to be an integral part of Israel.

10 December 1949: The UN General Assembly adopted a resolution seeking the internationalization of Jerusalem and surrounding areas.

14 December 1949: The Prime Minister's office was transferred from Tel-Aviv to Jerusalem.

26 December 1949: The Knesset was convened in Jerusalem at the office of the Jewish Agency, where it had previously held its inaugural session.

23 January 1950: The Knesset adopted a resolution declaring Jerusalem to be the capital of the State of Israel.

1 April 1950: The Council of the Arab League, meeting in Cairo, Egypt, unanimously adopted a resolution which stated, among other things, that 'No Arab State has the right to negotiate separate peace treaties or any political, military or economic agreement with Israel, or the right to ratify such an agreement'.

13 June 1950: The Knesset voted against the adoption of a formal written constitution in favour of a proposal that a constitution should instead be allowed to evolve during a period of unspecified length.

14 June 1950: The Israeli Government paid the UN a sum in excess of US $50,000 in reparation for the assassination of Count Folke Bernadotte in 1948.

July 1950: The Knesset adopted the Law of Return, which gave every Jew the right of immigration into Israel.

September 1950: The Knesset established a Development Authority to be charged with the disposal of property formerly owned by Arabs or controlled by the British mandatory authority. The Development Authority would enjoy the sole right of disposal, but it was stipulated that almost all of the land in question must be sold to the Jewish National Fund, which would not be allowed to resell it.

15 October 1950: The Government led by David Ben-Gurion resigned.

19 October 1950: President Weizmann requested Dr Pinchas Rosen to form an interim administration pending the organization of a general election; Rosen was unable to do so.

30 October 1950: David Ben-Gurion presented a new Cabinet to the Knesset, having been requested by the President to form a new coalition to govern.

9 July 1951: The Israeli Government protested at the decision of the United Kingdom, its Dominions and several other countries formally to end the state of war with Germany.

30 July 1951: At the general election Mapai gained the largest number of seats—but not an absolute majority—in the Knesset.

7 October 1951: A new Cabinet was formed, comprising members of Mapai and religious parties.

19 November 1951: Chaim Weizmann was re-elected as President of Israel.

14 July 1952: The Knesset adopted a nationality and citizenship law, with retroactive effect from 14 May 1948, stipulating that all Jews resident in Israel on 14 July 1952 would automatically acquire Israeli citizenship, whether they were nationals of other countries or not; that Jewish immigrants arriving in Israel after that date would automatically acquire citizenship; that Arabs and other non-Jews were eligible for Israeli citizenship provided that they were citizens of Palestine during the period of the British Mandate, were legally resident in Israel, and that their names were included in the population register on 1 March 1952.

27 October 1952: An agreement was signed between the Federal Republic of Germany (FRG—'West' Germany) and Israel in respect of reparations to be paid to Israel for the National Socialist (Nazi) regime's crimes against the Jews and to meet the cost of absorbing refugees from the Nazi regime into Israel.

9 November 1952: President Weizmann died.

9 December 1952: Itzhak Ben-Zvi was elected President of Israel.

22 December 1952: His previous administration having resigned to the new President, Ben-Gurion formed a new Cabinet, comprising Mapai, the General Zionists and the Progressive (Liberal) party.

11 February 1953: The USSR severed diplomatic relations with Israel following a bomb attack on the Soviet Legation in Tel-Aviv two days previously; relations were restored in July.

10 July 1953: Israel announced that its Ministry of Foreign Affairs would be transferred from Tel-Aviv to Jerusalem.

20 August 1953: The Knesset conferred 'memorial citizenship' on the 6m. European Jews who had died under the Nazi regime.

14–15 October 1953: Israeli armed forces launched an attack on the Jordanian village of Qibya in retaliation for recent Jordanian raids on Israeli villages in the area.

8 November 1953: Ben-Gurion resigned as Prime Minister and Minister of Defence, and retired from political life.

25 November 1953: Mapai nominated Moshe Sharett to succeed Ben-Gurion as Prime Minister and Pinchas Lavon to succeed him as Minister of Defence.

2 December 1953: The USSR recognized Jerusalem as the capital of Israel.

9 December 1953: President Itzhak Ben-Zvi requested Moshe Sharett to form a new Cabinet; the resultant coalition, which took office in January, comprised Mapai, the General Zionists, Mizrachi and Hapoel Hamizrachi.

17 March 1954: An Israeli bus was ambushed by unidentified Arab assailants at Scorpion's Pass in the Negev desert; 11 civilians were killed. Israel accused Jordan of responsibility for the attack. Despite Jordan's denial, Israel subsequently withdrew from the Israeli-Jordanian Mixed Armistice Commission.

25 September 1954: Israel appealed to the Arab states for a peaceful settlement of their disputes.

28 September 1954: An Israeli freighter, the *Bat Galim*, was seized by Egyptian authorities when it attempted to pass through the Suez Canal.

17 January 1955: The Mizrachi and Hapoel Hamizrachi political parties announced decision to merge.

17 February 1955: Ben-Gurion rescinded his retirement and was appointed Minister of Defence.

28 February 1955: Egyptian and Israeli armed forces engaged in hostilities near Gaza.

29 March 1955: The UN Security Council unanimously adopted a Resolution in which it described the fighting in Gaza on 28 February as a violation by Israel of its obligations under the general armistice agreement and the UN Charter.

26 July 1955: The general election resulted in victory for Mapai.

18 September 1955: The Israeli Prime Minister, Moshe Sharett, urged the Western powers to supply arms to Israel.

2 November 1955: A new Cabinet was formed, under Ben-Gurion.

11–12 December 1955: Israeli armed forces attacked Syrian positions north of Lake Tiberias.

29 December 1955: Israel announced its intention to propose that a peace conference with Egypt should be held under the terms of the Egyptian-Israeli armistice agreement.

5 April 1956: Exchanges of artillery fire took place between Egyptian and Israeli armed forces in the Gaza area.

3 May 1956: Ben-Gurion assured the UN Secretary General of Israel's full and unconditional acceptance of armistice agreements previously concluded with Jordan, Lebanon and Syria. A similar assurance regarding the agreement with Egypt had previously been given on 12 April.

18 June 1956: Moshe Sharett resigned as Minister of Foreign Affairs. He was replaced by Golda Myerson, the Minister of Labour.

29 October 1956: Israeli armed forces attacked Egyptian positions in the Sinai peninsula.

30 October 1956: France and the United Kingdom issued 12-hour ultimatums to Egypt and Israel to cease hostilities and withdraw their forces from the immediate vicinity of the Suez Canal; and requested the Egyptian Government to allow Anglo-French forces to occupy positions at three points on the Canal.

1 November 1956: The Egyptian garrison in Gaza surrendered to Israeli armed forces.

2 November 1956: Israel took control of almost all of the Sinai peninsula.

6 November 1956: A cease-fire halted an advance by British, French and Israeli armed forces on Egypt.

9 November 1956: The Israeli Prime Minister announced that Israel would withdraw its forces from the Sinai peninsula after an international force had taken up positions in the Suez Canal area.

19 January 1957: The UN General Assembly adopted a resolution expressing its concern at Israel's failure to comply with Resolutions adopted in November 1956 regarding its withdrawal to the 1949 armistice lines in respect of the Gaza Strip and the Gulf of Aqaba.

22 January 1957: Israeli armed forces completed their withdrawal from most of the Sinai peninsula.

23 January 1957: Ben-Gurion stated that Israel required UN guarantees regarding freedom of navigation in the Gulf of Aqaba and the resumption of Palestinian guerrilla raids in the Gaza Strip before it would withdraw its armed forces from those areas.

2–3 February 1957: The UN General Assembly deplored Israel's failure to withdraw its armed forces (in the Gulf of Aqaba and the Gaza Strip) behind the armistice demarcation lines of 1949, and recognized that the 'scrupulous maintenance of the armistice agreement requires the placing of the UN Emergency Force on the Egyptian-Israeli armistice demarcation line'.

3 February 1957: Israel reiterated its refusal to comply with UN General Assembly Resolutions of November 1956 in respect of the Gaza Strip and the Gulf of Aqaba without UN guarantees, as detailed above.

6–8 March 1957: Israeli armed forces withdrew from the Gaza Strip and the west coast of the Gulf of Aqaba.

28 October 1957: Itzhak Ben-Zvi was re-elected as President of Israel.

21 May 1959: The United Arab Republic (UAR—formed by the union of Egypt and Syria) prevented a Danish freighter from carrying Israeli cargo through the Suez Canal.

3 November 1959: Following a general election Ben-Gurion was able to remain in power.

16 November 1959: Israel announced a Five-Year Transport Plan.

31 January 1961: Ben-Gurion tendered his resignation.

15 August 1961: Following legislative elections Ben-Gurion was able to form a new coalition Government.

9 February 1962: The Israeli Pound was devalued.

23 April 1963: President Ben-Zvi died.

21 May 1963: Zalman Shazar was elected President, in succession to the late Ben-Zvi.

16 June 1963: Ben Gurion again resigned his post of Prime Minister.

24 June 1963: Levi Eshkol formed a new coalition Government.

13–16 January 1964: An Arab League conference was held in Cairo to discuss Israeli plans for the diversion of the River Jordan.

10 February 1965: The FRG ceased arms supplies to Israel.

6 March 1965: President Bourguiba of Tunisia proposed Arab recognition of Israel, on the terms of the 1947 UN Resolution.

12 May 1965: Diplomatic relations with the FRG were formally established; in October the first FRG Ambassador (who had served in the German Army during the Second World War) arrived in Israel, amid demonstrations.

13 November 1966: Israeli forces raided the Jordanian village of Samu; attacks on Israel by groups based in its neigbouring Arab states had increased in frequency throughout the mid-1960s.

25 November 1966: The UN Security Council condemned the Israeli raid on Samu.

7 April 1967: Fighting occurred between Israeli and Syrian forces on the countries' border.

18 May 1967: The UAR officially requested that the UN force be withdrawn from the area of its border with Israel.

23 May 1967: The UAR imposed a blockade on Israeli shipping in the Straits of Tiran.

5 June 1967: A period of military tensions between Israel and its neighbouring Arab countries was ended when Israel attacked the air bases of Jordan, Syria and the UAR. The Arab countries' air forces were severely damaged, and Israel was swiftly able to capture territory from each of the Arab combatants (notably the West Bank and Old Jerusalem from Jordan, the Golan Heights from Syria and the Sinai peninsula from the UAR).

10 June 1967: Syria and the UAR signed a cease-fire with Israel, as Jordan had done some days earlier, thus concluding the conflict, which came to be known as the 'Six-Day War'; Israel retained the territories it had gained in the conflict.

10–13 June 1967: Diplomatic relations with Israel were discontinued by Bulgaria, Czechoslovakia, Hungary, Poland, the USSR and Yugoslavia.

21 October 1967: The Israeli destroyer *Eilat* was sunk off Sinai, with many casualties, by UAR warships.

25 October 1967: Israeli shelling at Suez succeeded in disabling the UAR's principal petroleum refineries for several months.

22 November 1967: Gunnar Jarring was appointed UN Special Representative to mediate between Israel and the Arab states.

22 November 1967: The UN Security Council adopted Resolution 242, which urged the withdrawal of Israeli forces from the Occupied Territories, the acknowledgement by all countries in the region of the others' sovereignty, a solution to the problem of Palestinian refugees and advocated a negotiated settlement to the region's disputes. The Resolution became the basis of international efforts to agree a settlement to the Israeli-Palestinian question.

21 January 1968: The new 'Israel Labour Party', formed from the Mapai, Ahdut Ha'avoda and Rafi parties, became the dominant party in the governing coalition.

21 March 1968: Israeli forces attacked the Jordanian village of Karameh, claimed to be the headquarters of the al-Fatah guerrilla organization.

5 June 1968: Israeli forces bombarded the Jordanian village of Irbid as a reprisal for what it termed an 'incessant artillery barrage' by groups based in the area against Israeli settlements.

23 July 1968: An Israeli airliner was hijacked by Arab commandos and flown to the Algerian capital, Algiers.

22 November 1968: A car filled with explosives by Arab guerrillas exploded in a Jerusalem market, killing 13.

26 December 1968: An Israeli passenger aircraft was the subject of a machine-gun attack by Arab guerrillas at an airport in Greece.

28 December 1968: Israeli commandos raided the airport of the Lebanese capital, Beirut, destroying 13 Arab aircraft.

31 December 1968: The UN Security Council unanimously condemned the Israeli raid on Beirut.

6 January 1969: The Government announced that France had imposed a ban the export of arms to Israel.

27 January 1969: Fourteen men (nine of whom were Jewish) were executed in Iraq amid much publicity, after being convicted of spying for Israel.

26 February 1969: The Prime Minister, Eshkol, died.

11 March 1969: Golda Meir became Prime Minister of Israel, leading an unchanged Cabinet.

21 August 1969: Fire caused severe damage to the Al-Aqsa Mosque in Jerusalem.

9 September 1969: The Israeli army launched a major raid on the UAR.

28 November 1969: Following a general election the governing 'Alignment' lost its majority in the Knesset.

9 December 1969: The USA's ten-point peace plan for the Middle East was publicly announced.

11 December 1969: A new coalition Government took office.

25 December 1969: Israeli crews boarded 6 gunboats, built in France for Israel but withheld by the French Government, and sailed them out of the port of Cherbourg *en route* to Haifa.

January 1970: Israeli aircraft bombarded a number of targets in the UAR, including some in the Cairo area.

23 January 1970: The High Court adjudged that Israelis could register children as Jewish by nationality if not religion, even if their mother was a Gentile—religious groups protested strongly.

12 February 1970: An Israeli air raid on a scrap-metal processing plant in Egypt killed a reported 70 civilians.

15 February 1970: A petroleum pipeline linking the port of Eilat, on the Red Sea, to the Mediterranean port of Ashqelon was opened.

1 May 1970: Israel claimed that Soviet pilots were flying operational missions based in the UAR.

8 August 1970: A cease-fire between Israel and its Arab neighbours came into effect, on Israel's post-1967 frontiers.

31 August 1970: The Arab 'Eastern Front' against Israel was split into separate national fronts.

6–13 September 1970: Arab-Israeli peace talks were held in New York (USA); Israel withdrew.

7 March 1971: The President of the UAR, Anwar Sadat, announced that the cease-fire with Israel would not be renewed.

1–8 May 1971: The US Secretary of State, William Rogers, visited Israel, Jordan, Lebanon, Saudi Arabia and the UAR to discuss plans for reopening the Suez Canal, which had been closed since the Six-Day War.

18 May 1971: An organization known as the 'Black Panthers' demonstrated in Jerusalem against discrimination against Jews of oriental origin.

13 January 1972: President Sadat said that a plan for action against Israel by the end of 1971 had been abandoned owing to the conflict between India and Pakistan.

24–28 February 1972: Israel attacked targets in Lebanon.

8 May 1972: Members of an Islamic group seized a Belgian passenger aircraft and ordered it to be flown to Israel, where the passengers were held hostage—Israeli commandos subsequently freed the hostages and killed or captured the suspected hijackers.

21–23 June 1972: Israeli forces carried out further attacks on Lebanon; 36 civilians and 30 guerrillas were reported to have been killed and 80 civilians and 50 guerrillas wounded; five Syrian army officers were taken captive.

5 September 1972: Eleven Israeli athletes were abducted and killed by Arab activists at the Olympic Games in Munich (Germany).

8 September 1972: The Israeli air force bombarded sites believed to be guerrilla bases in Lebanon and Syria; further raids were carried out on 15 October.

19–20 September 1972: A letter-bomb killed an Israeli diplomat in London; 17 other letter bombs addressed to Israelis were discovered elsewhere in the world.

9 November 1972: Israeli and Syrian fighter aircraft were involved aerial combat over the disputed Golan Heights.

8 December 1972: The UN General Assembly advocated prompt implementation of UN Security Council Resolution 242, adopted in 1967.

28–29 December 1972: The Israeli Embassy in Bangkok (Thailand) was occupied by four armed members of the Palestinian Black September Organization.

21 February 1973: A Libyan passenger aircraft was shot down by Israeli fighters over the Sinai desert; 108 people on board were killed.

9 April 1973: Arab guerrillas made unsuccessful attempts to kill the Israeli Ambassador in Nicosia (Cyprus).

10 April 1973: Israeli troops in civilian dress killed three Palestinian Arab guerrilla leaders in Beirut.

10 April 1973: Professor Ephraim Katzir (Katchalski) was elected President.

September 1973: The Likud (Consolidation) party was formed.

6 October 1973: Egyptian armed forces crossed the Suez Canal into the Sinai desert to begin an offensive against Israel; Syrian armed forces began simultaneous attack against Israel through the Golan Heights; the conflict became known as the 'Yom Kippur War', after the Jewish religious festival during which the offensives began.

16 October 1973: Israeli armed forces made an incursion west of the Suez Canal against Egyptian forces; an attack on Egyptian positions in Sinai began the following day.

22 October 1973: Egypt and Israel agreed to a cease-fire, but were unable to maintain the truce; a renewed, UN-monitored cease-fire was agreed two days later, and Israel signed a cease-fire with Syria on 26 October.

1 December 1973: Ben-Gurion died.

3 December 1973: Golda Meir was endorsed as leader of Labour Alignment (a coalition of the Labour Party, Mapam, the National Religious Party (NRP) and independents).

31 December 1973: A general election was held, with inconclusive results.

22 January 1974: The Knesset ratified the Israeli-Egyptian Agreement for the disengagement of forces on the Suez-Sinai front.

6 March 1974: A new Cabinet was formed by Labour Alignment; the Government was endorsed by the Knesset on 10 March.

2 April 1974: Gen. David Elazar resigned as Chief of Staff of the Israeli armed forces.

10 April 1974: Golda Meir resigned as Prime Minister.

14 April 1974: Maj.-Gen. (subsequently Lt.-Gen.) Mordechai Gur was appointed Chief of the General Staff of the IDF.

May 1974: A cease-fire between Israel and Syria took effect.

28 May 1974: Gen. Itzhak Rabin formed a new coalition Government comprising Labour Alignment (Labour Party and Mapam), Independent Liberals and the Civil Rights Movement.

28 October 1974: The Civil Rights Movement withdrew from the governing coalition; the NRP joined the following day.

7 November 1974: Israel was excluded from activities of UNESCO.

13–23 January 1975: Israeli forces made an incursion into southern Lebanon.

2 February 1975: The Israeli Cabinet established a special ministerial committee for defence.

10–15 February 1975: The US Secretary of State, Dr Henry Kissinger, visited the Middle East (including Israel) with aim of securing the basis for agreement between Israel and Egypt on a further disengagement of forces in the Suez-Sinai sector; Kissinger repeated his visit in March.

8–11 July 1975: Itzhak Rabin made the first visit by an Israeli Prime Minister to the FRG.

1 September 1975: Egypt and Israel signed a further limited agreement on military disengagement in the Sinai peninsula.

22 February 1976: The implementation of the second Egyptian-Israeli disengagement agreement of 1975 was completed.

29 February 1976: The Cabinet's approval of a plan to expropriate Arab land in Galilee subsequently provoked a general strike by Israeli Arabs and widespread disturbances.

12 April 1976: Municipal elections were held in 24 towns in the Israeli-occupied West Bank.

27 June 1976: An Air France passenger aircraft was hijacked *en route* from Tel-Aviv to Paris, France, by the 'Che Guevara' cell of the Popular Front for the Liberation of Palestine (PFLP); the aircraft was redirected to Entebbe, Uganda.

3–4 July 1976: Israeli troops mounted a successful operation to rescue the passengers held captive by the PFLP hijackers at Entebbe.

11 November 1976: The UN Security Council issued a consensus statement deploring Israeli attempts to modify the demographic nature of the occupied territories through the establishment of Jewish settlements there.

21 November 1976: Syrian military deployment in southern Lebanon provoked fears of a confrontation between Israel and Syria.

19 December 1976: Three NRP members of the coalition Government were dismissed.

20 December 1976: Rabin submitted his Government's resignation; President Katzir requested him to form a new administration in early January.

29–30 December 1976: The Egyptian President, Anwar Sadat, made new proposals as part of an attempt to revive the Geneva Middle East peace conference. The proposals urged the USA to apply pressure on Israel to accept a settlement based on UN Security Council Resolution 242.

5 January 1977: The Knesset adopted a bill providing for the holding of a general election on 17 May. Rabin was thus confirmed in office in an interim capacity until that date.

14 January 1977: The Israeli High Court ruled that the two Independent Liberal members remained part of the governing coalition, whereas the three members belonging to the NRP did not.

18 January 1977: Rabin appointed three Labour members to portfolios vacated by deputies from the NRP.

8 March 1977: Rabin stated that Israel would not participate in a renewed Geneva Middle East peace conference which included the PLO.

8 April 1977: Itzhak Rabin resigned as Labour's candidate for the premiership at the forthcoming general election; Shimon Peres subsequently assumed the party leadership.

11 April 1977: The Central Committee of Mapam voted in favour of remaining in coalition with Labour, despite Peres's leadership, to which it had originally objected.

22 April 1977: Rabin relinquished all effective power as interim head of government to Peres.

17 May 1977: Following the general election, the Likud party emerged as the largest group in the Knesset.

19 June 1977: The Likud leader, Menachem Begin, formed a centre-right coalition Government comprising, initially, Likud, the NRP and one independent deputy; Agudat Israel subsequently pledged its parliamentary support, and the new Cabinet was endorsed by the Knesset on 21 June.

19–20 July 1977: Begin made procedural proposals with regard to a renewed Geneva Middle East peace conference.

12 September 1977: The US stated publicly, for the first time, that a settlement of the Palestinian question was vital to the success of a renewed Geneva Middle East peace conference.

25 September 1977: The Israeli Cabinet accepted that a unified Arab delegation to a renewed Geneva Middle East peace conference should include a Palestinian component. However, it insisted that Palestinian representatives should be attached to the Jordanian component of such a delegation and should not be members of the PLO.

20 October 1977: the Democratic Movement for Change decided to join the governing coalition, four cabinet posts had been reserved for it.

18–20 November 1977: President Sadat visited Israel. Addressing the Knesset, he accepted the existence of Israel, but stated that peace in the Middle East depended on Israel's withdrawal from occupied Arab territory and on recognition of Palestinian rights.

14 December 1977: A preparatory conference aiming to facilitate the resumption of the Geneva Middle East peace conference commenced in Cairo.

25 December 1977: Begin made an official visit to Egypt, the first such visit by an Israeli Prime Minister. During the visit he detailed new Israeli proposals regarding Sinai, the West Bank and Gaza Strip.

28 December 1977: The Knesset approved a 26-point government plan regarding the restoration of Egyptian sovereignty in the Sinai peninsula, and for the West Bank and Gaza Strip.

January 1978: The Cabinet was expanded from 17 to 19 members.

11–13 January 1978: The Egyptian-Israeli military committee met for the first time in Cairo.

11 March 1978: PLO guerrillas attacked numerous Israeli targets.

14–15 March 1978: Israel invaded southern Lebanon with the declared aim of eradicating Palestinian guerrilla bases there.

19 March 1978: The UN Security Council adopted Resolution 425, in which it urged 'strict respect for the territorial integrity, sovereignty and political independence of Lebanon within its internationally recognized boundaries'; sought the immediate cessation of Israeli 'military action against Lebanese territorial integrity' and the immediate withdrawal of Israeli forces from all Lebanese territory; and decided 'to establish immediately under its authority a

United Nations Interim Force for Southern Lebanon (UNIFIL) for the purpose of confirming the withdrawal of Israeli forces, restoring international peace and security and assisting the Government of Lebanon in ensuring the return of its effective authority in the area'.

23 March 1978: Israel indicated that it would co-operate fully with the UN over southern Lebanon.

1 April 1978: Maj.-Gen. Rafael Eitan was appointed Chief of the General Staff of the IDF.

11 April 1978: Israel implemented a partial withdrawal of its armed forces from southern Lebanon.

19 April 1978: Itzhak Navon was elected as President of Israel.

21 May 1978: Israel announced that it would withdraw all of its armed forces from southern Lebanon by 13 June, provided that Palestinian guerrillas were not permitted to return there; that no further attacks against Israel took place; and that the security of southern Lebanon's inhabitants was guaranteed.

24 May 1978: The PLO undertook not to oppose the UN mission in southern Lebanon and the reassertion of Lebanese sovereignty there.

13 June 1978: The withdrawal of Israeli armed forces from southern Lebanon was completed. Final positions were, however, transferred to the Lebanese Christian militia.

18 June 1978: The Cabinet approved a statement in which Israel agreed that five years after the application of 'administrative autonomy' in the West Bank and Gaza Strip negotiations would commence on 'the nature of the future relations between the parties'.

14 September 1978: The Democratic Movement for Change split into two factions; consequently seven Knesset members withdrew support for Begin's coalition.

17 September 1978: Following negotiations at the US President's residence at Camp David, Maryland, Begin and Sadat signed two agreements: 'A Framework for Peace in the Middle East' and 'A Framework for the Conclusion of a Peace Treaty between Egypt and Israel'.

28 September 1978: The Knesset approved the Camp David Agreements.

12 October 1978: Negotiations commenced between Egypt and Israel on the text of a formal peace treaty in the context of the Camp David Agreements.

27 October 1978: Begin and Sadat were awarded the Nobel Peace Prize.

17 December 1978: The formal deadline for the conclusion of a peace treaty between Egypt and Israel passed, without agreement.

18 February 1979: Iran severed diplomatic relations with Israel, following that country's Islamic Revolution.

26 March 1979: Egypt and Israel signed a peace treaty, by which Israel agreed to return Sinai to Egypt, while retaining control of the Gaza Strip.

1 April 1979: The Cabinet approved the peace treaty with Egypt (which also ratified the treaty in April).

29 April 1979: The Cabinet approved a proposal by Begin, that prosecutors should be able to seek the death penalty for 'terrorists who commit acts of inhuman cruelty'.

7 May 1979: In a speech to the Knesset, Begin offered to engage in peace negotiations with Lebanon.

25 May 1979: Israeli, Egyptian and US negotiating teams commenced talks on Palestinian autonomy.

27 June 1979: Israeli and Syrian fighter aircraft engaged in hostilities over southern Lebanon.

1 July 1979: The Cabinet endorsed policy of pre-emptive attacks against Palestinian guerrillas in Lebanon.

10 August 1979: President Carter denied that the USA supported the creation of an independent Palestinian state and declared that the USA would not negotiate with the PLO unless it accepted UN Security Council Resolution 242.

26 August 1979: The UN brokered a cease-fire between Israeli and Palestinian forces after an intensification in hostilities between them throughout the month in southern Lebanon.

29–30 August 1979: The UN Security Council held an extraordinary session to address the deteriorating security situation in southern Lebanon.

25 September 1979: The USA announced that it would attempt to mediate a solution to the crisis in Lebanon and envisaged the holding of an international peace conference in which both Israel and the PLO, among others, would participate.

21 October 1979: Moshe Dayan resigned as Minister of Foreign Affairs in protest at the Government's inflexibility with regard to negotiations with Egypt and the USA on Palestinian autonomy in the West Bank and Gaza Strip.

25 January 1980: The first phase of Israeli military withdrawal from the Sinai peninsula was completed.

26 January 1980: Egypt and Israel formally established diplomatic relations.

7 February 1980: Begin warned that Israel would not remain passive in the event of attacks on the Christian minorities in Lebanon.

25 May 1980: Ezer Weizman resigned as Minister of Defence, in protest at reductions in defence expenditure.

30 July 1980: The Knesset adopted legislation declaring a unified Jerusalem to be the capital and an integral part of Israel.

20 August 1980: The UN Security Council adopted a Resolution urging all states with diplomatic missions in Jerusalem to withdraw them.

26–30 October 1980: President Navon made first official visit by an Israeli head of state to Egypt.

19 December 1980: Labour elected Peres as its candidate for the premiership at the next general election.

January 1981: Yigael Hurwitz resigned as Minister of Finance.

10 February 1981: The Knesset approved a bill providing for its premature dissolution and the holding of a general election on 30 June.

7 June 1981: Israel attacked and destroyed a nuclear reactor close to the Iraqi capital, Baghdad.

30 June 1981: The general election resulted in a narrow victory for the Likud bloc.

4 August 1981: Begin formed a new coalition, in which Likud was the dominant component, in alliance with the NRP, Tami and Agudat Israel.

14 December 1981: Israeli 'law, jurisdiction and administration' was extended to the Golan Heights, an action widely interpreted as annexation.

22 December 1981: The formation of a 'ministerial defence committee' was announced.

25 April 1982: Israel completed its military withdrawal from the Sinai peninsula.

6 June 1982: Israel launched 'Operation Peace for Galilee', an armed incursion into Lebanon.

1 September 1982: The US President, Ronald Reagan, announced that while the USA would not accept the establishment of a Palestinian state, it would support the granting of some autonomy to the West Bank Palestinians, in association with Jordan; the policy became known as the 'Reagan Plan'.

6–9 September 1982: Arab leaders meeting in Fez, Morocco, adopted a Middle East peace plan (the 'Fez plan') that envisaged, among other things, the establishment of an independent Palestinian state.

15 September 1982: Israeli armed forces occupied positions around Palestinian refugee camps in Muslim areas of West Beirut.

17 September 1982: Palestinian refugees at the Sabra and Chatila camps were massacred, apparently by Lebanese Phalangists.

28 September 1982: The Israeli Government initiated a full judicial inquiry into the massacres at Sabra and Chatila.

28 December 1982: Direct talks began between Israel and Lebanon on the withdrawal of foreign forces from Lebanon.

1983: Opposition to the 'Reagan Plan' from Palestinians, Arab states and elements within Israel ensured it could not be implemented.

8 February 1983: The Israeli Supreme Court concluded that the Lebanese Phalangist militiamen were responsible for Sabra and Chatila massacres, but also that Israel's political and military leaders bore indirect responsibility through negligence.

22 February 1983: The USA announced that it would guarantee the security of Israel's northern border after the withdrawal of Israeli armed forces from Lebanon.

22 March 1983: Chaim Herzog was elected as President of Israel.

10 April 1983: The Ministry of Agriculture and the WZO announced plans to increase the number of settlements in the occupied West Bank from 108 to 165 in 1983-87.

24 April 1983: Arafat and King Hussein of Jordan failed to establish a joint negotiating position based on a compromise between the Reagan and Fez peace proposals.

17 May 1983: Israel, Lebanon and the USA signed an agreement providing, among other things, for the withdrawal of Israeli armed forces from Lebanon and the termination of the state of war between Israel and Lebanon.

28 August–7 September 1983: The 'International Conference on the Question of Palestine' was organized by the UN in Geneva.

30 August 1983: Begin resigned as Prime Minister and as leader of the Likud bloc.

2 September 1983: Itzhak Shamir was elected leader of Herut, the dominant component of the Likud bloc.

4 September 1983: Israel redeployed its forces in Lebanon south of Beirut along the Awali river.

21 September 1983: Itzhak Shamir was invited to form a new coalition to govern.

10 October 1983: Itzhak Shamir's Cabinet was endorsed by the Knesset; Shamir was sworn in as Prime Minister.

1 February 1984: The Government was defeated in the Knesset over an opposition demand that a debate should be held on the proposed reconstruction of the Jewish quarter in the West Bank town of Hebron.

22 March 1984: The opposition presented in the Knesset a bill providing for an early general election to be held; the chamber approved the bill (the Government would normally have remained in office until November 1985).

30 May 1984: The UN Security Council voted unanimously to prolong the mandate of its peace-keeping force in the Golan Heights, for an additional six months.

23 July 1984: The general election proved inconclusive, as neither Labour Alignment nor Likud was able to form a coalition from among the new deputies.

5 August 1984: President Herzog nominated Peres as Prime Minister-designate, as a prelude to the formation of a Labour-Likud government of national unity.

31 August 1984: Likud bloc and Labour Alignment announced that they were broadly in agreement on the structure of a government of national unity, which would incorporate the principle of an alternating premiership.

13 September 1984: A Labour-Likud coalition, to be led by Peres, was agreed.

22 November 1984: At the 17th session of the Palestine National Council, King Hussein of Jordan proposed that the PLO and Jordan should pursue a peace initiative based on UN Security Council Resolution 242 of 1967.

14 January 1985: The Cabinet voted in favour of a unilateral withdrawal from Lebanon; the withdrawal began in February.

23 February 1985: King Hussein of Jordan and Arafat made formal provision for a joint Jordanian-Palestinian delegation to attend future peace talks.

May 1985: An 'Inner Cabinet' of 10 ministers (five each from the Likud bloc and the Labour Alignment) was established to deliberate on issues of defence, foreign affairs and Jewish settlements.

June 1985: Israel completed the third and final phase of its withdrawal from Lebanon.

10 June 1985: Peres suggested that Israel and Jordan should engage in direct peace negotiations. Proposing a five-year timetable, he advocated the formation of a joint Jordanian-Palestinian-Israeli committee to draft an agenda for a peace conference.

16 July 1985: The Cabinet rejected as unacceptable seven Palestinians proposed as potential nominees for a Palestinian component of a joint Jordanian-Palestinian delegation to peace talks.

October 1985: The Israeli press published a secret government document, which suggested the establishment of an interim Israeli-Jordanian condominium of the West Bank, granting a degree of Palestinian autonomy and gave details of an Israeli-Jordanian mutual agreement on the need for a forum for peace talks.

1 October 1985: Israeli aircraft bombarded the PLO headquarters in Tunis, Tunisia.

17 October 1985: Peres informed President Reagan that he was prepared to participate, without preconditions, in negotiations with Jordan, and to consider 'territorial compromises'.

19 February 1986: King Hussein of Jordan formally severed political links with the PLO.

25 May 1986: The Cabinet ordered a police investigation of Avraham Shalom, the director of the internal security service, Shin Bet. Shalom had been accused of suppressing evidence concerning the killing of two Palestinian guerrillas in 1984.

11 September 1986: President Mubarak of Egypt and Peres met in Egypt to discuss ways of reviving the Middle East peace process.

5 October 1986: A British newspaper, *The Sunday Times*, claimed that Israel had amassed an arsenal of nuclear weapons in the Negev desert. Mordechai Vanunu, a former employee of the Israeli Atomic Energy Commission and the 'source' of the story, was subsequently abducted and taken to Israel by Mossad agents.

20 October 1986: The Knesset approved a new Cabinet, with Shamir replacing Peres as Prime Minister.

6–10 April 1987: President Herzog made an unofficial visit to the FRG, the first such visit by an Israeli head of state.

17 May 1987: Amon Rubinstein, the Minister of Communications and leader of the Shinui party, resigned from the Cabinet.

15 June 1987: The Tami party announced its decision to merge with Likud.

9 December 1987: Amid increasing Palestinian anger at Israel's continued occupation of the West Bank and Gaza Strip, and frustration with Jordanian policy, the Palestinian *intifada* (uprising) began in those territories.

22 December 1987: The UN Security Council adopted Resolution 605, condemning Israel's violent methods of suppressing Palestinian demonstrations.

5 January 1988: The UN Security Council adopted Resolution 607, urging Israel to comply with the International Red Cross's fourth Geneva Convention of 1949 concerning the treatment of civilians in wartime. The resolution was supported by the USA, voting in favour of the censure of Israel for the first time since 1981.

1 February 1988: The US proposed a new plan for the resolution of the Arab-Israeli conflict, which did not provide for a Palestinian State, but would permit the PLO to participate in the peace process.

2 February 1988: The Centre Party was formed.

23 February 1988: Chaim Herzog was re-elected for a second term of office as President of Israel.

10 March 1988: The European Parliament condemned 'the instances of torture, arbitrary arrest, reprisals, expulsions, and all acts of violence committed by the Israeli Army against the Palestinian population'.

16 April 1988: Khalil al-Wazir, the PLO deputy leader and commander of the Palestine Liberation Army (PLA), was assassinated by Israeli agents in Tunis.

28 July 1988: Jordan cancelled its Five-Year Development Plan for the West Bank.

31 July 1988: Jordan severed its legal and administrative links with the West Bank and renounced its claim to the West Bank and East Jerusalem.

1 November 1988: In elections to the Knesset, Likud and Labour gained approximately the same number of seats, and neither was able to form a coalition without the participation of the other—negotiations for a new government of national unity began.

15 November 1988: The PLO declared an independent Palestinian State and endorsed UN Security Council Resolutions 242 and 338, thereby implicitly recognizing Israel's right to exist.

December 1988: A new Labour-Likud coalition Government was formed, under Shamir, with Peres as Deputy Prime Minister and Minister of Finance.

14 December 1988: Arafat presented a three-point peace initiative to the UN General Assembly.

7 February 1989: The US State Department criticized a 'substantial increase of human rights violations' by Israel against the Palestinian population of the West Bank and the Gaza Strip.

22 February 1989: The Soviet Minister of Foreign Affairs, Eduard Shevardnadze, met separately with his Israeli counterpart, Moshe Arens, and with Arafat, in Cairo.

26 February 1989: Israel agreed to return an area of the Red Sea town of Taba to Egyptian control.

14 May 1989: The Cabinet approved Shamir's proposal that Palestinian elections should be held in the Occupied Territories; the proposal was subsequently approved by the Knesset.

22 May 1989: The US Secretary of State, James Baker, urged the Israeli Government to abandon its 'unrealistic vision of a "Greater Israel"', while urging the Palestinians to abandon violence and concentrate their efforts on diplomacy.

23 July 1989: Attempts by the Minister of Trade and Industry, Ariel Sharon, and other Cabinet ministers to amend Shamir's proposal for Palestinian elections were unsuccessful.

15 September 1989: President Mubarak of Egypt proposed a 10-point plan aiming to revive Israeli-Palestinian peace negotiations.

18 September 1989: Hungary restored diplomatic relations with Israel.

3 November 1989: Ethiopia and Israel restored diplomatic relations.

14 January 1990: The Prime Minister, Itzhak Shamir, claimed that the Occupied Territories would be used to settle Jewish immigrants from the USSR.

18 February 1990: Ariel Sharon resigned his position as Israel's Minister of Trade and Industry; he was subsequently replaced by Moshe Nissim.

13 March 1990: The Government collapsed, following the dismissal of the Deputy Prime Minister and Minister of Finance, Shimon Peres.

15 March 1990: The Knesset adopted a motion of 'no confidence' in the Government of Itzhak Shamir.

18 March 1990: President Herzog invited Shimon Peres to form a new Government.

7 April 1990: A demonstration demanding electoral reform was held in Tel-Aviv.

11 April 1990: Jewish settlers occupied the St John's Hospice in Jerusalem.

27 April 1990: Following Peres' failure to reach an agreement on a coalition, President Herzog invited Shamir to form a Government.

20 May 1990: Widespread rioting occurred in the Gaza Strip, following the murder of a number of Palestinian civilians by an Israeli civilian.

28–30 May 1990: An emergency Arab League 'summit' meeting was held in Baghdad (Iraq) to discuss the increased emigration of Soviet Jews to Israel, and their potential settlement in the Occupied Territories.

30 May 1990: The Palestine Liberation Front launched a seaborne attack on Israeli beaches.

8 June 1990: Shamir announced the formation of a new Government; the Knesset endorsed the administration three days later.

30 September 1990: Israel and the USSR agreed to upgrade their diplomatic links to ambassadorial level.

8 October 1990: Israeli security forces killed 21 Palestinians during unrest in Jerusalem; the action was subsequently condemned by the UN Security Council.

24 October 1990: Israel banned all movement in or out of the Occupied Territories amid increasing tension between Jewish and Arab communities.

4 November 1990: The Israeli Cabinet rejected proposals made by the UN Secretary-General for the protection of Palestinians living in the Occupied Territories.

16 November 1990: The Agudat Israel party joined the governing coalition.

20 December 1990: The UN Security Council adopted Resolution 681, condemning Israeli conduct in the Occupied Territories.

17 January 1991: Iraq, which was being attacked by a multi-national force in response to its annexation of Kuwait (see chapter on Iraq), commenced attacks with *Scud* missiles against Israeli and Saudi Arabian targets.

19 January 1991: King Hussein stated that Jordan would defend its airspace in the event of any incursion by the Israeli air force.

3 February 1991: The Cabinet approved the admission of the Moledet party to the governing coalition.

20 February 1991: The US Secretary of State signed a guarantee for a US $400m. loan to Israel for the purpose of housing immigrants.

6 March 1991: The US President, George Bush, identified the resolution of the Arab-Israeli conflict as one of his administration's principal aims in the period following the Iraqi conflict.

7–14 March 1991: The US Secretary of State visited Egypt, Israel, Kuwait, Saudi Arabia and Syria.

31 March 1991: The Israeli Cabinet introduced new measures to combat the Palestinian *intifada*.

16 April 1991: The first new Israeli settlement in the West Bank for two years was established.

22 May 1991: The US Secretary of State identified Israel's policy of establishing settlements in the Occupied Territories as the biggest obstacle to US efforts to achieve a Middle Eastern peace settlement.

14 July 1991: Syria agreed to participate in direct negotiations with Israel at a regional Middle East peace conference.

29–31 July 1991: The Minister of Foreign Affairs, David Levy, visited Egypt for talks with his Egyptian counterpart and with President Mubarak.

31 July 1991: The Presidents of the USA and the USSR announced that they would co-sponsor a regional Middle East peace conference which they scheduled to take place in October 1991.

4 August 1991: The Cabinet formally agreed that Israel would participate in a regional Middle East peace conference on the terms proposed by the USA and the USSR.

7 October 1991: The Prime Minister annouced that any proposals involving the exchange of land for peace at the forthcoming Middle East peace conference would be rejected; he subsequently announced that he would lead the Israeli delegation to the conference himself.

30 October 1991: The Middle East peace conference commenced in Madrid (Spain), attended by representatives from Egypt, Israel, Lebanon and Syria, in addition to a joint Palestinian-Jordanian delegation.

3 November 1991: The first sessions of bilateral talks between Arab and Israeli delegations took place within the framework of the Middle East peace conference.

14 November 1991: The USSR appointed an Ambassador to Israel.

10 December 1991: A second round of bilateral negotiations between Israeli and Arab delegations commenced in the US capital, Washington, DC; a third round took place there in January 1993.

19 January 1992: Tehiya and Moledet withdrew from the governing coalition.

24 January 1992: Israel and the People's Republic of China established diplomatic relations.

16 February 1992: Sheikh Abbas Moussawi, Secretary-General of Lebanese Hezbollah, was killed in an attack by the Israeli air force.

19 February 1992: Itzhak Rabin was elected Chairman of the Labour Party.

20 February 1992: Itzhak Shamir was re-elected as leader of Likud.

24 February 1992: A fourth round of bilateral negotiatios between Israeli and Arab delegations commenced in Washington, DC; the same city hosted further rounds in April, August and October and November.

11 May 1992: Multilateral negotiations between Israeli and Arab delegations resumed in various locations.

23 June 1992: The Labour Party won 44 of the 120 seats in the Knesset, compared with 32 won by Likud.

28 June 1992: The Labour Party was invited to form a new coalition Government; the Cabinet was appointed on 13 July.

21 July 1992: The Prime Minister, Rabin, visited Egypt.

16 December 1992: The Israeli Cabinet approved a mass deportation of alleged Palestinian supporters of the Islamic Resistance Movement (Hamas) from Israel to Lebanon.

17 December 1992: Arab delegations withdrew from the eighth round of bilateral negotiations with Israel.

11–12 January 1993: The foreign ministers of the Arab League member states met in Cairo to discuss the deportation of Palestinians from Israel to Lebanon.

28 January 1993: The Israeli High Court ruled that deportation of Palestinians to Lebanon in December 1992 had been lawful; the following week the Government offered to allow 101 of the deportees to return.

15 March 1993: The Prime Minister, Rabin, visted the USA for talks with that country's newly inaugurated President, Bill Clinton.

24 March 1993: Ezer Weizmann was elected President of Israel; on the same day, Binyamin Netanyahu was elected leader of Likud.

11 April 1993: Israel announced the indefinite 'closure' of the Occupied Territories.

27 April 1993: A ninth round of bilateral negotiations between Israeli and Arab delegations commenced in Washington, DC; a 10th round began in June.

30 May 1993: The Cabinet was reshuffled.

25 July 1993: Israeli armed forces initiated intense air and artillery attacks against Hezbollah fighters and Palestinian guerrillas in southern Lebanon.

15 August 1993: Palestinian deportees in southern Lebanon approved an offer by the Israeli Government permitting their staged return to Israel by December 1993.

30 August 1993: A secretly negotiated draft peace agreement between Israel and the PLO was announced; the negotiations had taken place in the Norwegian capital, Oslo.

13 September 1993: The Declaration of Principles on Palestinian Self-Rule in the Occupied Territories (known informally as the Oslo Agreement) was signed by Israel and the PLO in Washington, DC. Israel and the PLO formally recognized each other.

15 September 1993: Israel and Jordan agreed an agenda for future bilateral negotiations between their respective delegations to the Middle East peace conference.

20 September 1993: An Israeli delegation arrived in Tunisia for talks with that country's Government and with PLO officials.

13 October 1993: Israeli and Palestinian negotiators commenced talks in Taba, Egypt.

24 November 1993: Imad Akel, a commander of Qassem (the military wing of Hamas), was shot dead by Israeli forces.

13 December 1993: By this date, Israeli forces should have begun to withdraw from the Gaza Strip and the Jericho area under the terms of the Declaration of Principles on Palestinian Self-Rule; however, a failure to agree on security arrangements for border crossings led to the process being delayed.

30 December 1993: Israel and the Vatican signed an agreement on mutual recognition.

22–29 January 1994: The twelfth round of bilateral negotiations in the Middle East peace process commenced in Washington, DC.

25 February 1994: The PLO and other Arab delegations withdrew from the Middle East peace negotiations, following the murder of some 30 worshippers at a mosque in Hebron by an Israeli civilian.

13 March 1994: The Kach and Kahane Chai political parties were proscribed by the Government.

18 March 1994: The UN Security Council adopted a Resolution condemning the killings in Hebron.

29 April 1994: Israel and the PLO signed an economic agreement, concerning the relations between Israel and the autonomous Palestinian entity in the five-year period prior to self-rule.

4 May 1994: Israel and the PLO signed an agreement providing for Palestinian Self-Rule in the Gaza Strip and Jericho; Israel was to withdraw its forces from the areas, and a Palestinian National Authority (PNA) would assume the powers of the Israeli military governments (with the exceptions of external security and foreign affairs). Elections to the Palestinian National Council (PNC), which had been sceduled to take place in July, were postponed until October.

13 May 1994: The Israeli armed forces completed their withdrawal from the Gaza Strip.

1 June 1994: Israeli forces launched a major attack on a Hezbollah training camp in Lebanon.

15 June 1994: Israel and the Vatican established full diplomatic relations.

25 July 1994: Israel and Jordan signed a joint declaration formally ending the state of war between them.

1 September 1994: Morocco announced its decision to open a liaison office in Tel-Aviv.

30 September 1994: The Gulf Co-operation Council ended its secondary and tertiary trade boycott of Israel.

20 October 1994: Following an attack in Tel-Aviv by a suicide bomber representing Hamas, Israel temporarily closed its borders with the West Bank and Gaza Strip.

26 October 1994: Israel and Jordan signed a comprehensive peace treaty.

10 November 1994: King Hussein of Jordan made his first public visit to Israel.

21 December 1994: The Yi'ud party joined the governing coalition.

22 January 1995: The Islamic Jihad movement claimed responsibility for bomb attacks in Netanya, which killed 21 people.

9 February 1995: Israeli armed forces completed their withdrawal from Jordanian territory.

14 March 1995: The US Secretary of State, Warren Christopher, announced that peace negotiations between Israel and Syria were to resume.

24 May 1995: Israel and Syria concluded a 'framework understanding' on security arrangements in the disputed Golan Heights.

27–29 June 1995: Israeli and Syrian Chiefs of Staff met in Washington, DC.

17 July 1995: The Government was reorganized.

28 September 1995: The Israeli-Palestinian Interim Peace Agreement on the West Bank and Gaza Strip was signed; the accord (known informally as the Taba Agreement or 'Oslo II') provided for elections to an 82-member Palestinian Council, and for a Palestinian Executive President, in addition to the progressive withdrawal of Israeli forces from West Bank towns and the release of Palestinian prisoners.

10 October 1995: The President of Syria, Hafiz al-Assad, stated that Syria would not conclude a peace agreement with Israel which did not meet all of its aspirations.

11 October 1995: The first Palestinian prisoners to be released under the Second Israeli-Palestinian Interim Peace Agreement were freed.

25 October 1995: The PNA took control of the West Bank town of Jenin; Israeli forces completed their withdrawal from the town in November, and from five other towns in December.

4 November 1995: Rabin was assassinated by a Jewish student opposed to the peace process. Peres was appointed acting Prime Minster and was subsequently invited (with the approval of Likud) to form a new administration.

21 November 1995: The new Government, a coalition of the same parties as in the previous administration, was endorsed by the Knesset.

27–29 December 1995: Peace negotiations between Israel and Syria resumed.

5 January 1996: Yahya Ayyash, a leading figure in the Hamas movement, was killed in Gaza; the group alleged that Israeli agents were responsible.

February 1996: Peres announced legislation providing for the direct election of the Prime Minister—the election would be held concurrently with legislative elections in May.

8 February 1996: The Likud and Tzomet parties formed an electoral alliance.

20 February 1996: A new political party, Gesher, was founded—the new party joined the Likud-Tzomet allance shortly after its foundation.

25 February–4 March 1996: Suicide-bomb attacks were carried out in Jerusalem and in several other cities.

13 March 1996: A 'Peacemakers summit meeting' was convened in Sharm esh-Sheikh, Egypt; Lebanon and Syria boycotted the meeting.

14 March 1996: President Clinton began a visit to Israel.

7 April 1996: Israel and Turkey signed a series of military co-operation agreements.

11 April 1996: Israel launched a campaign of aerial and artillery bombardment of Hezbollah targets in southern Lebanon (known as 'Operation Grapes of Wrath'), with the stated aim of preventing rocket attacks on northern Isaeli towns.

18 April 1996: More than 100 Lebanese civilians were killed in an attack by Israeli armed forces on UN base at Qana; Israel claimed the base had been attacked in error.

27 April 1996: A cease-fire between Israel and Lebanese Hezbollah came into force.

5–6 May 1996: Israeli and Palestinian delegations commenced 'final status' negotiations.

29 May 1996: Israeli legislative and prime-ministerial elections were held; Netanyahu was elected Prime Minister, unexpectedly defeating his only opponent, Peres. In the election to the Knesset, Labour secured 34 seats and the Likud-Tzomet-Gesher alliance 32; two ultra-orthodox Jewish parties, Shas and the National Religious Party (NRP), won 10 and nine seats, respectively.

18 June 1996: The new Israeli Government (a coalition formed by the Likud alliance, Shas, the NRP and several smaller parties) was approved by the Knesset.

21–23 June 1996: An Arab 'summit' meeting was held in Cairo in response to Likud's victory in the Israeli elections.

2 August 1996: Israel relaxed restrictions on the expansion of Jewish settlements in the West Bank and Gaza Strip.

28 August 1996: Israel and Turkey signed a defence agreement.

29 August 1996: A Palestinian general strike was organized in the West Bank and Gaza Strip.

25 September 1996: Violent disturbances occurred in the West Bank and Gaza Strip after the Israeli Government opened a tunnel close to al-Aqsa mosque.

30 December 1996: Some 250,000 Israeli workers observed a general strike in protest at reduced government spending.

10 January 1997: Roni Bar-On was appointed Attorney-General; however, he resigned within 12 hours, after allegations of corruption surrounded the promotion.

15 January 1997: Palestinian and Israeli officials signed an agreement on the redeployment of Israeli troops in Hebron; Binyamin Begin resigned the science portfolio in protest.

17 January 1997: The redeployment of Israeli troops in Hebron began.

29 January 1997: Elyaqim Rubenstein was appointed Attorney-General.

16 February 1997: The Israeli Minister of Foreign Affairs, David Levy, and the chief Palestinian negotiator, Mahmoud Abbas, attended the first session of renewed bilateral negotiations.

26 February 1997: The construction of 6,500 new homes for Jewish settlers at Har Homa, in East Jerusalem, was approved; despite condemnation of the decision by Palestinian groups and Arab governments, construction commenced in March.

7 March 1997: The PNA rejected the Israeli government interpretation of the terms agreed for future troop deployment in the Occupied Territories.

18 March 1997: Construction of new Jewish homes at Har Homa, East Jerusalem, commenced.

21 March 1997: A proposed UN Security Council Resolution to halt the Har Homa development was vetoed by the USA for a second time.

21 March 1997: A suicide-bomb attack carried out in Tel-Aviv by a member of Hamas resulted in the deaths of three Israelis and injuries to at least 40 others; Israel closed the West Bank and Gaza Strip in response.

16 April 1997: Israeli police recommended that Prime Minister Netanyahu should be indicted on charges of fraud and breach of trust following preliminary investigation into the January appointment of Roni Bar-On as Attorney-General.

29 April 1997: The Israeli Government announced that it would allow 55,000 Palestinian workers to enter Israel from 30 April.

3 June 1997: The election to the leadership of the Labour Party was won by Ehud Barak.

15 June 1997: The US House of Representatives recognized Jerusalem as the undivided capital of Israel.

18 June 1997: The Minister of Finance, Dan Meridor, resigned; a government reorganization was carried out in July.

20 June 1997: The Attorney-General ruled that Netanyahu would not be charged in connection with the appointment of Roni Bar-On.

9 July 1997: The Cabinet was reshuffled.

22 July 1997: Levy and Arafat met in Brussels, Belgium, for preliminary discussions concerning the peace process.

28 July 1997: Israeli and Palestinian officials announced that peace talks were to be resumed in early August.

30 July 1997: An attack by two Palestinian suicide bombers resulted in the deaths of 14 Israelis in Jerusalem; in response Israel closed the West Bank and Gaza Strip and withheld the payment of some US $50m. in tax revenues owed to the PNA.

18 August 1997: One-third of the PNA funds being withheld by the Israeli Government was released.

1 September 1997: The West Bank and Gaza Strip were reopened by Israel.

5 September 1997: Twelve Israeli soldiers were killed by Lebanese armed forces while attempting to enter a Lebanese village known to be inhabited by Hezbollah members.

14 September 1997: The Israeli Government released 50% of the PNA funds withheld since 30 July and relaxed restrictions on the movement of Palestinians in the Occupied Territories.

15 September 1997: Netanyahu vetoed an Israeli housing project in East Jerusalem which had been anticipated to cause disruption to the peace process.

25 September 1997: The leader of the Palestinian Hamas group, Khalid Meshaal, was the subject of a failed assassination attempt by Israeli agents in Amman; diplomatic activity to preserve cordial relations between Israel and Jordan ensued.

1 October 1997: A number of Arab prisoners, including Sheikh Ahmad Yassin—one of the founders of Hamas, were released from Israeli prisons, reportedly in exchange for the return of two Israeli secret-service agents who had been detained in Jordan following the attempted assassination of Hamas bureau chief, Meshaal.

8 October 1997: Arafat and Netanyahu had their first direct discussions for eight months at the Erez check-point between Israel and the Gaza Strip.

16–18 November 1997: The Fourth Middle East and North Africa (MENA) economic conference was convened in Doha, Qatar; the event was the subject of a wide-spread Arab boycott, owing to the participation of an Israeli delegation.

30 November 1997: The Israeli Cabinet agreed, in principle, to a partial withdrawal from the West Bank, but did not agree the timing or scale of such a withdrawal; the Government also undertook to create a team of Ministers to decide which areas of the West Bank should be permanently retained by Israel.

4 January 1998: David Levy, the Minister of Foreign Affairs and leader of the Gesher party, resigned, and Gesher withdrew from the Government, ostensibly owing to the lack of progress in the peace process and the Government's indifference to the needs of low-income workers in Israel.

20 January 1998: During a visit to the USA Netanyahu held talks with US President Clinton, at which he reportedly rejected US proposals for a second-stage redeployment of forces from 10%–15% of West Bank territory, proposing instead redeployment from no more than 9.5% of the territory.

20 January 1998: The Deputy Prime Minister, Minister of Education, Culture and Sport and leader of the NRP, Zevulun Hammer, died. Itzhak Levi assumed his ministerial portfolio and the leadership of the NRP. Levi's previous responsibilities as Minister of Transport and Energy were taken by NRP deputy Shaul Yahalom.

31 January 1998: The US Secretary of State, Madeleine Albright, visited the Middle East region and held talks with Netanyahu and Arafat, the effort failed to restart the peace process.

16 February 1998: The commission of investigation into the Israeli military intelligence agency's alleged involvement in the attempted assassination of the Hamas official Khalid Meshaal in September 1997 published its report; Netanyahu was absolved of responsibility for the operation. Maj.-Gen. Danny Yatou, the head of agency (known as Mossad), who had been severely criticized in the report, resigned and was replaced by Ephraim Halevy.

4 March 1998: The Knesset re-elected Ezer Weizman as President of Israel for a futher five-year term.

15–18 March 1998: The British Secretary of State for Foreign and Commonwealth Affairs, Robin Cook, visited the Middle East on a tour intended to raise the profile of the EU in the peace process. During his time in the region, Cook made a controversial visit to the Har Homa settlement.

29 March 1998: The discovery in the West Bank of the body of Muhiad-Din Sharif, a leader of the armed wing of Hamas, led to fears of reprisal attacks against Israel; however, Hamas members were later arrested for the murder, which was reportedly the result of an internal power struggle.

1 April 1998: Israel's 'inner' Security Cabinet voted unanimously to accept UN Security Council Resolution 425 (adopted in March 1978) and withdraw from southern Lebanon, conditional upon Lebanese guarantees of the security of Israel's northern border. Lebanon continued to assert that Resolution 425 required an unconditional withdrawal from its territory, and refused to accede to Israel's terms for departure.

16–21 April 1998: The British Prime Minister, Tony Blair, undertook a tour of the Middle East region during which he invited Arafat and Netanyahu, to attend a 'summit' for peace in the British capital, London, in early May. During his visit Blair signed an EU-Palestinian security agreement.

4–5 May 1998: The US Secretary of State, Madeleine Albright, held separate talks with Netanyahu and Arafat, in London. No significant progress was made and although both parties were invited to Washington, DC, for further talks, Netanyahu declined to attend since the talks were made conditional on Israeli support for a US plan for a 13.1% redeployment in the West Bank.

26 May 1998: Serious clashes erupted in East Jerusalem after a Jewish settler organization began construction work on a religious settlement on disputed territory in the Arab quarter of the city.

21 June 1998: The Israeli Cabinet approved a draft plan to widen Jerusalem's municipal boundaries; the decision was condemned by the Palestinians, the Arab states and the international community.

19–22 July 1998: Israeli and Palestinian negotiators held their first direct peace talks for some 16 months; however, the talks failed to secure agreement on redeployment.

22 July 1998: The Knesset gave preliminary approval to a bill which required a majority vote in the Knesset and a referendum to be held prior to allowing an Israeli withdrawal from either the Golan Heights or any part of Jerusalem; this action was condemned by Syria.

28 September 1998: At a US-mediated meeting in Washington, DC, the Israeli and Palestinian leaders agreed to attend a tripartite peace 'summit' in the USA in mid-October 1998; in an address to the UN General Assembly, Netanyahu had previously stated that a unilateral declaration of an independent Palestinian state would occasion the end of the peace process.

15 October 1998: US-brokered talks between Netanyahu and Arafat opened in the Wye Plantation, Maryland, USA.

23 October 1998: Following nine days of negotiations Arafat and Netanyahu signed the Wye River Memorandum in the presence of President Clinton and King Hussein; the agreement outlined a three-month timetable for the imple-metation of the 1995 Interim Agreement and facilitated the beginning of the 'final status' talks. The Wye River Memorandum was the first development in Israeli-Palestinian relations for some 19 months.

17 November 1998: The Knesset ratified the Wye River Memorandum by 75 votes to 19.

20 November 1998: Israel implemented the first stage of troop redeployment from the West Bank and released 250 Palestinian prisoners, as agreed under the Wye River Memorandum.

15 December 1998: A 'summit' meeting was held between President Clinton, Netanyahu and Arafat at the Erez check-point; Netanyahu announced that Israel would not proceed with the second troop redeployment prescribed by the Wye River Memorandum—Arafat demanded that no further Jewish settlements be constructed in disputed territory and refused to exclude the possibility of a unilateral declaration of Palestinian statehood.

16 December 1998: The Minister of Finance, Yaacov Ne'eman, resigned, citing the ineffectiveness of the governing coalition.

20 December 1998: The Cabinet voted to suspend the implementation of Wye River Memorandum.

21 December 1998: An opposition motion resulted in the dissolution of the Knesset and the organization of early legislative elections.

1 January 1999: The Security Cabinet voted to respond to future Hezbollah offensives by targeting infrastructure in central and northern Lebanon.

23 January 1999: The Minister of Defence, Itzhak Mordechai, was dismissed; Moshe Arens was appointed to the position some days later.

18 February 1999: Israeli forces annexed the Lebanese village of Arnoun, on the edge of the Israeli 'security zone'; Arnoun was subsequently liberated by thousands of Lebanese students.

28 February 1999: The Commander of the Israeli army's liaison unit with its client South Lebanon Army (SLA), Brig.-Gen. Erez Gerstein, was killed in a Hezbollah ambush in southern Lebanon—the most senior Israeli officer to be killed there since the 1982 invasion; Israel responded with series of air raids against Hezbollah targets in southern Lebanon.

26 March 1999: EU leaders, meeting in Berlin, Germany, issued the 'Berlin Declaration', which urged Israel to conclude 'final status' negotiations with the PNA within one year.

14–15 April 1999: Israeli forces reannexed the Lebanese village of Arnoun.

15 April 1999: The leader of Shas, Aryeh Der'i, was sentenced to four years' imprisonment and fined, having been found guilty of bribery and fraud; the sentence was subsequently suspended on appeal, although Der'i resigned as Shas leader in June.

4 May 1999: The 'Oslo interim period', as outlined in the Interim Agreement signed by Israel and the PNA on 28 September 1995, ended.

17 May 1999: The Labour leader, Ehud Barak, defeated Netanyahu in the election to the premiership, obtaining 56.1% of the votes cast. In the concurrent elections to the Knesset the Labour-led One Israel alliance became the largest grouping, securing 26 of the 120 seats, while Likud's representation decline from 32 seats to 19; Shas obained 17 seats, an increase of seven. Netanyahu resigned from both the Knesset and the leadership of Likud.

27 May 1999: Ariel Sharon, the outgoing Minister of Foreign Affairs, became Chairman of Likud.

1–3 June 1999: The Israeli-supported SLA completed unilateral withdrawal from enclave of Jezzine, in the north-east of Lebanon's 'security zone'.

3 June 1999: Palestinians in the West Bank declared a 'day of rage' against the continuing expansion of Israeli settlements.

24–25 June 1999: The outgoing Israeli administration initiated a series of aerial attacks on infrastructure targets in central and southern Lebanon, the heaviest raids since 'Operation Grapes of Wrath' in 1996; at least eight civilians were killed and as many as 70 were injured.

6 July 1999: The new Cabinet (comprising ministers from Labour, the Centre Party, Shas, Meretz, Israel B'Aliyah and the NRP, and including leading figure such as Levy, Mordechai and Peres) was presented to the Knesset; in his opening speech to the chamber, Barak (who assumed the defence portfolio himself) promised to negotiate a bilateral peace with Syria, based on the relevant UN Security Council Resolutions.

9 July 1999: Barak began a series of 'summit' meetings with Arab and other world leaders; the first was with the Egyptian President, Mubarak.

11 July 1999: Barak and Arafat held their first direct discussions at the Erez check-point.

20 July 1999: Syria declared a cease-fire with Israel.

1 August 1999: Talks between Israeli and Palestinian delegations collapsed after Arafat rejected Barak's proposal to delay implementation of the Wye River Memorandum and to combine further Israeli troop withdrawals from the West Bank with 'final status' negotiations.

4 September 1999: Israel and the PNA signed the 'Wye Two' agreement in the Egyptian resort of Sharm esh-Sheikh, detailing a revised timetable for outstanding provisions of the original Wye River Memorandum.

9 September 1999: Israel released 199 Palestinian prisoners, as agreed under 'Wye Two'.

10 September 1999: Israel transferred a further 7% of West Bank territory to Palestinian self-rule.

2 November 1999: Barak and Arafat held discussions in Oslo, while attending a ceremony marking the fourth anniversary of the assassination of Itzhak Rabin.

8 November 1999: Israeli and Palestinian negotiators began negotiations on 'final status' issues in the West Bank town of Ramallah.

15–16 December 1999: Following an agreement reached earlier in the month to resume peace talks suspended since 1996, Barak and the Syrian Minister of Foreign Affairs, Farouk ash-Shara' met in Washington, DC, for talks hosted by President Clinton.

21 December 1999: Arafat and Barak met for talks in Ramallah—the first occasion on which an Israeli premier had attended peace talks in Palestinian-controlled territory.

3–9 January 2000: Israeli-Syrian peace talks at Shepherdstown, West Virginia, USA, attended by the Israeli Prime Minister and Syrian Minister of Foreign Affairs, proved inconclusive. A further round of talks, scheduled for 19 January, was subsequently postponed indefinitely.

17 January 2000: At a meeting in Tel-Aviv between Barak and Arafat, the Israeli premier required flexibility in respect of deadlines for troop redeployments and for reaching agreement on 'final status' issues.

20 January 2000: The Attorney-General ordered a criminal investigation into the financial dealings of President Ezer Weizman during his time as a member of the Knesset.

3 February 2000: Talks in Gaza between Arafat and Barak ended in acrimony, following disagreement over the third Israeli troop redeployment.

7 February 2000: Israel launched a series of bombing raids on Hezbollah positions and infrastructure targets in Lebanon, in reprisal for the deaths of Israeli military and SLA personnel in assaults at the end of January.

13 February 2000: The deadline expired for agreement on a framework agreement on permanent status (FAPS) by Israel and the PNA, as stipulated in the 1999 Sharm esh-Sheikh agreement.

5 March 2000: Israel declared that it would unilaterally withdraw from southern Lebanon by 7 July.

9 March 2000: Meeting at Sharm esh-Sheikh for talks hosted by President Hosni Mubarak, Arafat and Barak agreed a formula for the resumption of peace talks.

20–26 March 2000: Pope John Paul II undertook a millennium pilgrimage to the Christian 'Holy Land', including visits to Israel, Jordan and the Palestinian self-rule areas.

21 March 2000: Israeli troops completed the final phase of the second-stage redeployment, as agreed in the 1998 Wye Memorandum. Israeli and Palestinian negotiators resumed 'final status' negotiations in Washington, DC.

26 March 2000: A 'summit' meeting in Geneva between President Assad and President Clinton failed to find a formula for the resumption of negotiations on the Israeli-Syrian track of the peace process.

6 April 2000: Corruption charges against President Weizman were dismissed owing to lack of evidence.

13 April 2000: Israel announced an end to the suspension of settlement construction in the Golan Heights.

30 April 2000: Palestinian negotiators withdrew from 'final status' negotiations in Eilat, in protest at Israeli proposals to expand the settlement of Ma'aleh Edomin.

7 May 2000: Arafat and Barak met in Ramallah for 'crisis' talks, mediated by US special envoy Dennis Ross, ahead of the impending expiry of the extended deadline of 13 May for agreement on FAPS.

15–18 May 2000: A Palestinian 'day of rage', declared in commemoration of the 52nd anniversary of the declaration of the State of Israel, resulted in violent confrontations with Israeli security forces throughout the West Bank and Gaza; at least six Palestinians were killed, and several hundred injured.

24 May 2000: The accelerated Israeli withdrawal from southern Lebanon was completed, several weeks ahead of the original deadline, after Hezbollah forces and civilian supporters overran positions abandoned by the Israeli proxy SLA.

22 June 2000: Meretz ministers resigned from the Cabinet, in protest at concessions made to the ultra-orthodox Shas party regarding state funding for religious schools.

9 July 2000: Israel B'Aliyah, the NRP and Shas withdrew from Israel's governing coalition, in protest at the lack of consulation over concessions to be made by Barak at the scheduled Camp David 'summit' meeting with Arafat.

10 July 2000: Barak narrowly survived a Knesset vote of 'no confidence' in his premiership.

11–25 July 2000: Arafat and Barak attended a peace meeting at Camp David, Maryland, USA, in the presence of President Clinton; negotiations failed to achieve agreement on the issue of the status of Jerusalem.

2 August 2000: Gesher leader David Levy resigned as Minister of Foreign Affairs, following differences with Barak over the peace process; the Minister of Public Security, Shlomo Ben-Ami, was given temporary responsibility for foreign affairs.

31 August 2000: Moshe Katsav was elected to the presidency by the Knesset.

6 September 2000: President Clinton held separate meetings with Arafat and Barak in New York, where the leaders were to attend the UN 'millennium summit'.

19 September 2000: Israel cancelled a scheduled round of talks with Palestinian negotiators in Jerusalem, citing the Palestinians' failure to resolve the impasse in the peace process.

25 September 2000: Barak and Arafat met at the Israeli premier's home for their first peace talks since the Camp David 'summit' in July, amid reported preparations by negotiators from both sides for further talks in the USA.

27 September 2000: The Attorney-General closed criminal cases against the former Likud Prime Minister, Binyamin Netanyahu, and his wife Sara, despite a police recommendation that they should stand trial on corruption charges.

28 September 2000: The Likud leader, Ariel Sharon, visited the disputed sacred site known as Temple Mount by Jews and Haram ash-Sharif by Muslims; this provoked violent protests by Palestinians, which subsequently escalated throughout the West Bank and the Gaza Strip.

5 October 2000: Barak left US-sponsored peace talks in France early and announced that he would not be attending further discussions in Egypt.

6 October 2000: Israeli police stormed the compound of the al-Aqsa mosque in Jerusalem in order to apprehend a group of Palestinian youths who had attacked them several hours previously; the action provoked violent protests among Palestinians and Israeli Arabs throughout the country and was condemned by the international community.

7 October 2000: Lebanese Hezbollah guerrillas captured three Israeli soldiers as violence spread to the Shebaa Farms area near the Israeli-Lebanese border.

7 October 2000: Barak announced that Arafat must suppress the violence in East Jerusalem, Gaza and the West Bank—which had become known as the Al-Aqsa *intifada*—within 48 hours, otherwise the armed forces would intensify offensives on Palestinian targets. The UN Security Council issued a Resolution condemning Israel's excessive use of force against Palestinians.

12 October 2000: Israel criticised the Palestinian authorities for releasing significant numbers of Hamas prisoners. On the same day, Palestinian demonstrators stormed a police station in Ramallah and killed two members of the Israeli security forces detained there; the Israelis subsequently launched a rocket attack on the building and on the headquarters of Arafat's Fatah movement.

16–17 October 2000: At a UN-mediated summit meeting led by President Clinton in Sharm esh-Sheikh, Israel agreed with the Palestinians to end the violence, and establish a mission to investigate its causes, to end the closure of Palestinian-controlled areas and redeploy troops stationed there and to reopen Gaza airport. Barak also demanded that Arafat re-arrest 65 Islamic militants whom the PNA had freed earlier in the month.

18 October 2000: Barak and Arafat met to discuss the implementation of the peace agreement; the following day Israeli troops began to withdraw from their positions in the West Bank and Gaza. The Karni border crossing to the Gaza Strip was also reopened after its closure during unrest two weeks previously.

21–22 October 2000: At a meeting in Cairo, the Arab leaders determined that Israel bore full responsibility for the recent violence. In the enusing weeks Morocco, Oman and Tunisia terminated diplomatic ties with Israel, followed by Egypt and Qatar in November.

22 October 2000: The Government announced that Israel was taking a formal pause from the peace process owing to renewed Palestinian violence; Israeli troops had shot dead nine Palestinians since the implementation of the cease-fire agreement.

26 October 2000: Islamic Jihad carried out a suicide bomb attack on an Israeli security post in Gaza.

29 October 2000: Israel sent tanks and armoured vehicles into the Gaza Strip to open the road to the Jewish settlement of Netzarim; one Palestinian was killed and several others wounded in the operation.

2 November 2000: Peres, the Minister of Regional Co-operation, held talks with Arafat in Gaza; the following day two Israelis were killed in a car bomb attack perpetrated by Islamic Jihad.

17 November 2000: The Government imposed an economic blockade on the West Bank and Gaza.

20 November 2000: A bomb exploded near an Israeli school bus in the Gaza Strip, killing two adults and injuring a further nine adults and children. In retaliation, the Israeli forces shelled the Palestinian security forces and the Fatah party buildings, killing four Fatah officials.

28 November 2000: Barak announced that prime-ministerial elections would take place in February 2001. The following day Ariel Sharon announced his candidacy.

29 November 2000: Russia mediated a further round of peace talks between the Israelis and Palestinians. Barak announced that Israel would withdraw its armed forces from the West Bank, on the condition that the PNA would agree to postpone any discussion of remaining 'final status' issues; this was rejected by the PNA.

10 December 2000: Barak announced his resignation as Prime Minister and his intention to represent Labour in the approaching elections.

10 December 2000: The former Prime Minister, Netanyahu, announced his candidacy for election, providing that the Knesset would either enact new legislation removing the requirement for candidates for the premiership to be members of parliament, or vote to to dissolve itself.

11 December 2000: An inquiry was begun into the recent violence by an international delegation, led by a former US Senator, George Mitchell.

18 December 2000: The Knesset voted against a bill to dissolve itself; Netanyahu subsequently cancelled his candidacy for the premiership.

27 December 2000: US-mediated peace talks collapsed following further explosions in the Gaza Strip and Tel-Aviv. President Clinton was believed to have proposed the creation of a Palestinian state, including the Gaza Strip and 95% of the West Bank, on the condition that the PNA relinquish their demand that Palestinian refugees be allowed to return to the areas they left in 1948. The plan was rejected by the Palestinians.

31 December 2000: The leader of the extremist Jewish settler movement Kahane Chai, Binyamin Kahane, was shot dead. On the same day, a senior Fatah official was killed in the West Bank.

1 January 2001: Three bombs exploded in the Netanya, injuring more than 40 people; the previous day Israeli forces had shot five Palestinians.

5–16 January 2001: US-mediated talks resumed, however, they ended shortly after the killing of a Jewish settler in the Gaza Strip; revenge attacks by Jewish settler extremists on Palestinians ensued.

21 January 2001: Peace talks took place in Taba, Egypt; proceedings were soon suspended, however, after Israeli civilians were killed in a gun attack in the West Bank, for which Hamas later claimed responsibility.

21 January 2001: The Government announced that it would boycott the Mitchell inquiry into the recent violence, after the commission visited Haram ash-Sharif without permission from the Israeli authorities. The commission was subsequently suspended.

6 February 2001: Ariel Sharon won the prime-ministerial election, receiving 62.4% of the votes cast; 62.3% of those eligible to vote participated. Following his defeat, Barak resigned as leader of the Labour Party and announced his retirement from political life.

26 February 2001: The Central Committee of the Labour Party voted to join Ariel Sharon's coalition administration.

2 March 2001: The composition of the new 26-member Cabinet was announced. The Shas leader, Eliyahu Yishai, was appointed Deputy Prime Minister and Minister of the Interior. Salah Tarif, a member of the Arab Druze community, was designated as a minister without portfolio.

19–20 March 2001: Amid continued violence, Sharon visited Washington, DC, for talks with the new US President, George W. Bush.

21 March 2001: A Jerusalem Court convicted the former Minster of Defence, Itzhak Mordechai, of indecently assaulting two women who had worked for him in the 1990s.

5 April 2001: The Supreme Court rejected a petition from the ultra-nationalist Temple Mount Faithful to be allowed to celebrate Passover at Temple Mount. The court ruled that such an event could lead to Palestinian rioting.

24 April 2001: The Israeli authorities closed off all access to and from the West Bank and the Gaza Strip, ostensibly to protect Israel from potential Palestinian attacks during independence celebrations.

28–29 April 2001: Peres held discussions with President Mubarak of Egypt regarding a joint Egyptian-Jordanian peace plan; the proposals suggested that the Israelis and Palestinians should maintain a month-long truce, followed by talks on a future peace deal. At the conclusion of the negotiations, Peres announced that the border restrictions on the Palestinian territories would be relaxed.

30 April 2001: Peres met the UN Secretary-General, Kofi Annan, to discuss the peace plan; he suggested that the truce period should be extended before peace talks commenced; in the subsequent days he discussed the Egyptian-Jordanian peace proposals with President Bush and the US Secretary of State, Colin Powell.

10 May 2001: The armed forces carried out missile attacks on the headquarters of the Palestinian police buildings and the Fatah headquarters in Gaza city.

16 May 2001: Helicopter gunships carried out further attacks on Palestinian security force buildings.

18 May 2001: Peres declared that Israel would be prepared to stop any further seizures of land around the Palestinian territories.

19 May 2001: Following a suicide-bomb attack on an Israeli shopping centre by Islamic militants, the Israelis launched rocket attacks on the towns of Tulkarm and Jenin, in which three people were wounded.

21 May 2001: The Israelis carried out air raids on what it believed to be a Palestinian mortar factory in Jabilya, outside Gaza city. Israeli tanks also moved into the town of Qarara.

22 May 2001: The report of the international inquiry into the causes of the recent Arab-Israeli violence was published; the Mitchell Report emphasized that Jewish settlement expansion was the main obstacle to peace and recommended that it be halted; it also called for an immediate cease-fire in preparation for peace negotiations. In a change of policy, the Israeli Government refused to halt Jewish settlement programmes but declared a unilateral cease-fire.

24 May 2001: The armed forces shot down a Lebanese light aircraft which had crossed into Israeli airspace near the port city of Haifa, killing the pilot.

25 May 2001: Sharon stated that Israel would maintain its unilateral cease-fire for several more days, despite further suicide-bomb attacks.

27 May 2001: Following a meeting with the new US envoy to the region, William Burns, the Government proposed a return to co-operation with the Palestinians. As the discussions were taking place, two bomb attacks were carried out in Jerusalem by the PFLP.

1 June 2001: A total of 18 Israelis were killed and over 100 others were injured during a Palestinian suicide-bomb attack on a night-club in Tel-Aviv. Arafat denounced the attack and advocated an immediate cease-fire; numerous armed Palestinian groups rejected the demand.

6 June 2001: Some 20,000 Israeli settlers demonstrated in Jerusalem, demanding that the Government end its unilateral cease-fire.

12 June 2001: Following meetings mediated by the Director of the US Central Intelligence Agency, George Tenet, the Government and the PNA signed a cease-fire, which was to come into effect the following day.

19–20 June 2001: Continuing bomb attacks on Israelis by Palestinians prompted the Government to reconsider the cease-fire, however, they decided to maintain their position.

4 July 2001: The Government gave the army permission to use more force against the Palestinians, effectively ending the cease-fire.

9 July 2001: The Minister of Defence, Binyamin Ben-Eleizer, travelled to Ankara to meet his Turkish counterpart, Sabahattin Cakmakoglu; the two ministers discussed military co-operation.

10 July 2001: The security forces demolished 17 Palestinian houses in the Gaza Strip; a gun battle between the Palestinians and security forces ensued.

11 July 2001: The UN admitted that a video reording which showed fake UN vehicles and uniforms believed to have been used by Hezbollah during its kidnapping of Israeli soldiers in October 2000 had been made by a member of UNIFIL. Kofi Annan ruled that an edited version of the recording could be shown to the Israeli Government and ordered an investigation into the handling of the evidence by the UN.

13 July 2001: Following allegations apparently made by an unidentified peace-keeper in an Israeli newspaper, the UN announced a further investigation into whether its troops had collaborated with Hezbollah in the capture of the Israeli soldiers.

29 July 2001: Palestinians attempted to stop a group of messianic Jews from placing a symbolic cornerstone in the Temple Mount/Haram ash-Sharif complex; police stormed the al-Aqsa mosque to end the violence and several Israelis and Palestinians were injured. The Palestinians dispersed after the intervention of the Israeli Arab politician, Ahmed Tibi.

Jordan

2000 BC–1500 BC: The Amorites, a tribe of Semitic nomads, arrived in Palestine and established the state of Canaan in the region.

14th–13th centuries BC: The towns of Ammon, Bahan, Edom, Gilead and Moab were established; they benefited from trade routes from Egypt and the Mediterranean to the Arabian peninsula to the Persian (Arabian) Gulf, which passed through the region now occupied by Jordan.

1220 BC–1190 BC: Canaan was conqered by Israelite tribes; the Philistines—sea-faring peoples from the Peloponnese—also attacked Canaan and came into confrontation with the Israelites.

965 BC–928 BC: During the reign of King Solomon, the Israelite lands were extended from the upper Euphrates to the Gulf of Aqaba; the territory was eventually divded into two Jewish kingdoms: Israel in the north and Judah in the south.

722 BC: Israel was conquered by Assyrian forces led by King Shalmaneser and the Israelites were deported. The Assyrians made Judea a tributary kingdom and divided the remainder of the region into provinces for administrative purposes.

612 BC: The Assyrian Empire fell and the region was absorbed into the Chaldean (Neo-Babylonian) Empire. While under Chaldean rule the Jordan valley was the subject of incursions by several neighbouring civilizations.

6th century BC: The Nabateans, an Arabic tribe, established their capital at Petra, in the south of modern Jordan.

586 BC: Jerusalem (al-Quds in Arabic) was destroyed by the Babylonian forces of King Nebuchadnezzar; most of the Jewish population were captured and taken to Babylon.

333 BC: Alexander III ('the Great') of Macedon, the Greek warrior, conquered the region. Following his death in 323 BC, the region came under the rule of one of his generals, Seleucus Nicator.

301 BC: Palestine, including the modern countries of Israel and Jordan, came under the control of another of Alexander's followers, Ptolemy I of the Macedonian dynasty in Egypt. The region's cities prospered from trade links with Egypt and were influenced by Hellenistic culture.

1st century BC: The Nabateans took advantage of hostilities between the Seleucids of Persia and the Ptolemies to extend their own territory northwards.

64 BC–63 BC: Under the leadership of the Emperor Pompei, the kingdom of Nabatea was conqered by the Romans; it retained political autonomy but was required to pay imperial taxes.

37 BC: The Romans installed Herod as King of Judea; with their support, he was able to extend his rule over both sides of the Jordan valley.

AD 106: Nabatea was absorbed into the Roman Empire as Palaestine Tertia; the region prospered and new settlements were established.

4th century: Christianity became widely established throughout the region and a large number of churches were built.

395: The Roman Empire was partitioned for administrative purposes; the Byzantine Empire, which was ruled from Constantinople (now Istanbul, Turkey), assumed control over the Levant.

6th–7th centuries: Constant warfare between the Byzantine Empire and the Persian Sassanid (Sassanian) Empire devastated the Jordan valley.

627: The Roman Emperor Heraclius defeated the Persians and re-established order in the region.

636: Khalid ibn al-Walid ('the Sword of Islam') led an army of Muslim Arabs to victory against the Byzantines at the Battle of Uhudat; Syria and Palestine consequently came under Muslim rule.

660: The Umayyad dynasty established the Muslim Caliphate at Damascus (Syria). Jordan subsequently prospered as a result of its proximity to the centre of the Muslim world and the use of Arabic spread throughout the region.

750: The Abbasids took control of the Caliphate and established their capital at Baghdad (in modern Iraq). The use of trade routes which passed through the Jordan valley declined as goods were increasingly transported by sea rather than by land. Settlements fell into decay and many of the population reverted to a nomadic way of life.

969: The Shi'a Muslim Fatimids of Egypt, who had seized the Caliphate from the Abbasids, took control of the region.

1071: The Fatimids were supplanted in control of the Caliphate by the Seljuq Turks.

1099: Jerusalem was captured by Western Christian forces during the Crusades, who established the principality of Oultre Jordain, with a capital at Al-Karak.

1174: Salah ad-Din Yusuf ibn Ayyub (Saladin), deposed the Fatimids and established himself as the sultan of Egypt.

1187: Salah ad-Din captured Jerusalem from the Christians.

1260: The Ayyub dynasty was deposed by the Mamelukes—former Christian slaves of Kurdish and Circassian origin who had converted to Islam; the region became a province of Mameluke territory, which extended from the Nile to the Euphrates.

1517: The Ottoman Sultan, Selim I ('the Great'), took control of the region and Jordan became incorporated into the *vilayet* (province) of Damascus. Under the Ottoman rule, the region's economy declined and its population decreased.

1831–39: The Governor of Egypt, Muhammad Ali, led a revolt against the Ottomans and stationed his troops in the Jordan valley. With the assistance of British and Russian forces, however, Ottoman rule was restored.

late 19th century: In an attempt to counteract depopulation, the Ottomans granted asylum to Palestinian and Syrian refugees, and to Chechens and Circassian Muslims fleeing Russian persecution, allowing them to settle in the Jordan valley.

1900–06: With the assistance of Germany, the Ottomans built the Hedjaz Railway between Damascus and Medina (Saudi Arabia), passing through the Jordan valley.

1905: A revolt by the Bedouin tribes of the desert was violently suppressed by the Ottomans; a similar revolt occurred in 1910.

November 1914: At the outbreak of the First World War, the Ottomans allied themselves with Germany.

1916: Hussein ibn Ali Al-Hashimi, the Grand Sharif and Amir of Mecca, proclaimed himself 'King of the Arabs' and initiated an Arab revolt against the Ottomans.

May 1916: Under the Asia-Minor Agreement ('Sykes-Picot Treaty') signed by France and Russia and the United Kingdom, Jordan became a British Mandate.

July 1917: Aqaba was captured by Arab nationalist troops under the leadership of Faisal ibn Hussein, the third son of King Hussein.

November 1917: The 'Balfour Declaration', a statement made by the British Foreign Secretary, Arthur Balfour, to Baron Rothschild, leader of the British Jewry, proclaimed the Jordanian Mandate to be within the area to be allocated as a Jewish 'national home' in Palestine.

September 1918: The Arabs captured Amman and Deraa; the following month, the towns were occupied by the European Allies.

7 November 1918: The Arab nationalist Government, established in Jordan and Syria by Faisal, was recognised by the British and French governments.

June 1919: At a peace conference held in Paris (France) at the end of the First World War, Faisal proclaimed independent rule for Arabs throughout the Middle East.

March 1920: Faisal and his brother, Abdullah, declared the independence of Iraq, Jordan and Syria; the declarations were denounced by the British and French Governments.

April 1920: At the San Remo Conference in Italy, the Palestinian Mandate, including Jordan, was awarded to the United Kingdom.

March 1921: The Palestinian Mandate was divided along the line of the River Jordan; the eastern bank, which was to be known as Transjordan, was placed under a separate Arab administration, to be advised by the United Kingdom. Abdullah was appointed as Amir.

September 1922: The League of Nations approved a British goverment memorandum stating that Transjordan would be excluded from the Jewish settlement programme in the Middle East.

15 May 1923: The United Kingdom formally recognized Transjordan as an independent constitutional state ruled by Abdulllah, under British guidance. The British Government subsidized the development of infrastructure, education and health care; an Arab Legion, comprising mainly Bedouin troops, was also trained by British officers.

5 March 1924: In Amman, Abdullah's father, King Hussein, was proclaimed Caliph.

June 1925: Ma'an and Aqaba were incorporated into Transjordan.

February 1928: The British agreed to grant Transjordan greater autonomy in a new treaty, although finance and foreign policy were to remain under the control of a British Resident.

April 1928: A new Constitution was promulgated, providing for a Legislative Council to replace the Executive Council; the first meeting of the new body took place the following year.

January 1934: The United Kingdom permitted Transjordan to appoint consular delegates in Arab countries.

1938: The Arab Legion, led by the British officer, John Bagot Glubb (known as 'Glubb Pasha'), began a campaign to end tribal feuding among the Bedouins.

May 1939: The Legislative Council was replaced by a Cabinet led by the Amir; ministers were given specific portfolios.

May 1939: Government representatives prticipated in the 'Round Table' Conference on Palestinian issues in London (United Kingdom).

1941: Arab Legion troops participated in several British operations in the Second World War; they assisted in the overthrow of the pro-German Iraqi leader, Rashid Ali, defeated the forces of the German-approved Vichy Government of occupied France in Syria and guarded British installations in Egypt.

March 1945: Egypt, Iraq, Lebanon, Saudi Arabia, Syria, Transjordan and Yemen founded the League of Arab States (Arab League), which aimed to promote political, cultural, economic and social co-operation between its members and act as mediator in regional disputes.

22 March 1946: By the Treaty of London, the United Kingdom agreed to grant independence to Transjordan; Amman was declared the capital of the new state.

25 May 1946: Abdullah was proclaimed King of Transjordan; a new Constitution was subsequently promulgated, superseding that of 1928.

1947: The Government applied for membership of the UN; the application was opposed by the USA and the USSR, who refused to recognize Transjordan as an independent state.

March 1948: A new agreement was signed with the United Kingdom, permitting that country to maintain military air bases and communications and transit facilities in Transjordan, in return for continued economic support.

14–15 May 1948: Following the proclamation of the State of Israel, Transjordanian troops were among the Arab forces who invaded Palestine at the start of the first major conflict between the Arab states and Israel.

December 1948: Abdullah was proclaimed King of All Palestine at Jericho.

31 January 1949: Jordan was recognized by the USA.

3 April 1949: Israel and Jordan signed an armistice; the territory on the west bank of the River Jordan (West Bank) and Eastern Jerusalem were incorporated under Jordanian rule.

2 June 1949: The state was renamed the Hashemite Kingdom of Jordan.

April 1950: In accordance with Arab League policy, Jordan agreed to refrain from the annexation of Palestinian territory and from entering into negotiations with Israel.

12 April 1950: Following general elections in Jordan and Arab Palestine, the Prime Minister, Tewfiq Pasha Abd el-Muda, resigned; King Abdullah appointed Sa'id al-Mufti to replace him; al-Mufti formed a new Governent, which included five Palestinian members.

24 April 1950: Abdullah formally annexed Arab Palestine; the annexation was recognized by the United Kingdom but condemned by the Arab League.

March 1951: The Government signed an agreement with the USA, securing development aid.

20 July 1951: Abdullah was assassinated by a Palestinian as he entered the Al-Aqsa Mosque in Jerusalem; he was succeeded by his eldest son, Talal ibn Abdullah.

January 1952: A new Constitution was promulgated, by which the monarch was granted powers to dismiss the National Assembly and appoint the Prime Minister and other ministers. In the same month Jordan joined its fellow Arab League member states in the Arab Collective Security Pact.

August 1952: Talal, who was suffering from mental illness, abdicated in favour of his son, Hussein ibn Talal, who was 16 years of age. A Regency Council was formed to act on Hussein's behalf until his majority.

February 1953: Jordan and Syria signed an economic and financial agreement. The two countries also announced plans to dam the Yarmouk River to facilitate irrigation and the generation of hydroelectricity.

2 May 1953: Hussein formally acceded to the throne on his 18th birthday.

early 1954: The Government rejected a US-sponsored scheme for the distribution of water taken from the River Jordan among Iraq, Israel, Jordan and Syria because it necessitated co-operation with, and therefore recognition of, the state of Israel.

December 1954: The Government signed an agreement on financial aid with the United Kingdom; however, ngotiations on the revision of the treaty signed by the two countries in 1948 were unsuccessful.

November 1955: The Government announced that it would not align Jordan with either of the proposed strategic alliances in the region: the bloc formed by Egypt, Saudi Arabia and Syria, or the pact being negotiated by Iran, Iraq, Pakistan and the United Kingdom, which became known as the 'Baghdad Pact'.

15 December 1955: Al-Mufti resigned as Prime Minister, he was replaced by Hazza al-Majali, who announced that Jordan would join the Baghdad Pact; this precipitated three days of rioting and demonstrations in Amman. The Arab Legion was used to restore order and the Government resigned after only seven days in power.

20 December 1955: Ibrahim Hashim was appointed Prime Minister.

9 January 1956: Hashim was dismissed; Samir Rifai was appointed to succeded him.

2 March 1956: 'Glubb Pasha' was dismissed as commander-in-chief of the Arab Legion; he was replaced by Maj.-Gen. Radi Annab.

May 1956: Al-Mufti was reappointed to the premiership; Lt-Col (later Gen.) Ali Abu Nuwar replaced Annab as leader of the Arab Legion, which subsequently became known as the Jordan Arab Army. The Government also signed an agreement for military co-operation with Egypt, Lebanon and Syria.

30 June 1956: Al-Mufti resigned as Prime Minister owing to disputes within the Cabinet.

July 1956: Jordan and Syria formed an economic union.

2 July 1956: Ibrahim Hashim replaced al-Mufti as acting Prime Minister and formed a provisional cabinet.

21 October 1956: Following a general election, the National Socialist Suliman Nabulsi was able to form a comparatively left-wing government.

13 March 1957: Following negotiations with the British Government, the bilateral agreement of 1948 was abrogated; Jordan had already secured financial aid from Egypt, Saudi Arabia and Syria to offset the resultant loss of British subsidies.

10 April 1957: King Hussein dismissed Nabulsi as Prime Minister, owing to his communist sympathies; two weeks of unrest and political uncertainty ensued, during which time a number of short-lived administrations were formed.

13 April 1957: Fighting occurred between left-wing and royalist elements in the army; Gen. Nuwar fled to exile in Syria.

22–24 April 1957: Demonstrations demanding the reinstatement of Nablusi and the former Government took place in Amman and other towns.

25 April 1957: King Hussein installed a right-wing cabinet, led by Ibrahim Hashim, which imposed martial law, prohibited all political parties and removed many perceived radicals from the Civil Service.

May 1957: The Government requested the removal of Syrian troops stationed in Jordan as part of the joint Egyptian-Jordanian-Syrian command.

2 July 1957: The last British troops stationed in Jordan under the countries' bilateral agreement were withdrawn.

September 1957: In response to Syria's alignment with the USSR, the USA announced its intention to preserve Jordan's autonomy and made a substantial delivery of arms to the country.

November 1957: Egypt and Syria condemned Jordan's relations with the USA and accused it of entering into covert negotiations with Israel.

14 February 1958: King Hussein and his cousin, King Faisal of Iraq, proclaimed the unification of their kingdoms in a new Arab Federation, formed in response to the creation of the United Arab Republic (UAR) by Egypt and Syria at the beginning of the month.

May 1958: Ibrahim Hashim resigned as Prime Minister, to assume the post of Vice-Premier of the Arab Federation; he was succeeded by Samir Rifai.

July 1958: Ibrahim Hashim was assassinated in Baghdad, during the revolution in Iraq which precipitated the dissolution of the Arab Federation. Disorder spread throughout Jordan, and in August a plot to oust King Hussein was discovered.

17 July 1958: British troops were flown to Amman in response to King Hussein's appeal for military assistance against a possible revolt; the troops had left the country by November.

20 July 1958: Jordan suspended relations with the UAR.

1 August 1958: The Arab Federation was formally suspended.

10 November 1958: King Hussein was forced to return to Jordan after Syrian fighter aircraft intercepted him on his way by air to Europe.

11 January 1959: The statute of the Arab Development Bank was signed by Jordan, Lebanon, Libya, Saudi Arabia, the UAR and Yemen.

15 April 1959: The British Government announced grants to Jordan totalling US $5,600,000.

29 August 1960: Hazza al-Majali, who had succeeded Samir Rifai as Prime Minister in May 1959, was assassinated.

1 October 1960: Jordan recognized the republican regime in Iraq.

27 January 1962: A new Government, led by Wasfi at-Tal, was formed.

March 1963: At-Tal's Government was dismissed; Rifai returned as Prime Minister.

20 April 1963: Rifai resigned, amid severe unrest provoked by the announcement of plans to form a federation with Iraq and Syria. A transitional Government, led by the king's great-uncle, Sharif Hussein bin Nasir, took office, with the task of overseeing the dissolution of the House of Representatives prior to legislative elections.

July 1963: Following the legislative election, Sharif Hussein was returned to office.

22 August 1963: Jordan established diplomatic relations with the USSR.

13 August 1964: A Common Market of Iraq, Jordan, Kuwait and Syria was established, under the aegis of the Arab League.

5–11 September 1964: A second summit meeting of Arab leaders was held in Alexandria (Egypt) to discuss strategy and plans for the development of the Jordan waters.

1 January 1965: The provisions of the Arab Common Market entered into force.

February 1965: Bahjat Talhouni, who had replaced Sharif Hussain the previous year, himself resigned as Prime Minister; Wasfi at-Tal returned to the office.

April 1965: King Hussein nominated his brother, Hassan, as Crown Prince.

13 November 1966: Israeli forces raided the Jordanian village of Samu; attacks on Israel by groups based in its neigbouring Arab states had increased in frequency throughout the mid-1960s. The raid, which was subsequently condemned by the UN Security Council, increased pressure on King Hussein to resume his support for the Palestine Liberation Organization (PLO), withdrawn in July; when the King refused, the PLO urged Arabs to overthrow him.

27 February 1967: Jordan resumed diplomatic relations with the Federal Republic of Germany (FRG), which had been suspended when the FRG recognized Israel in May 1965 .

23 April 1967: A new Government was formed by Saad Jumaa.

30 May 1967: Jordan and the UAR signed a mutual-defence pact.

5 June 1967: A period of military tensions between Israel and its neighbouring Arab countries was ended when Israel attacked the air bases of Jordan, Syria and the UAR. The Arab countries' air forces were severely damaged, and Israel was swiftly able to capture territory from each of the Arab combatants (notably the West Bank and Old Jerusalem from Jordan, the Golan Heights from Syria and the Sinai peninsula from the UAR).

6 June 1967: The United Kingdom and the USA were accused by President Nasser of the UAR and King Hussein of Jordan of military collusion with Israel; 10 Arab states imposed an embargo on petroleum supplies to the two countries. Diplomatic relations with the USA were suspended by Algeria, Iraq, Sudan, Syria, the UAR and Yemen; Iraq and Syria terminated relations with the United Kingdom.

7 June 1967: Unable to defend its territory, Jordan was forced to seek a UN-sponsored cease-fire with Israel; both the other Arab combatants signed similar truces by 10 June—Israel retained the territory it had gained in what became known as the 'Six-Day War'.

29–31 August 1967: At a conference of Arab heads of state in Khartoum (Sudan), the petroleum-producing states agreed a substantial aid programme for Jordan and the UAR; Syria, which did not send a delegation to the conference, was excluded from the agreement.

7 October 1967: A new cabinet was formed by Bahjat Talhouni.

21 March 1968: Israeli forces attacked the Jordanian village of Karameh, claimed to be the headquarters of the al-Fatah guerrilla organization.

5 June 1968: Israeli forces bombarded the Jordanian village of Irbid as a reprisal for what it termed an 'incessant artillery barrage' by groups based in the area against Israeli settlements.

4 November 1968: Extensive fighting took place between the army and Palestinian guerrilla forces.

24 March 1969: A new Government was formed by Abdul Moniem Rifai.

12 August 1969: Baghat Talhouni formed a new administration, following the resignation of Moniem Rifai.

7–11 June 1970: Heavy fighting occurred between guerrillas and the armed forces; following a cease-fire agreement, the King dismissed some of his officials.

5–6 August 1970: The foreign and defence ministers of Jordan, Libya, Sudan, Syria and the UAR met in Tripoli (Libya); Algeria and Iraq refused to send delegations.

6–13 September 1970: Four Western passenger airliners were hijacked by Palestinian groups; the aircraft were flown to Cairo and northern Jordan, where the passengers were removed and the aircraft destroyed in explosions; the passengers were subsequently released in exchange for the freedom from detention of Palestinian commandos held in Western countries.

16–27 September 1970: Exceptionally fierce fighting between the army and Palestinian commandos led to an agreement being signed by King Hussein and the leader of the PLO, Yasser Arafat; despite the signature of a further accord in October, the Civil War in Jordan continued.

14 January 1971: A new agreement was reached between Jordanian Government and Palestinian guerrillas after continuing fighting between the two sides.

4 March 1971: Amid continued conflict in the country, a royal decree extended the term of House of Representatives for two years.

28 March 1971: The Libyan leader, Col Muammar al-Qaddafi of Libya urged Jordanians to overthrow King Hussein.

28 March 1971: Bahi Ladgham, the chairman of the committee supervising the agreements reached by the Government and the PLO, accused the Government of violating their terms.

1–8 May 1971: The US Secretary of State, William Rogers, visited Israel, Jordan, Lebanon, Saudi Arabia and the UAR to discuss plans for reopening the Suez Canal, which had been closed since the Six-Day War.

3 June 1971: Palestinian guerrilla movements, including al-Fatah, advocated that King Hussein be overthrown.

13–16 June 1971: The Jordanian army attacked Palestinian guerrilla positions; Iraq and Syria closed their borders with Jordan in protest, and Algeria suspended relations; at the conclusion of the operations, King Hussein declared the guerrilla problem to be 'solved'.

11–13 August 1971: Altercations occurred on the border between Jordan and Syria; the latter country suspended diplomatic relations the following day.

7 September 1971: The formation of the Jordanian National Union, Jordan's only legal political organization, was announced; the party was renamed the Arab National Union on 16 March 1972.

28 September 1971: Wasfi at-Tal, the Jordanian Prime Minister, was assassinated in Cairo by members of the extremist Black September Organization.

15–16 December 1971: The Jordanian ambassadors to Switzerland and the United Kingdom survived assassination attempts.

15 March 1972: King Hussein announced a plan for a United Arab Kingdom.

21 August 1972: King Hussein carried out a major reorganization of the Government.

13 February 1973: Abu Daoud and other Palestinian guerrillas were arrested for subversive activities in Jordan.

26 May 1973: Ahmed Louzi resigned as Prime Minister, citing ill health; he was succeeded by Zaid Rifai.

September 1973: King Faisal of Saudi Arabia mediated a reconciliation in the dispute between King Hussein of Jordan and the Egyptian and Syrian leaders.

October 1973: Conflict between Arab nations and Israel resumed; Jordan sent troops to assist in Syrian offensives on the Golan Heights, occupied by Israel in 1967.

November 1973: Following the declaration of a cease-fire, Jordanian officials attended a peace conference in Algiers (Algeria), during which they demanded that Israel evacuate territory gained in 1967 that the Arab forces had failed to regain during the conflict.

December 1973: Government representatives attended further peace negotiations in Geneva, Switzerland.

April 1974: King Hussein announced that the Arab National Union was to be reorganized, with the formation of an executive and a council of reduced numbers.

September 1974: Following the agreement made by Egypt, Syria and the PLO, which identified the PLO as the sole legitimate representative of the Palestinian People, Jordan announced its intention to boycott any further Arab-Israeli peace talks.

October 1974: At a 'summit' meeting of the Arab League in Rabat, Morocco, the members' resolution to unanimously resolved to recognize the PLO as the sole legitimate representative of Palestinians, with the right to establish national authority over any liberated Palestinian territory, King Hussein was reported to have supported the resolution with reluctance.

November 1974: The House of Representatives was dissolved.

9 November 1974: The Constitution was amended to allow King Hussein to dissolve the National Assembly and postpone legislative elections; the Assembly was dissolved later that month.

March 1975: The scheduled general election was postponed.

June 1975: A Supreme Joint Committee was set up to co-ordinate military and political planning between Jordan and Syria.

August 1975: A Supreme Command Council, directed by King Hussein of Jordan and President Hafiz al-Assad of Syria, was established to co-ordinate political and military action against Israel.

February 1976: King Hussein convened an extraordinary session of the National Assembly to enact legislation enabling him to suspend general elections indefinitely.

July 1976: Zaid ar-Rifai resigned as Prime Minister; he was replaced by the chief of the royal court, Mudar Badran. Badran set up a Bureau of Occupied Homeland Affairs, ostensibly to co-ordinate and advise on relations with Palestinians in Israeli-occupied territory.

November 1976: The PLO was recognized by the UN and granted observer status.

March 1977: The King held talks with Arafat, concerning the situation in Israel.

July 1977: The Presidents of Egypt, Jordan and the USA discussed the possiblity of a link between Jordan and a future Palestinian entity; the concept was condemned by the PLO.

April 1978: A 60-member National Consultative Council (NCC) was appointed by royal decree.

September 1978: The Government refused to participate in the US-sponsored Camp David peace negotiations with Israel.

November 1978: Jordan accepted a grant of US $1.25m from Iraq to attend a conference of the Arab League regarding the situation in Israel.

March 1979: Following the signature of a peace accord between Egypt and Israel, the Government severed diplomatic relations with Egypt.

March 1979: The Israeli agriculture minister, Ariel Sharon, stated that the Palestinians should take control of Jordan and establish a government there.

4–6 March 1979: Iraq, Jordan and Syria attended negotiations in Kuwait to mediate a cease-fire between the People's Democratic Republic of Yemen and the Yemen Arab Republic.

December 1979: Sharif Abd al-Hamid Sharaf replaced Mudar Badran as Prime Minister.

3 July 1980: Following the sudden death of Sharaf, the former Minister of Agriculture, Qassim ar-Rimawi, was appointed Prime Minister.

August 1980: A new Government, led by Badran, was inaugurated.

December 1980: Syria accused Jordan of supporting the Muslim Brotherhood movement in a conspiracy to undermine its Government; both countries began to station troops on their common border.

1981: The membership of the NCC was increased from 60 to 75.

February 1981: The Jordanian ambassdor in the Lebanese capital, Beirut, was abducted; the Government blamed Syria for the incident and abrogated a six-year economic and customs agreement with the country.

October 1981: Iraq and Jordan established a joint Committee for Economic and Technical Co-operation.

January 1982: King Hussein announced the formation of the 'Yarmouk Force', a Jordanian volunteer force to assist Iraq in its war with Iran.

April 1982: The King acted as intermediary in an attempt to negotiate a settlement between Iran and Iraq, without success.

1 September 1982: The US President, Ronald Reagan, announced that while the USA would not accept the establishment of a Palestinian state, it would support the granting of some autonomy to the West Bank Palestinians, in association with Jordan; the policy became known as the 'Reagan Plan'.

October 1982: The King and Arafat held a series of meetings to discuss a common response to the 'Reagan Plan'.

November 1982: The Government and the PLO agreed to create a Higher Jordanian-Palestinian Committee, jointly chaired by the Prime Minister, Mudar Badran, and Arafat.

December 1982: Jordan and the USA held discussions on the 'Reagan Plan'.

January 1983: The Government held further discussions regarding the regional peace process with Arafat.

April 1983: Jordan announced that it would not support the 'Reagan Plan'.

May 1983: Relations with the USA were strained when the US Senate sanctioned the sale of military aircraft to Israel.

July 1983: At a meeting of the UN Security Council, the US vetoed a draft resolution submitted by Jordan, proclaiming Israeli settlement of the West Bank to be illegal.

December 1983: Egypt and Jordan signed a trade agreement and discussed future co-operation on scientific and agricultural matters.

January 1984: The Government resigned; the new administration, led by Ahmed Ubeidat, included a greater number of Palestinians.

5 January 1984: King Hussein dissolved the NCC and reconvened the National Assembly. The former West Bank deputies were permitted by Israel to attend the Assembly, which unanimously approved constitutional amendments enabling legislative elections to be held solely in the East Bank; the House of Representatives would, in turn, elect deputies from the West Bank.

February 1984: Following the destruction of the Jordanian embassy in the Libyan capital, Tripoli, the Government severed diplomatic links with Libya. Throughout 1984 and 1985, several attacks on Jordanian diplomats in European countries occurred, for which extremist Islamic groups claimed responsibility.

12 March 1984: Elections were held to replace the eight East Bank members of the House of Representatives who had died since the chamber was last convened—women were granted the vote for the first time.

September 1984: Jordan re-established diplomatic relations with Egypt.

October 1984: The Government rejected an Israeli offer of direct peace negotiations; King Hussein suggested instead a conference attended by delegations from all the states in the region.

November 1984: The Palestinian National Council held its 17th session in Amman.

January 1985: The Government purchased an air-defence system from the USSR; Jordan had already agreed to buy several anti-aircraft missiles from France.

23 February 1985: King Hussein and Arafat announced the co-operation of the Government and the PLO in a joint peace initiative. It was agreed that any peace proposals should be discussed by the five permanent member countries of the UN Security Council and all parties concerned in the conflict. The Palestinian people would exercise the right to self-determination in the context of a proposed confederate state of Jordan and Palestine.

March 1985: President Muhammad Hosni Mubarak of Egypt proposed negotiations between Egypt, the USA and a joint Jordanian-Palestinian delegation; the PLO rejected the proposal, however, claiming that it deviated from its accord with Jordan.

April 1985: Ahmad Ubeidat resigned the premiership; Zaid ar-Rifai returned to the post and formed a new cabinet.

May 1985: King Hussein proposed a four-stage plan for Middle East peace negotiations, consisting of separate meetings between the USA and a Jordanian-Palestinian delegation, in addition to wider discussions involving the UN Security Council.

12 June 1985: The US Government announced that it was to grant Jordan additional economic aid totalling US \$250m. during the two subsequent years.

October 1985: The Israeli press published a secret government document, which suggested the establishment of an interim Israeli-Jordanian condominium of the West Bank, granting a degree of Palestinian autonomy and gave details of an Israeli-Jordanian mutual agreement on the need for a forum for peace talks.

19 February 1986: Following Arafat's refusal to accept resolutions of the UN Security Council as the foundation for peace negotiations, King Hussein suspended relations with the PLO and repudiated the Amman agreement.

March 1986: The number of seats in the House of Representatives was increased from 60 to 142, to allow for greater representation of West Bank Palestinians in the chamber.

August 1986: The Government announced the introduction of a five-year development programme for the West Bank and the Gaza Strip; the project was to cost US \$1,300m. and was supported by the Israeli Government.

September 1986: Jordan restored diplomatic relations with Libya.

April 1987: King Hussein and the Israeli Minister of Foreign Affairs, Shimon Peres, agreed to proposals for a peace conference involving all parties concerned, under the auspices of the UN.

April 1987: A number of bomb attacks occurred in Amman; Black September later claimed responsibility.

May 1987: At the conclusion of a series of secret negotiations with King Hussein, Peres claimed that enough progress had been made regarding the issue of Palestinian representation at peace negotiations to seek the consent of Egypt, Jordan and the USA to convene an international conference.

November 1987: Amman hosted the first full 'summit' meeting of the Arab League for eight years; the discussions principally concerned the ongoing conflict between Iran and Iraq.

December 1987: An *intifada* (uprising) occurred among the Palestinians on the West Bank in opposition to Israeli rule and the policies of King Hussein.

February 1988: The US Secretary of State, George Shultz, devised a new peace initiative. The 'Shultz Plan' provided for an international conference to be attended by all parties involved the Arab-Israeli conflict and the permanent members of the UN Security Council, in addition to separate talks between Israel and each of its Arab neighbours. Shultz also recommended a three-year transitional period of autonomy for the 1.5m. Palestinians in the West Bank and Gaza Strip territories.

June 1988: At a meeting of the Arab League in Algiers, King Hussein expressed Jordan's unconditional support for the PLO as representatives of the Palestinians and relinquished its claim to the West Bank.

July 1988: King Hussain cancelled the West Bank development plan and severed all Jordan's legal and administrative ties with the West Bank.

December 1988: The Minister of Foreign Affairs, Taher al-Masri, a principal opponent of the King's decision to abandon Jordan's claim to the West Bank, was dismissed; he was replaced by Marwan al-Qassim.

April 1989: The Government's imposition of price increases of up to 20% on basic commodities and services caused severe unrest in Amman and several other Jordanian cities. The Government resigned; the former Commander-in-Chief of the armed forces, Field Marshal Zaid ibn Shaker, was appointed Prime Minister and formed a new administration.

8 November 1989: Full parliamentary elections were held in Jordan for the first time since 1967.

4 December 1989: Mudar Badran was appointed Prime Minister, at the head of a new Cabinet.

9 April 1990: King Hussein appointed a royal commission to draft a national political charter.

22 August 1990: Jordan temporarily closed its border with Iraq to halt the influx of refugees (mostly non-Arab Asians) from that country and from Kuwait.

23 September 1990: King Hussein demanded the immediate and unconditional withdrawal of multinational forces from the Persian (Arabian) Gulf region; the forces had been stationed in Saudi Arabia, pending possible action against Iraq if it did not withdraw its forces from Kuwait.

1 January 1991: The Cabinet was reorganized.

14 January 1991: Iran and Jordan restored diplomatic relations; the respective embassies reopened in March.

19 January 1991: King Hussein stated that Jordan would defend its airspace in the event of any incursion by the Israeli air force.

9 June 1991: King Hussein and Jordan's principal political movements endorsed a new National Charter.

19 June 1991: A new Jordanian Government was formed; it was reorganized in October.

13 October 1991: King Hussein announced Jordan's unconditional acceptance of the terms for participation in a regional Middle East peace conference to be held in Madrid (Spain).

30 October 1991: The Middle East peace conference commenced in Madrid (Spain), attended by representatives from Egypt, Israel, Lebanon and Syria, in addition to a joint Palestinian-Jordanian delegation.

16 November 1991: The Prime Minister, Taher al-Masri, resigned.

21 November 1991: A new Jordanian Government was appointed.

20 August 1992: The formal legalization of political parties was approved.

17 February 1993: The Jordanian Cabinet announced the appointment of Sheikh Sulaiman al-Ja'bari as the new Mufti of Jerusalem.

29 May 1993: Abd as-Salam al-Majali, who had led the Jordanian delegation to the Madrid peace conference, was appointed Prime Minister of a transitional Government, pending the result of the country's first multi-party elections, scheduled for November.

4 August 1993: King Hussein of Jordan dissolved the country's House of Representatives, despite its scheduled debate on amendments to the electoral legislation for the forthcoming multi-party elections.

17 August 1993: The new electoral law was announced by the King.

15 September 1993: Israel and Jordan agreed an agenda for future bilateral negotiations between their respective delegations to the Middle East peace conference.

8 November 1993: Some 68% of the electorate was reported to have participated in the elections to the House of Representatives. The majority of deputies returned were independent royalists; the King appointed a new Senate on 18 November and a new Cabinet, led by al-Majali, was announced on 1 December.

January 1994: Jordan and the PLO signed an agreement on economic co-operation and the co-ordination of financial policy in the Occupied Territories.

3 March 1994: Jordan and the Vatican established diplomatic relations.

8 June 1994: Ministerial portfolios were reorganized.

25 July 1994: Israel and Jordan signed a joint declaration formally ending the state of war between them.

26 October 1994: Israel and Jordan signed a comprehensive peace treaty.

6 November 1994: The National Assembly ratified the peace treaty with Israel.

10 November 1994: King Hussein made his first public visit to Israel.

8 January 1995: Al-Majali was dismissed and a new Government, led by Zaid ibn Shaker, appointed.

9 February 1995: Israeli armed forces completed their withdrawal from Jordanian territory.

7–9 August 1995: Lt-Gen. Hussein Kamil al-Majid, the Iraqi Minister of Industry, Minerals and Military Industrialization, defected to Jordan.

29–31 October 1995: The second Middle East and North Africa Economic Summit took place in Amman.

4 February 1996: King Hussein reorganized the Government, appointing Abd al-Karim Kabariti as Prime Minister.

13 August 1996: Unrest spread throughout Jordan in protest at the removal of subsidies on wheat; King Hussein suspended the legislature and deployed the army to suppress the most serious disturbances.

15 October 1996: King Hussein visited the West Bank for the first time since 1967.

19 March 1997: Kabariti was dismissed by King Hussein and replaced by al-Majali; a new Government was appointed, in which al-Majali also held the defence portfolio.

29 August 1997: King Hussein dissolved the House of Representatives in preparation for general elections scheduled for November 1997.

25 September 1997: The leader of the Palestinian Hamas group, Khalid Meshaal, was the subject of a failed assassination attempt by Israeli agents in Amman; diplomatic activity to preserve cordial relations between Israel and Jordan ensued.

4 November 1997: A parliamentary election was conducted in Jordan, although it was boycotted by Islamic parties; 62 of the 80 seats in the House of Representatives were won by pro-Government candidates, amid widespread allegations of electoral malpractice.

8 December 1997: Four Jordanians were executed in Iraq, following smuggling convictions, despite appeals by the Jordanian Government for the sentences to be commuted.

10 December 1997: King Hussein of Jordan expelled several Iraqi diplomats from the country and recalled the Jordanian chargé d'affaires from Baghdad, in protest at the executions.

17 January 1998: Iraq's chargé d'affaires in Jordan was killed; despite speculation that Iraqi government agents were responsible the Jordanian interior ministry announced the arrest of several Jordanians in connection with the incident, and claimed that the crime was not politically motivated.

13 February 1998: Riot police suppressed pro-Iraqi demonstrations in the southern town of Ma'an; a number of arrests were made.

17 February 1998: King Hussein effected a cabinet reorganization.

9 July 1998: The Minister of Water and Irrigation, Mundhir Haddadin, resigned following a scandal involving contaminated drinking water and severe water shortages in Amman.

late August 1998: King Hussein, who was undergoing treatment for lymphatic cancer in the USA, issued a decree vesting certain executive powers, including the power to appoint ministers, in his brother, Crown Prince Hassan.

20 August 1998: Al-Majali resigned the premiership and was replaced by Fayez at-Tarawneh; a cabinet reshuffle ensued.

24 September 1998: A motion of 'no confidence' in the Government of at-Tarawneh was defeated in the House of Representatives.

24 January 1999: Upon his return from the USA, King Hussein issued royal decrees naming his eldest son, Abdullah, as Crown Prince in place of his brother, Hassan, who was styled the King's 'deputy'. King Hussein was believed to have been dissatisfied with Hassan's conduct of the country's affairs in his absence.

26 January 1999: King Hussein travelled to the USA for emergency medical treatment; he returned to Jordan on 5 February.

7 February 1999: King Hussein died in Amman; Crown Prince Abdullah was sworn in as King Abdullah ibn al-Hussein of Jordan, while the late King's youngest son, Prince Hamzeh ibn Hussein, was designated Crown Prince.

8 February 1999: The state funeral of King Hussein, held in Amman, was attended by more than 50 heads of state or government.

3 March 1999: Full diplomatic relations were restored by Jordan and Kuwait; the respective embassies were reopened.

4 March 1999: A new Cabinet was appointed in Jordan; Abd ar-Raouf ar-Rawabdeh was named Prime Minister; the former premier, Abd al-Karim al-Kabariti, was appointed Chief of the Royal Court.

3 July 1999: The Minister of Youth and Sports, Muhammad Kheir Mamsar, resigned following controversy over his handling of preparations for the 9th Pan-Arab Games, scheduled to be held in Jordan in August.

14–15 July 1999: Municipal elections were held throughout Jordan.

25 August 1999: Security forces closed the offices of Hamas in Amman; Meshaal's home was raided and a number of leading Hamas activists arrested.

1 September 1999: A government reorganization was effected.

22 September 1999: Three Hamas leaders, including Khalid Meshaal, were detained by Jordanian security forces on their arrival at Amman airport; they faced charges of organizing illegal political activities and involvement in terrorism.

21 November 1999: Jordan expelled Khalid Meshaal and other senior members of the guerrilla group Hamas to Qatar.

15 January 2000: Al-Kabariti resigned, citing 'political and personal reasons'; in the ensuing cabinet reshuffle, he was replaced by at-Tarawneh, while the other principal portfolios remained with their incumbents.

16 February 2000: The Prime Minister, ar-Rawabdeh was cleared of corruption allegations relating to the construction of a tourism complex by an investigating parliamentary commission.

24 February 2000: The Deputy Prime Minister and Minister of Planning, Dr Rima Khalaf al-Hunaidi, resigned in protest at the direction of economic reforms.

20–26 March 2000: Pope John Paul II undertook a millennium pilgrimage to the Christian 'Holy Land', including visits to Israel, Jordan and the Palestinian self-rule areas.

18 June 2000: The Prime Minister, ar-Rawabdeh, was dismissed and replaced by Ali Abu ar-Ragheb; a new Council of Ministers was announced the following day.

18 September 2000: A military court sentenced six Islamic militants to death for their role in a bombing campaign against European and Israeli tourists during the country's millennium celebrations; a further 16 defendants were sentenced to terms of imprisonment ranging from seven years to life.

27 September 2000: A Jordanian aircraft carrying government officials, in addition to medical personnel and humanitarian aid, arrived in Baghdad, in contravention of UN sanctions on Iraq.

4 October 2000: King Abdullah met the military ruler of Libya, Col al-Qaddafi, to discuss the Arab-Israeli conflict and bilateral relations.

6 October 2000: The Government banned public protests following violent disturbances at anti-Israeli demonstrations, during which one demonstrator was killed and several other protesters and police-officers were injured.

24 October 2000: An anti-Israeli demonstration took place near the Israeli border; the participants demanded that Palestinian refugees in Jordan be allowed to return to their homes.

24 October 2000: Jordan signed a free-trade agreement with the USA, which proposed the progressive elimination of all trade restrictions between the two countries over the subsequent ten years.

9 January 2001: King Abdullah and Gen. Pervez Musharraf, the military leader of Pakistan, signed an agreement on co-operation in the areas of science and technology.

27–28 March 2001: Amman hosted a 'summit' meeting of Arab leaders, which was also attended by the UN Secretary-General, Kofi Annan. The leaders pledged more financial support for the Palestinians, but failed to agree common policies regarding the sanctions on Iraq and the reconciliation of Iraq and Kuwait.

1 May 2001: A new road bridge across the River Jordan was opened, linking Jordan and the West Bank.

6 May 2001: King Abdullah and the Egyptian President, Mubarak, discussed their joint proposal for peace negotiations to end the Arab-Israeli conflict. The two countries urged the Israelis to withdraw from reoccupied territory in the Palestinian Autonomous Areas and proposed the imposition of restrictions on construction in the territories and the renewal of peace negotiations. The following day, King Abdullah travelled to France to discuss the proposals with that country's President, Jacques Chirac, and its Prime Minister, Lionel Jospin.

14–30 June 2001: The Jordanian authorities detained a Qatar Airways aircraft carrying the exiled Hamas activist, Ibrahim Gosheh, at Amman airport. Gosheh was denied entry to Jordan and the aircraft refused permission to leave unless Gosheh was on board. The Palestinian activist was eventually granted entry to Jordan; Qatari Airways subsequently announced that it would take legal action against the Jordanian Government for its conduct during the incident.

27 June 2001: The Minister of Transport, Muhammad al-Kalaldeh, met his Iraqi counterparts in Baghdad, to discuss the future transport of goods and passengers between the two countries.

Kuwait

***c.* 4000 BC:** Semite peoples began to migrate from the Arabian peninsula to Mesopotamia, which extended from the northern part of the Persian Gulf to incorporate modern Iraq and parts of Armenia and Syria.

2000 BC: Arab tribes began incursions on the Persian (Arabian) Gulf coast.

***c.* 1000 BC:** Trade routes were established from the interior of the Arabian peninsula to the Gulf coast, further increasing Arab influence in the area.

325 BC: Followers of Alexander III ('the Great'), the Macedon King and Greek military leader who had defeated the Persians, sent an expeditionary fleet along the Persian Gulf to the Tigris and Euphrates rivers.

250 BC: The Gulf came under the influence of the Persian dynasty, the Parthians.

c. AD 200: Another Persian tribe, the Sassanids (Sassanians), succeeded the Parthians. Under their rule, agricultural colonies were established in the area and inland nomadic tribes were employed to protect the region from attacks by the Romans. Also, at this time, Judaism and Christianity arrived in the Gulf region.

7th century: Islam spread throughout Arabia and the Middle East and gained popularity among the peoples of the Gulf region.

750: The Abbasids overthrew the Umayyad Caliphate and established Baghdad (Iraq) as the centre of the Islamic world, bringing increased prosperity to the Persian (Arabian) Gulf.

985: The Buyids drove the Ismailis out of Iraq and proceeded to entend their influence along the Gulf coast as far as Oman.

1000: Gulf merchants travelled regulary to India and China and spread the influence of Islam.

15th century: The Portuguese arrived in the Persian (Arabian) Gulf. They captured coastal cities in Oman and Iran and began to control trade in the waterway.

***c.* 1500:** The Safavids from Iran made incursions into the Gulf region. They established some Shi'a religious groups in what is now Kuwait.

1546: The Ottomans conquered Iraq and the area surrounding Kuwait.

early 18th century: The Bani Utb, a group of families belonging to the Anziah tribe from the interior of the Arabian peninsula, migrated to the Gulf coast, settling the area of present-day Kuwait.

1756: The head of the Sabah family was appointed as Sheikh by the settlers, to address security matters and represent them in dealings with the Ottoman Government.

1765: The town of Kuwait was estimated to have a population of 10,000, who were mainly engaged in fishing and pearling.

1775–79: During the Persian occupation of the Iraqi port of Basra, the British East India Company used Kuwait as the southern terminal of its overland mail route from Aleppo (Syria). Kuwait also benefited from the migration of many merchant families from Basra.

late 18th century: Groups of Wahhabi religious extremists carried out a series of attacks on Kuwait.

1871: Sheikh Abdullah bin Sabah al-Jabir took the title of Qa'immaqam (District Governor), under the Turkish Vali (Governor) of Basra.

1892: The Sheikh was assasinated by his brother, Murbarak, who subsequently assumed the Sheikdom.

1899: Concerned that the Ottomans would occupy Kuwait and impose direct rule, Sheikh Murbarak signed an agreement with the British not to cede, mortgage or otherwise dispose of any parts of their territory to anyone except the British Government, in return for British protection.

1904: A British political agent to Kuwait was appointed.

1909: The Ottoman Empire and the United Kingdom began discussions regarding proposals for legislation to guarantee the autonomy of Kuwait; the outbreak of the First World War prevented the successful conclusion of these negotiations however.

1917: Sheikh Murbarak's second son, Salim, succeeded him and supported the Ottomans in the First World War; Kuwait was consequently blockaded by the British.

1921: Murbarak's nephew, Ahmad al-Jabir became Sheikh; the state prospered under his governance.

1934: A joint concession was granted to the Gulf Oil Corporation of USA and the British Anglo-Persian Oil Company to exploit the sheikhdom's oil reserves; they consequently formed the Kuwait Oil Co Ltd.

1936: The first deep drilling for petroleum began.

1942: Following the outbreak of the Second World War in 1939, the petroleum wells were sealed and drilling suspended.

1950: Sheikh Ahmad died, he was succeeded by Abdullah as-Salim. During his reign he used petroleum revenues to improve public services in Kuwait.

1 April 1961: The Kuwaiti dinar replaced the Indian external rupee as the unit o currency in Kuwait.

19 June 1961: The 1899 Agreement between Kuwait and the United Kingdom was cancelled, and Kuwait became fully independent.

22 June 1961: Kuwait applied for membership of the Arab League.

25 June 1961: Gen. Kassem of Iraq laid claim to Kuwait.

1 July 1961: Amid concern at a possible Iraqi invasion, a British force arrived in Kuwait.

10 September 1961: An Arab League force replaced the British force in Kuwait.

30 November 1961: The USSR vetoed proposals by the United Arab Republic to admit Kuwait to the UN.

16 November 1962: A new Constitution was promulgated in Kuwait.

23 January 1963: Elections to the first Assembly were held.

14 May 1963: Kuwait was accepted as the 111th member of the UN.

13 August 1964: A Common Market of Iraq, Jordan, Kuwait and Syria was established, under the aegis of the Arab League.

1 January 1965: The provisions of the Arab Common Market entered into force.

23 November 1965: Sheikh Abdullah al-Salim al-Sabah died and was succeeded by his brother, Sheikh Sabah al-Salim al-Sabah.

18 December 1966: Kuwait purchased British aircraft valued at some £20m.

14 February 1971: A new, five-year agreement was signed by 23 international petroleum companies and the governments of Abu Dhabi, Iran, Iraq, Kuwait, Qatar and Saudi Arabia.

5 October 1972: Agreement was reached between Abu Dhabi, Iraq, Kuwait, Qatar and Saudi Arabia for one part, and representatives of various petroleum companies for the other, on the eventual 51% participation of the producing countries in the various concessions.

September 1973: Armed Arab terrorists attacked the Saudi Arabian embassy in Paris and took five hostages to Kuwait, where they subsequently surrendered. The Kuwaiti authorities transferred the terrorists to the Palestine Liberation Organization (PLO), who had condemned the incident.

October 1973: Kuwait sent troops to assist the Palestinians in the Arab-Israeli conflict. The Government also hosted a meeting of the Organization of Arab Petroleum Exporting Countries (OAPEC) to discuss proposals to use the price of petroleum as an instrument against Western countries who supported the Israeli cause.

17 October 1973: Delegates at the meeting of OAPEC decided to decrease shipments of petroleum to Western countries by five per cent each month until Israeli forces withdrew from Palestinian territory. The price of crude petroleum was to be increased by 70% from November and Kuwait imposed a total embargo on shipments to USA and subsequently, the Netherlands.

4 November 1973: OAPEC reduced the production of petroleum by an additional 5%.

March 1974: Abu Dhabi, Algeria, Bahrain, Egypt, Kuwait and Saudi Arabia agreed to lift the embargo on petroleum supplies to the USA imposed following US support for Israel the previous year; shipments to the Netherlands were resumed in July.

1975: Legislation to introduce conscription was approved.

August 1976: The Amir suspended the National Assembly owing to its delaying of legislation; he ordered a committee to be formed to review the Constitution.

31 December 1977: Sheikh Abdullah as-Salim died, he was succeeded by his cousin, Sheikh Jaber al-Ahmad as-Sabah. Sheikh Saad al-Abdullah as-Salim as-Sabah became Crown Prince and Prime Minister. It was announced that the National Assembly would be reconvened and democratic government restored by August 1980.

November 1978: Following a meeting of Arab nations concerning the Egyptian-Israeli peace agreeement and the imposition of sanctions against Egypt, the Kuwaiti ambassador was recalled from Cairo and all aid was withdrawn.

4–6 March 1979: Iraq, Jordan and Syria attended negotiations in Kuwait to mediate a cease-fire between the People's Democratic Republic of Yemen and the Yemen Arab Republic.

24 August 1980: A committee was established to consider constitutional amendments and means of reforming the legislature. The Amir decreed that a new assembly would be elected by February 1981.

September 1980: Kuwait supported Iraq on the outbreak of its conflict with Iran; the Government allowed the Iraqi navy to use its strategic ports and provided financial aid.

23 February 1981: A general election was held; the franchise was limited to male citizens whose family had resided in Kuwait since before 1920. Twenty-three conservative tribal elders, 13 younger technocrats and four Shi'a candidates were elected; radical Arab nationalist candidates were unsuccessful.

May 1981: Bahrain, Kuwait, Oman, Qatar, Saudi Arabia and the United Arab Emirates founded the Co-operation Council for Arab states of the Gulf (Gulf Co-operation Council—GCC) to promote economic and military co-operation in the region.

December 1983: Bombs exploded at the French and US embassies, a power station and the airport in Kuwait City; five people were killed and 61 wounded. A group of pro-Iranian Shi'ite Muslims belonging to al-Jihad al-Islami (Islamic Jihad), claimed they had carried out the attack.

early 1984: The authorities deported some 600 Iranian workers from Kuwait.

May 1984: Unidentified aircraft bombed two Kuwaiti and several other Saudi Arabian oil tankers in the Gulf. The GCC blamed Iran and withdrew its offers to mediate in the conflict with Iraq.

November 1984: GCC members agreed to form a joint military force with the potential to contain any spread of the conflict between Iran and Iraq.

1985–1986: Some 27,000 expatriates were deported, most of them Iranian.

January 1985: The Government announced plans to construct military bases on the islands of Bubiyan and Warba.

March 1985: The Goverment declared Bubiyan to be a war zone and forbade access to the area.

May 1985: The Amir survived an assassination attempt by an Iraqi member of the banned organization, ad-Dawa al-Islamiya (Call of Islam).

July 1985: Legislation which instituted the death penalty for terrorist acts resulting in loss of life was approved and the Government announced plans to set up popular security committees in all districts.

February 1986: Iran captured the Iraqi port of Faw, close to the border with Kuwait.

June 1986: Explosions occurred at the Mina al-Ahmadi petroleum-export refinery. The Arab Revolutionaries Group later claimed that they had perpetrated the attack in an attempt to force Kuwait to reduce its petroleum output.

3 July 1986: Following frequent disputes with the National Assembly, the Council of Ministers resigned. The Amir dissolved the National Assembly, suspended several articles of the Constitution and declared rule by Amiri decree. Crown Prince Sheikh Saad was reappointed Prime Minister and ordered to nominate a new Government, which was given greater powers of censorship, including the right to close newspapers for up to two years.

13 July 1986: The Amir announced the formation of a new Council of Ministers, which included seven new ministers and three new portfolios.

24 July 1986: The USS *Bridgeton*, a former Kuwaiti vessel, struck a mine in the Gulf near Farsi Island.

August 1986: Belgium, France, Italy and the United Kingdom sent mine-sweeping vessels to the Persian Gulf.

October 1986–April 1987: Iranian forces attacked and seized the cargoes of merchant ships sailing to Kuwait in retaliation for the Government's sales of petroleum on Iraq's behalf and allowing its ports to be used for Iraqi imports. Saudi Arabia and the USA subsequently provided assistance in clearing mines from the shipping lane leading to the Mina al-Ahmadi petroleum terminal and Kuwaiti vessels were re-registered under flags of various other nations.

9 March 1987: The first session of the new National Assembly, the Majlis al-Umma, was convened. Crown Prince Sheikh Saad was sworn in as Prime Minister and formed a new fifteen-member Council of Ministers.

June 1987: Six Shi'a Muslims recieved death sentences following their conviction for plotting against the Government and sabotaging petroleum installations.

September 1987: Six Iranian diplomats were expelled following further Iranian attacks on the country's petroleum industry.

October–December 1987: Following an Iranian attack, the Government closed the main offshore loading terminal at Sea Island.

November 1987: The Government restored full diplomatic relations with Egypt.

28 December 1987: At a meeting of the GCC, the members resolved to urge the UN Security Council to enforce a cease-fire between Iran and Iraq.

January 1988: Legislation which aimed to control the movements of foreign nationals was enacted; persons who violated temporary residence permits or illegaly sold permits and visas were liable to a fine of 3,000 dinars and up to three years' imprisonment.

March 1988: Three Iranian gunboats attacked Bubiyan Island; two Kuwaiti soldiers were wounded in the attack.

April 1988: An Iranian missile landed on the al-Wafra oilfield, south of Kuwait City; the attack was believed to be in retaliation for Kuwait's permission for Iraqi armed forces to use Bubiyan Island to recapture the Faw peninsula.

20 August 1988: A cease-fire was declared by Iran and Iraq.

22 March 1989: A new law banning foreign workers in the private sector from taking up employment with anyone other than their official sponsor was introduced.

April 1989: The Prime Minister announced a normalization of relations with Iran.

June 1989: A total of 22 people were sentenced up to 15 years' imprisonment for conspiring to overthrow the royal family.

10 June 1990: Fifty members were elected to the new Kuwaiti National Assembly.

20 June 1990: A new Council of Ministers was appointed.

15 July 1990: Iraq accused Kuwait, via the Arab League, of unlawfully exploiting Iraqi petroleum resources by conducting exploration in a disputed border area.

18 July 1990: The Kuwaiti army was placed on alert.

24 July 1990: President Mubarak of Egypt visited Iraq, Kuwait and Saudi Arabia in pursuit of a solution to the dispute developing between Iraq and Kuwait.

31 July 1990: Iraqi and Kuwaiti delegations met in Jeddah (Saudi Arabia) to seek a solution to the dispute between the two countries; the meeting ended without resolution within two hours.

2 August 1990: Iraq invaded Kuwait; the UN Security Council adopted Resolution 660, demanding Iraq's immediate and unconditional withdrawal.

3 August 1990: Fourteen Arab League member states condemned the Iraqi invasion of Kuwait and demanded the immediate withdrawal of Iraqi armed forces; the United Kingdom and the USA announced their decision to send naval forces to the Gulf.

6 August 1990: The UN Security Council adopted Resolution 661, imposing economic sanctions on Iraq and Kuwait.

8 August 1990: Iraq announced the formal annexation of Kuwait.

9 August 1990: Iraq closed its own and Kuwait's borders to foreigners. The UN Security Council adopted Resolution 662, rejecting Iraq's annexation of Kuwait.

10 August 1990: Iraq ordered the closure of foreign embassies in Kuwait by 24 August.

18 August 1990: The UN Security Council adopted Resolution 664, urging Iraq to allow all foreign nationals to leave Iraq and Kuwait.

24 August 1990: Many foreign embassies in Kuwait refused to comply with Iraqi orders that they should close.

28 August 1990: Iraq declared northern Kuwait to be part of Basra province, and the remainder to be the 19th province of Iraq.

13 September 1990: The Muslim World League condemned Iraq's invasion of Kuwait.

15 September 1990: Iraq opened Kuwait's border with Saudi Arabia to allow some Kuwaiti refugees to leave.

24 September 1990: French proposals to resolve the crisis were unsuccessful.

3 October 1990: Saddam Hussain visited Kuwait for the first time since the Iraqi invasion.

29 November 1990: UN Security Council Resolution 678 authorized member governments to employ 'all necessary means' to ensure Iraq's withdrawal from Kuwait if it had not removed its forces from the country by 15 January 1991.

16–17 January 1991: The US-led multinational force commenced an air offensive against Iraqi forces and installations in Iraq and Kuwait, known as 'Operation Desert Storm'.

15 February 1991: Iraq made a conditional offer to withdraw from Kuwait.

18 February 1991: President Gorbachev of the USSR proposed an eight-point peace plan to resolve the conflict.

24 February 1991: The multi-national force commenced a ground offensive against Iraqi forces in Kuwait and southern Iraq.

25 February 1991: Iraqi forces evacuated Kuwait City.

27 February 1991: Iraq agreed to observe all UN Security Council Resolutions adopted from August 1990 in respect of its occupation of Kuwait.

27 February 1991: The US President, George Bush, declared the defeat of the Iraqi army and the liberation of Kuwait.

28 February 1991: Hostilities between Iraq and the multi-national force were suspended.

2 March 1991: The UN Security Council adopted Resolution 686, which announced a cease-fire in the conflict over Kuwait; Iraq accepted its terms the following day.

7–14 March 1991: The US Secretary of State visited Egypt, Israel, Kuwait, Saudi Arabia and Syria.

20 March 1991: The Kuwaiti Government resigned.

30 March 1991: Kuwait's principal political groups refused to participate in a new government in the absence of a schedule for political reform.

3 April 1991: The detailed terms of the cease-fire were stipulated in UN Security Council Resolution 687.

9 April 1991: By the terms of UN Security Council Resolution 689, a demilitarized zone (DMZ) was created between Iraq and Kuwait.

12 April 1991: The Kuwaiti Government estimated the cost of the country's reconstruction at US $50,000m.–$100,000m; the UN estimated that the process would take 10 years.

20 April 1991: A new Kuwaiti Government was appointed.

2 June 1991: The Amir of Kuwait scheduled elections to a new National Assembly for October 1992.

3 June 1991: Egypt, Syria and the GCC states agreed, in accordance with the 'Damascus declaration', to supply ground forces for the defence of Kuwait.

26 June 1991: Martial law was lifted.

19 September 1991: Kuwait and the USA signed a defence agreement.

5 October 1992: Elections to the National Assembly were held; pro-Government candidates enjoyed considerable success.

17 October 1992: A new Kuwaiti Government was appointed; members of the ruling family retained the foreign affairs, finance and interior portfolios.

13 April 1994: The Council of Ministers was reorganized.

6 October 1994: Iraqi armed forces advanced southward towards the Iraq-Kuwait border; they withdrew the following week.

10 November 1994: Iraq gave formal recognition to the demarcation of its border with Kuwait.

7 October 1996: Kuwaiti legislative elections took place; pro-Government candidates were again successful, and Sheikh Saad was reappointed Prime Minister.

20 May 1997: A new political organization, the National Democratic Rally, was formed.

22 October 1997: The Minister of Health resigned, citing personal reasons for his decision.

15 March 1998: The Council of Ministers resigned in protest at a forthcoming vote of 'no confidence' in the Minister of Information, Sheikh Sa'ud Nasir as-Sa'ud as-Sabah; a new Government was formed the following week, with Sheikh Sa'ud Nasir being allocated the post of Minister of Oil, regarded as a promotion.

8 December 1998: Two new members were appointed to the Council of Ministers, following resignations.

15 January 1999: The Deputy Prime Minister and Minister of State for Cabinet Affairs visited Jordan, the first Kuwaiti minister to do so since 1990.

3 March 1999: Full diplomatic relations were restored by Jordan and Kuwait; the respective embassies were reopened.

4 May 1999: The Amir dissolved the National Assembly and decreed early elections.

16 May 1999: The Government granted women full suffrage from 2003; the National Assembly was to approve the measure when it reconvened after elections in July.

3 July 1999: Elections to the National Assembly were held, with the electorate greatly extended. Islamist candidates secured 20 of the 50 seats in the Assembly, compared with 14 by liberal candidates and only 12 (less than one-half the previous total) by pro-Government candidates.

13 July 1999: Sheikh Saad, despite having resigned after the general election, was reappointed Prime Minister and led a new Council of Ministers.

November 1999: Legislation approving the granting of female suffrage was defeated, as liberal deputies, who had been expected to support the measures, opposed them as they had originated as legislation by royal decree. The liberals subsequently resubmitted identical legislation, which was narrowly defeated.

2 July 2000: Kuwait and Saudi Arabia signed an agreement on the demarcation of their joint border.

September 2000: Iraq renewed its allegations that Kuwait was unlawfully exploiting Iraqi petroleum reserves by drilling in the border area.

late Sepember 2000: The UN Compensation Council announced that it was to make a payment of US $15,900m. in compensation for lost production and sales of petroleum during the 1990–91 occupation by Iraq. The Iraqi Government had threatened to withdraw business contracts from any country that contributed to this fund.

October 2000: Kuwait accused Iraq of 78 violations of the DMZ and increased the strength of its security force in the border region.

3 October 2000: Some 120,000 stateless bedouin tribesmen attempted to enter Kuwait from the Iraqi side of the DMZ; the Prime Minister accused Iraq of orchestrating the protest.

7–12 October 2000: Thousands of people participated in demonstrations against recent Israeli attacks on Palestinians; several members of the national Assembly were among the protestors.

29 October 2000: The Government announced that it would contribute US $150m. towards the establishment of a fund for the Palestinian groups involved in the so-called Al-Aqsa *intifada* against Israel.

1 November 2000: Following the visit of the Prime Minister of Bangladesh, Sheikh Hasina, the ban on the employment of Bangladeshi workers in Kuwait was lifted.

5 November 2000: The Amir accepted the resignation of the Minister of Information, Dr Saad Muhammad bin Tefiah al-Ajmi.

8 November 2000: Following reports of threatened bomb attacks on US military bases in the Gulf states, the police began investigations into Islamic fundamentalists in Kuwait.

9 November 2000: Some 20 suspected Islamic militants were arrested in connection with the threatened sabotage against US installations.

18 November 2000: The First Deputy Prime Minister and Minister of Foreign Affairs, Sheikh Sabah, received a visit from the Russian Foreign Minister, Igor Ivanov; the two ministers discussed bilateral relations and the situation regarding Iraq.

19 November 2000: The Deputy Prime Minister and Minister of Defence, Sheikh Salim al-Sabah met the US Secretary of Defense, William Cohen, for discussions concerning regional security.

20 November 2000: Muhammad al-Dawsari, the principal suspect in the sabotage investigations confessed that had planned to attack US bases in Qatar. He also implicated a senior officer in the Kuwaiti army, who was subsequently arrested.

22 November 2000: The First Deputy Prime Minister and Minister of Foreign affairs met Wu Bangguo, the Chinese Vice-Premier, for talks on issues of common concern.

23 November 2000: Iraq lodged a complaint with the Secretary-General of the Arab League, concerning alleged aggressive behaviour by a Kuwaiti patrol boat against an Iraqi vessel in Iraqi territorial waters; the allegation was later denied by Kuwait.

4 December 2000: The Minister of Electricity and Water and Minister of State for Housing Affairs, Dr Adil Khalid as-Sahib, defeated a vote of 'no confidence' brought against him in Parliament. He had been closely questioned the previous month regarding the affairs of a business he owned.

7 December 2000: Jamal al-Omar, an independent businessman, won a by-election to the National Assembly; his predecessor, the late Sami al-Mumais, had been a supporter of women's political rights.

13 December 2000: Algeria, Egypt, Iran, Kuwait, Morocco, Saudi Arabia, Syria and Tunisia signed the UN Convention Against Organized Crime, which provided for co-ordination between national crime-fighting bodies, the protection of witnesses, measures to combat money-laundering and the acceleration of extradition proceedings.

28 December 2000: The Interior Minister announced the Government's intention to establish a female police force.

early 2001: The US-based organization, Human Rights Watch, published a report which criticized the authorities for alleged continuing violations of human rights and systematic discrimination against the Bedouin community.

16 January 2001: The Foreign Ministry sent letters and memoranda to the Arab League, the Organization of the Islamic Conference and several other international organizations, urging them to condemn recent Iraqi aggression towards Kuwait. It had recently been reported that Saddam Hussain's eldest son, Uday, had called for the drawing a new map of Iraq to include the state of Kuwait.

16 January 2001: The Constitutional Court rejected a further attempt to grant women the vote; one man initiated legal proccedings against the elections department for failing to register the names of the women in his family.

19 January 2001: During a visit of the Lebanese Prime Minister, several economic agreements were made.

27 January 2001: A member of the National Assembly requested that the Minister of Justice, Saad Jasem Yousuf al-Hashil, be questioned in Parliament over his perceived failure to combat corruption.

29 January 2001: The Prime Minister and the Government resigned, claiming that tensions with the National Assembly had hindered their work; National Assembly members accused the Government of protecting its members from questioning regarding alleged corruption. The Amir immediately ordered the Prime Minister to form a new government.

30 January 2001: The Saudi and Kuwaiti governments co-ordinated an agreement on plans to launch a joint diplomatic initative to urge international organizations and the UN Security Council to confront Iraqi hostility.

31 January 2001: Kuwait and Saudi Arabia signed maps on the demarcation of their maritime borders.

2 February 2001: The Governments of Iran and Kuwait announced plans to construct a 540-km pipeline to supply Kuwait with drinking water; the existing method of desalination was believed to be causing environmental damage in Kuwait.

6 February 2001: The Egyptian President, Mubarak, arrived in Kuwait to discuss relations between the two countries, the Israeli-Palestinian conflict and the issue of Iraq with government officials and with the Amir.

14 February 2001: The new Council of Ministers was anounced, it included four elected members of the National Assembly and five younger members of the royal family; the former education minister, Yousuf Hamad al-Ibrahim, was appointed Minister of Oil.

20 February 2001: The British Government renewed its pledge to safeguard Kuwait's territorial integrity and sovereignty.

24 February 2001: The Kuwait-US security agreement was automatically renewed for 10 years.

13 March 2001: The death sentence originally imposed in May 2000 on Alaa Hussein, who had acted as the country's pro-Iraqi leader during its occupation in 1990–91, was commuted to life imprisonment by the Cassation Court. Hussein had repeatedly protested his innocence, claiming that the Iraqi authorities had threatened to 'dishonour' his family if he failed to take up the post.

20 March 2001: A women's rights campaigner and editor of a political magazine, *Hidayat al-Salam*, was assassinated following the publication of an article in which she criticized the police for treating women unfairly. Two days later, a police-officer confessed to having carried out the murder.

28–29 March 2001: At a 'summit' meeting of the Arab League in Jordan, Kuwait opposed Iraq's proposal that the members contravene the UN sanctions imposed upon it.

21 April 2001: The Constitutional Court dismissed a petition brought by two women activists, Lowlowa al-Mulla and Hind al-Shalfan, to grant full political rights to women in the emirate.

22 May 2001: The Government signed a number of accords with Jordan reviving economic links, which had been terminated following Jordan's percieved support for Iraq during its occupation of Kuwait in 1991.

30 May 2001: Members of the National Assembly protested at the visit of PLO minister in charge of Jerusalem affairs for the Palestinian National Authority, Faisal Husseini (who died of a heart complaint the following day).

4 June 2001: In an effort to attract more foreign investment, the Cabinet approved a bill to reduce the rate of taxation on foreign companies operating in the country from 55% to 25%.

Lebanon

***c*. 3000 BC:** The Semitic Canaanites migrated to the area of modern-day Lebanon from the interior of the Arabian peninsula. They founded the independent coastal city-states of Tyre, Sidon, Gubla (Byblos—later known as Jubayl) and Berytus (Beirut).

***c*. 2700 BC:** Gubla—and subsequently Byblos—began to export cedar timber, olive oil and wine to Egypt, in exchange for gold and ivory.

2200 BC: The Amorites, another Semitic tribe, entered the region from Arabia and Syria.

***c*. 1490 BC–1436 BC:** Having defeated domestic adversaries, the Egyptians invaded Syria and annexed the Canaanite territories.

12th century BC: The Egyptian Empire weakened; the Canaanites were able to recover their autonomy and propsperity. The production of textiles, carved ivory, glass and metals flourished.

***c*. 1000 BC:** The Canaanites invented the first known alphabet, which facilitated the expansion of trade and communication links with other civilizations, such as the Greeks, who named the northern Canaanites, the Phoenicians.

969 BC–936 BC: During the reign of Hiram I of Tyre, the city grew wealthy through trade in the Mediterranean and the Red Sea. Hiram also formed an alliance with King Solomon of the Hebrews.

867 BC: The Assyrians of the Tigris Valley invaded and subsequently conquered Phoenicia.

814 BC: The Phoenicians of Tyre established the colony of Carthage (in present-day Tunisia); other trading colonies were also founded on Crete, Cyprus and Rhodes.

mid-8th century BC: The citizens of Tyre and Byblos rebelled against the Assyrian ruler, Tiglath-Pileser III; they were defeated, and subjected to increased taxation.

721 BC: Following a further rebellion by Tyre, Sargon II beseiged the city.

7th century BC: Following a rebellion, Sidon was destroyed by Esarhaddon; the Assyrian ruler enslaved its citizens and ordered that a new city be built on its ruins.

***c*. 672 BC:** The Phoenicians are believed to have made the first circumnavigation of the continent of Africa.

650 BC: Carthage established its own navy fleet and army and assumed responsibility for the defence of the Phoenician colonies in the Mediterranean Sea.

590s BC: Nebuchadnezzar III of Babylon invaded and conquered Phoenicia, only Tyre resisted. Following a siege which lasted 13 years, the King of Tyre was eventually deposed and its citizens enslaved.

539 BC: Cyrus II ('the Great'), founder of the Achaemenid Empire overthrew the Babylonians and incorporated Phoenicia into the Persian Empire.

5th century BC: A series of rebellions against Persian rule occurred, owing to poverty and increasingly higher taxation.

333 BC: Alexander III ('the Great') of Macedon led the Greek army to victory against the Persians. His troops began to advance towards the Mediterranean coast and at first encountered little resistance from the Phoenicians.

332 BC: Following a siege of six months' duration, the Phoenicians were defeated by Alexander's forces. Phoenicia became subjugated to the Greek Empire and heavily influenced by Hellenistic culture.

321 BC: Following the death of Alexander, one of his generals, Seleucus Nicator, took control of the Greek colonies in the East, including Phoenicia. During the first 40 years of his rule, he was engaged in constant conflict with the Greek rulers of Egypt, the Ptolemies, over sovereignty of Phoenicia.

AD 64: The Romans conquered Phoenicia; the region became part of the Roman and subsequently, the Byzantine Empire. Under their rule, the Phoenicians enjoyed a period of prosperity and cultural enlightenment. Aramaic became the principal language and Christianity was introduced.

632–34: The Caliph Abu Bakr, the successor of the founder of the Islamic faith, the Prophet Muhammad, established Islam in the area surrounding Lebanon.

c. 661: The Umayyad Caliph Mu'awiya was appointed Governor of Syria; he subsequently attempted to assert control over Phoenicia. Umayyad troops were stationed on the Mediterranean coast in anticipation of an attack by forces of the Byzantine (Eastern) Roman Empire.

667: Mu'awiya negotiated an agreement with the Byzantine Emperor Constantine IV, by which he agreed to pay an annual fee in return for an end to the Byzantine-supported Christian incursions.

late 7th century: The Christian Maronites migrated from Syria into the mountains of northern Phoenicia; the region became known as Lebanon. They united with native Aramean Christians and Mardaites from Byzantium to challenge the rule of Mu'awiya.

750: The Abbasids succeeded the Umayyads to the Caliphate; their treatment of Lebanon and Syria as subordinate territories caused several revolts in the region.

late 10th century: The Amir of Tyre proclaimed the city's independence from Abbasid Caliphate; shortly afterwards however, the Fatimids of Egypt, an independent Arab Muslim dynasty, assumed control.

early 11th century: The Druze, a sect of the Ismailite Shi'ites, settled in the Mount Hermon area.

1095: Following the capture of the 'Holy Land' by the Muslims, led by the Fatimid Caliph Al-Hakim, Pope Urban II proclaimed the First Crusade; in 1109, the Franks marched through Lebanon on their way to Jersualem.

1102: The French Count, Raymond VI Saint Gilles of Toulouse, began a conquest of the Emirate of Tripoli. His forces defeated the Amirs of Homs and Damascus at the Battle of Banu Ammars outside Tripoli, but failed to capture the city itself.

June 1109: In alliance with King Baldwin I of Jerusalem, Bertrand, the son of Raymond, conquered Tripoli following some six years of siege. Bertrand was installed as the Count of Tripoli and a vassal of Jerusalem.

1110: Bertrand of Toulouse captured Beirut; Sidon was captured in the same year.

November 1111: Baldwin attempted to conquer Tyre; his troops besieged the city for four months before abandoning the campaign.

February 1124: The Crusaders laid seige to Tyre by land and sea; the Tyrians received assistance from the Tughtinin, the King of Damascus; however, Tyre was forced to surrender in June.

1183: Following his accession to the throne of Egypt and Syria, Salah ad-Din (Saladin) began to challenge the Crusaders' control of the Lebanese coastal towns. The Muslim army laid seige to Beirut but was forced to withdraw with the arrival of Crusader reinforcements.

1187: After the fall of Palestine to the Muslims, Salah ad-Din's army captured Sidon, Beirut and Jubayl (formerly Gubla). Salah ad-Din attempted to conquer Tyre but was forced to abandon the campaign the following year.

1192: The leader of the Third Crusade, King Richard I of England, negotiated a truce with Salah ad-Din, which was to last three years.

1197: Jubayl was recaptured by the Crusaders.

July 1198: A peace agreement was negotiated by Salah ad-Din's successor, al-Adil, with King Almaric of Jerusalem; the Crusaders ceded the Jaffa (modern-day Tel-Aviv, Israel) to the Muslims in return for control of the cities of Jubayl and Beirut; Sidon was divided between the two rulers.

1252: Muez Aibak, a Mameluke (Caucasian slave soldiers employed by the Eyptian Ayyubids as bodyguards), assassinated Sultan Al-Ashraf Musa and founded the Mameluke dynasty which was to rule Egypt and Syria for the next two centuries. He declared his intention to recapture the territories held by the Crusaders.

1291: The Mameluke Malik al-Ashraf Salah ad-Din captured Tyre, Sidon and Beirut. During their reign, the coastal cities prospered from trade with Western Europe and intellectual life flourished.

1291: Shi'a Muslims allied with Druze in the Beka'a Valley and Kasrawan region to rebel against the Mamelukes; since the Mamelukes were distracted with their campaigns against the Crusaders, the rebellion was at first successful.

1308: The Mamelukes suppressed the rebellion in the Beka'a Valley and Kasrawan; the defeated Shi'a and Druze fled to southern Lebanon.

1516: The Ottoman Sultan Selim I conquered Lebanon; the Amirs were allowed to maintain a degree of autonomy but were required to pay tribute to the Ottoman rulers. In the 16th century northern Lebanon became dominated by the Turkoman Banu Saifa dynasty and the southern regions ruled by the Druze house of Ma'an.

1584–85: An attack on a tribute convoy passing through Lebanon on its way to the Ottoman capital, Constantinople, provoked Sultan Murad III to launch an offensive against the Banu Saifa and the Ma'an.

1608: The Ma'an ruler, Fakhr ad-Din, sought to extend his power over the whole of Lebanon; he made a commercial agreement with the Italian Grand Duke of Tuscany, which included a secret military clause directed against the Ottomans.

1613: The Ottoman navy attacked the territories of Fakhr ad-Din; the Amir was forced to take refuge in Tuscany.

1618: Fakhr ad-Din returned and established himself as ruler of a region extending from Aleppo in the north to Egypt in the south. He equipped the army with Tuscan weapons and engaged Italian engineers and agricultural experts to improve the efficiency of agriculture and manufacturing.

1635: Following a campaign against the Ma'an by the Pasha (governor) of Damascus, Fakhr ad-Din was executed at Constantinople.

1697: The House of Ma'an was replaced by another Druze dynasty, the Chehab. Over the course of the 18th century, the Chehab consolidated their authority over Lebanon.

1788–1840: During the reign of Bashir II, the House of Chehab reached its zenith.

1810: Bashir's forces assisted the Ottomans to repel an invasion by the Arabian Wahhabi army.

1831: Bashir entered into an alliance with the Egyptian ruler, Muhammad Ali, and assisted him in his campaign against Syria.

1834: The American Press of Beirut was established; the Catholic Press was founded later in the century.

1840: A popular rebellion against his rule forced Bashir to flee to Egypt. The Ottomans subsequently asserted more direct control over Lebanon; two local officials, one Druze and one Maronite, were appointed to supervise the pashas of Sidon and Beirut.

1858–60: Amid severe economic and social discontent, the Maronite peasantry revolted against their aristocracy and created a system of independent small-holdings. Fearing similar attacks by their own Maronite peasants, the Druze massacred more than 10,000 Maronites in northern Lebanon. French forces intervened to end the conflict.

1864: The French assisted the Ottomans to draft an Organic Statute, which defined Lebanon as an autonomous province under the jurisdiction of a non-Lebanese Ottoman Christian governor, who was appointed by the Sultan. The governor was to be assisted by an elected administrative council and a locally recruited police force. Feudalism was abolished.

1866: The Syrian Protestant College was founded in Beirut; it later became the American University of Beirut.

1875: St Joseph University was founded in Beirut by French Jesuit priests.

1914: At the outbreak of the First World War, the Ottomans terminated Lebanon's semi-autonomous status. Jamal Pasha, the Commander-in-Chief of the Turkish forces in Syria, occupied Lebanon.

1915: In an attempt to prevent the delivery of supplies to British and French forces in the region, Jamal Pasha implemented a military blockade of the entire eastern Mediterranean coast; a severe famine ensued in Lebanon.

1916: The Ottoman authorities publicly executed 21 Lebanese and Syrians who had been convicted of engaging in anti-Turkish activities.

1918: The coastal areas were occupied by British and French forces.

September 1918: British and Arab forces, led by Gen. Edmund Allenby and Faisal, the son of Sharif Hussain of Mecca, captured Palestine and subsequently occupied Syria and Lebanon.

April 1920: At the San Remo Conference in Italy, Lebanon was designated as a French mandate.

September 1920: The French Governor, Gen. Gouraud, declared the establishment of the state of Greater Lebanon, within its modern borders, and designated Beirut as the capital.

1925–26: A revolt against the French authorities in Syria caused some unrest in southern Lebanon.

23 May 1926: The country's first Constitution was promulgated; it provided for a President, Council of Ministers and Chamber of Deputies. The deputies were to be elected according their confessions by their own communities and would, in turn, elect the President for a six-year term.

26 May 1926: Charles Dabbas, a member of the Greek Orthodox Church, was elected President.

1932: In the first national census, the religious confessions of the population were monitored; the results of the census were used to appoint government positions in accordance with the faiths represented in Lebanese society.

May 1932: Following a dispute in the Chamber of Deputies over the election of a new President, the Muslim Sheikh Muhammad al-Jisr was suggested as a compromise candidate. Apparently in order to prevent the election of a Muslim President, the French High Commissioner, Henri Ponsot, suspended the Constitution and extended the term of President Dabbas for a further year.

30 January 1934: Comte Damien de Martel replaced Ponsot; he appointed Habib as-Saad as President.

1936: The Franco-Lebanese Treaty was negotiated between French and Lebanese leaders; the agreement accorded France considerable military powers.

30 January 1936: Emile Iddi was elected President.

1937: Iddi attempted to revive part of the Constitution of 1926; the French, however, refused to ratify the document.

September 1939: At the outbreak of the Second World War, the Constitution was again suspended by the French authorities.

1941: The Free French Commander, Gen. Catroux, declared Lebanon to be an independent state.

1943: Christian and Muslim leaders concluded an oral agreement, the *al-Mithaq al-Watani* (National Covenant), by which the principles of the new state were established. It stated that: Lebanon should be independent of the West and Arab states, although intellectual ties and nieghbourly relations should be retained; public offices should be distributed in proportion with the religious groupings of the population; the President of the Republic should be Christian Maronite, the Prime Minister Sunni Muslim and the Speaker of the Chamber of Deputies Shi'a.

September 1943: A new parliament was elected and Bishara al-Khuri was elected as President. The large nationalist majority in the Government came into conflict with the French authorities over the transfer of control over the administrative services.

November 1943: Legislation to remove from the Constitution all provisions inconsistent with the independence of Lebanon was enacted. The French Delegate-General responded by arresting the President and suspending the Constitution; this was condemned by other Arab nations and the Governments of the United Kingdom and USA.

January 1944: Control of all public services, except for the *Troupes spéciales* (local units of troops commanded by the French), was transfered to the Lebanese authorities; the process of Lebanese independence was thus completed.

1945: The Lebanese assumed command over the *Troupes spéciales.*

March 1945: Egypt, Iraq, Lebanon, Saudi Arabia, Syria, Transjordan and Yemen founded the League of Arab States (Arab League), which aimed to promote political, cultural, economic and social co-operation between its members and act as mediator in regional disputes.

April 1945: Government delegates participated in the San Francisco Conference of the UN and Lebanon subsequently became a member.

1946: The Government negotiated the withdrawal of French troops.

February 1948: Following the devaluation of the French currency, the franc, to which the Lebanese and Syrian currencies were linked, the Government was compelled to conclude an economic agreement with France. This led to a dispute with Syria over economic and financial relations between the two countries.

May 1948: The Government sent troops to assist the Arabs in their war against the newly-created state of Israel.

1949: Following the esablishment of the State of Israel, and during the subsequent Arab-Israeli wars, thousands of Palestinians fled to Lebanon and were housed in refugee camps in the south of the country.

1949: Al-Khuri was re-elected President.

March 1949: The Government agreed to an armistice with Israel; which Lebanon had joined its Arab neighbours in attacking.

June 1949: A nationalist conspiracy against the Government was discovered; its leader, Antun Sa'ade, was executed.

March 1950: Syria demanded a full economic and financial union with Lebanon; the Government refused. An economic agreement, providing for the division of petroleum revenues and confirming customs arrangements, was signed in 1952, however.

May 1952: The SNF organized a mass demonstration in Dayr al-Qamar; the participants protested at the high cost of living and mass unemployment and demanded the resignation of al-Khuri.

June 1952: The Social National Front (SNF), was founded by Kamal Jumblatt, the head of the Progressive Socialist Party, the former ambassador to the United Kingdom, Camille Chamoun, and other prominent deputies. The organization aimed to end sectarianism and eradicate corruption; it swiftly gained popularity and demonstrated against unemployment and the high cost of living, and urged President al-Khuri to resign.

11 September 1952: The SNF instigated a general strike to force the resignation of the President. The armed forces refused al-Khuri's request to end the strike and he was forced to resign on 18 September.

23 September 1952: Chamoun was elected President and Amir Khalid Chehab Prime Minister. The new Government reorganized the judicial system and revised the press law. A new electoral law was also instituted, which provided for the election of the Chamber of Deputies on a sectarian basis; thus of the 44 available seats, the Christian Maronites recieved 13, Sunni Muslims nine, Shi'a Muslims eight, the Greek Orthodox community five, the Druze three, Greek Meklite Catholics three, Armenian Catholics two and other confessions one.

November 1953: The Government held discussions with Syria regarding problems in the financial arrangements between the two countries; little progress was attained.

August 1955: The Government received a loan of US $27m. from the World Bank to finance a hydro-electricity and irrigation programme in the Litani river area.

October 1956: Following attacks on Egypt by British and French forces in response to Egypt's nationalization of the Suez Canal, the Government declared a state of emergency; unlike several other Arab states, however, Lebanon retained diplomatic ties with France and the United Kingdom.

November 1956: There were disturbances in the mainly Muslim areas of Tripoli and Beirut over the perceived pro-Western attitude of the Government.

January 1957: The Government announced the 'Eisenhower Doctrine', a scheme by which the USA would distribute military and economic aid to Middle-Eastern states to ensure their loyalty in the event of conflict with the USSR. Lebanon's participation in the scheme was approved by the Chamber of Deputies and US military equipment began to arrive in June.

May–June 1957: Elections to the Chamber of Deputies and subsequently for the office of President took place. Chamoun retained his post; the number of seats in the Chamber was also increased from 44 to 66.

November 1957: Anti-Government demonstrations occurred; the protesters were mainly Muslim pan-Arab groups who accused the Government of favouring Chrisitians and criticized its acceptance of the Eisenhower Doctrine.

December 1957: Following further unrest in the area, martial law was declared in northern Lebanon.

March 1958: The Government was reorganized, ostensibly to remove anti-Western elements; the new administration announced that Lebanon would not be joining either the United Arab Republic (UAR—created earlier that year by Egypt and Syria) or the Arab Federation of Jordan and Iraq. These events provoked unrest among Arab nationalists in major cities.

10 May 1958: Anti-Government rioting worsened throughout the country; the Government appealed to the USA for assistance; shipments of US arms were accelerated and the US Navy presence in the eastern Mediterranean reinforced.

15 July 1958: US marines landed at Beirut following a further appeal to the USA by President Chamoun (a *coup d'état* had taken place in Iraq the previous day).

31 July 1958: Gen. Fuad Chehab was elected President by the Chamber of Deputies; he took office in September upon the expiry of Chamoun's term of office.

August 1958: Amid Arab and interntional condemnation of the presence of US forces in Lebanon, the USA agreed to evacuate its troops from the country under the supervision of the UN and the Arab League.

11 January 1959: The statute of the Arab Development Bank was signed by Jordan, Lebanon, Libya, Saudi Arabia, the UAR and Yemen.

16 January 1960: The Lebanese Council of Ministers decided to increase the number of Deputies in the next Chamber to be elected by 33, to a total of 99.

2 August 1960: A new Government, led by Saeb Salem, took office.

23 October 1961: Saeb Salem resigned; Rashid Karami was subsequently appointed Prime Minister.

1964: Following the formation of the Palestine Liberation Organization (PLO), training centres for guerrilla fighters were established among the refugee camps of southern Lebanon.

23 August 1964: Charles Helou was elected President by the Chamber of Deputies.

17 November 1964: Hussein Oweini formed a new administration, which remained in office until his resignation in July 1965.

26 July 1965: Following Oweini's resignation, Karami returned to the premiership and appointed a new Council of Ministers; the Cabinet was subsequently modified several times, in an attempt to fully implement a programme of military reform.

March 1966: Amid demands for the Council of Ministers to be composed mainly of elected Deputies, Karami, whose Cabinet contained a number of unelected figures, resigned; President Hélou appointed Dr Abdallah Yafi as the new premier.

7 December 1966: Following Yafi's resignation, Karami was again appointed premier; his third Government resigned in February 1968, and Yafi was charged with the formation of an interim administration, pending legislative elections in March.

5–10 June 1967: Unlike other Arab states bordering Israel, Lebanon did not participate in the Arab-Israeli conflict which came to be known as the Six-Day War.

9 April 1968: The results of the general election gave no party an absolute majority; Yafi's interim Government remained in office.

9–20 October 1968: Internal discord within the Cabinet and the inability to command a majority in the legislature forced Yafi to resign. President Hélou tendered his resignation in response, but withdrew the offer. Yafi formed a new Government, with only four Ministers; political instability persisted throughout late 1968 and early 1969.

28 December 1968: In an apparent response to an Arab group's assault on an Israeli aircraft in Greece, Israeli commandos raided Beirut airport, destroying 13 Arab aircraft.

7 January 1969: The Lebanese Government resigned, following the Israeli raid; Karami subsequently formed a new ministry.

25 April 1969: Amid tensions between the Christian and Muslim communities, Karami resigned; however, as no stronger administration could be formed, Karami's Government continued in an interim capacity.

October–November 1969: Extensive fighting between the Lebanese Army and guerrilla forces threatened civil war.

3 November 1969: The Commander-in-Chief of the armed forces signed a pact on the supervision of the guerrilla movement with the leader of the al-Fatah movement and of the PLO, Yasser Arafat, in Cairo (Egypt).

25 November 1969: Karami formed a new administration, as tensions eased following the agreement with Arafat.

17 August 1970: Sulayman Franjiya was elected President.

October 1970: President Franjiya charged Saeb Salam with the formation of a new cabinet, whose members came from outside parliament.

1–8 May 1971: The US Secretary of State, William Rogers, visited Israel, Jordan, Lebanon, Saudi Arabia and the UAR to discuss plans for reopening the Suez Canal, which had been closed since the Six-Day War.

24–28 February 1972: Israeli forces attacked military and guerrilla installations in Lebanon.

April–May 1972: Left-wing candidates performed strongly in the legislative elections.

27 May 1972: Salam, the outgoing Prime Minister, formed a new Government.

21–23 June 1972: Israeli forces carried out further attacks on Lebanon; 36 civilians and 30 guerrillas were reported to have been killed and 80 civilians and 50 guerrillas wounded; five Syrian army officers were taken captive.

8 September 1972: The Israeli air force bombarded sites believed to be guerrilla bases in Lebanon and Syria; further raids were carried out on 15 October.

8 December 1972: A confrontation took place between Lebanese regular troops and Palestinian Arab guerrillas in southern Lebanon.

27 February 1973: Israeli commandos conducted a raid into Lebanon against Palestinian Arab guerrilla-training bases.

13 April 1973: Following Israeli raids on Beirut, in which troops in civilian dress killed three guerrilla leaders, Salam presented his resignation. Dr Amin Hafez subsequently formed a new Government; fighting between the military and Palestinian forces resumed.

17 May 1973: Lebanese authorities and Palestinian guerrillas reached agreement on terms under which guerrillas would remain in Lebanon. Heavy fighting between the guerrillas and the Lebanese army had preceded the settlement.

14 June 1973: Dr Amin Hafez resigned as Prime Minister of Lebanon.

8 July 1973: Takieddine Solh formed a 22-member Cabinet.

October 1973: Palestinian guerrillas used southern Lebanon as a base from which to launch attacks on Israel; the region was the victim of several Israeli reprisals.

February 1974: The Government proposed a number of reforms to the civil service, in an attempt to change the sectarian nature of the Government. The proposals were opposed by the Maronites, the right-wing Christian Phalange movement and the Bloc National; the Parti National Libéral also threatened to withdraw three cabinet members in protest.

July 1974: The Phalange demanded that the Government do more to control guerrilla activities in the south; this led to prolonged conflict with the Palestinians.

September 1974: Owing to his failure to contain the violence, Takieddine Solh resigned.

October 1974: A new Government was formed under Rashid Solh; the new members disagreed over Muslim proposals to grant citizenship to long-term residents of the country.

February 1975: A group of Muslim fishermen demonstrated in Sidon at the granting of favourable fishing rights to a group of Christians; the Government deployed the army to quell the resultant violence.

13 April 1975: Four Phalangists were killed when gunmen attempted to assassinate their leader, Pierre Jumayyil. Believing the perpetrators to be Palestinians, the Phalangists retaliated with an attack on a bus carrying Palestinian passengers, killing 26. The incidents led to prolonged sectarian conflict between Christians and Muslims, eventually developing into civil war.

May 1975: Rashid Solh and his Government resigned; a new Government was formed by Karami.

September 1975: A National Dialogue Committee was formed; it comprised 20 members representing all the political and confessional groups in Lebanon and aimed to discuss ways of restoring order.

1976: Syrian-based PLO guerrillas assisted Muslim groups in their conflict against the Christian community.

March 1976: Some 70 deputies singed a petition demanding Franjiya's resignation.

23 April 1976: The Chamber of Deputies unanimously approved an amendment of the Constitution to allow Presidential elections to be held up to six months before the incumbent's term of office expired. It was also announced that the scheduled legislative elections were to be postponed, owing to the continued unrest.

May 1976: Some 40,000 Syrian troops entered the civil war in order to prevent an outright victory by the left-wing, mainly Muslim, Lebanese National Movement.

June 1976: Syria began a series of successful offensives against nationalist positions.

September 1976: Elias Sarkis was elected President. In the same month, numerous Maronite armed groups united to form the Lebanese Forces—these forces took control of east Beirut and northern Lebanon, while Muslim groups dominated the west of the capital and Palestinians the south of the country.

October 1976: At Arab League conferences in Riyadh, Saudi Arabia, and subsequently Cairo, it was agreed that the Syrian troops should withdraw from Lebanon and a pan-Arab peace-keeeping force, the Arab Deterrent Force (ADF) should oversee a cease-fire in the conflict (in practice, the ADF was composed mainly of Syrians). A four-party disengagement committee was also established to implement the terms of the 1969 Cairo agreement between Lebanon and the Palestinian guerrillas.

December 1976: Dr Selim al-Hoss was appointed Prime Minister; he formed a Cabinet of technocrats who were charged with the task of post-war reconstruction.

1977: There was renewed conflict in the southern regions; a 'proxy war' developed between Syrian-supported Palestinian guerrillas and pro-Government Israeli troops.

16 March 1977: The Druze chief, Kamal Joumblatt, was assassinated; the incident precipitated several revenge killings.

July 1977: The Shtaura agreement was concluded between the Government and the Palestinians in an attempt to regulate guerrilla activity in the south.

January 1978: The Chamber of Deputies' term was extended until June 1980.

11 March 1978: Palestinian al-Fatah guerrillas launched an attack on Tel-Aviv, Israel, from Lebanon; Israeli forces retaliated with an incursion into Lebanese territory.

19 March 1978: The UN Security Council urged Israel to cease incursions into Lebanese territory and withdraw its forces; the United Nations Interim Force in Lebanon (UNIFIL) was established to secure the withdrawal of the Israelis and restore peace.

May 1978: UNIFIL was increased in strength from 4,000 to 6,000.

June 1978: Following the withdrawal of the Israeli troops, a right-wing Christian militia, led by Maj. Saad Haddad, took control of the southern region.

July 1978: Fighting between Syrian ADF troops and right-wing Christians occurred in Beirut.

October 1978: At a conference of the participating countries of the ADF, which included Kuwait, Lebanon, Qatar, Saudi Arabia, Sudan, Syria and the United Arab Emirates a cease-fire agreement was concluded.

March 1979: The Chamber of Deputies was renamed the National Assembly.

April 1979: Maj. Haddad proclaimed the state of 'Free Lebanon' in the south; the state was recognized and supported by Israel.

July 1979: A new Cabinet was formed, seven of whom had previously been deputies.

5 March 1980: President Sarkis issued a message to the nation, in which he promised that the Government would achieve unity and sovereignty; he also asserted Lebanon's status as an Arab country which rejected the peace agreement reached by Egypt and Israel.

April 1980: The National Assembly's term was extended for a further three years.

7 June 1980: Hoss resigned as Prime Minister, owing to his Government's failure to restore order.

July 1980: Phalangist troops, led by Bachir Gemayel, occupied the town of Zahle in the Beka'a valley.

16 July 1980: Takieddine Solh was invited to form a government, but was unable to do so.

October 1980: Chafic al-Wazzan was appointed Prime Minister.

April 1981: Syrian ADF troops besieged the town of Zahle; the siege remained in place until June 1981.

May 1981: The Syrian Government stationed surface-to-air missile launchers in the Beka'a valley following an Israeli attack on Syrian helicopters.

24 July 1981: The US envoy to the Middle East, Philip Habib, arranged a cease-fire between the Syrian and Israeli forces.

6 June 1982: Following PLO shelling of northern Israel, the Israeli army launched a full-scale invasion of Lebanon. Towns and villages were heavily bombarded, causing many civilian casualties.

July–August 1982: The Israeli forces subjected west Beirut to persistent bombardment.

August 1982: A withdrawal of PLO troops from Beirut was negoitiated by US diplomats.

23 August 1982: The Phalangist Bachir Gemayel was elected President; most Muslim members of the National Assembly boycotted the ballot.

14 September 1982: President-elect Gemayel was assassinated in a bomb attack on the Phalangist headquarters; his brother, Amin, was elected to succeed him the following week.

15 September 1982: The Israeli army again advanced into Beirut.

16 September 1982: Apparently in revenge for the assassination of Bachir Gemayel, Phalangist extremists massacred Palestinian refugees in camps at Sabra and Chatila.

February 1983: Under pressure from the US Government, the Government began peace talks with Israel. Israel demanded the right to maintain military bases in Lebanon and the recognition of Maj. Haddad's Free State; the Government rejected these demands.

17 May 1983: The Government and Israel signed an agreement, which provided for the withdrawal Israeli troops. The Israeli Government, however, did not consider itself bound to the agreement unless Syrian troops also withdrew.

July 1983: Israel began to redeploy its troops; by the end of the year the number of its soldiers in Lebanon had been reduced from 30,000 to 10,000.

July 1983: Violence errupted between Phalangist and Druze militias in Chouf. The opposition National Salvation Front was formed the Druze leader, Walid Joumblatt, the former Prime Minister, Rashid Karami and the former President, Sulayman Franjiya; the movement was supported by Syria.

September–December 1983: A dispute over control of al-Fatah took place in Tripoli, between Arafat and Abu Musa and Abu Saleh, who were supported by Syria. A truce was eventually mediated by Saudi Arabian diplomats.

23 September 1983: A cease-fire was declared in the inter-factional fighting in Beirut; al-Wazzan offered to resign the premiership, but was persuaded to maintain his post.

23 October 1983: Two seperate suicide-bomb attacks were perpetrated on international peace-keeping forces by members of a Muslim militia; 241 US and 58 French marines were killed.

31 October–4 November 1983: The Conference of National Reconciliation was convened in Geneva, Switzerland; the delegates agreed on the necessity for increased representation for Muslims (it was widely recognized that they, and not Christians, now formed the najority of the country's population), although Israel and Syria remained hostile towards each other.

February 1984: Factional fighting intensified; Beirut became divided into eastern (Christian) and western (Muslim) areas along the so-called 'Green Line'. Following attacks on their troops, Italy, the United Kingdom and the USA withdrew their components of the peace-keeping forces; al-Wazzan again tendered his resignation.

16 February 1984: President Gemayel offered to abrogate the 1983 agreement with Israel, give greater representation to the Muslims, and to form a government of national unity. These reforms would be accompanied by the withdrawal of all foreign forces, and new security arrangements for southern Lebanon. The measures were found to be unacceptable by both Muslims and Christians.

5 March 1984: In return for guarantees of internal security from President Hafiz al-Assad of Syria, Gemayel abrogated the 1983 agreement with Israel; al-Wazzan subsequently withdrew his resignation.

12 March 1984: The Conference of National Reconciliation reconvened in Lausanne (Switzerland).

April 1984: At a conference in Damascus, President Assad of Syria approved plans for the creation of a Lebanese government of national unity, in which both Muslims and Christians were equally represented.

30 April 1984: Rahsid Karami was appointed Prime Minister of a Government of National Unity, arranged by President Gemayel. He announced his objectives to be the removal of the Israeli presence in the south, the restoration of civil order and an amendment to the Constitution to reflect the Muslim majority.

7 May 1984: Nabih Berri was appointed to the newly created position of Minister of State for the Affairs of the South and Reconstruction.

June 1984: A Military Council, whose members represented each religious group in the country, was established to discuss ways to reintegrate the army and disband the militias.

July 1984: Despite sporadic fighting, Beirut port and airport were reopened; they had been closed since February.

September 1984: Walid Joumblatt vetoed the Military Council's proposed security plan and accused the Lebanese army of having Phalangist sympathies.

September 1984: Following disagreements in the Government over the proportion of National Assembly seats to be appointed to each religious grouping; a special committee was subsequently appointed to draft proposals for political reform.

October 1984: Walid Joumblatt and Nabih Berri threatened to resign unless further progress was made in amending the Constitution.

November 1984: The Government met Israeli representatives to discuss the withdrawal of the Israeli Defence Force (IDF) from the south. The two sides failed to agree on the role of the UNIFIL and the Lebanese army in the patrolling of the evacuated area.

November 1984: Under the supervision of the Syrian Government, a new security plan was formulated; once control of Beirut had been gained, the army was to extend its authority to Tripoli, the Chouf mountains and south to the Israeli-occupied territories.

21 December 1984: The army gained control of Tripoli.

February 1985: Following a decision taken by the Israeli Government the previous month, the IDF began to evacuate its forces from the south-west.

March 1985: President Gemayel approved a security plan proposed by Syria; the plan granted more political and constitutional power to the Muslim majority and deprived the Christian militias of control of the check-point on the road between Beirut and Tripoli. The proposals provoked renewed fighting between the Christians and Muslims in Beirut.

March 1985: Rebel Christian guerrillas launched an offensive against a Palestinian refugee camp at Ain al-Hinweh; they also attacked Muslim militiamen and troops of the Lebanese army in the Muslim suburbs of Sidon.

3 March 1985: Israeli forces began to withdraw from the Beka'a valley. Shi'ite guerrillas attacked the retreating troops; this prompted a programme of retaliation by the Israeli army against the Shi'ite communities.

10 April 1985: Owing to the Government's failure to quell the unrest in Sidon, the Prime Minister, Rashid Karami, announced that he would boycott meetings until a cease-fire had been agreed.

17 April 1985: Following sectarian fighting between Muslims in west Beirut, Karami announced his resignation; he was subsequently persuaded to withdraw it.

May–June 1985: The Shi'ite Amal militia and the Shi'ite Sixth Brigade of the Lebanese army, with the support of Syria, launched a joint initiative to aimed at preventing Arafat from establishing his influence in Lebanon. They besieged Palestinian refugee camps at Sabra, Chatila and Bourj el-Barajneh. The Palestinian National Salvation Front (PNSF) later intervened to assist Arafat's supporters.

9 May 1985: Elie Hobeika was elected Commander of the Christian Lebanese Forces (LF); he announced that the militia was ready for cease-fire negotiations with Druze and Shi'ite leaders. He also acknowledged the role of Syria in the creation of a stable Lebanon and announced the withdrawal of LF forces from the Christian enclave at Jezzine.

10 June 1985: The withrawal of IDF forces was officially completed; however some units remained to support the Israeli proxy South Lebanon Army (SLA).

14 June 1985: Two Shi'ite Muslims, allegedly members of Hezbollah (Party of God), hijacked a passenger aircraft flying between Athens and Rome. The hijackers forced the aircraft to fly to Beirut and Algiers twice, releasing some 100 hostages in the process.

17 June 1985: A cease-fire agreement was negotiated between Amal and the Palestinians; however the conditions were not upheld.

17 June 1985: The hijacked aircraft was forced to land in Beirut for a third time; Nabih Berri, the hijackers' spokesman, announced that the remaining passengers, who were mostly US citizens, had been taken to secret locations in the city where they would be detained until 766 Lebanese nationals held in Israeli prisons were released. Israel refused and the US Government threatened to impose sanctions on Lebanon. Following the intervention of President Assad, the prisoners were eventually set free at the end of the month.

July 1985: During talks between 13 spiritual and temporal leaders of the Muslim community in Damascus, a new security plan for west Beirut was proposed; the city was to be divided into five security zones and Muslim militias to withdraw. The plans were disrupted by further fighting.

6 August 1985: In the town of Shtoura, representatives of most of the religious communities formed a pro-Syrian national unity front; the organisation aimed to end the civil war and the sectarian form of government.

September–October 1985: Some 500,000 citizens of Tripoli were forced to flee when fighting between rival militias intensified. A cease-fire was eventually negotiated in Damascus and the Syrian army patrolled the city.

28 December 1985: Following discussions in Damascus, the leaders of the Druze militia and Amal concluded an agreement for the settlement of the civil war. It provided for an immediate cease-fire, an end to the state of civil war within one year and included proposals for a non-sectarian form of Government. However neither Hezbollah nor the Sunni Murabitoun were included in the agreement, the Christians were divided and the problem of the Palestinian refugees and the PLO was not addressed. President Gemayel refused to endorse it.

January 1986: Owing to divisions in the LF over acceptance of the Damascus accord, Elie Hobeika was forced into exile. Samir Geagea was elected as his successor and he demanded an immediate renegotitiation of the Damascus accord. However, sectarian clashes resumed.

14 June 1986: Following fighting between Syrian-supported Amal militia and Palestinian forces, Muslim leaders met in Damascus and agreed to impose a cease-fire in the Palestinian refugee camps around Beirut.

2 September 1986: Following the resumption of peace negotiations between the various factions in the civil war, a new truce was concluded. A new national charter was also drafted, which aimed to end the civil war and form the confessional system of political representation.

November 1986–February 1987: Palestinian refugee camps in Tyre and Sidon were besieged by Amal forces.

February 1987: Syrian 'special forces' were deployed around the camps of Hezbollah militiamen, who aimed to create an Islamic state in Lebanon. In response several hundred Iranian Revolutionary Guards were stationed at Ba'albek in the Beka'a valley.

22 February 1987: Some 4,000 Syrian troops were deployed after Muslim leaders appealed for Syria to intervene following fighting between Amal forces and an alliance of Druze, Murabitoun and Communist Party militias in west Beirut. Syria succeeded in imposing a cease-fire and then moved into areas occupied by Hezbollah, killing 23 Hezbollah members and forcing others to return to their strongholds in the southern suburbs.

6 April 1987: A Syrian-brokered cease-fire was established in the Palestinian refugee camps in Beirut. It was negotiated by representatives of Syria, Amal and the pro-Syrian PNSF.

4 May 1987: Karami and his Government resigned owing to the Cabinet's failure to agree on measures to alleviate the country's acute economic problems.

21 May 1987: The National Assembly voted to abrogate an agreement signed by the Government and Arafat in Cairo in 1969, which had legitimized the PLO's presence in Lebanon.

June 1987: An American journalist, Charles Glass, was abducted in west Beirut, allegedly by Hezbollah; this was the first abduction that had taken place since the Syrian army had assumed responsibility there in February.

1 June 1987: Karami was assassinated; responsibility for the attack was unclear but the Muslim community strongly suspected the Christian section of the divided Lebanese army and the LF. Gemayel subsequently appointed Dr Selim al-Hoss as acting Prime Minister.

5 June 1987: Husain al-Hussaini, the Shi'ite President of the National Assembly, resigned; he had accused Gemayel of attempting to conceal evidence concerning the circumstances of Karami's assassination.

11 September 1987: An agreement was made between Amal and the PLO, lifting the seige of the Palestinian refugee camps and providing for the withdrawal of Palestinian fighters surrounding the Ain al-Hinweh camp, east of Sidon. However, there was renewed fighting in October.

16 January 1988: The leader of Amal, Nabih Berri, announced that his militias would withdraw from the Palestinian refugee camps in Beirut and southern Lebanon.

21 January 1988: Syrian troops replaced Amal militiamen and soldiers of the Sixth Brigade of the Lebanese army in positions around the Beirut camps and the 14-month seige of Rashidiya camp near Tyre was lifted.

April 1988: Syrian forces prevented a Kuwaiti passenger aircraft which had been hijacked by Islamic fundamentalists (allegedly Lebanese citizens) from landing at Beirut airport.

April 1988: Arafat loyalists in the Palestinian refugee camps of Chatila and Bourj al-Barajneh attempted to drive out fighters belonging to the Syrian-backed group, al-Fatah Intifada, led by the PLO dissident Abu Musa. Syrian troops who had surrounded the camps in April 1987 did not attempt to intervene in the fighting but allowed reinforcements to reach the rebel Fatah group.

13 May 1988: Syrian troops became involved in the fighting between Amal and Hezbollah militias when the Hezbollah guerrillas, having taken control of the majority of the southern suburbs, advanced into Syrian-held west Beirut.

27 May 1988: Several hundred Syrian troops moved into the southern suburbs of Beirut to enforce a cease-fire agreement reached by Syria, Iran and their militia proxies on the previous day. After the Syrians troops had been deployed, Amal and Hezbollah were to close down their military operations in all parts of the southern suburbs, except in areas adjoining the 'Green Line'.

3 June 1988: In accordance with the cease-fire agreement, Nabih Berri announced the disbandment of the Amal militia in Beirut and the Beka'a valley and all other areas of the country except the south.

27 June 1988: The Arafat loyalists in the camp at Chatila surrendered to the forces of Abu Musa.

28 June 1988: Syria granted 100 PLO guerrillas safe passage from Chatila to the Palestinian camp at Ain al-Hilweh near Sidon.

7 July 1988: Bourj al-Barajneh, Arafat's last stronghold in Beirut, fell to Abu Musa and 120 Arafat loyalists were evacuated to Ain al-Hilweh.

September 1988: Following the failure of the National Assembly to elect a successor to Gemayel, whose term expired that month, representatives from Syria and the USA held discussions regarding a compromise candidate. It was reported that they had both agreed to support the candidacy of Mikhail ad-Daher, a deputy in the National Assembly; Christian leaders in Lebanon reiterated their rejection of any candidate imposed upon them by foreign powers.

22 September 1988: Minutes before the expiry of his term of office, Gemayel appointed a six-member interm military Government composed of three Christian and three Muslim officers, led by Gen. Michel Awn. The three Muslim officers refused to take up their positions, which were subsequently occupied by Christians.

24 September 1988: Selim al-Hoss withdrew the Government's resignation, which had been tendered by Karami in 1987 and appointed the Greek Orthodox Christian, Abdullah ar-Rassi as Deputy Prime Minister. The Government vied with Gen. Awn's military administration for control of the country.

October 1988: The National Assembly failed to elect a successor to Hussain al-Hussaini, or to renew its one-year mandate.

November 1988: Gen. Awn was dismissed as Commander-in-Chief of the army by the Minister of Defence in al-Hoss's Government, Adel Osseiran.

March 1989: The most violent clashes for two years erupted along the 'Green Line' between the Christian and Muslim brigades of the Lebanese army loyal to General Awn, leader of the interim Military Government, and Syrian-backed Muslim militia.

14 March 1989: Gen. Awn announced that his Government had decided to take all measures to secure the immediate withdrawal of Syrian forces from Lebanon. Fighting continued between his troops and the Syrian-backed militias for the ensuing six months.

19 April 1989: Twenty-three members of the National Assembly demanded an immediate cease-fire and appealed to the Arab League, UN and the European Community (EC—the precursor of the European Union, EU) to intervene to end the fighting. A subsequent cease-fire negotiated at the end of the month by the Arab League was unsuccessful.

May 1989: Fighting between the Christian and Muslim communities intensified.

23–25 May 1989: At an emergency 'summit' meeting of Arab leaders in Casablanca (Morocco), Egypt, Iraq, Jordan and the PLO proposed that Syria should immediately withdraw its troops from Lebanon; Syria rejected the motion.

28 June 1989: A tripartite committee consisting of King Hassan of Morocco, King Fahd of Saudi Arabia and President Chadli of Algeria, issued a peace plan, which involved the removal of blockades of Muslim and Christian ports in Lebanon and the opening of roads between east and west Beirut. The committee also suggested the meeting of the National Assembly in an unspecified foreign country; this proposal was rejected by Gen. Awn.

6 September 1989: The USA evacuated its diplomatic personnel from Beirut.

16 September 1989: The Arab League Tripartite Committee on Lebanon proposed a peace plan for the country.

30 September 1989: The Lebanese National Assembly convened in Ta'if, Saudi Arabia, to discuss the Arab League's peace plan for Lebanon; they voted to endorse the plan in late October.

5 November 1989: René Mouawad was elected President; he was assassinated less than three weeks later.

24 November 1989: Elias Hrawi was elected President, in succession to Mouawad.

25 November 1989: A new Cabinet was appointed, led by Dr Selim al-Hoss.

11 July 1990: The Government initiated a new attempt to implement the 1989 Ta'if agreement.

21 September 1990: President Hrawi signed the amendments to the Lebanese Constitution stipulated by the Ta'if agreement, inaugurating the second Lebanese Republic.

28 September 1990: President Hrawi ordered the blockade of Gen. Awn's headquarters in east Beirut; he subsequently requested Syrian assistance to remove Gen. Awn.

13 October 1990: Gen. Awn was evicted from east Beirut and sought refuge in the French embassy.

24 October 1990: President Hrawi ordered all militias to leave Beirut and relinquish their positions to the Lebanese army.

3 December 1990: The army began to deploy in Beirut in accordance with the 'Greater Beirut Security Plan' contained in the Ta'if agreement.

19 December 1990: Al-Hoss submitted his Government's resignation.

24 December 1990: Omar Karami formed a new Government of National Unity, as stipulated in the Ta'if agreement.

20 March 1991: The Government declared the disbandment of all Lebanese and non-Lebanese militias in the country.

28 March 1991: The Cabinet approved an increase in the number of deputies in the National Assembly from 99 to 108.

30 April 1991: The Government stated its intention to deploy the Lebanese army in the whole of the country by 20 September 1991.

22 May 1991: Lebanon and Syria signed a 'treaty of brotherhood, co-operation and co-ordination'.

7 June 1991: The Cabinet appointed 40 new deputies to the National Assembly.

August 1991: The National Assembly approved an amnesty for crimes committed during the civil war, and permitted Gen. Awn to depart for exile.

10 August 1991: A British national being held hostage in Lebanon, apparently by Islamic Jihad, John McCarthy, was released with a message for the UN Secretary-General from that organization regarding a settlement of the hostage issue.

30 October 1991: The Middle East peace conference commenced in Madrid (Spain), attended by representatives from Egypt, Israel, Lebanon and Syria, in addition to a joint Palestinian-Jordanian delegation.

18 November 1991: Further Western hostages in Lebanon were released by Islamic Jihad.

4 December 1991: The last US hostage in Lebanon was released by Islamic Jihad.

16 February 1992: Sheikh Abbas Moussawi, Secretary-General of Lebanese Hezbollah, was killed in an attack by the Israeli air force.

6 May 1992: The Government resigned; a new administration was formed by Rashid Solh.

23 August 1992: The first regional round of elections to the National Assembly (the first legislative elections in more than 20 years) was held; the second round of ballots took place on 30 August and the third group on 6 September; the overall rate of participation was some 32%.

22 October 1992: Rafik Hariri, a Lebanese-born Saudi Arabian business executive, was appointed Prime Minister; he announced a largely technocratic Government the following week.

16 December 1992: The Israeli Cabinet approved a mass deportation of alleged Palestinian supporters of the Islamic Resistance Movement (Hamas) from Israel to Lebanon.

17 March 1993: The Council for Development and Reconstruction informed the Cabinet of details of its planned reconstruction programme.

25 July 1993: Israeli armed forces initiated intense air and artillery attacks against Hezbollah fighters and Palestinian guerrillas in southern Lebanon.

15 August 1993: Palestinian deportees in southern Lebanon approved an offer by the Israeli Government permitting their staged return to Israel by December 1993.

27 February 1994: Lebanon and Syria withdrew from the Middle East peace process.

23 March 1994: The Lebanese Forces organization was proscribed.

8 May 1994: Hariri withdrew from his official duties; he resumed the premiership following Syrian intervention.

1 June 1994: Israeli forces launched a major attack on a Hezbollah training camp in Lebanon.

2 September 1994: A minor reorganization of the Cabinet was effected.

19 November 1994: The trial on charges of murder of the former LF leader, Samir Geagea, commenced in Beirut.

19 May 1995: Rafik Hariri resigned as Prime Minister, amid disagreements over possible amendments to the Constitution, enabling President Hrawi to serve a second term in the interests of national stability. Following Syrian mediation, Hariri was invited to resume his role and form a new administration.

24 June 1995: Geagea was sentenced to death; however, the sentence was immediately commuted to life imprisonment.

19 October 1995: The National Assembly approved the extension of President Hrawi's term of office by three years.

11 April 1996: Israel launched a campaign of aerial and artillery bombardment of Hezbollah targets in southern Lebanon (known as 'Operation Grapes of Wrath'), with the stated aim of preventing rocket attacks on northern Isaeli towns.

18 April 1996: More than 100 Lebanese civilians were killed in an attack by Israeli armed forces on UN base at Qana; Israel claimed the base had been attacked in error.

27 April 1996: A cease-fire between Israel and Lebanese Hezbollah came into force.

10 July 1996: A new electoral law was adopted; Maronite groups claimed the law discriminated against them; the legislation was subsequently modfied to ensure the disputed provisions applied only to the impending elections.

18 August–16 September 1996: Voting in the legislative elections, again organized in regional rounds, was held; Syrian forces were deployed in the Beka'a valley, prior to the fifth round of voting, which encompassed that area.

7 November 1996: A new Government, led by Hariri, was appointed.

5 December 1996: The Government announced that the first municipal elections since 1963 were to be scheduled for mid-1997.

16 December 1996: The 'Friends of Lebanon' conference was organized in Washington, DC (USA).

22 April 1997: The municipal elections scheduled for mid-1997 were postponed by one year.

30 July 1997: The US Secretary of State, Madeleine Albright, announced the end of a ten-year prohibition on US civilians travelling to Lebanon.

5 September 1997: Twelve Israeli soldiers were killed by Lebanese armed forces while attempting to enter a Lebanese village known to be inhabited by Hezbollah members.

12 November 1997: The Lebanese Government ordered the deployment of troops in the eastern Beka'a valley, in response to a campaign of civil disobedience (the 'revolution of the hungry') orchestrated by Sheikh Sobhi Tufayli, Hezbollah Secretary-General in 1989–91.

30–31 January 1998: At least eight people were killed as a result of a confrontation in the Beka'a valley, between supporters of Sheikh Sobhi Tufayli, recently expelled from Hezbollah, and local Hezbollah officials, and of subsequent army intervention.

1 April 1998: Israel's 'inner' Security Cabinet voted unanimously to accept UN Security Council Resolution 425 (adopted in March 1978) and withdraw from southern Lebanon, conditional upon Lebanese guarantees of the security of Israel's northern border. Lebanon continued to assert that Resolution 425 required an unconditional withdrawal from its territory, and refused to accede to Israel's terms for departure.

24 May 1998: The first of four rounds of voting in Lebanon's first municipal elections since 1963 was held.

15 October 1998: Gen. Emile Lahoud was elected Lebanese President, having received the approval of all 118 deputies present at the National Assembly's ballot.

24 November 1998: President Lahoud took office in Lebanon; Prime Minister Hariri subsequently declined an invitation from Lahoud to form a new government.

2 December 1998: Selim al-Hoss was appointed Prime Minister; he subsequently formed a new, 16-member administration.

18 February 1999: Israeli forces annexed the Lebanese village of Arnoun, on the edge of the Israeli 'security zone'; Arnoun was subsequently liberated by thousands of Lebanese students.

28 February 1999: The Commander of the Israeli army's liaison unit with its client South Lebanon Army (SLA), Brig.-Gen. Erez Gerstein, was killed in a Hezbollah ambush in southern Lebanon—the most senior Israeli officer to be killed there since the 1982 invasion; Israel responded with series of air raids against Hezbollah targets in southern Lebanon.

1–3 June 1999: The Israeli-supported SLA completed unilateral withdrawal from enclave of Jezzine, in the north-east of Lebanon's 'security zone'.

8 June 1999: Four judges were assassinated while conducting the trial of two Palestinians in Sidon.

24–25 June 1999: The outgoing Israeli administration initiated a series of aerial attacks on infrastructure targets in central and southern Lebanon, the heaviest raids since 'Operation Grapes of Wrath' in 1996; at least eight civilians were killed and as many as 70 were injured.

7 February 2000: Israel launched a series of bombing raids on Hezbollah positions and infrastructure targets in Lebanon, in reprisal for the deaths of Israeli military and SLA personnel in assaults at the end of January.

5 March 2000: Israel declared that it would unilaterally withdraw from southern Lebanon by 7 July.

24 May 2000: The accelerated Israeli withdrawal from southern Lebanon was completed, several weeks ahead of the original deadline, after Hezbollah forces and civilian supporters overran positions abandoned by the Israeli proxy SLA.

27 August 2000: Voting in the first round of the general election indicated a decisive rejection of the Government of Selim al-Hoss.

3 September 2000: The second round of voting in Lebanon confirmed the likelihood that Rafik Hariri would form the next Government, following resounding victories by candidates allied to the former premier.

7 October 2000: In protest at the detention of Palestinian and Lebanese prisoners held by the Israeli authorities, Hezbollah guerrillas captured three Israeli soldiers in the disputed Shebaa Farms area near the Syrian border.

11–12 October 2000: The UN Secretary-General, Kofi Annan, visited Beirut in an attempt to negotiate the release of the Israeli soldiers detained at the Shebaa Farms.

23 October 2000: Rafik Hariri was formally appointed Prime Minister.

14 November 2000: The Government rejected a demand from the UN Security Council to take control of the the south of the country, in particular the Shebaa Farms area.

16 November 2000: Hezbollah perpertated a further bomb attack in Shebaa Farms, in which two Israeli soldiers were injured; one soldier was killed and a further two injured in another bomb attack in the area later in the month.

11 December 2000: Syria released 48 Lebanese prisoners who had been captured at the end of the 1975–90 civil war.

30 January 2001: The UN Security Council voted to extend UNIFIL's mandate to the end of July 2001. It was also agreed that the strength of the force was to be reduced from 5,700 to 4,500.

30 January 2001: The Government ordered that an inquiry be carried out into allegations that the Israeli army had employed depleted uranium (DU) during its occupation of southern Lebanon.

5 February 2001: Following criticism from the UN, Israel agreed to demolish a security barrier which it had constructed inside Lebanese territory evacuated by Israeli troops eight months previously.

15 April 2001: Israel carried out air raids on a Syrian air base in eastern Lebanon; three Syrian soldiers were killed.

24 May 2001: The Israeli airforce shot down a Lebanese civilian light aircraft near the Israeli town of Netanya, killing the pilot. Israel claimed that the pilot had failed to respond to warnings; Lebanon accused the Israeli forces of forcing the pilot to fly into Israeli airspace.

14–18 June 2001: Following public protests over Syrian interference in government affairs, Syria withdrew its remaining troops from Beirut.

26 June 2001: Hariri announced that the Government would debate whether to sue Israel for compensation for the damage caused during its occupation of the country.

28 June 2001: The UN envoy to Beirut announced that Israel had agreed to cease military flights over Lebanon; this was later denied by Israel.

29 June 2001: Hezbollah guerrillas fired mortars on Israeli positions in the Shebaa Farms area. Israeli forces retaliated with attacks on the town of Kfor Shouba. The following week, the UN Security Council expressed its concern over the escalating violence in the region.

11 July 2001: The UN admitted that a video reording which showed fake UN vehicles and uniforms believed to have been used by Hezbollah during its kidnapping of Israeli soldiers in October 2000 had been made by a member of UNIFIL. Kofi Annan ruled that an edited version of the recording could be shown to the Israeli Government and ordered an investigation into the handling of the evidence by the UN.

13 July 2001: Following allegations apparently made by an unidentified peace-keeper in an Israeli newspaper, the UN announced a further investigation into whether its troops had collaborated with Hezbollah in the capture of the Israeli soldiers.

16 July 2001: A new political party, the Movement for Democratic Renewal, was formed by a group of Christian and Muslim politicians, led by the Opposition MP, Nassib Lahoud. The movement aimed to end the confessional system of government and combat sectarianism and corruption.

Oman

1st–2nd centuries AD: Following the collapse of the Marib dam in Yemen, the territory constituting modern Oman was invaded by Malik ibn Farhan.

630: Envoys from Medina converted the Arab tribes to Islam; they, in turn, attempted to convert the Persians based at Rostaq. The Persians resisted with force, but were defeated.

705: The region was invaded by the Umayyad governor, al-Hajjaj, in order to crush dissident Shi'a elements, incluidng Kharijites and Ibadites.

749: The Ibadi Imam, al-Julanda bin Ma'ud, was elected.

752: Al-Julanda was killed in battle against the armies of the Abbasid Caliphs.

793: A new Imam, Muhammad bin Abi 'Aflan, was elected.

10th century: Sohar was a major trading port with Omani merchants travelling to India and China.

985–86: The Karmatians, an Ismaili sect, were driven out of Oman.

15th century: The Ibadi community resumed its previous practice of electing Imams.

1507: Afonso de Albuquerque and a fleet of Portuguese ships arrived at Sohar (which, at that time, was under the suzerainty of the King of Hormuz). The Portuguese were able to conquer the region and came to dominate its trade.

1587: The Portuguese built the fort of Merani at Sohar; a fort was built at Muscat the following year.

1617: The Imamate was assumed by Nasir bin Murshid of the Yaariba tribe. His capital was established at Rostaq.

1650: Imam Nasir bin Murshid expelled the Portugese from Muscat and the rest of Oman.

1692–1711: During the Imamate of Saif, Omanis, assisted by their commercial power, expanded their territory significantly, coming to control settlements in India and East Africa.

1698: Oman took control of Mombasa, on the East African coast (now in Kenya).

1718: Upon the death of Saif, a dispute over the succession led to a long-running civil war. The parties enlisted assistance from other nations, most notably the Persians, who were able to establish Saif bin Sultan as Imam.

1730: The Omanis controlled the Portuguese settlements on the east coast of Africa, including Mogadishu, Mombasa and Zanzibar.

1742: Ahmad bin Said, the governor of Suhar, expelled the Persians and gained control of the Omani coast.

1749: Ahmad bin Said was elected Imam and founded the Al Bu Said dynasty.

1786: The capital was transferred from Rostaq to Muscat.

1798: Oman agreed with the British to exlude French warships during the Napoleonic Wars.

1811: Imam Said bin Ahmad died; as no other family was able to command sufficient religious respect, the title of Imam was discontinued, and the Omani rulers from that point used the style of Sultan.

1829: Dhofar became part of the Sultanate of Oman.

1839: The British negotiated with the Sultan Said bin Sultan for the establishment of consular relations; further treaties aimed at protecting British trade routes were signed throughout the 19th century.

1856: Upon the death of Sultan Said bin Sultan, Omani possessions were divided between his sons, Thuwayn assuming control of Oman, Majid receiving the African possessions, based at Zanzibar—Zanzibar subsequently became an independent Sultanate, although it continued to pay a subsidy to Oman until the Sultan was overthrown in January 1964.

1868: A rebellion installed Imam 'Azzan bin Qais as ruler of Oman.

1871: The Said branch of the ruling family was restored to power; however, the historic difficulty of administering the interior from the coast re-emerged.

1876: Following persistent British lobbying, the trade in slaves was abolished.

1891: A non-alienation agreement was signed with the British, confirming their administrative control over Oman.

1913: Upon the death of Sultan Faisal bin Turki, a rebellion in the interior of the country, where Faisal's son, Taimur bin Faisal, was not considered an acceptable successor; a new Imam was elected.

1915: The British army successfully defended Muscat from attacks by the Imam's forces.

1920: The Treaty of al-Sib was reached between the Sultan and the rebels; the Sultan was to administer the coastal regions and the rebels the interior. The agreement allowed for free movement of persons between the interior and the coast, limitations of customs duties and autonomy for tribal groups.

1932: Sultan Said bin Taimur succeeded his father; Omani isolation from the rest of the world grew, as Said rejected modernization of the country.

20 December 1951: A friendship treaty was signed with the United Kingdom, recognizing the independence of the Sultanate of Muscat and Oman.

1952: Saudi forces occupied the oasis of Al-Burayami in Oman, which was believed to be a potential source of petroleum; King Ibn Sa'ud justified this action by stating that the border with Oman had never been formally demarcated.

January 1953: With the assistance of British forces, Oman regained possession of Al-Burayami.

1954: Imam Muhammad bin Abdullah al-Khalili died; a rebellion broke out under his successor, Ghalib bin Ali.

December 1955: The Sultan's forces took control of the principal inhabited areas of the interior without encountering any resistance. The Imam was allowed to stay in his village, although his brother, Talib, fled to Saudi Arabia and then to Cairo (Egypt) where he established an Omani Imamate office.

1957: Talib returned and established a centre of resistance to the Sultan in the mountains north-west of Nizwa. The Sultan appealed for British military assistance.

1963: Rebels based in Dhofar province resisted the control of the Sultan.

24 July 1970: Sultan Said was overthrown by his son, who became Sultan Qabus bin Said.

9 August 1970: The name of the state was changed from Muscat and Oman to Oman.

5 May 1972: The Omani air force attacked border positions of the People's Democratic Republic of Yemen (PDRY).

1973: Iranian troops were sent to Oman to support the Sultan in the ongoing conflict against rebels in Dhofar province. Assistance was also sent from Jordan, Pakistan, Saudi Arabia and the United Arab Emirates (UAE).

1974: The Dhofar rebels became known as the People's Front for the Liberation of Oman (PFLO) and were supported by the PDRY.

April 1975: The emirate of Abu Dhabi, Oman and Saudi Arabia signed a demarcation agreement, which ended the territorial dispute over the Al-Burayami oasis.

December 1975: A new offensive was initiated against the rebels; the Sultan claimed victory.

March 1976: Saudi Arabia acted as intermediary in the negotiation of a cease-fire; an amnesty was offered to all Omanis who had fought with the PFLO.

1977: The United Kingdom's forces withdrew from their military base on the island of Masairah.

January 1977: The greater part of Iranian forces withdrew from Dhofar.

June 1978: A party of British engineers was attacked by rebels near Dhofar.

1979: The Governor of Dhofar was assassinated.

June 1980: A defence pact was signed with the USA on the use of port and air-base facilities in the Persian (Arabian) Gulf, which included the use of the former British base on Masairah.

1981: The USA established a communications centre in Oman.

January 1981: The Omani government closed its border with the PDRY, following that country's disapproval of Oman's agreement with the USA; British officers were seconded to the Omani forces.

May 1981: Bahrain, Kuwait, Oman, Qatar, Saudi Arabia and the United Arab Emirates founded the Co-operation Council for Arab states of the Gulf (Gulf Co-operation Council—GCC) to promote economic and military co-operation in the region.

October 1981: A Consultative Assembly was created in response to suggestions that Sultan Qaboos did not have sufficient access to public opinion.

December 1981: US forces made landings in Oman during the 'Bright Star' military exercises, occasioning protests from the pro-Soviet PDRY. Other Gulf states sought to discourage both countries' links with the 'superpowers'.

October 1982: Following mediation by Kuwait and the UAE, Oman and the PDRY re-established diplomatic relations.

1983: Membership of the Consultative Assembly was expanded from 45 to 55.

July 1983: The GCC (Gulf Cooperation Council) gave Oman a five-year defence grant; the Council conducted military exercises in Oman in October.

September 1985: Oman established diplomatic relations with the USSR.

October 1988: Oman signed a co-operation agreement with the PDRY, in the fields of trade and communications.

March 1989: Oman and Iran set up an economic co-operation committee; Oman stipulated that any such co-operation depended on Iran contributing towards the political stability of the region.

2 January 1990: Changes to the Cabinet were announced.

18 November 1990: Sultan Qaboos announced plans to create a 'Consultative Council' (Majlis ash-Shoura) to replace the Consultative Assembly; the new body, which was to be composed of representatives of the Government and private enterprise, as well as regional representatives approved by the Sultan, was intended to allow 'wider participation' by Omani citizens in ther country's affairs.

5 January 1994: The Council of Ministers was reshuffled.

14 June 1994: The membership of the Majlis was increased from 59 to 80, to allow greater representation of larger towns; in certain regions, women were permitted to be nominated for appointment for the first time—two women were appointed to the enlarged body.

August 1994: An estimated 200 members of an allegedly foreign-sponsored Islamist organization, including two junior ministers, were detained; most were later released, although several were sentenced to death in November, having been found guilty of conspiracy to foment sedition (the Sultan subsequently commuted the sentences to life imprisonment).

November 1995: The Sultan granted a general amnesty to those imprisoned for membership of proscribed organizations.

4–6 December 1995: A GCC 'summit' meeting was held in Muscat.

19 December 1995: The Council of Ministers was reorganized.

2 November 1996: The Deputy Prime Minister for Security and Defence, Faher bin Taimur, died.

6 November 1996: The Sultan issued a decree promulgating the 'Basic Statute of the State', providing for a Council of Oman, to be composed of the Majlis ash-Shoura and a new Majlis ad-Dawlah (Council of State), to be appointed by the Sultan. The Basic Statute also formalized the process of the succession to the throne.

26 May 1997: The Governments of Oman and Yemen signed maps officially demarcating their joint border.

16 October 1997: Elections to select the list of candidates from whom the members of the Majlis would be appointed were held; 164 nominees were elected from amongst 736 candidates—82 of whom were then appointed to the Majlis by Sultan Qaboos.

16 December 1997: The Sultan reorganized the Cabinet, most notably creating a new post, that of Minister of Awqaf (Religious Endowments) and Religious Affairs; on the same day, the Majlis ad-Dawlah (Council of State) was established by royal decree. The Council of Oman was, in turn, inaugurated on 27 December.

2 February 2000: The Government was reorganized; the Ministry of Communications was merged with the Ministry of Housing to becaome the Ministry of Transport and Housing, while the Ministry of Posts, Telegraphs and Telephones was renamed the Ministry of Communications.

14 September 2000: Direct elections to the Majlis ash-Shoura were held for the first time.

15 September 2000: The results of the elections to the Majlis ash-Shoura were announced; government figures placed the participation rate at approximately 90% of eligible voters. Among the 83 new members, selected from among 541 candidates, were two women.

12 October 2000: The Government closed its trade office in Tel Aviv, Israel and the Israeli office in Muscat, in protest at Israel's treatment of the Palestinians.

27 October 2000: It was reported that the Government had prohibited foreign nationals from taking jobs in certain industries as part of its policy to create more jobs for the expanding Omani labour force.

4 November 2000: The Council of Oman convened for a second term.

5 January 2001: The Palestinian leader, Yasser Arafat, visited Oman to brief Sultan Qaboos on the latest round of talks in the Middle East Peace Process.

27 January 2001: The Sultan met the Lebanese Prime Minister, Rafik Hariri, to disuss bilateral relations.

March 2001: It was announced that Oman was to buy 12 military aircraft from the USA.

25 April 2001: The police reported that they had arrested more than 100 illegal immigrants, most of whom were from Afghanistan, Iran, Pakistan, Somalia and Yemen; it was announced that all foreign nationals employed illegally in Oman would be deported if they were unable to provide the appropriate documentation within two months.

9 May 2001: A former minister, Muhammad Bin Musa al-Yousef, was sentenced to six years' imprisonment and fined approximately US $15,000, having been convicted of defrauding the Muscat Securities Market.

15 May 2001: The Sultan effected a government reorganization, in which several ministries were merged; the new ministries created were: the Ministry of Housing, Electricity and Water; the Ministry of Transport and Telecommunications and the Ministry of Regional Municipalities.

22 June 2001: Sultan Qaboos appointed Hamed bin Muhammad bin Mohsin al-Rashidi as the new Minister of Information.

20 July 2001: Three Pakistani men convicted of drugs-trafficking were executed.

Palestinian Autonomous Areas

24 October 1915: Sir Henry McMahon, on behalf of the British Government, declared support for post-war Arab independence in an area possibly including Palestine (then administered by the Ottoman Empire).

February 1916: France, Russia and the United Kingdom signed the Asia Minor Agreement (also known as the 'Sykes-Picot Treaty'), under which Palestine was to be administered as a British, French and Russian condominium.

November 1917: The 'Balfour Declaration', a statement made by the British Foreign Secretary, Arthur Balfour, to Baron Rothschild, leader of the British Jewry, proclaimed the Jordanian Mandate to be within the area to be allocated as a Jewish 'national home' in Palestine.

9 December 1917: Jerusalem was captured from Ottoman forces by the British.

31 October 1918: The entirety of Palestine was taken under British military rule.

July 1920: Palestine became a British Mandated Territory.

24 July 1922: The Council of the League of Nations approved the terms of the British Mandate for Palestine.

September 1922: The British Government promulgated a Constitution providing for a legislative council and the creation of a joint Arab-Jewish Palestinian State. Arab opposition, however, meant that the Constitution did not supersede British direct rule.

22 September 1922: The British Government announced that the Balfour Declaration would not be applied to the area east of the river Jordan, which would be closed to Jewish immigration.

1936: A general strike was observed by the Arab population of Palestine.

April 1936: The Palestinian revolt commenced. An Arab High Committee (AHC) was formed to co-ordinate Palestinian opposition to Jews.

November 1936: A British investigatory commission, the Peel Commission, was despatched to Palestine to study the situation there.

1937: The Palestinian revolt was suppressed by the British, both by use of force and by negotiation with the AHC.

July 1937: The Peel Commission's report declared that co-operation between Arabs and Jews in a Palestinian state would be impossible, and recommended partition.

September 1937: Unofficial representatives of various Arab states, meeting in Bludan, Syria, rejected the recommendations of the Peel Commission.

October 1937: The Palestinian revolt resumed.

May 1939: British Government legislation ('The White Paper') stated that there would be no partition in Palestine, that Jewish immigration and land purchase should cease, and that the British Government did not support the establishment of either an Arab or a Jewish state in the region. Instead, the establishment of an independent Palestinian State, within 10 years, was envisaged. Jewish groups in Palestine opposed the White Paper policy, but abandoned the opposition at the start of the Second World War, in order to present a 'united front' against Germany.

2 April 1947: The United Kingdom referred its Palestinian Mandate to the UN.

15 May 1947: The UN General Assembly voted to create a Special Committee on Palestine (UNSCOP); which subsequently recommended the partition of Palestine.

31 August 1947: The UN General Assembly proposed two plans concerning the future of Palestine: a majority plan for the partition of Palestine into two states, one Jewish and one Arab, with economic union; and a minority plan for a federal state.

29 November 1947: The UN General Assembly adopted the majority plan for Palestine.

14 May 1948: The British Mandate for Palestine was terminated. The State of Israel was officially declared in Palestine by the Jewish authorities; it was granted immediate recognition by the USA and the USSR.

September 1948: An Arab government was formed in Palestine at Gaza under Egyptian tutelage.

1964: The Palestinian Liberation Organization (PLO) was formed to co-ordinate the activities of various Palestinian political and military groups; its activities were initially concentrated in southern Lebanon, where many displaced Palestinians lived in refugee camps and sites for the training of guerrillas had been established.

5 June 1967: A period of military tensions between Israel and its neighbouring Arab countries was ended when Israel attacked the air bases of Jordan, Syria and the UAR. The Arab countries' air forces were severely damaged, and Israel was swiftly able to capture territory from each of the Arab combatants (notably the West Bank and Old Jerusalem from Jordan, the Golan Heights from Syria and the Sinai peninsula from the UAR).

22 November 1967: The UN Security Council adopted Resolution 242, which urged the withdrawal of Israeli forces from the Occupied Territories, the acknowledgement by all countries in the region of the others' sovereignty, a solution to the problem of Palestinian refugees and advocated a negotiated settlement to the region's disputes. The Resolution became the basis of international efforts to agree a settlement to the Israeli-Palestinian question.

1968: Yasser Arafat, the leader of the al-Fatah movement, became Chairman of the PLO.

21 August 1969: Fire caused severe damage to the Al-Aqsa Mosque in Jerusalem.

9 August 1970: The Central Committee for Palestinian Resistance announced its rejection of American peace proposals for the Middle East.

6–13 September 1970: Four Western passenger airliners were hijacked by Palestinian groups; the aircraft were flown to Cairo and northern Jordan, where the passengers were removed and the aircraft destroyed in explosions; the passengers were subsequently released in exchange for the freedom from detention of Palestinian commandos held in Western countries.

16–27 September 1970: Exceptionally fierce fighting between the army and Palestinian commandos led to an agreement being signed by King Hussein and the leader of the PLO, Yasser Arafat; despite the signature of a further accord in October, the Civil War in Jordan continued.

13 February 1973: Abu Daoud and other Palestinian guerrillas were arrested for subversive activities in Jordan.

October 1974: At a 'summit' meeting of the Arab League in Rabat, Morocco, the members' resolution to unanimously resolved to recognize the PLO as the sole legitimate representative of Palestinians, with the right to establish national authority over any liberated Palestinian territory, King Hussein was reported to have supported the resolution with reluctance.

16 March 1977: The US President, Jimmy Carter, stated publicly that the establishment of a 'homeland' for Palestinian refugees was imperative.

20 March 1977: The Palestine National Council (PNC) adopted a 15-point policy programme that sought, among other things, to establish an 'independent national state on national soil'.

26 August 1977: The Central Council of the PLO repeated its rejection of UN Security Council Resolution 242 as a basis for negotiations with Israel.

12 September 1977: The US stated publicly, for the first time, that a settlement of the Palestinian question was vital to the success of a renewed Geneva Middle East peace conference.

1 October 1977: The USA and USSR issued a joint statement which emphasized that any Middle East peace settlement should guarantee 'the legitimate rights of the Palestinian people'.

6–8 July 1979: Dr Bruno Kreisky, the Federal Chancellor of Austria, became the first western European head of government to receive Arafat formally.

21 August 1982: The evacuation of some 15,000 Palestinian and Syrian troops trapped in west Beirut by the Israeli army commenced.

1 September 1982: The evacuation of Palestinian forces from West Beirut was completed. The US President, Ronald Reagan, announced new proposals (the 'Reagan Plan') for achieving a Middle East peace settlement, that envisaged self-determination for West Bank and Gaza Palestinians within a polity linked to Jordan.

15 September 1982: Israeli armed forces occupied positions around Palestinian refugee camps in Muslim areas of west Beirut.

17 September 1982: Palestinian refugees at the Sabra and Chatila camps were massacred, apparently by Lebanese Phalangists.

10–13 October 1982: Arafat and King Hussein of Jordan agreed to explore the concept of federation between the Jordan and a Palestinian entity.

28 August–7 September 1983: The 'International Conference on the Question of Palestine' was organized by the UN in Geneva.

20 December 1983: Pro-Arafat Fatah forces besieged in the Lebanese city of Tripoli by rebel factions since November were evacuated.

22 November 1984: At the 17th session of the Palestine National Council, King Hussein of Jordan proposed that the PLO and Jordan should pursue a peace initiative based on UN Security Council Resolution 242 of 1967.

23 February 1985: King Hussein and Arafat announced the co-operation of the Government and the PLO in a joint peace initiative. It was agreed that any peace proposals should be discussed by the five permanent member countries of the UN Security Council and all parties concerned in the conflict. The Palestinian people would exercise the right to self-determination in the context of a proposed confederate state of Jordan and Palestine.

March 1985: President Muhammad Hosni Mubarak of Egypt proposed negotiations between Egypt, the USA and a joint Jordanian-Palestinian delegation; the PLO rejected the proposal, however, claiming that it deviated from its accord with Jordan.

1 October 1985: Israeli aircraft bombarded the PLO headquarters in Tunis, Tunisia.

19 February 1986: Following Arafat's refusal to accept resolutions of the UN Security Council as the foundation for peace negotiations, King Hussein suspended relations with the PLO and repudiated the Amman agreement.

19 February 1986: King Hussein formally severed political links with the PLO.

20–25 April 1987: The PNC expressed support, at its 18th session in Algiers, Algeria, for 'the convening of an international conference under UN auspice, to be attended by the five permanent members of the Security Council and the parties to the conflict in the region, including the PLO on equal footing with the other parties'.

9 December 1987: Amid increasing Palestinian anger at Israel's continued occupation of the West Bank and Gaza Strip, and frustration with Jordanian policy, the Palestinian *intifada* (uprising) began in those territories.

22 December 1987: The UN Security Council adopted Resolution 605, condemning Israel's violent methods of suppressing Palestinian demonstrations.

16 April 1988: Khalil al-Wazir, the PLO deputy leader and commander of the Palestine Liberation Army (PLA), was assassinated by Israeli agents in Tunis.

15 November 1988: The PLO declared an independent Palestinian State and endorsed UN Security Council Resolutions 242 and 338, thereby implicitly recognizing Israel's right to exist.

14 December 1988: Arafat presented a three-point peace initiative to the UN General Assembly.

2–3 May 1989: Arafat made a visit to France, during which he declared the PLO's National Charter to be 'obsolete'.

3–9 August 1989: The fifth Congress of Fatah, the largest PLO faction, endorsed a 'dual-state' solution to the Arab-Israeli conflict, as favoured by Arafat.

11 April 1990: Jewish settlers occupied the St John's Hospice in Jerusalem.

20 May 1990: Widespread rioting occurred in the Gaza Strip, following the murder of a number of Palestinian civilians by an Israeli civilian.

21 May 1990: The PLO urged the USA to defend the Palestinian people.

25–26 May 1990: The UN Security Council convened in Geneva to discuss the Palestinian question.

30 May 1990: The Palestine Liberation Front launched a seaborne attack on Israeli beaches.

20 June 1990: The USA suspended its dialogue with the PLO.

24 October 1990: Israel banned all movement in or out of the Occupied Territories amid increasing tension between Jewish and Arab communities.

6 March 1991: The US President, George Bush, identified the resolution of the Arab-Israeli conflict as one of his administration's principal aims in the period following the Iraqi conflict.

16 April 1991: The first new Israeli settlement in the West Bank for two years was established.

23 September 1991: Arafat stated the PLO's commitment to the success of the proposed regional Middle East peace conference.

29 September 1991: The PNC approved Palestinian participation in the proposed regional Middle East peace conference.

19–22 October 1991: A conference was held in Tehran to rally support for Palestinians opposed to a 'compromise' peace settlement with Israel.

30 October 1991: The Middle East peace conference commenced in Madrid (Spain), attended by representatives from Egypt, Israel, Lebanon and Syria, in addition to a joint Palestinian-Jordanian delegation.

16 December 1992: The Israeli Cabinet approved a mass deportation of alleged Palestinian supporters of the Islamic Resistance Movement (Hamas) from Israel to Lebanon.

11–12 January 1993: The foreign ministers of the Arab League member states met in Cairo to discuss the deportation of Palestinians from Israel to Lebanon.

28 January 1993: The Israeli High Court ruled that deportation of Palestinians to Lebanon in December 1992 had been lawful; the following week the Government offered to allow 101 of the deportees to return.

11 April 1993: Israel announced the indefinite 'closure' of the Occupied Territories.

25 July 1993: Israeli armed forces initiated intense air and artillery attacks against Hezbollah fighters and Palestinian guerrillas in southern Lebanon.

15 August 1993: Palestinian deportees in southern Lebanon approved an offer by the Israeli Government permitting their staged return to Israel by December 1993.

30 August 1993: A secretly negotiated draft peace agreement between Israel and the PLO was announced; the negotiations had taken place in the Norwegian capital, Oslo.

13 September 1993: The Declaration of Principles on Palestinian Self-Rule in the Occupied Territories (known informally as the Oslo Agreement) was signed by Israel and the PLO in Washington, DC. Israel and the PLO formally recognized each other.

12 October 1993: The PLO Central Council approved the Declaration of Principles signed with Israel in September.

13 October 1993: Israeli and Palestinian negotiators commenced talks in Taba, Egypt.

24 November 1993: Imad Akel, a commander of Qassem (the military wing of Hamas), was shot dead by Israeli forces.

10 December 1993: Hanan Ashrawi resigned as spokeswoman of the Palestinian delegation to the Middle East peace talks.

13 December 1993: By this date, Israeli forces should have begun to withdraw from the Gaza Strip and the Jericho area under the terms of the Declaration of Principles on Palestinian Self-Rule; however, a failure to agree on security arrangements for border crossings led to the process being delayed.

25 February 1994: The PLO and other Arab delegations withdrew from the Middle East peace negotiations, following the murder of some 30 worshippers at a mosque in Hebron by an Israeli civilian.

18 March 1994: The UN Security Council adopted a Resolution condemning the killings in Hebron.

29 April 1994: Israel and the PLO signed an economic agreement, concerning the relations between Israel and the autonomous Palestinian entity in the five-year period prior to self-rule.

4 May 1994: Israel and the PLO signed an agreement providing for Palestinian Self-Rule in the Gaza Strip and Jericho; Israel was to withdraw its forces from the areas, and a Palestinian National Authority (PNA) would assume the powers of the Israeli military governments (with the exceptions of external security and foreign affairs). Elections to the Palestinian National Council (PNC), which had been sceduled to take place in July, were postponed until October.

13 May 1994: The Israeli armed forces completed their withdrawal from the Gaza Strip.

26–28 May 1994: The newly-appointed PNA met for first time in Tunis.

26 June 1994: The PNA met in Gaza for the first time.

1 July 1994: Arafat arrived in the Gaza Strip.

7 September 1994: The PNA signed a loan agreement with World Bank.

20 October 1994: Following an attack in Tel-Aviv by a suicide bomber representing Hamas, Israel temporarily closed its borders with the West Bank and Gaza Strip.

18 November 1994: Twelve people were killed in clashes between Palestinian police and supporters of Hamas and Islamic Jihad in Gaza.

12 February 1995: The US-based organization Human Rights Watch published a report which criticized the policies of the PNA.

1 September 1995: The Libyan leader, Col Muammar al-Qaddafi, announced the expulsion from Libya of 30,000 Palestinians.

28 September 1995: The Israeli-Palestinian Interim Peace Agreement on the West Bank and Gaza Strip was signed; the accord (known informally as the Taba Agreement or 'Oslo II') provided for elections to an 82-member Palestinian Council, and for a Palestinian Executive President, in addition to the progressive withdrawal of Israeli forces from West Bank towns and the release of Palestinian prisoners.

11 October 1995: The first Palestinian prisoners to be released under the Second Israeli-Palestinian Interim Peace Agreement were freed.

25 October 1995: The PNA took control of the West Bank town of Jenin; Israeli forces completed their withdrawal from the town in November, and from five other towns in December.

25 October 1995: Libya suspended expulsions of Palestinian refugees.

5 January 1996: Yahya Ayyash, a leading figure in the Hamas movement, was killed in Gaza; the group alleged that Israeli agents were responsible.

20 January 1996: Palestinian presidential and legislative elections took place. In the Presidential election, Arafat received 88.1% of the votes cast and was duly elected; Fatah won 54 of the 88 elective seats in the Palestinian Legislative Council (PLC—one seat was reserved for the President, *ex officio*).

7 March 1996: The inaugural session of the PLC opened in Gaza City.

24 April 1996: The PNC voted in favour of amending the Palestinian Covenant and elected a new Executive Committee.

5–6 May 1996: Israeli and Palestinian delegations commenced 'final status' negotiations.

9 May 1996: The Palestinian Cabinet was announced.

29 May 1996: Binyamin Netanyahu, the leader of the conservative Likud party, was elected Prime Minister of Israel.

2 August 1996: Israel relaxed restrictions on the expansion of Jewish settlements in the West Bank and Gaza Strip.

29 August 1996: A Palestinian general strike was organized in the West Bank and Gaza Strip.

25 September 1996: Violent disturbances occurred in the West Bank and Gaza Strip after the Israeli Government opened a tunnel close to al-Aqsa mosque.

2 October 1996: The European Union pledged to continue financial support of Palestinian authorities.

25 October 1996: President Chirac of France became first foreign head of state to address the PLC.

14 January 1997: Libya formally revoked the expulsion order affecting Palestinian refugees.

16 February 1997: The Israeli Minister of Foreign Affairs, David Levy, and the chief Palestinian negotiator, Mahmoud Abbas, attended the first session of renewed bilateral negotiations.

26 February 1997: The construction of 6,500 new homes for Jewish settlers at Har Homa, in East Jerusalem, was approved; despite condemnation of the decision by Palestinian groups and Arab governments, construction commenced in March.

7 March 1997: A UN Security Council Resolution to halt the Har Homa development in East Jerusalem was vetoed by the USA.

7 March 1997: The PNA rejected the Israeli government interpretation of the terms agreed for future troop deployment in the Occupied Territories.

18 March 1997: Construction of new Jewish homes at Har Homa, East Jerusalem, commenced.

21 March 1997: A proposed UN Security Council Resolution to halt the Har Homa development was vetoed by the USA for a second time.

21 March 1997: A suicide-bomb attack carried out in Tel-Aviv by a member of Hamas resulted in the deaths of three Israelis and injuries to at least 40 others; Israel closed the West Bank and Gaza Strip in response.

29 April 1997: The Israeli Government announced that it would allow 55,000 Palestinian workers to enter Israel from 30 April.

6 May 1997: The PNA announced new legislation sentencing to death Palestinians found guilty of selling land to Jewish settlers.

27 May 1997: The PNA audit office announced that US $326m. of Palestinian funds had been misappropriated by PNA ministers.

5 June 1997: Arafat established a parliamentary committee to investigate the misappropriation of PNA funds; Khalid al-Quidram resigned as General Prosecutor.

22 July 1997: Levy and Arafat met in Brussels, Belgium, for preliminary discussions concerning the peace process.

28 July 1997: Israeli and Palestinian officials announced that peace talks were to be resumed in early August.

29 July 1997: The PLC urged Arafat to dissolve his Cabinet following further investigation of the misappropriation of state funds.

30 July 1997: An attack by two Palestinian suicide bombers resulted in the deaths of 14 Israelis in Jerusalem; in response Israel closed the West Bank and Gaza Strip and withheld the payment of some US $50m. in tax revenues owed to the PNA.

1 August 1997: Sixteen members of the PNA's Cabinet reportedly offered their resignations after a parliamentary report implicated them in a corruption investigation.

1 September 1997: The West Bank and Gaza Strip were reopened by Israel.

14 September 1997: The Israeli Government released 50% of the PNA funds withheld since 30 July and relaxed restrictions on the movement of Palestinians in the Occupied Territories.

15 September 1997: Netanyahu vetoed an Israeli housing project in East Jerusalem which had been anticipated to cause disruption to the peace process.

25 September 1997: The leader of the Palestinian Hamas group, Khalid Meshaal, was the subject of a failed assassination attempt by Israeli agents in Amman; diplomatic activity to preserve cordial relations between Israel and Jordan ensued.

1 October 1997: A number of Arab prisoners, including Sheikh Ahmad Yassin—one of the founders of Hamas, were released from Israeli prisons, reportedly in exchange for the return of two Israeli secret-service agents who had been detained in Jordan following the attempted assassination of Hamas bureau chief, Meshaal.

8 October 1997: Arafat and Netanyahu had their first direct discussions for eight months at the Erez check-point between Israel and the Gaza Strip.

30 November 1997: The Israeli Cabinet agreed, in principle, to a partial withdrawal from the West Bank, but did not agree the timing or scale of such a withdrawal; the Government also undertook to create a team of Ministers to decide which areas of the West Bank should be permanently retained by Israel.

20 January 1998: During a visit to the USA Netanyahu held talks with US President Clinton, at which he reportedly rejected US proposals for a second-stage redeployment of forces from 10%–15% of West Bank territory, proposing instead redeployment from no more than 9.5% of the territory.

31 January 1998: The US Secretary of State, Madeleine Albright, visited the Middle East region and held talks with Netanyahu and Arafat, the effort failed to restart the peace process.

15–18 March 1998: The British Secretary of State for Foreign and Commonwealth Affairs, Robin Cook, visited the Middle East on a tour intended to raise the profile of the EU in the peace process. During his time in the region, Cook made a controversial visit to the Har Homa settlement.

29 March 1998: The discovery in the West Bank of the body of Muhiad-Din Sharif, a leader of the armed wing of Hamas, led to fears of reprisal attacks against Israel; however, Hamas members were later arrested for the murder, which was reportedly the result of an internal power struggle.

16–21 April 1998: The British Prime Minister, Tony Blair, undertook a tour of the Middle East region during which he invited Arafat and Netanyahu, to attend a 'summit' for peace in the British capital, London, in early May. During his visit Blair signed an EU-Palestinian security agreement.

27 April 1998: The PNA Minister of Awqaf (Religious Endowments), Hassan Tahboob, died.

4–5 May 1998: The US Secretary of State, Madeleine Albright, held separate talks with Netanyahu and Arafat, in London. No significant progress was made and although both parties were invited to Washington, DC, for further talks, Netanyahu declined to attend since the talks were made conditional on Israeli support for a US plan for a 13.1% redeployment in the West Bank.

26 May 1998: Serious clashes erupted in East Jerusalem after a Jewish settler organization began construction work on a religious settlement on disputed territory in the Arab quarter of the city.

21 June 1998: The Israeli Cabinet approved a draft plan to widen Jerusalem's municipal boundaries; the decision was condemned by the Palestinians, the Arab states and the international community.

24 June 1998: Arafat accepted the resignation of his Cabinet (10 months after parliament had first demanded it).

7 July 1998: The UN voted to upgrade the status of the PLO at the UN, despite objections from the Israel and the USA, to allow the organization greater participation.

19–22 July 1998: Israeli and Palestinian negotiators held their first direct peace talks for some 16 months; however, the talks failed to secure agreement on redeployment.

5 August 1998: Arafat announced a cabinet reshuffle within the PNA. Members of the legislature who had demanded the dismissal of key ministers for corruption and mismanagement were extremely critical of the reshuffle in which only one prominent cabinet member was removed from the Government. An additional 10 ministers were appointed, bringing the total to 28.

6 August 1998: Hanan Ashrawi, the Minister of Higher Education, and Abd al-Jawad Saleh, Minister of State (and formerly Minister of Agriculture) resigned from the newly formed Palestinian Cabinet, stating that the recent reshuffle had failed to address the internal problems of the PNA.

28 September 1998: At a US-mediated meeting in Washington, DC, the Israeli and Palestinian leaders agreed to attend a tripartite peace 'summit' in the USA in mid-October 1998; in an address to the UN General Assembly, Netanyahu had previously stated that a unilateral declaration of an independent Palestinian state would occasion the end of the peace process.

15 October 1998: US-brokered talks between Netanyahu and Arafat opened in the Wye Plantation, Maryland, USA.

23 October 1998: Following nine days of negotiations Arafat and Netanyahu signed the Wye River Memorandum in the presence of President Clinton and King Hussein; the agreement outlined a three-month timetable for the implemetation of the 1995 Interim Agreement and facilitated the beginning of the 'final status' talks. The Wye River Memorandum was the first development in Israeli-Palestinian relations for some 19 months.

20 November 1998: Israel implemented the first stage of troop redeployment from the West Bank and released 250 Palestinian prisoners, as agreed under the Wye River Memorandum.

24 November 1998: Arafat formally opened Gaza International Airport.

12–15 December 1998: President Clinton visited the Palestinian territories; violent clashes between Palestinian demonstrators and Israeli security forces in the West Bank and Gaza preceded the visit.

14 December 1998: The PLC reconfirmed, in a session attended by President Clinton, the deletion of those articles of the Palestinian National Charter (PLO Covenant) deemed to be anti-Israeli.

15 December 1998: A 'summit' meeting was held between President Clinton, Netanyahu and Arafat at the Erez check-point; Netanyahu announced that Israel would not proceed with the second troop redeployment prescribed by the Wye River Memorandum—Arafat demanded that no further Jewish settlements be constructed in disputed territory and refused to exclude the possibility of a unilateral declaration of Palestinian statehood.

29 April 1999: The PLO Central Council announced the postponement of any unilateral declaration of Palestinian statehood until after the Israeli general election; violent protests against the decision occurred in the West Bank, Gaza and East Jerusalem.

4 May 1999: The 'Oslo interim period', as outlined in the Interim Agreement signed by Israel and the PNA on 28 September 1995, ended.

17 May 1999: Ehud Barak, of the LAbour Party, won the Israeli prime-ministerial election.

3 June 1999: Palestinians in the West Bank declared a 'day of rage' against the continuing expansion of Israeli settlements.

1 August 1999: Talks between Israeli and Palestinian delegations collapsed after Arafat rejected Barak's proposal to delay implementation of the Wye River Memorandum and to combine further Israeli troop withdrawals from the West Bank with 'final status' negotiations.

25 August 1999: Security forces closed the offices of Hamas in Amman; Meshaal's home was raided and a number of leading Hamas activists arrested.

4 September 1999: Israel and the PNA signed the 'Wye Two' agreement in the Egyptian resort of Sharm esh-Sheikh, detailing a revised timetable for outstanding provisions of the original Wye River Memorandum.

9 September 1999: Israel released 199 Palestinian prisoners, as agreed under 'Wye Two'.

10 September 1999: Israel transferred a further 7% of West Bank territory to Palestinian self-rule.

22 September 1999: Three Hamas leaders, including Khalid Meshaal, were detained by Jordanian security forces on their arrival at Amman airport; they faced charges of organizing illegal political activities and involvement in terrorism.

2 November 1999: Barak and Arafat held discussions in Oslo, while attending a ceremony marking the fourth anniversary of the assassination of Itzhak Rabin.

8 November 1999: Israeli and Palestinian negotiators began negotiations on 'final status' issues in the West Bank town of Ramallah.

21 December 1999: Arafat and Barak met for talks in Ramallah—the first occasion on which an Israeli premier had attended peace talks in Palestinian-controlled territory.

17 January 2000: At a meeting in Tel-Aviv between Barak and Arafat, the Israeli premier required flexibility in respect of deadlines for troop redeployments and for reaching agreement on 'final status' issues.

3 February 2000: Talks in Gaza between Arafat and Barak ended in acrimony, following disagreement over the third Israeli troop redeployment.

13 February 2000: The deadline expired for agreement on a framework agreement on permanent status (FAPS) by Israel and the PNA, as stipulated in the 1999 Sharm esh-Sheikh agreement.

9 March 2000: Meeting at Sharm esh-Sheikh for talks hosted by President Hosni Mubarak, Arafat and Barak agreed a formula for the resumption of peace talks.

20–26 March 2000: Pope John Paul II undertook a millennium pilgrimage to the Christian 'Holy Land', including visits to Israel, Jordan and the Palestinian self-rule areas.

7 May 2000: Arafat and Barak met in Ramallah for 'crisis' talks, mediated by US special envoy Dennis Ross, ahead of the impending expiry of the extended deadline of 13 May for agreement on FAPS.

15–18 May 2000: A Palestinian 'day of rage', declared in commemoration of the 52nd anniversary of the declaration of the State of Israel, resulted in violent confrontations with Israeli security forces throughout the West Bank and Gaza; at least six Palestinians were killed, and several hundred injured.

11–25 July 2000: Arafat and Barak attended a peace meeting at Camp David, Maryland, USA, in the presence of President Clinton; negotiations failed to achieve agreement on the issue of the status of Jerusalem.

6 September 2000: President Clinton held separate meetings with Arafat and Barak in New York, where the leaders were to attend the UN 'millennium summit'.

10 September 2000: Following a two-day meeting in Gaza, the PNC adopted a recommendation by Arafat to delay the unilateral declaration of a Palestinian state on 13 September, upon the expiry of the deadline for the conclusion of permanent status negotiations.

19 September 2000: Israel cancelled a scheduled round of talks with Palestinian negotiators in Jerusalem, citing the Palestinians' failure to resolve the impasse in the peace process.

25 September 2000: Barak and Arafat met at the Israeli premier's home for their first peace talks since the Camp David 'summit' in July, amid reported preparations by negotiators from both sides for further talks in the USA.

28 September 2000: The Israeli Likud Party leader, Ariel Sharon, visited the disputed sacred site known as Temple Mount by the Jews and Haram ash-Sharif by Muslims; this provoked violent protests throughout the West Bank and the Gaza Strip.

6 October 2000: Israeli police stormed the compound of the al-Aqsa mosque in Jerusalem in order to apprehend a group of Palestinian youths who had attacked them several hours previously; the action provoked violent protests among Palestinians and Israeli Arabs throughout the country and was condemned by the international community.

7 October 2000: Barak announced that Arafat must suppress the violence in East Jerusalem, Gaza and the West Bank—which had become known as the Al-Aqsa *intifada*—within 48 hours, otherwise the armed forces would intensify offensives on Palestinian targets. The UN Security Council issued a Resolution condemning Israel's excessive use of force against Palestinians.

9 October 2000: The Iraqi Government called for a *jihad* (holy war) to liberate Palestine and announced that it would donate US $5m. to the cause.

12 October 2000: The Israeli armed forces responded to the killing of two Israeli soldiers by launching rocket attacks on the headquarters of Arafat's Fatah movement.

12 October 2000: Israel criticised the Palestinian authorities for releasing significant numbers of Hamas prisoners. On the same day, Palestinian demonstrators stormed a police station in Ramallah and killed two members of the Israeli security forces detained there; the Israelis subsequently launched a rocket attack on the building.

16–17 October 2000: At a UN-mediated summit meeting led by President Clinton in Sharm esh-Sheikh, Israel agreed with the Palestinians to end the violence, and establish a mission to investigate its causes, to end the closure of Palestinian-controlled areas and redeploy troops stationed there and to reopen Gaza airport. Barak also demanded that Arafat re-arrest 65 Islamic militants whom the PNA had freed earlier in the month.

18 October 2000: Barak and Arafat met to discuss the implementation of the peace agreement; the following day Israeli troops began to withdraw from their positions in the West Bank and Gaza. The Karni border crossing to the Gaza Strip was also reopened after its closure during unrest two weeks previously.

22 October 2000: Israel announced that it was taking a formal pause from the peace process owing to renewed Palestinian violence; Israeli troops had shot dead nine Palestinians since the implementation of the ceasefire agreement.

26 October 2000: Islamic Jihad carried out a suicide bomb attack on an Israeli security post in Gaza.

29 October 2000: Israel sent tanks and armoured vehicles into the Gaza Strip to open the road to the Jewish settlement of Netzarim; one Palestinian was killed and several others wounded in the operation.

1 November 2000: Shimon Peres, the Israeli Minister of Regional Co-operation, held crisis talks with Arafat in Gaza; truce agreements made at the meeting collapsed the following day when two Israelis were killed in a car bomb attack perpertrated by Islamic Jihad.

15 November 2000: A report by the UN High Commissioner for Human Rights, Mary Robinson, expressed concerns regarding the deterioration of human rights in the Palestinian territories and recommended that international monitors be installed.

17 November 2000: The Israeli Government imposed an economic blockade of the West Bank and Gaza.

20 November 2000: A bomb exploded near an Israeli school bus in the Gaza Strip, killing two adults and injuring a further nine adults and children. In retaliation, the Israeli forces shelled the Palestinian security forces and the Fatah party buildings, killing four Fatah officials.

29 November 2000: Russia mediated a further round of peace talks between the Israelis and Palestinians. Barak announced that Israel would withdraw its armed forces from the West Bank, on the condition that the PNA would agree to postpone any discussion of remaining 'final status' issues; this was rejected by the PNA.

7 December 2000: A court in Nablus convicted a man of collaborating with the Israeli secret services in the assassination of a Hamas commander and sentenced him to death. Later in the month, two more alleged collaborators were assassinated.

11 December 2000: An inquiry was begun into the recent violence by an international delegation, led by a former US Senator, George Mitchell.

27 December 2000: US-mediated peace talks collapsed following further explosions in the Gaza Strip and Tel-Aviv. President Clinton was believed to have proposed the creation of a Palestinian state, including the Gaza Strip and 95% of the West Bank, on the condition that the PNA relinquish their demand that Palestinian refugees be allowed to return to the areas they left in 1948. The plan was rejected by the Palestinians.

30 December 2000: The Democratic Front for the Liberation of Palestine (DFLP), called on Arafat to issue weapons to all Palestinians, following the wounding of one of its leaders in an Israeli gun attack.

31 December 2000: The leader of the extremist Jewish settler movement Kahane Chai, Binyamin Kahane, was shot dead. On the same day, a senior Fatah official was killed in the West Bank.

31 December 2000: Israeli forces shot five Palestinians, including a 10 year-old boy. The Palestinians retaliated with three bomb attacks in the Israeli town of Netanya, injuring more than 40 people.

5–16 January 2001: US-mediated talks resumed, however, they ended shortly after the killing of a Jewish settler in the Gaza Strip; revenge attacks by Jewish settler extremists on Palestinians ensued.

18 January 2001: The Chairman of Palestinian Satellite Television and the director of the state broadcasting corporation, Hisham Mekki, was assassinated by an unidentified gunman in Gaza. The al-Aqsa Martyrs Brigade claimed responsibility for the attack.

21 January 2001: Peace talks took place in Taba, Egypt; proceedings were soon suspended, however, after Israeli civilians were killed in a gun attack in the West Bank, for which Hamas later claimed responsibility.

21 January 2001: The Israeli Government announced that it would boycott the inquiry into the recent violence, led by former US Senator George Mitchell, after the commission visited al-Haram al-Sharif without permission from the Israeli authorities. The commission was subsequently suspended.

6 February 2001: There were violent demonstrations in the West Bank and Gaza following the election of Ariel Sharon as Prime Minister in Israel; it was widely believed that he was responsible for the massacre of Palestinian refugees in Lebanese camps in 1982 and it was his visit to Temple Mount/Haram ash-Sharif that was widely held responsible among Palestinians for the unrest in 2000–01.

19–20 March 2001: As Sharon visited Washington, DC, for talks with the newly inaugurated US President, George W. Bush, Palestinian guerrillas shot dead a Jewish settler on the West Bank; in Gaza, Israeli troops injured a Palestinian spokeswoman, Dr Hanan Ashwari, and four children.

24 April 2001: The Israeli authorities closed off all access to and from the West Bank and the Gaza Strip, ostensibly to protect Israel from potential Palestinian attacks during independence celebrations.

28–29 April 2001: The Israeli Minister of Foreign Affairs, Shimon Peres, held discussions with President Mubarak of Egypt regarding a joint Egyptian-Jordanian peace plan; the proposals suggested that the Israelis and Palestinians should maintain a month-long truce followed by talks on a future peace deal. At the conclusion of the talks, Peres announced that the border restrictions on the Palestinian territories would be relaxed.

10 May 2001: The Israeli armed forces carried out missile attacks on the headquarters of the Palestinian police buildings and the Fatah headquarters in Gaza city.

16 May 2001: Israeli helicopter gunships carried out further attacks on security-force buildings, killing 12 Palestinian police officers.

16 May 2001: The Secretary-General of the PLO, Mahoud Abbas, met the US Secretary of State, Colin Powell. During talks regarding the peace process, Abbas asked the US Government to formally endorse the findings of Mitchell's inquiry.

19 May 2001: Following a suicide-bomb attack on an Israeli shopping centre by Islamic militants, the Israelis launched rocket attacks on the towns of Tulkarm and Jenin, in which three people were wounded.

21 May 2001: The Israelis carried out air raids on what it believed to be a Palestinian mortar factory in Jabilya, outside Gaza city. Israeli tanks also moved into the town of Qarara.

22 May 2001: The report of the international inquiry into the causes of the recent Arab-Israeli violence was published; the Mitchell Report emphasized that Jewish settlement expansion was the main obstacle to peace and recommended that it be halted; it also called for an immediate cease-fire in preparation for peace negotiations. In a change of policy, the Israeli Government refused to halt Jewish settlement programmes but declared a unilateral cease-fire.

26 May 2001: At an emergency meeting of the foreign ministers of the Organisation of the Islamic Conference, Arafat accused the UN Security Council of failing to protect the Palestinians.

27 May 2001: As the UN envoy to the region, William Burns, held discussions with Israeli and Palestinian leaders, two bomb attacks were carried out in Jerusalem by the Popular Front for the Liberation of Palestine.

1 June 2001: A total of 18 Israelis were killed and over 100 others were injured during a Palestinian suicide-bomb attack on a night-club in Tel-Aviv. Arafat denounced the attack and advocated an immediate cease-fire; numerous armed Palestinian groups rejected the demand.

12 June 2001: The Israeli Goverment made a cease-fire agreement with the Palestinians, which was to come into effect the following day, in a series of meetings mediated by the US Central Intelligence Agency Director, George Tenet. The Israeli defence minister anounced that the blockade of Palestinian towns would cease and that the armed forces would be deployed.

2 July 2001: Following Israeli air-raids on Hamas targets, during which three Palestinians were killed, Islamic militants detonated two car bombs in the town of Yehud, near Tel Aviv.

4 July 2001: The Israeli Government gave the army permission to use more force against the Palestinians, effectively ending the cease-fire.

10 July 2001: Israeli security forces demolished 17 Palestinian houses in the Gaza Strip; a gun battle between the Palestinians and security forces ensued.

29 July 2001: Palestinians attempted to stop a group of messianic Jews from placing a symbolic cornerstone in the Temple Mount/Haram ash-Sharif complex; police stormed the al-Aqsa mosque to end the violence and several Israelis and Palestinians were injured. The Palestinians dispersed after the intervention of the Israeli Arab politician, Ahmed Tibi.

Qatar

late 7th century AD: The Islamic religion spread to the peninsula comprising modern Qatar, which was largely inhabited by sea-faring tribes, with some nomadic groups in the interior. The area eventually became part of the Arab Caliphate.

8th century: Qatar began to benefit from its commercially strategic position in the Persian (Arabian) Gulf.

1507: Portuguese commercial vessels, which had begun to conduct trade in East Africa and India, were supported in the Persian (Arabian) Gulf area by military vessels—Portugal took control of much of north-eastern Arabia.

17th century: Forces of the Shah of Persia expelled the Portuguese from the coast of the Persian (Arabian) Gulf. A struggle for dominance of trade in the Gulf took place between the British and Portuguese merchants; the British, with Persian support, eventually prevailed. Urban centres began to emerge at Zubarah and at Doha.

18th century: Wahhabi Islam, a sect urging more rigorous adherence to Islamic principles, gained popularity among the tribes of Arabia, including Qatar, where a major family, the ath-Thani, embraced Wahhabism.

1760s: The al-Khalifa dynasty moved from Kuwait to north-eastern Arabia.

1776–1779: Merchants fleeing the Persian occupation of Basra (now Iraq) settled in Zubarah, making it the centre of the Gulf's pearl trade.

1783: A Persian attack on Zubarah was defeated. The al-Khalifa invaded Bahrain.

1810–1811: Abdallah bin Ufaysan, a Wahhabi, governed Bahrain, Qatar and Qatif.

1811: Sultan Said of Oman defeated the Wahhabis, who withdrew from Bahrain, enabling the al-Khalifa to return to power.

1867: Bahrain and Abu Dhabi launched a joint attack on Doha; the city was destroyed.

1868: Muhammad bin Thani signed an agreement with the British which established his dominance in the partially rebuilt Doha.

1871: A Turkish deputation persuaded the ath-Thani to acknowledge Ottoman rule; the peninsula formally became part of the Ottoman Empire the following year.

1872: The Ottomans landed troops and guns to pacify Wahhabi elements, and used Qatar as a base for raids.

1890–1913: Doha and, increasingly, the remainder of the peninsula was governed by Sheikh Qasim ath-Thani.

1893: An Ottoman attack on Doha was repelled by Sheikh Qasim.

1913: A Wahhabi resurgence resulted in a decline in Ottoman power over Qatar. In the same year, Sheikh Qasim died, and was succeeded by his son, Sheikh Abdullah ath-Thani.

1914: Ottoman forces evacuated Qatar.

1916: The United Kingdom recognized Sheikh Abdullah ath-Thani as the legitimate ruler of Qatar; the two countries signed a treaty, by which Qatar undertook not to enter into any political arrangements with powers other than the United Kingdom and agreed not to trade in slaves or commit acts of piracy, in exchange for British protection in case of aggression against Qatar from land or sea.

1934: A further treaty was signed with the British, extending their protection of Qatar.

1939: Petroleum was discovered on Qatari territory; Sheikh Abdullah occupied Zubarah.

July 1939: The dispute between Bahrain and Qatar over sovereignity of the Hawar islands was settled in favour of Bahrain by the United Kingdom.

1949: Sheikh Abdullah died and was succeeded by his son, Shiekh Ali ath-Thani. The production of petroleum on a commercial scale began. Saudi Arabia made a territorial claim on land in southern Qatar.

24 October 1960: Sheikh Ali ath-Thani abdicated in favour of his son, Sheikh Ahmad ath-Thani.

1961: Qatar joined the Organization of Petroleum Exporting Countries (OPEC).

1968: Qatar joined Bahrain and the Trucial States to form the Federation of Arab Emirates in preparation for British withdrawal from the administration of the region.

14 February 1971: A new, five-year agreement was signed by 23 international petroleum companies and the governments of Abu Dhabi, Iran, Iraq, Kuwait, Qatar and Saudi Arabia.

1 September 1971: Following the failure of negotiations for union among the member states of the Federation of Arab Emirates upon British withdrawal, the Federation was dissolved and Qatar became fully independent.

22 February 1972: A bloodless *coup d'état* in Qatar deposed the Amir, Sheikh Ahmad; his cousin, Sheikh Khalifa, assumed power.

5 October 1972: Agreement was reached between Abu Dhabi, Iraq, Kuwait, Qatar and Saudi Arabia for one part, and representatives of various petroleum companies for the other, on the eventual 51% participation of the producing countries in the various concessions.

1975: The membership of the Advisory Council, whose members were selected with limited suffrage, was increased from 20 to 30.

May 1981: Bahrain, Kuwait, Oman, Qatar, Saudi Arabia and the United Arab Emirates founded the Co-operation Council for Arab states of the Gulf (Gulf Co-operation Council—GCC) to promote economic and military co-operation in the region.

1982: Qatar signed a bilateral defence agreement with Saudi Arabia.

October 1983: Qatari forces participated in the GCC 'Peninsula Shield' military exercises.

April 1986: Qatar raided the artificially constructed island of Fasht al-Dibal, near the disputed Hawar islands, and seized the 29 foreign workers who were constructing a Bahrain coast-guard station on the island.

May 1986: After mediation by fellow-members of the GCC Qatar released the workers and the Bahraini and Qatari governments agreed to destroy the island which had been created on an coral reef in the Gulf.

1988: The membership of the Advisory Council was increased to 35.

May 1989: The Supreme Council for Planning was formed to co-ordinate plans for the country's social and economic development under the direction of the heir apparent, Sheikh Hamad bin Khalifa ath-Thani.

July 1989: There was a government reorganization, in which five new portfolios were created and 11 new ministers appointed.

1991: Qatari forces participated in the campaign to liberate Kuwait, following the Iraqi invasion.

July 1991: Qatar instigated proceedings at the International Court of Justice (ICJ) regarding the disputed Hawar islands, awarded to Bahrain by the British in 1939.

September 1992: Qatar accused Saudi Arabia of attacking a Qatari border post, killing two border guards and capturing a third. Relations were consequently strained—Saudi Arabia claimed the incident occurred as a result of fighting between Bedouin tribes. Following mediation by Kuwait, the guard was released and relations improved.

1 September 1992: A new Government was appointed.

20 December 1992: Qatar and Saudi Arabia agreed to establish a committee to delineate their disputed border by 1994.

March 1995: Qatar agreed to permit US forces to station military equipment on its territory—this was the latest of a series of defence agreements signed in the 1990s, most notably with the United Kingdom and the USA.

27 June 1995: The Amir, Sheikh Khalifa, was deposed in a bloodless *coup d'état* by his son, Sheikh Hamid bin Kahlifa ath-Thani.

11 July 1995: A new Council of Ministers was announced; Sheikh Hamad assumed the role of Prime Minister.

20 February 1996: An attempted *coup d'état* was reported to have failed; the following year, relations with Egypt were strained, when the Qatari Minister of Foreign Affairs suggested potential Egyptian involvement in the coup. Following Saudi Arabian mediation, the situation improved.

July 1996: Legal proceedings were instituted by the Government against the former Amir, Sheikh Khalifa, who was alleged to have retained control over some US $3,000m.—$8,000m. in state assets following his removal from power. In October it was reported that the Amir and his father had been reconciled and a settlement reached.

30 October 1996: The Council of Ministers was reshuffled; the Amir's younger brother, Sheikh Abdullah bin Khalifa ath-Thani, was appointed Prime Minister (he retained the post of Minister of the Interior).

16–18 November 1997: The Fourth Middle East and North Africa (MENA) economic conference was convened in Doha, Qatar; the event was the subject of a wide-spread Arab boycott, owing to the participation of an Israeli delegation.

19 December 1997: Draft legislation granting universal suffrage was presented.

20 January 1998: The Cabinet was reorganized.

21 July 1998: Plans for elected municipal councils were approved; women were to be granted the vote in these elections.

8 October 1998: The Minister of Municipal Affairs and Agriculture resigned.

13 January 1999: In a government reorganization, three new ministries were created.

8 March 1999: Elections to the Municipal Council were held under full adult suffrage.

22 June 1999: Two new ministers were appointed.

13 July 1999: A Constitutional Committee, charged with drafting a permanent Constitution by 2002, was approved.

21 November 1999: Jordan expelled Khalid Meshaal and other senior members of the guerrilla group Hamas to Qatar.

January 2000: The Amir of Bahrain visited Qatar. The two countries agreed to open embassies in each other's capitals.

September 2000: A meeting took place between the Amir of Qatar and the Israeli Prime Minister Ehud Barak; other Arab states deplored Qatar.

22 October 2000: Morocco and Qatar restored diplomatic relations; they had been terminated when Qatar had supported Germany's bid to hold the 2006 football World Cup competition rather than Morocco's.

9 November 2000: The Government announced the closure of the Israeli trade mission, following threats from Iran and Saudi Arabia to boycott a forthcoming meeting of the Organization of the Islamic Conference (OIC) in Doha.

12 November 2000: An OIC 'summit' meeting took place in Doha; delegates discussed the recent escalation in violence between the Palestinians and Israelis and were urged to withdraw diplomatic ties with Israel.

2 January 2001: The Minister of State for Interior Affairs, Sheikh Abdullah bin Khalid ath-Thani, was promoted to the office of Minister of the Interior; the post had previously been held by the Prime Minister.

16 March 2001: The ICJ confirmed Bahrain's sovereignty over the Hawar Islands, and Qatar's over Zubarah and the Fasht ad-Dibal reefs. Both Bahrain and Qatar agreed to abide by the verdict; the Amir of Bahrain claimed that the judgement was a significant victory for his country. The two countries subsequently agreed to resume the activities of the Bahrain-Qatar Supreme Joint Committee, and the construction of a causeway linking Bahrain with the Arabian mainland in Qatar was scheduled to commence later in 2001.

21 March 2001: The Minister of Foreign Affairs, Sheikh Hamad bin Jasim bin Jaber ath-Thani, signed an agreement with his Saudi counterpart, Prince Sa'ud al-Faisal, settling a border dispute which had lasted 35 years.

7–8 April 2001: The Amir met senior officials of the Afghan Taliban regime; the visiting delegates expressed their need for policital recognition and humanitarian aid.

13 May 2001: Dr Fidel Castro Ruz, the Cuban leader, held talks with the Amir on improving bilateral relations in the areas of economy, health and science.

21 May 2001: An appeal court sentenced 19 people to death for their role in the abortive *coup d'état* in 1996; the decision overruled life sentences imposed by a lower court in February. A further 20 people, 14 of whom had originally been acquitted, were also sentenced to life imprisonment.

14–30 June 2001: The Jordanian authorities detained a Qatar Airways aircraft carrying the exiled Hamas activist, Ibrahim Gosheh, at Amman airport. Gosheh was denied entry to Jordan and the aircraft refused permission to leave unless Gosheh was on board. The Palestinian activist was eventually granted entry to Jordan; Qatari Airways subsequently announced that it would take legal action against the Jordanian Government for its conduct during the incident.

Saudi Arabia

6th century BC: The Hedjaz region on the Red Sea coast of the Arabian peninsula was developed by the Chaldean civilization as a summer administrative centre.

5th century BC: The Hedjaz town of Mecca became dominated by the Quraish tribe.

4th century BC: The Minaean kingdom evolved to become an important trading civilization; establishing trade routes across the interior of the Arabian peninsula.

1st century AD: The Nabateans took control of the Hedjaz and founded the commercial centre of Mada'in Salih.

2nd century: The Minaean kingdom was conquered by the Sabaeans.

400: The Persian and Roman Empires encouraged Arab tribes to harass the borders of each other's territories.

570: The Prophet Muhammad bin 'Abdullah was born into a noble family in Mecca.

613: Muhammad began to preach the Islamic faith, most notably denouncing the polytheism of the Quraish religions.

618: Several followers of Muhammad were attacked by city authorities in Mecca. The Prophet subsequently sent his followers to Ethiopia to be protected by the Christian king there.

622: Muhammad left Mecca for the town of Yathrib (Medina); this event became known as the *hijra* (emigration) and was subsequently used to mark the beginning of the Islamic calendar.

630: Muhammad returned to Mecca and took control of the city and its territory; Mecca and Medina were established as the holy cities of Islam.

632: Muhammad died; Abu Bakr, who had accompanied him on the *hijra*, was appointed his successor, or Caliph. The *riddah* (apostasy wars), in which rival prophets and their followers challenged Bakr's authority, followed.

May 633: Musaylimah, Abu Bakr's strongest opponent, was killed at the Battle of Agraba. This severely weakened the opposition and by the following year, the Caliphate regained control over most of its territory.

634–44: During the reign of the Caliph Omar, the Arabians invaded Egypt, Palestine, Persia and Syria.

644–56: Caliph Uthman oversaw the production of the official text of the Koran, the sacred book of Islam, as revealed to Muhammad.

656: Uthman was assassinated and the succession was again disputed. In 661 the Umayyads, led by Mu'awiya, established a hereditary line of caliphs in Damascus (Syria).

8th century: The codification of Islamic law (*Shari'a*) took place in Medina.

750: The Abbasids overthrew the Umayyads and ruled the Islamic Empire from Baghdad (now in Iraq).

mid-10th century: Mecca replaced Medina as the capital of the state of Hedjaz in western Arabia.

1181–82: The French knight Reynaud de Châtillon raided the Red Sea coast. The Ayyubid sultan Salah ad-Din (Saladin) destroyed his vessels before he reached Mecca.

1269: The Hedjaz came under nominal rule of the Egyptian Mamluks.

mid-15th century: The Sa'ud dynasty was founded by Muhammad ibn Sa'ud, who ruled the area surrounding the town of Diriyah.

1517: The Ottoman Turks gained control of Arabia when they conquered Egypt but were unable to extend their authority to the interior.

early 16th century: The Portuguese were active in the Indian Ocean and the Red Sea. They blockaded Indian trade routes to Europe via the Persian (Arabian) Gulf and Red Sea, which caused severe damage to the economies of the Arabian states.

18th century: British, Dutch and French merchant adventurers were active in the Persian (Arabian) Gulf.

1703: The theologian Muhammad ibn Abd al-Wahhab was born in Uyaynah.

1744: Wahhab and Muhammad ibn Sa'ud took an oath to work together to establish a state organized according to Islamic principles.

1745: Wahhab began to teach fundamental Islamic principles in Diriyah.

1765: Sa'udi political authority and Wahhabism were established over most of the Najd region.

1801: Sa'udi-Wahhabi troops attacked Karbala, a Shi'ite shrine in eastern Iraq.

1802: Mecca was captured by the Sa'udi-Wahhabi army; the following year Sunni towns in the Hedjaz also fell to Sa'udi control. Muhammad ibn Sa'ud was assassinated by Shi'ite activists in revenge for the attack on Karbala.

1804: The Sa'udis captured Medina from the Ottomans.

1812: An Egyptian force commanded by Tusun landed on the Hedjaz coast.

1815: The Egyptians captured Ar-Ra's in Al-Qasim; Abd Allah ibn Sa'ud negotiated a cease-fire which lasted until 1816.

1818: The Saudi army was overpowered at Diriyah; Abd Allah was captured by the Egyptians and sent to the Ottoman capital, İstanbul (in modern Turkey), where he was subsequently beheaded; the remaining members of the Sa'ud family were imprisoned in Egypt.

1824: Turki ibn Abd Allah, a grandson of Muhammad ibn Sa'ud, captured Riyadh; he established the town as a capital and from there began to re-conquer the land the Sa'udis had lost.

1834: Turki was murdered by a cousin, who, in turn, was deposed and executed by Turki's son, Faisal.

1838: The Egyptians captured Faisal and detained him in Cairo (Egypt), following his refusal to recognise their rule. Khalid, the brother of Abd Allah was installed as the ruler of Najd by the Egyptians.

1841: Abd Allah ibn Thunayan led a revolt against the rule of Khalid, who was forced to flee to Jeddah.

1843: Faisal killed Thunayan and regained control of Riyadh.

1865: Faisal died; there followed a dispute among his sons over the succession.

1870: Civil war broke erupted among Faisal's sons and their supporters. Abd Allah (the eldest son) appealed to the Ottomans in Baghdad, who subsequently occupied the province of Al-Hasa.

1871: Abd Allah was defeated at the battle of Judah by his younger brother, Sa'ud, who became Sa'ud II.

1875: Sa'ud died and further conflict over the succession ensued; Abd Allah eventually returned to the throne in 1876.

1887: The Emir of Jabal Shammar, ibn Rashid, brought Abd Allah to his court at Ha'il and installed his own governor in Riyadh.

1889: Abd Allah died; his younger brother, Abd ar-Rahman, succeeded to the throne.

1891: Abd ar-Rahman attempted to rebel against the rule of the Rashidis but was defeated at the battle of Al-Mulaida. Rahman took refuge with the rulers of Kuwait.

15 January 1902: Rahman's son, Abd al-Aziz led an army estimated to number 200 in a surprise attack on the Rashidi regime in Riyadh; he defeated the Rashidis and was welcomed by the citizens as their new ruler.

1905: Najd fell to the Sa'udi forces and Abd al-Aziz , who subsequently became known as Ibn Sa'ud, was recognized as an Ottoman client in the region.

1906: Ibn Rashid was killed in battle and Ottoman presence in central Arabia was diminished.

1912: A Wahhabi Ikhwan (brethren) colony, dedicated to the Islamic faith and the Sa'ud family, was established by Ibn Sa'ud among some Bedouin tribes. As more of these colonies were established, the Bedouin renounced their nomadic way of life and began to practise agriculture.

1913: Sa'udi forces took the province of Al-Hasa from the Ottomans, although the following year, Ibn Sa'ud was forced to reaffirm Ottoman sovereignty over all his territory.

June 1916: With British support, Sharif Hussein of Mecca declared war on the Ottomans (the British and Ottomans were in conflict during the First World War); by November he was able to proclaim himself King of the Hedjaz.

July 1917: The Arab army captured the port of Aqaba from the Ottomans, which left Medina as the only Ottoman stronghold in Arabia.

1919: The Ikhwan inflicted a heavy defeat on Sharif Hussein's forces in the Hedjaz.

1920: Faisal, the son of Ibn Sa'ud, captured the province of Asir.

1921: The Sa'udi forces defeated the last Rashidi emir, Muhammad ibn Talal, and occupied most of northern Arabia; Ibn Sa'ud adopted the title of Sultan of Najd. In response, the British Government placed the sons of Sharif Hussein, Faisal and Abdullah, on the thrones of Iraq and Transjordan.

May 1922: The border between Iraq and Saudi Arabia was defined in the Treaty of Mohammara; subsequent Saudi concerns over the loss of traditional grazing rights led to the establishment of 7,000 sq km of neutral territory near Kuwait.

1923: Frequent border incidents between the Arabian states and Iraq and Transjordan led the British to organize a conference for the respective leaders to resolve the disputes; no such resolution was achieved.

5 March 1924: Following the deposition of the Ottoman sultan, Sharif Hussein claimed the title of the Caliph; this was challenged by Ibn Sa'ud and received little international recognition.

September 1924: Ibn Sa'ud's Wahhabi army attacked the Hedjaz and successfully captured At-Taif and Mecca, forcing Sharif Hussein to abdicate. Sa'ud's sons also laid seige to Jeddah and Medina, which fell in 1925.

8 January 1926: Ibn Sa'ud was proclaimed King of the Hedjaz in the Great Mosque in Mecca.

1927: Ibn Sa'ud changed his title of Sultan to King of Najd and its dependencies; in an agreement made at Jeddah, the British recognized the independence of the Sa'udi territories in return for Sa'ud's acceptance of Sharif Hussein's sons, Faisal and Abdullah, as the rulers of Iraq and Transjordan, and the special status of the British-protected sheikhdoms on the coast of the Persian (Arabian) Gulf.

1928: Two Ikhwan leaders, Faisal ad-Dawish and Sultan ibn Bijad, led a rebellion against Ibn Sa'ud, whose efforts to unite his newly-acquired territories and centralize power, they claimed, compromised Wahhabi practices.

1930: The rebels were captured by the British in Kuwait, who transferred them to the authority of Ibn Sa'ud.

18 September 1932: The kingdoms of Najd and Hedjaz were officially united to form the Kingdom of Saudi Arabia.

1933: The King announced that his son, Sa'ud ibn Abd al-Aziz, would succeed him upon his death.

1934: A dispute arose with Yemen over the countries' mutual border and Yemen's assistance of an Asiri prince in a revolt against Ibn Sa'ud. Following a seven-week campaign, Saudi Arabia took control of the disputed district of At-Ta'if.

1936: Diplomatic relations were renewed with Egypt; they had been terminated in 1926 owing to an incident during the *Hajj* (the pilgrimage made by Muslims to Mecca).

1945: In spite of having at declared its neutrality at the outbreak of the Second World War in 1939, Saudi Arabia declared war on Germany, following the receipt of subsidies from the United Kingdom and the USA.

March 1945: Egypt, Iraq, Lebanon, Saudi Arabia, Syria, Transjordan and Yemen founded the League of Arab States (Arab League), which aimed to promote political, cultural, economic and social co-operation between its members and act as mediator in regional disputes.

October 1945: As the exploitation of petroleum reserves developed, and new reserves were discovered, a petroleum refinery was opened at Ras Tanura.

1947: Work commenced on the Trans-Arabian pipeline (Tapline), which was to connect the Arabian oilfields with the Mediterannean ports of Lebanon.

1948: Saudi Arabia sent one battalion to assist the Palestinians in the Arab-Israeli war.

1949: The Government announced a Four-Year Plan of industrial and economic development for Saudi Arabia, with a budget of US $270m.; the principal objective of the Plan was the construction of a railway network.

2 December 1950: The first Saudi Arabian petroleum emerged from the Tapline at the Lebanese port of Sidon. The Government negotiated an agreement with the Arab-American Oil Company (Aramco), by which it received 50% of the company's net income.

1951: The USA agreed to loan the Government US $15m. and the two countries signed a mutual assistance pact.

1952: Saudi forces occupied the oasis of Al-Burayami in Oman, which was believed to be a potential source of petroleum; King Ibn Sa'ud justified this action by stating that the border with Oman had never been formally demarcated.

January 1953: With the assistance of British forces, Oman regained possession of Al-Burayami.

9 November 1953: King Ibn Sa'ud died; Crown Prince Sa'ud ibn al-Aziz, who had been appointed Prime Minister the previous month, succeeded him—his brother, Faisal ibn Abd al-Aziz, was appointed Crown Prince and Prime Minister.

October 1955: The Government signed a mutual defence pact with Egypt and Syria; this agreement was joined by Jordan and Yemen a year later.

1956: The state-owned National Oil Company was established to exploit petroleum reserves in areas not covered by Aramco's concession. In the same year, a strike by Saudi Aramco workers took place; King Sa'ud issued a royal decree forbidding further strikes on the penalty of dismissal.

November 1956: King Sa'ud terminated diplomatic relations with France and the United Kingdom and granted Egypt US $10m. in assistance, following British and French military action on the Sinai peninsula, owing to Egypt's nationalization of the Suez Canal in July.

January 1957: At a meeting with the US President, Dwight D. Eisenhower, Sa'ud expressed his support for the 'Eisenhower Doctrine', which promised US aid to any Middle Eastern country threatened by communism. The US Air Force's lease on the Dhahran air base was subsequently renewed for a further five years.

January 1958: The Saudi currency, the riyal, was devalued by nearly 80%, osensibly owing to the increasing cost of maintaining the King's palace guard.

March 1958: In order to strengthen the machinery of Government, King Sa'ud increased Faisal's powers over internal, foreign and economic affairs.

3 March 1958: President Gamal Abd an-Nasser of the United Arab Republic (UAR), which had been formed by Egypt and Syria in February, accused King Sa'ud of financing a military conspiracy to assassinate him; Sa'ud denied the allegations and relations with the UAR were severely strained.

11 January 1959: The statute of the Arab Development Bank was signed by Jordan, Lebanon, Libya, Saudi Arabia, the UAR and Yemen.

21 December 1960: Crown Prince Faisal resigned as Prime Minister; King Sa'ud assumed the premiership himself.

25 July 1961: King Sa'ud formed a National Defence Council.

6 November 1962: Saudi Arabia severed diplomatic relations with the UAR; tensions between the two countries had continued to increase, and had further deteriorated since 1961, when Saudi Arabia supported Syria's secession from the union.

24 March 1963: Aramco concluded a settlement with th Saudi authorities, involving the return to Saudi control of 64% of the concession territory.

March 1964: Diplomatic relations between Saudi Arabia and Egypt were restored.

28 March 1964: King Sa'ud relinquished all active personal authority to Crown Prince Faisal, who had again acted as Prime Minister since mid-1963.

2 November 1964: King Sa'ud, whose health had deteriorated significantly, was forced to abdicate; Crown Prince Faisal was proclaimed King, and retained the role of premier.

March 1965: King Faisal appointed his half-brother, Khalid ibn Abd al-Aziz, to the position of Crown Prince.

24 August 1965: King Faisal and President Nasser agreed proposals aimed at settling the conflict in Yemen.

27–28 January 1967: The UAR air force bombarded the Saudi town of Najran.

August 1967: Saudi Arabia, whose forces had assisted the Arab combatants in the so-called 'Six-Day' war against Israel in June, agreed to provide £50m. to a fund aimed at restoring the economic strength of Jordan and the UAR, following their defeat in the conflict.

24 October 1968: Iran and Saudi Arabia signed an agreement delineating territorial claims in the Persian (Arabian) Gulf.

5 September 1969: Arrests were made in Saudi Arabia following reports of an abortive *coup d'état.*

25 November–3 December 1969: Armed conflict took place on the border between Saudi Arabia and the YR.

23–26 March 1970: Islamic countries' foreign ministers met in Jeddah and decided to establish a permanent secretariat. Saudi Arabian and Yemen representatives also met there.

14 February 1971: A new, five-year agreement was signed by 23 international petroleum companies and the governments of Abu Dhabi, Iran, Iraq, Kuwait, Qatar and Saudi Arabia.

2 April 1971: An agreement was reached in Tripoli between international petroleum companies and the Libyan Government (which was also acting on behalf of Algeria, Iraq and Saudi Arabia); the posted price for Libyan crude petroleum was increased by US $0.90.

1–8 May 1971: The US Secretary of State, William Rogers, visited Israel, Jordan, Lebanon, Saudi Arabia and the UAR to discuss plans for reopening the Suez Canal, which had been closed since the Six-Day War.

5 October 1972: Agreement was reached between Abu Dhabi, Iraq, Kuwait, Qatar and Saudi Arabia for one part, and representatives of various petroleum companies for the other, on the eventual 51% participation of the producing countries in the various concessions.

1973: The Government negotiated direct ownership of one-quarter of Aramco.

September 1973: Armed Arab terrorists attacked the Saudi Arabian embassy in Paris and took five hostages to Kuwait, where they subsequently surrendered. The Kuwaiti authorities transferred the terrorists to the Palestine Liberation Organization (PLO), who had condemned the incident.

October 1973: Conflict resumed between Israel and its Arab neighbours; the Government sent a small number of troops to aid the Arabs. The Organization of Petroleum Exporting Countries (OPEC) reduced its supplies to the Western supporters of Israel and the price of crude petroleum on Western markets increased four-fold.

November 1973: At a conference of Arab leaders in the Algerian capital, Algiers, all participants, except Jordan, recognized the PLO as the legitimate representatives of the Palestinian people.

March 1974: Following the defeat of the Arab states in their conflict with Israel, Saudi Arabia (estimated to control one-quarter of the world's petroleum reserves) urged fellow OPEC members to resume supplies of petroleum to Israel's Western allies, apparently threatening to leave OPEC and lower prices unilaterally in order to achieve this aim.

March 1974: Abu Dhabi, Algeria, Bahrain, Egypt, Kuwait and Saudi Arabia agreed to lift the embargo on petroleum supplies to the USA imposed following US support for Israel the previous year; shipments to the Netherlands were resumed in July.

May 1974: The Government signed an economic and military co-operation agreement with the USA.

October 1974: King Hussein of Jordan agreed to the proposal that the PLO should be the negotiators with Israel over the establishment of a Palestinian entity, in return for an annual grant of US $300m. from Saudi Arabia over the next four years.

25 March 1975: Faisal was assassinated by his nephew, Prince Faisal ibn Masaed ibn Abd al-Aziz. Crown Prince Khalid immediately acceeded to the throne and assumed the office of Prime Minister.

April 1975: The emirate of Abu Dhabi, Oman and Saudi Arabia signed a demarcation agreement, which ended the territorial dispute over the Al-Burayami oasis.

7 October 1975: In a cabinet reorganization, Crown Prince Fahd was appointed First Deputy Prime Minister and Abd Allah, his half-brother, Second Deputy Prime Minister.

March 1976: Diplomatic relations were established with the People's Democratic Republic of Yemen (PDRY); in return for a Saudi loan, the PDRY was also to cease its support of the People's Front for the Liberation of Oman.

April 1976: Khalid made official visits to all the Gulf states to promote closer relations between Saudi Arabia and its neighbours.

18 October 1976: At the conclusion of a series of meetings in Riyadh and following the direct appeal of the Government, Syria, Lebanon and the PLO agreed to a ceasefire and peace plan to resolve the civil war in Lebanon.

December 1976: At an OPEC conference in Qatar, jointly with the United Arab Emirates, Saudi Arabia restricted the increase in the price of petroleum to 5%, rather than the 10% sought by other members.

November 1977: The Government expressed its support for the initiative for peace with Israel proposed by the Egyptian President, Anwar Sadat.

3 January 1978: At a meeting with the US President, Jimmy Carter, in Riyadh, King Khalid declared that the Arab-Israeli question could only be resolved by a complete Israeli withdrawal from occupied territories and resettlement rights for Palestinians; the two leaders also discussed increasing Soviet influence on the two Yemeni states.

14 February 1978: The US Government announced that it was to sell Saudi Arabia several fighter aircraft to help maintain peace in the region.

April 1979: The Government suspended diplomatic relations with Egypt following its signature of the 'Camp David' peace agreement with Israel; Saudi participation in an arms-manufacturing consortium with Egypt was supended in July.

20 November 1979: Some 250 armed 'purist' dissidents, led by Juhaiman ibn Seif al-Otabi seized and occupied the Grand Mosque at Mecca and attempted to force the congregation to recognize Muhammad ibn Abdullah al-Qatami as the Mahdi ('Guided One'—an Islamic prophet whose coming is held to be a precursor of the end of time). The seige lasted two weeks, although most of the congregation, estimated to number 50,000, were released earlier. The Council of the Ulema—

the country's most senior religious authority—issued a special dispensation for the security forces to use force to end the seige. In the operation to relieve the Mosque, 102 of the insurgents (including al-Qatami), some 100 soldiers and 27 civilians were killed; al-Otaibi was one of 63 rebels subsequently executed.

December 1979: Shi'a riots took place in Al-Qatif in support of the Islamic Revolution in Iran. Some 20,000 national guard troops were mobilized in the area.

February 1980: In response to further Shi'a demonstrations, the Minister of the Interior, Amir Ahmad ibn Abd al-Aziz, announced plans to improve the standard of living in Shi'a communities.

March 1980: Amid increasing criticism of the opulence and privilege enjoyed by the extended royal family, a committee led by Prince Nayef was appointed to draft a 200-article 'system of rule' based on Islamic principles; a consultative assembly was intended to act as an advisory body but was not inaugurated until 1993.

September 1980: Tensions between Iran and Iraq escalated into war; Saudi Arabia and Kuwait supported Iraq by donating its Government the proceeds of the sale of 310,000 barrels per day of petroleum through the Arabian Oil Co, as compensation for lost export capacity.

November 1980: Khalid announced the release of 100 of the Shi'a demonstrators.

January 1981: The Government hosted a meeting of the Organization of the Islamic Conference (OIC), which was attended by 38 Muslim heads of state.

March 1981: The USA agreed to sell the Government five airborne warning and control systems (AWACS) aircraft.

May 1981: Bahrain, Kuwait, Oman, Qatar, Saudi Arabia and the United Arab Emirates founded the Co-operation Council for Arab states of the Gulf (Gulf Co-operation Council—GCC) to promote economic and military co-operation in the region.

August 1981: Crown Prince Fahd announced the 'Fahd Plan', which had been drawn up by the Government as a solution to the Arab-Israeli question; the document recieved little support from the Arab states owing to its apparent recognition of the legitimacy of Israel.

November 1982: The GCC made preparations for the co-ordination of defences and agreed to establish a Rapid Defence Force.

3 June 1983: Khalid died suddenly; Crown Prince Fahd became King and Prime Minister and appointed his half-brother Abdullah ibn Abd al-Aziz Crown Prince and First Deputy Prime Minister.

February 1984: Crown Prince Abdullah expressed his support for the Syrian position in the Lebanese conflict and demanded the withdrawal of US troops from the region.

April 1984: A Saudi Arabian tanker loading at the Iranian Kharg island petroleum terminal was struck by missiles from an Iraq fighter aircraft. The following month, the Iranians retaliated by striking two more tankers, one of which was sailing in Saudi waters.

February 1985: The Government announced the 'Peace Shield' programme, which aimed to provide the country's air defences with computerized command, control and communications systems; factories producing avionics and tele-communications equipment were to be established and conscription to be introduced.

18 May 1985: Two bombs exploded in the Sulmaniya district of Riyadh; the Iranian-based Islamic Jihad group claimed responsibilty for the attack and warned that it was the beginning of a continuing campaign against Saudi Arabia.

18–20 May 1985: The foreign minister, Prince Sa'ud, visited Iran for talks on improving bilateral relations with the President, the Speaker of the Majlis (Parliament) and the Minister of Foreign Affairs.

1986: King Fahd adopted the title of Custodian of the Two Holy Mosques.

June 1986: The Government made controversial arrangements to buy military equipment from the US Government, including five more AWACS aircraft.

29 October 1986: Sheikh Ahmand Zaki Yamani was dismissed as Minister of Petroleum and Mineral Resources following OPEC's abandonment of official production quotas for each member country; he had held the post for 24 years.

20 July 1987: At a meeting of the Arab League in Jordan, Saudi Arabia joined several other countries in urging Iran to accept a recent UN resolution and negotiate a cease-fire with Iraq.

31 July 1987: Iranian pilgrims performing the *Hajj* came into conflict with Saudi security forces; 402 people were killed, 275 of them Iranians. Mass demonstrations took place in the Iranian capital, Tehran; the Saudi embassy was attacked and the Iranian Government warned that they would avenge the deaths by overthrowing the Sa'ud family.

November 1987: The Government restored diplomatic relations with Egypt.

March 1988: At a meeting of the OIC, the Government announced that it intended to introduce quotas on the number of pilgrims from each country permitted to undertake the *Hajj* in Mecca, as a temporary security measure. The Iranian leader, the Ayatollah Khomeini, declared that his country would ignore the decree. No Iranians performed the *Hajj* that year.

19 March 1988: It was reported by the press agency that a number of Chinese medium-range missiles had been delivered to Saudi Arabia. Israel threatened to carry out a pre-emptive strike on the al-Kharj missiles base; the following month the US Ambassador delivered an official complaint to the Government concerning the purchase of the missiles, which prompted Fahd to demand his replacement.

April 1988: Sheikh Hisham Nazer, the Minister of Petroleum and Mineral Resources, became the first Saudi chairman of Aramco; the Government had become full owners of the company earlier in the decade.

27 April 1988: Saudi Arabia terminated diplomatic relations with Iran.

May 1988: The British Government agreed to supply Saudi Arabia with fighter-bomber aircraft, trainer aircraft, helicopters and naval vessels. In the same month, the US Senate issued a ban on sales of military equipment to Saudi Arabia, unless the President could certify that the country had no biological or nuclear warheads with which to equip them.

October 1988: Four Shi'a Muslims, who had been convicted of sabotaging a petrochemical plant in collaboration with Iran, were executed.

28 October 1988: A senior Saudi Arabian intelligence officer was assassinated in Turkey; he had been posing as a diplomat in an attempt to trace members of a pro-Iranian Shi'a group.

December 1988: The Soviet Deputy Minister of Foreign Affairs held talks with the Government concerning the conflict in Afghanistan; following this, Saudi Arabia and Sudan recognized the Afghan Mujahidin Government-in-exile.

2 July 1990: 1,426 pilgrims died in Mecca when a tunnel collapsed during the *Hajj*.

21 July 1990: Saudi Arabia and the People's Republic of China established diplomatic relations.

24 July 1990: President Mubarak of Egypt visited Iraq, Kuwait and Saudi Arabia in pursuit of a solution to the dispute developing between Iraq and Kuwait.

7 August 1990: The USA announced its decision to send ground forces to Saudi Arabia as part of a multi-national force (requested by King Fahd) to deter Iraqi aggression against that country.

9 August 1990: King Fahd denounced the Iraqi invasion of Kuwait.

10 August 1990: Twelve Arab League member states approved a proposal to send a pan-Arab deterrent force to Saudi Arabia.

19 August 1990: Saudi Arabia announced it would unilaterally increase production of petroleum if OPEC did not convene an emergency meeting.

29 August 1990: The Saudi Arabian proposal to increase OPEC production of crude petroleum was approved by a majority of OPEC member states.

7 September 1990: Saudi Arabia and the USSR agreed to restore diplomatic relations.

14 September 1990: The USA announced the sale of weapons with a value in excess of US $20,000m. to Saudi Arabia.

19 September 1990: Saudi Arabia terminated the privileges of Yemeni workers in the country and discontinued emergency supplies of petroleum to Jordan.

17 January 1991: Iraq, which was being attacked by a multi-national force in response to its annexation of Kuwait (see chapter on Iraq), commenced attacks with *Scud* missiles against Israeli and Saudi Arabian targets.

7–14 March 1991: The US Secretary of State visited Egypt, Israel, Kuwait, Saudi Arabia and Syria.

26 March 1991: Iran and Saudi Arabia restored diplomatic relations.

1 March 1992: A royal decree provided for the creation, within six months, of a 'Consultative Council' in Saudi Arabia.

September 1992: Qatar accused Saudi Arabia of attacking a Qatari border post, killing two border guards and capturing a third. Relations were consequently strained—Saudi Arabia claimed the incident occurred as a result of fighting between Bedouin tribes. Following mediation by Kuwait, the guard was released and relations improved.

20 December 1992: Qatar and Saudi Arabia agreed to establish a committee to delineate their disputed border by 1994.

12 May 1993: The Committee for the Defence of Legitimate Rights (CDLR), established by a group of prominent Isamic scholars and lawyers, was declared illegal and disbanded; the organization's spokesman, Muhammad al-Masari, was arrested. In April 1994 the CDLR (including al-Masari, who had been released in the previous month) relocated to London, United Kingdom.

11 July 1993: The Saudi Arabian Council of Ministers was reshuffled.

20 August 1993: It was decreed that the Consultative Council (Majlis ash-Shoura) would be composed of 80 men, appointed by the King, to review the Government's activities. A further decree established limits for the terms of office of the Cabinet and of each of its members.

20–22 December 1993: A GCC 'summit' meeting was held in Riyadh.

29 December 1993: The Consultative Council was inaugurated.

23 May 1994: 270 pilgrims died during crushing among those performing the *Hajj* in Mecca.

26 February 1995: Yemen and Saudi Arabia signed a memorandum of understanding on their border dispute.

2 August 1995: A new Council of Ministers was appointed, in which many portfolios (though none of those held by members of the royal family) were redistributed.

1 January 1996: A royal decree charged Crown Prince Abdullah ibn Abd al-Aziz with responsibility for affairs of state, following King Fahd's admission to hospital.

21 February 1996: King Fahd was reported to have resumed full control of affairs of state.

25 June 1996: Some 19 US military personnel were killed when an explosive device attached to a petroleum tanker was detonated at a military installation near Dhahran.

7 July 1997: The Consultative Council began its second term, with an increased membership of 90.

13 May 1999: The Grand Mufti of Saudi Arabia died; his deputy, Abd al-Aziz bin Abdullah ash-Sheikh, was appointed as his successor on 15 May.

16 June 1999: The Cabinet was reshuffled.

12 June 2000: The Ministers of Foreign Affairs of Saudi Arabia and Yemen signed an agreement delineating two countries' mutual land and maritime borders.

2 July 2000: Kuwait and Saudi Arabia signed an agreement on the demarcation of their joint border.

7 September 2000: The Government ratified the UN Convention on Elimination of All Forms of Discrimination Against Women, provided that it did not contravene *shari'a* law.

5 October 2000: The Saudi ambassador to the UN, Fauzi Abd-al-Majid Shabakshi requested that the Al-Judaydah-Ar'ar border post with Iraq be reopened to facilitate trade in accordance with the 'oil-for-food' programme established by the UN for Iraq.

6 October 2000: The Government condemned Israel for its recent attacks on the Palestinian community, which they claimed violated international law and displayed contempt for the Middle East peace process.

10 October 2000: The Libyan leader, Col Muammar Al-Qaddafi, made his first visit to Saudi Arabia in two decades. He met senior government officials for discussions on bilateral ties and the Arab-Israeli conflict.

14–15 October 2000: Two Saudi men hijacked a Saudi passenger aircraft on a flight to London, forcing it to land in Baghdad, where the Iraqi authorities were able to end the hijack peacefully. The hijackers said that they had seized the aircraft in protest at the Government's repression of ordinary citizens; the Goverment sought their extradition from Iraq, but abandoned the attempt in December.

19 October 2000: Crown Prince Abdullah discussed bilateral relations with the Algerian President.

21 October 2000: The Government announced that it would be granting Palestinian groups involved in the al-Aqsa *intifada* US $800m. to fund their activities and a further US $200m. to assist the families of members who had died during the conflict.

30 October 2000: Prince Nayef, the Minister of the Interior, held meetings with Dr Nobil Sha'th, minister of planning and international co-operation of the Palestinian Authority.

7 November 2000: Prince Walid ibn Talal met the Palestinian leader, Yasser Arafat in Gaza; during his visit he donated 20m. riyals to Palestinian workers.

8 November 2000: The Goverment announced its intention to boycott an impending meeting of the OIC in Qatar, owing to the country's refusal to terminate trade relations with Israel. Two days later, Qatar declared that it would close its Israeli trade mission; Crown Prince Abdullah subsequently attended the conference.

17 November 2000: A car bomb exploded in Riyadh, killing a British national; another bomb injured three British nationals and one Irish national the following week.

31 November 2000: The Saudi Fund for Development (SFD) announced that it would provide a loan of 45m. riyals to Kazakhstan to assist in the construction of a major road.

3 December 2000: The Government ratified documents relating to agreements on economic, communications and investment co-operation with Yemen.

10 December 2000: The former Prime Minister of Pakistan, Nawaz Sharif, began a term of exile in Saudi Arabia.

13 December 2000: Algeria, Egypt, Iran, Kuwait, Morocco, Saudi Arabia, Syria and Tunisia signed the UN Convention Against Organized Crime, which provided for co-ordination between national crime-fighting bodies, the protection of witnesses, measures to combat money-laundering and the acceleration of extradition proceedings.

15 December 2000: It was reported that a US national had been arrested in connection with the car bomb attack on 17 November; on the same day a further car-bomb attack injured a British national.

29 December 2000: Prince Sultan announced that an agreement had been made with the USA for the purchase of military equipment for the National Guard; the contract provided for a number of F-16 fighter aircraft, anti-tank rockets, communications equipment and armoured vehicles.

8 January 2001: The Government announced the resumption of passenger flights to Iran, of trade relations, and the establishment of a news agency in Tehran.

19–21 January 2001: India and Saudi Arabia signed a memorandum of understanding on bilateral relations.

31 January 2001: Kuwait and Saudi Arabia signed maps on the demarcation of their maritime borders.

4 February 2001: A British national appeared to confess on a Saudi television programme that he had recieved orders to carry out the car bomb attack in Riyadh on 17 November 2000. Nine other non-Saudis, including a Belgian and an American, were also arrested in connection with the attack.

22 February 2001: The Government expressed concern over joint British-US bombardment of Iraq.

26 February 2001: It was reported that Saudi companies had won contracts to export medicine and building material supplies to Iraq as part of the eighth stage of the 'oil-for-food' agreement with the UN.

March 2001: A total of 35 pilgrims of various nationalities died during a stampede at the *Hajj*.

7 March 2001: The military leader of Pakistan, Gen. Pervez Musharraf, visited Saudi Arabia for a meeting with King Fahd and Crown Prince Abdullah.

15 March 2001: A bomb exploded in Riyadh, outside a building reported to house the offices of the international Arabic newspaper, *al-Hayat*.

16 March 2001: Chechen activits seized a passenger aircraft on a flight from Turkey to Russia and forced it to land in Medina. Saudi troops boarded the aircraft to end the hijack, resulting in three deaths.

18 April 2001: Iran and Saudi Arabia signed a security accord to combat terrorism, drugs-trafficking and organised crime; the agreement also contained messures on border surveillance and co-operation between police forces.

May 2001: Saudi Arabia made a complaint to the UN over continued unprovoked Iraqi attacks on its territory. The Government's ambassador to the UN reported that in one such incident three weeks previously, Iraqi troops had crossed the border and shot at a Saudi border patrol; the Saudis returned fire and one Iraqi soldier was killed.

12–13 May 2001: The Iranian foreign minister, Kamal Kharazi, met the Minister of Foreign Affairs, Prince Sa'ud, and other senior government officials; in addition to bilateral ties, the delegates discussed ways in which the Muslim nations could assist the Palestinian people.

26 May 2001: Four British men were sentenced to fines, flogging and imprisonment following their conviction of illegal alcohol trading. The British Government subsequently announced that it regarded the flogging of the men as an infringement of human rights.

4 June 2001: It was reported that the Government had signed several agreements worth millions of dollars with eight international petroleum companies, to develop three new natural-gas projects.

Syria

***c*. 2300 BC:** Ebla (near Aleppo and previously the dominant city in the region) was destroyed and the area became part of the Akkadian Empire.

15th century BC: Damascus was conquered by the Egyptian Pharaoh Thutmoses III.

1430 BC: Aleppo was conquered by the Hittites.

11th century BC: Damascus was the capital of the land of Aram.

734 BC–732 BC: The Assyrian King Tiglath-Pileser III, made war on the Kingdom of Damascus; following a two-year siege, the city fell. The King was executed and the Kingdom incorporated into the Assyrian Empire, which eventually conquered most of what is now Syria.

605 BC: Most of the Assyrian Empire had been conquered by Babylonian forces and their Median allies. Following their defeat of the Egyptians, all of Syria and Palestine were under Babylonian control.

333 BC: Damascus, now part of the Persian Empire, was conquered by the Macedon King and Greek military leader, Alexander III ('the Great').

301 BC–281 BC: Seleucus Nicator, Alexander's successor in Syria and Palestine, built the city of Beroia on the site of Aleppo.

111 BC–90 BC: Damascus was developed as a Greek city by the Seleucid succesors to Alexander in Syria.

64 BC: Syria was annexed by the Roman leader, Pompey; it became an important element in the defence of the eastern provinces of the Empire.

AD 500: The client Arab kingdom of Ghassan acted as a bulwark for the Byzantine Empire against the Sassanids in Persia.

613–614: The Sassanid Shahs invaded Byzantine lands, conquering Syria and penetrating as far as Egypt.

634: Arab armies under Khaild bin al-Walid deafeated Byzantine forces at Ajnadain, near Ramallah in Palestine.

14 September 635: The Arab armies entered Damascus.

August 636: The battle of Yarmuk effectively ended Byzantine rule in the region.

661: Following a struggle for the succession as leader of the Muslim Arab World, in succession to the Prophet Muhammad, Mu'awiya, who had been governor of Syria, was acclaimed Caliph (successor) in Jerusalem (Al-Quds in Arabic). The capital of the Islamic Empire was now at Damascus, the Umayyad dynasty of Caliphs was established and the Syria prospered as the focus of the Arab civilization.

705–11: The great mosque in Damascus was built by the Umayyad Caliph, Walid I.

750: The Abbasid revolt secured the defeat and virtual elimination of the Umayyads, the capital of the Islamic empire was moved to Mesopotamia and established at the newly created city of Baghdad.

9th century: There were a series of revolts against Abbasid rule by claimants to the Umayyad Caliphate often purporting to be al-Sufyani, a mythical descendent of the line of Mu'awiya who would inaugurate a resurgence in Umayyad power.

905–1004: The Hamdanid Amirs ruled northern Syria and parts of Mesopotamia from Mosul and Aleppo (from 944) as a largely autonomous dynasty.

963: The Byzantine Emperor Nicephorus Phocas invaded northern Syria.

October 968: The Byzantines took Antioch and Aleppo, ruling Antioch directly, while Aleppo became a Byzantine protectorate.

969: The Fatimids, after conquering Egypt, invaded Palestine and Syria and took Damascus.

997: Under a treaty between the Fatimid Caliphs and the Byzantine Empire, much of northern Syria came under Byzantine suzerainity, while the remainder of the country remained in the hands of the Fatimids.

1075: The Seljuq Turks, originally from Central Asia, invade Syria and captured Damascus; they gained much of the rest of the territory from the Byzantine Empire in 1084.

1084–1187: During the Christian Crusades, much of modern Syria was successively conquered by Muslim and Christian forces. The Muslim leader, Salah ad-Din (Saladin), was able to assert control over much of the territory concerned.

1250: The dynasty of Saladin's family, the Ayyubids, was removed from power by their elite 'slave' soldiers, the Mamelukes, and Syria came under Mameluke control. The Mamelukes retained control over the region (with the exception of a brief period of Mongol dominance in the early 14th century, and numerous subsequent Mongol incursions) until the 16th century.

24 August 1516: The Ottoman Sultan, Selim 'the Grim', invaded Mameluke territory and fought Sultan Kansuh al-Ghawri at Dabik, north of Aleppo. Ottoman artillery and the Janissary infantry secured a victory over the Mameluke cavalry and with the subsequent defeat of the Mamelukes in Egypt itself Ottoman rule in Syria was secured.

17th century: The English Levant Company established a factory at Aleppo and as a result of its geographical location it became the chief commercial centre of northern Syria for the next three centuries.

1810: Wahhabi nomads raiding from central Arabia threatened Damascus and the surrounding area.

1831: Egyptian troops invaded Syria under Ibrahim Pasha, son of Muhammad Ali Pasha, the ruler of Egypt. Ibrahim Pasha's rule was unpopular—although reformist in many aspects, his limits on the power of local leaders, high taxation and conscription attracted displeasure.

1833: Muhammad Ali signed a treaty with the Ottomans securing his administration of Lebanon, Palestine and Syria.

1839: A revolt broke out against Egyptian rule. The 'Great Powers' of Europe (France, Russia and the United Kingdom) intervened in support of the Ottoman Empire and Muhammad Ali was forced to renounce his claims to the region, which was returned to direct Ottoman rule.

1860: A Druze rebellion against the spread of Maronite Christian populations in Lebanon spread to Damascus, where the Christian quarter was pillaged and its inhabitants massacred.

September 1860: Supported by France, Ottoman forces arrived in Damascus and suppressed the revolt, including levying a collective fine of £200,000 on the city of Damascus. In subsequent years a period of emigration from Syria (most notably by Christians) began.

1876: The first Ottoman Constitution gave Syria representation in the Assembly in İstanbul (the Ottoman capital, now in Turkey). Nine individuals from leading families were selected.

1908: The Hedjaz railway, linking Damascus and Medina (Saudi Arabia) was opened.

1914–18: Ottoman entry into the First World War brought Syria into conflict with France and the United Kingdom; the Ottoman regime suppressed the growing Arab nationalist movement.

7 May 1918: Seven Syrian Arab leaders in Cairo (Egypt) submitted a memorandum to the British Foreign Secretary outlining Arab and Syrian aspirations for independence and seeking assurance of British support.

1 October 1918: Amir Faisal, the son of the Sharif of Mecca, who had become a focus for Arab nationalist aspirations, entered Damascus, which he hoped to establish as the capital of a Kingdom of Greater Syria.

31 October 1918: The Ottoman army withdrew from Syria into Anatolia.

8 March 1920: Syrian nationalists procaimed an independent kingdom of Greater Syria (including Lebanon and Palestine) under Amir Faisal. This was repudiated by the British and French, who imposed a system of mandates—the administration of the territories by one of the major European powers.

April 1920: The San Remo (Italy) conference gave France a mandate for Syria and Lebanon; French forces were subsequently deployed in the region, and defeated Arab resistance, occupying Damascus in July.

1925–26: Discontent with French rule escalated into revolt in Damascus and other cities, most notably in the north of the country.

October 1925–May 1926: During their operations against the Syrian uprising the French bombed Damascus.

April 1928: Elections were held for a Constituent Assembly and an indigenous Government, led by Sheikh Taj ad-Din al-Hasani was established.

August 1928: A draft constitution was completed, seen by many as a retreat from Arab nationalist aspirations; however, the French administrators refused to accept certain provisions of the document, notably the indivisibility of Syrian territory (France administered Jebel Druse and Latakia separately).

May 1930: The French High Commissioner dissolved the Assembly and on his own authority issued a new constitution for the state of Syria which included those amendments necessary for the maintainance of French control.

January 1932: New elections to a Chamber of Deputies were held and negotiations begun for a Franco-Syrian treaty modelled on that agreed by the British and Iraqi authorities.

1934: After repeated failures to secure a compromise between the French demands and those of the nationalists, the French High Commissioner suspended the Chamber of Deputies indefinitely.

1936: The National Bloc had an overwhelming majority in the elections.

9 September 1936: Following the visit of a Syrian delegation to the French capital, Paris, a Franco-Syrian treaty was signed, recognizing the principle of Syrian independence and stipulating that after ratification there should be a period of three years during which the apparatus of a fully independent state would be created. The districts of Jebel Druse and Latakia would be annexed to Syria, but would retain their special administrations. Other subsidiary agreements reserved to France important military and economic rights.

January 1937: Responding to Turkish expressions of concern, the League of Nations decided that the Sanjak of Alexandretta (a previously Turkish territory included in the French mandate) should be fully autonomous apart from its foreign and financial policies, which were to be under Syrian control.

June 1939: Alexandretta was ceded to Turkey by the French amid increasing international pressure; the concession was unpopular among Syrian nationalists.

December 1939: The French Government, concerned to secure its military position in the region at the start of the Second World War, declared that no ratification of the Franco-Syrian treaty could be expected.

1941: Open riots in major cities led the Vichy Government of France (installed after Germany had conquered that country) to promise the restoration of partial self-government.

8 June 1941: The Allies invaded Syria, mainly to prevent aid reaching the anti-British regime which had seized power in Iraq, and General Catroux, on behalf of the Free French Government, promised independence for Syria and an end to mandatory rule; the Vichy French forces in Syria surrendered in July.

September 1941: Syrian nationalists proclaimed an independent republic.

17 August 1943: Elections were held and the National Bloc was returned to power with Shukri al-Kuwatli as President of the Syrian Republic.

January 1944: Syria refused the French demand for a Franco-Syrian treaty as a condition for the final transfer of administrative and military services.

March 1945: Egypt, Iraq, Lebanon, Saudi Arabia, Syria, Transjordan and Yemen founded the League of Arab States (Arab League), which aimed to promote political, cultural, economic and social co-operation between its members and act as mediator in regional disputes.

May 1945: French forces responded to anti-French disturbances by shelling Damascus. The crisis ended following a threat of British armed intervention and the evacuation of French troops and administrative personnel; the last French troops withdrew in April 1946.

19 December 1949: After three *coups d'état* in one year Brig. Adib Shishakli established military government.

5 September 1950: A new Constitution was adopted; civil government appeared to be restored; however, the civilian Government resigned in March 1951 in protest at the continuing power of the military and, in November 1951 Brig. Shishakli resumed full control.

April 1952: All political parties were abolished.

February 1953: Jordan and Syria signed an economic and financial agreement. The two countries also announced plans to dam the Yarmouk River to facilitate irrigation and the generation of hydroelectricity.

July 1953: A new Constitution was approved; Brig. Shishakli became President in August.

October 1953: At elections to the Chamber of Deputies, supporters of President Shishakli won a large majority; the elections were boycotted by supporters of parties banned the previous year.

25 February 1954: Army intervention overthrew President Shishakli and the 1950 Constitution was restored.

September 1954: Elections to the new Chamber of Deputies were held—the majority of the seats were won by candidates regarded as independent of any political grouping.

August 1955: Shukri al-Kuwatli beame President. His appointment was perceived to indicate that pro-Egyptian factions had gained ascendancy over pro-Iraqi groups in Syria; a joint Egyptian-Syrian military command was established in October.

July 1956: Jordan and Syria formed an economic union.

30 October 1956: President al-Kuwatli visited the USSR; in his absence a state of emergency was declared.

November 1956: Amid the Israeli invasion of Sinai and the British and French military intervention in Egypt, following that country's nationalization of the Suez Canal, it was reported that Syrian forces had disrupted the flow of Iraqi petroleum through a major pipeline; Syria refused to repair the pipeline until Israeli forces withdrew.

November 1957: The Syrian National Assembly passed a resolution in favour of union with Egypt, the unified state to be known as the United Arab Republic (UAR).

1 February 1958: The union of Egypt and Syria, the UAR, was proclaimed; the Syrian National Assembly gave final assent to the creation of the new state four days later. The Egyptian President, Gamal Abd an-Nasser, became the first President of the UAR in late February.

2 March 1958: Yemen signed an agreement with the UAR to form a federal union known as the United Arab State.

13 March 1958: All political parties and organizations in the Syrian sector of the UAR were dissolved by decree.

19 July 1958: A defence pact between Iraq and the UAR was announced.

20 July 1958: Jordan suspended relations with the UAR.

10 November 1958: King Hussein was forced to return to Jordan after Syrian fighter aircraft intercepted him on his way by air to Europe.

11 January 1959: The statute of the Arab Development Bank was signed by Jordan, Lebanon, Libya, Saudi Arabia, the UAR and Yemen.

10 March 1959: The staff of the Embassy of the UAR in Baghdad were expelled from Iraq.

1 December 1959: The UAR and the United Kingdom re-established diplomatic relations.

21 July 1960: The first UAR Parliament was opened by President Nasser.

17 August 1961: The governmental system of the UAR was reorganized: one large central cabinet replaced a central cabinet and two regional cabinets.

28 September 1961: Amid increasing Syrian dissatisfaction at perceived Egyptian dominance of the UAR, a *coup d'état* took place in Syria; the new regime announced the secession of Syria from the UAR; President Nasser formally announced the separation on 5 October.

13 October 1961: Syria was readmitted to the UN.

1 December 1961: Following the promulgation of a provisional Constitution, elections to a Constituent Assembly were held; Dr Nazim Kudsi was subsequently elected President.

28 March 1962: The army resumed power in Syria, forcing the resignation of President Kudsi and of the Council of Ministers.

13 April 1962: Dr Kudsi was reinstated as President, following popular unrest; a new Government, led by Dr Bashir Azmeh, was subsequently formed.

9 September 1962: Syria resumed diplomatic relations with France.

8 March 1963: In a *coup d'état*, a military group styled the National Council of the Revolutionary Command (NCRC) seized power. Maj.-Gen. Atassi assumed the leadership of the NCRC.

17 April 1963: A proposal to create a federation of Iraq, Syria and the UAR was announced—the plans were abandoned in August.

13 May 1963: A new Government, dominated by members of the Baath party (an Arab nationalist socialist movement) was formed, led by Salah ad-Din al-Bitar.

18 July 1963: Pro-Egyptian elements attempted a *coup d'état*, but were defeated.

27 July 1963: Maj.-Gen Amin al-Hafiz, the Deputy Prime Minister and Minister of the Interior, became President of the NCRC, effectively head of state.

8 October 1963: Iraq and Syria announced a union of their military forces.

25 April 1964: A provisional Constitution was promulgated, defining Syria as a democratic socialist republic, and a part of the Arab nation. The NCRC was to exercise legislative authority, executive power being vested in a five-member Presidential Council. Gen. al-Hafiz was confirmed as President of the NCRC and of the Presidential Council, and was thus recognized as head of state.

13 August 1964: A Common Market of Iraq, Jordan, Kuwait and Syria was established, under the aegis of the Arab League.

4 November 1964: Gen. al-Hafiz formed a new Syrian cabinet, following the resignation of al-Bitar.

1 January 1965: The provisions of the Arab Common Market entered into force.

3–4 January 1965: A total of 112 companies in a number of industries were nationalized, numerous strikes arose in protest; a strike by merchants in Damascus was suppressed by military forces and the businesses were confiscated. The programme of nationalization continued throughout 1965 (a number of foreign-owned petroleum companies were nationalized in March).

23 February 1966: A Baathist military junta arrested President al-Hafiz and overthrew the Government; the new regime subsequently appointed Dr Nur ad-Din al-Atassi as President and Dr Yusuf Zeayen as Prime Minister.

18–23 April 1966: The Prime Minister, Zeayen, led an economic and military delegation to the Soviet capital, Moscow.

17–18 July 1966: Some 150 right-wing politicians were reported to have been arrested in a political purge.

8 September 1966: The Government announced the defeat of an attempted *coup d'état*, apparently led by elements supporting the regime ousted in February.

11 October 1966: Dr Zeayen declared Syria's support for the Palestinian al-Fatah organization.

4 November 1966: A mutual defence agreement was signed by Syria and the UAR.

7 April 1967: Fighting occurred between Israeli and Syrian forces on the countries' border.

14 May 1967: The Israeli Prime Minister, Levi Eshkol, stated that Israeli-Syrian war was inevitable if incursions into Israel by Syrian guerrillas continued.

5 June 1967: A period of military tensions between Israel and its neighbouring Arab countries was ended when Israel attacked the air bases of Jordan, Syria and the UAR. The Arab countries' air forces were severely damaged, and Israel was swiftly able to capture territory from each of the Arab combatants (notably the West Bank and Old Jerusalem from Jordan, the Golan Heights from Syria and the Sinai peninsula from the UAR).

6 June 1967: The United Kingdom and the USA were accused by President Nasser of the UAR and King Hussein of Jordan of military collusion with Israel; 10 Arab states imposed an embargo on petroleum supplies to the two countries. Diplomatic relations with the USA were suspended by Algeria, Iraq, Sudan, Syria, the UAR and Yemen; Iraq and Syria terminated relations with the United Kingdom.

10 June 1967: Syria and the UAR signed a cease-fire with Israel, as Jordan had done some days earlier, thus concluding the conflict, which came to be known as the 'Six-Day War'; Israel retained the territories it had gained in the conflict.

29–31 August 1967: At a conference of Arab heads of state in Khartoum (Sudan), the petroleum-producing states agreed a substantial aid programme for Jordan and the UAR; Syria, which did not send a delegation to the conference, was excluded from the agreement.

29 October 1968: Dr Atassi formed a new Government, with himself as Prime Minister; Gen. Hafiz al-Assad, a prominent supporter of Syria's Arab neighbours and opponent of Soviet influence on the country, was appointed Minister of Defence.

May 1969: A provisional constitution was published; however, it was never formally promulgated.

29 May 1969: A new Cabinet was formed in Syria, as the outcome of much reported strife between the army and the Baath Party leadership.

5–6 August 1970: The foreign and defence ministers of Jordan, Libya, Sudan, Syria and the UAR met in Tripoli (Libya); Algeria and Iraq refused to send delegations.

13 November 1970: Gen. Assad seized power, and was appointed Prime Minister and Secretary-General of the Baath party; Ahmed Katib became President.

29 January 1971: The flow of petroleum through the Syrian section of the American owned Trans-Arabian Pipeline (Tapline) resumed after Syria allowed repairs to be made; a section of the pipeline near the Syrian border with Israel had been damaged in early 1970, causing the flow of petroleum to be discontinued.

12 March 1971: Following amendments to the provisional constitution in February, Gen. Assad was elected to a seven-year term as President of Syria.

3 April 1971: A new Government was formed under Maj.-Gen. Abdal Rahman Khlefawi; Mahmoud Ayyoubi was appointed Vice-President.

13–14 April 1971: The heads of state of Libya, Sudan, Syria and the UAR met in Cairo and Benghazi (Libya); following the meeting, proposals to create a federation of Libya, Syria and the UAR, with Sudan joining at a later date, were announced.

14 June 1971: Syria closed its border with Jordan in protest at Jordanian raids on Palestinian guerrilla camps.

11–13 August 1971: Altercations occurred on the border between Jordan and Syria; the latter country suspended diplomatic relations the following day.

7 March 1972: The Syrian National Progressive Front was formed by five parties, including Baath and the Communists.

1 June 1972: Syria nationalized all petroleum installations.

8 September 1972: The Israeli air force bombarded sites believed to be guerrilla bases in Lebanon and Syria; further raids were carried out on 15 October.

9 November 1972: Israeli and Syrian fighter aircraft were involved aerial combat over the disputed Golan Heights.

24 December 1972: A new Government was formed in Syria under Ayyoubi, following the resignation on health grounds of Maj.-Gen. Khleifawi.

31 January 1973: A draft constitution, in which Islam received no official status, was approved by the People's Council.

25–26 March 1973: The draft constitution, which had been amended to stipulate that the President should be a Muslim, was approved in a referendum.

May 1973: At elections to the People's Council, the Progressive Front won 140 of the 186 seats; opposition candidates secured only 4 seats, while the remainder were won by independents.

5 July 1973: The first stage of the Euphrates Dam project was inaugurated by President Assad.

September 1973: King Faisal of Saudi Arabia mediated a reconciliation in the dispute between King Hussein of Jordan and the Egyptian and Syrian leaders.

October 1973: Syria and Egypt launched simultaneous attacks on Israeli-held territory. There was severe fighting on the Golan Heights until a cease-fire was agreed after 18 days.

October 1973: Diplomatic relations with Jordan were resumed.

May 1974: Henry Kissinger, the US Secretary of State, secured an agreement for the disengagement of forces on the Golan Heights.

April 1975: King Hussein of Jordan visited Syria.

August 1975: A Supreme Command Council, directed by King Hussein of Jordan and President Hafiz al-Assad of Syria, was established to co-ordinate political and military action against Israel.

January 1976: Syria intervened in the Lebanese Civil War, sending some 2,000 troops, in part to protect the position of the Palestinians. President Assad secured a cease-fire and pledged to control the Palestinians in the country.

June 1976: Renewed fighting in Lebanon brought about another Syrian intervention. It was welcomed by the Christian parties and condemned by the Palestinians and the Muslim left-wing, as well as by Egypt.

8–9 June 1976: A meeting of Arab League Ministers of Foreign Affairs agreed that a peace-keeping force should be sent to Lebanon. However, despite the presence of this force, fighting continued.

October 1976: Arab summit meetings in Riyadh (Saudi Arabia) and Cairo secured a more durable cease-fire; Syrian forces agreed to withdraw and a 30,000-strong Arab Deterrent Force (ADF), composed mainly of Syrian troops, was given authority to maintain peace. Iraq protested to Syria by restricting the flow of petroleum into the pipeline emerging at the Syrian port of Banias.

November 1976: Syrian forces occupied most of the suburbs of the Lebanese capital, Beirut, and dominated much of the rest of the country.

December 1976: The attempted assassination of the Syrian Deputy Prime Minister and Minister of Foreign Affairs was blamed on terrorists trained in Iraq.

April 1977: President Assad visited the Soviet capital, Moscow, as a sign of improved Syrian relations with the USSR.

May 1977: President Assad met the US President, Jimmy Carter, for talks in Geneva (Switzerland).

July 1977: Jordan and Syria came to an agreement to co-ordinate measures for closer economic integration.

December 1977: Syria strongly criticized President Anwar Sadat of Egypt, who had agreed a peace initiative with Israel (the 'Camp David Agreements'); Syria suspended diplomatic relations with Egypt.

26 October 1978: After a series of attempts at *rapprochement* between Iraq and Syria, including both countries' participation in the 'rejectionist movement' to the Camp David Agreements (see chapter on Israel), a 'Constitutional Union of Baathist Regimes' was simultaneously announced in their respective capitals.

March 1979: Syria joined most of the other Arab League member countries at a meeting in Baghdad which endorsed political and economic sanctions against Egypt.

4–6 March 1979: Iraq, Jordan and Syria attended negotiations in Kuwait to mediate a cease-fire between the People's Democratic Republic of Yemen and the Yemen Arab Republic.

1 April 1979: Fighting occurred in Aleppo between the Syrian army and dissident groups. In the same month, Governors in four provinces were replaced by the President.

16 June 1979: Some 32 army cadets, the majority thought to be from the same community as President Assad, were killed and 54 wounded in Aleppo. The attack was attributed to the Muslim Brotherhood, a proscribed Islamist organization.

late 1979: There was increasing violence and unrest in Syria, led by the Muslim Brotherhood.

26 June 1980: There was an assassination attempt on President Assad; the Muslim Brotherhood claimed responsibility.

27 June 1980: It was reported that some 550 members of the Muslim Brotherhood held in detention in Palmyra were killed in revenge for the assassination attempt on the President.

23 August 1980: Syrian troops bombarded Tripoli in northern Lebanon in order to end a confrontation between rival Muslim groups.

September 1980: Syria supported Iran in that country's developing conflict with Iraq.

2 September 1980: President Assad issued a declaration agreeing to unite his country with Libya; on the same day Syrian security forces killed a number of members of the Muslim Brotherhood.

October 1980: Syria signed a 20-year treaty of friendship and cooperation with the USSR.

December 1980: An estimated 200 members of the Muslim Brotherhood were believed to have been shot by Syrian security forces in Aleppo.

April 1981: Syrian forces beseiged Lebanese Phalange militiamen who had taken over the town of Zahle in the Beka'a valley in an attempt to link up with other Phalangists holding the area between Zahle and Beirut. The Syrians also moved anti-aircraft missiles into the Beka'a after two helicopters had been shot down by Israeli planes.

May 1981: The Syrian Government introduced drastic economic measures designed to counter the economic price of military involvement in Lebanon, including reducing the flow of imports and effecting a currency reform with the aim of suppressing illegal economic activity.

4 May 1981: Syria declined to accept a delimitation boundary in Lebanon beyond which Syria would not conduct military operations.

5 May 1981: Israeli forces shot down two Syrian helicopters; the following week two Syrian missiles were fired at Israeli aircraft over the Beka'a valley.

30 May 1981: The Syrians again bombarded Zahle.

August 1981: Some 150 individuals were killed as a result of bombings by dissidents in the city of Hama; in the same month, the Prime Minister's office was bombed, and further bombings against military and administrative targets occurred throughout late 1981.

December 1981: Israel formally annexed the disputed Golan Heights.

10 January 1982: A military revolt directed against the Baath party was suppressed; a similar, smaller incident took place later in the month.

February 1982: An uprising in Hama, led by the outlawed Muslim Brotherhood and other opposition elements lasted into March when it was suppressed by government forces with considerable damage to the town. Estimates of the number of deaths ranged from 8,000 to 30,000.

20 February 1982: An opposition group called the National Alliance of the Syrian People was formed, consisting of 19 factions drawn from various groupings, including the Muslim Brotherhood.

August 1982: An agreement was reached on the evacuation of Palestine Liberation Organization (PLO) and Syrian forces from Beirut; Syrian forces had withdrawn by 1 September.

May 1983: Syria supported a revolt against Yasser Arafat's leadership of the PLO; later in the year Syrian forces beseiged Arafat in the Lebanese city of Tripoli.

November 1983: President Assad suffered a heart attack. During his illness, displays of military strength were staged by rivals to the succession, including Colonel Rifaat al-Assad, the President's brother.

March 1984: The three main rivals for the succession to President Assad were appointed as Vice-Presidents, thus distributing power evenly between them.

5 March 1984: President Gemayel of Lebanon, responding to Syrian pressure, abrogated the May 1983 agreement with Israel, thus ensuring Syrian ascendancy in Lebanon's affairs. In return for Gemayel's concessions, President Assad undertook to guarantee Lebanon's internal security.

September 1984: Syria arranged a truce to end the fighting in Tripoli between the pro-Syrian Arab Democratic Party and the Sunni Muslim Tawheed Islami (Islamic Unification Movement).

January 1985: President Assad declared an amnesty for some members of the Muslim Brotherhood imprisoned in Syria and invited those in exile to return to the country.

February 1985: President Assad was re-elected for a third seven-year-term of office.

June 1985: Following the Israeli withdrawal to southern Lebanon, Syrian forces in the Beka'a valley were reduced.

30 June 1985: Syria secured the release of some 39 Americans taken hostage by Hezbollah militia after a TWA airliner was hijacked on 17 June by threatening to withdraw aid if the hostages were not freed.

July 1985: Syria attempted to broker a security plan for Beirut after weeks of fighting between Christians and Muslims along the 'Green Line' dividing east and west Beirut.

November 1985: King Hussein conceded that Jordan had unwittingly been a base for the Muslim Brotherhood in its attempts to overthrow President Assad but that members of the group would no longer receive shelter in his country.

December 1985: King Hussein travelled to Damascus to meet President Assad.

February 1986: The NFP and the Baath Party obtained 151 seats of the 195 seats in the People's Assembly. The Communist Party contested the elections separately and won nine seats and the independent candidates 35.

13 March 1986: A bomb exploded in Damascus, resulting in an estimated 60 deaths. Syria blamed Iraq for the attack.

April 1986: Jordan appointed its first ambassador to Syria since 1980.

15 April 1986: A total of 144 people were killed in a campaign of bombings in five Syrian towns including Damascus. A hitherto unknown Syrian group with possible pro-Iraqi and Islamic fundamentalist tendencies, the '17 October Group for the Liberation of the Syrian People', claimed responsibility for the attacks.

June 1986: A proposed meeting between the foreign ministers of Iraq and Syria, regarding a restoration of relations between the two countries, was cancelled by Syria shortly before it had been scheduled to take place.

24 October 1986: The British Government severed diplomatic relations with Syria after claiming that Syrian diplomats were implicated in the attempt by a Jordanian, Nezar Hindawi, to plant a bomb on an Israeli airliner at London airport the previous April.

November 1986: Three Syrian diplomats were expelled from the Federal Republic of Germany after a court in the city of West Berlin ruled that the Syrian embassy in East Berlin (in the Democratic Republic of Germany) was implicated in the bombing of a discotheque in West Berlin in 1986. The European Economic Community (EEC), Canada and the USA imposed limited diplomatic and economic sanctions against Syria and the Canadian and US ambassadors to Syria were recalled.

22 February 1987: Some 4,000 Syrian troops were redeployed in Lebanon, on the request of Muslim leaders.

April 1987: It was reported that the Presidents of Syria and Iraq had held secret conciliatory meetings in Jordan, although no public statements were made to confirm this.

April 1987: Various EEC countries sought to improve diplomatic relations with Syria, only the United Kingdom dissenting.

April 1987: President Assad and the Iraqi leader, Saddam Hussain, met secretly in Jordan at the instigation of King Hussein and Crown Prince Abdullah of Saudi Arabia.

June 1987: Syrian 'special forces' were deployed around the camps of Hezbollah militia fighters in the Beka'a valley.

June 1987: It was reported that the offices of the Palestinian Abu Nidal's Fatah Revolutionary Council near Damascus had been closed and many of its members had been expelled, Abu Nidal himself being moved to Libya.

July 1987: The EEC member states (with the exception of the United Kingdom) lifted the ban on ministerial contacts with Syria, although a ban on the sale of arms remained in force.

July 1987: Syria and Turkey signed a security protocol in which both agreed to curb the activities on their own soil of terrorist and separatist groups carrying out operations against the other. Turkey also assured Syria that the series of dams that it was building on the Euphrates river would not be deliberately used in such a way as to deprive Syria of water supplies further downstream.

September 1987: Syrian influence was held responsible for securing the release of a West German hostage held in Lebanon.

September 1987: The US Ambassador to Damascus returned to Syria and the US Government withdrew its opposition to operations by US petroleum companies in the country.

November 1987: A major government reshuffle took place after the resignation of the Prime Minister, Abd al-Rauf al-Kassem (his Government was accused of corruption and of failure to solve the country's severe economic problems). Mahmud az-Zoubi, the Speaker of the People's Assembly, was appointed to the post.

November 1987: President Assad and Saddam Hussain met again at the extraordinary summit meeting of the League of Arab States in Amman, Jordan. The summit was organized by King Hussein to discuss the conflict between Iran and Iraq, and it produced a unanimous statement condemning Iran for prolonging the war and for its occupation of Arab territory. However, Syria subsequently announced that a reconciliation with Iraq had not taken place, that its support for Iran remained and that it had succeeded in obstructing an Iraqi proposal that Arab states should sever diplomatic relations with Iran.

February 1988: President Assad did not endorse the plan for peace in the Middle East which was presented by the US Secretary of State, George Shultz in response to the Palestinian *intifada* (uprising) in the Occupied Territories. The 'Shultz Plan' was deemed unacceptable as it did not recognize the right of the Palestinians to self-determination; however, Assad chose not to condemn it.

March 1988: The Minister for Information, Muhammad Salman, announced that two months of Syrian mediation between Iran and the Arab states of the Gulf designed to prevent an escalation of the Iran-Iraq War had produced an Iranian undertaking to desist from attacks on tankers belonging to the members of the Gulf Co-operation Council (GCC).

April 1988: Further talks between President Assad and Shultz failed to reconcile their respective positions.

April 1988: A reconciliation was reported to have taken place between President Assad and Arafat. The two leaders held discussions when Arafat attended the funeral in Damascus of Khalil al-Wazir ('Abu Jihad', the military commander of the Palestine Liberation Army).

27 May 1988: Several hundred Syrian troops moved into the southern suburbs of Beirut to enforce a cease-fire agreement reached by Syria, Iran and their militia proxies on the previous day.

June 1988: An extraordinary summit meeting of the Arab League was held in Algiers to discuss the the Arab-Israeli conflict in general. The final communiqué of the summit, endorsed by all 21 League members, including Syria, rendered the Shultz Plan defunct.

23–25 May 1989: At the emergency summit meeting of Arab leaders in Casablanca the proposal supported by Egypt, Iraq, Jordan and the PLO, that Syria should immediately withdraw its troops from Lebanon was abandoned in response to Syrian opposition.

27 December 1989: Egypt and Syria restored full diplomatic relations.

2–3 May 1990: President Mubarak of Egypt visited Syria for talks with President Assad; the visit was reciprocated in July.

22–23 May 1990: Elections to the People's Assembly were held in Syria; the Baath party won 134 of the 250 seats available—the majority of the remainder were won by independent candidates.

14 September 1990: The US Secretary of State, James Baker, visited Syria for talks with President Assad.

28 November 1990: Syria and the United Kingdom restored diplomatic relations; the two countries exchanged ambassadors in February 1991.

5–6 March 1991: Egypt, Syria and the states of the Gulf Co-operation Council agreed, by the 'Damascus declaration', to form an Arab peace-keeping force to be stationed in Arabia as a supplement and, eventually, an alternative to the mult-national force stationed there following Iraq's invasion of Kuwait.

7–14 March 1991: The US Secretary of State visited Egypt, Israel, Kuwait, Saudi Arabia and Syria.

22 May 1991: Lebanon and Syria signed a 'treaty of brotherhood, co-operation and co-ordination'.

14 July 1991: Syria agreed to participate in direct negotiations with Israel at a regional Middle East peace conference.

30 October 1991: The Middle East peace conference commenced in Madrid (Spain), attended by representatives from Egypt, Israel, Lebanon and Syria, in addition to a joint Palestinian-Jordanian delegation.

12 March 1992: President Assad began a fourth seven-year term of office.

24 June 1992: The Government resigned; a new administration was formed on 29 June.

9–10 January 1994: The Ministers of Foreign Affairs of the Damascus Declaration signatories met in Damascus.

16 January 1994: The US President, Bill Clinton, met President Assad to discuss the Middle East peace process the two leaders met again in October.

5 February 1994: The Ministers of Foreign Affairs of Iran, Syria and Turkey met in Istanbul for talks on the implications of events in Iraqi Kurdistan. Turkey urged Iraq to prevent the Kurdistan Workers' Party (PKK, a proscribed party in Turkey) from maintaining bases on its territory.

27 February 1994: Lebanon and Syria withdrew from the Middle East peace process.

24 August 1994: Elections to the Syrian People's Assembly took place; the Baath party won 135 seats; independent candidates again secured the majority of the remaining seats.

14 November 1994: Syria announced a programme of economic reform.

14 March 1995: The US Secretary of State, Warren Christopher, announced that peace negotiations between Israel and Syria were to resume.

24 May 1995: Israel and Syria concluded a 'framework understanding' on security arrangements in the disputed Golan Heights.

27–29 June 1995: Israeli and Syrian Chiefs of Staff met in Washington, DC.

27–29 December 1995: Peace negotiations between Israel and Syria resumed.

3 July 1996: The Council of Ministers was reshuffled.

31 December 1996: A bomb exploded on a bus in Damascus; Syria held Israel responsible for the attack.

28 May 1997: Syria and Egypt signed an agreement to establish a bilateral free-trade zone.

2 June 1997: The border with Iraq was reopened after 18 years.

8 February 1998: Rifaat al-Assad, the younger brother of President Assad, was dismissed from his post as one of Syria's three Vice-Presidents.

10 February 1998: President Assad received the Iraqi Minister of Foreign Affairs, the first time that he had met publicly with a senior Iraqi official since the early 1980s.

5 July 1998: Maj.-Gen. Ali Aslan was appointed as Syria's Chief of Staff of the Armed Forces, replacing Maj.-Gen. Hikmat ash-Shehabi, who had held the position since 1973.

5 July 1998: Gen. Mahmoud ash-Shaqqa was appointed as head of Syria's general intelligence directorate.

16–18 July 1998: President Assad made a state visit to France, the first time since 1976 that he had ventured outside the Middle East (with the exception of his meetings in Switzerland with US Presidents Carter and Clinton).

22 July 1998: Syria condemned Israeli legislation stating that any withdrawal from the Golan hights would require the approval of the legislature and of the electorate in a referendum.

1 October 1998: Turkey threatened to invade Syria if its alleged support for the PKK continued and if Syria did not expel the PKK's leader, Abdullah Öcalan; both countries subsequently ordered troop redeployments along their joint border.

21 October 1998: Syria and Turkey signed a bilateral security agreement following two days of negotiations near the southern Turkish city of Adana.

30 December–1 January 1998: Elections to the People's Assembly were held in Syria; the National Progressive Front (led by the ruling Baath Party) won 167 of the 250 seats.

14 January 1999: The People's Assembly formally nominated President Assad for a fifth term in office.

10 February 1999: A national referendum endorsed the re-election of President Assad.

20 July 1999: Syria declared a cease-fire with Israel.

15–16 December 1999: Following an agreement reached earlier in the month to resume peace talks suspended since 1996, the Minister of Foreign Affairs, Farouk ash-Shara', met with the Israeli Prime Minister, Ehud Barak, in Washington, DC, for talks hosted by President Clinton.

3–9 January 2000: Israeli-Syrian peace talks at Shepherdstown, West Virginia, USA, attended by the Israeli Prime Minister and Syrian Minister of Foreign Affairs, proved inconclusive. A further round of talks, scheduled for 19 January, was subsequently postponed indefinitely.

11 January 2000: Pro-democracy activists claimed that over 1,000 intellectuals had signed a petition demanding political reform, including a suspension of martial law; the holding of free elections; freedom of the press; the release of political prisoners and end to discrimination against women.

27 January 2000: The Social Peace Movement was formed by the parliamentary deputy and businessman, Riad Seif; the organisation aimed to achieve democratic reform in Syria.

7 March 2000: Muhammad Mustafa Mero was named as Prime Minister of Syria, following the resignation of the Government led by Mahmoud az-Zoubi; a new Council of Ministers, containing 22 new appointees, was subsequently announced.

26 March 2000: A 'summit' meeting in Geneva between President Assad and President Clinton failed to find a formula for the resumption of negotiations on the Israeli-Syrian track of the peace process.

13 April 2000: Israel announced an end to the suspension of settlement construction in the Golan Heights.

21 May 2000: The Syrian authorities announced that former Prime Minister Mahmoud az-Zoubi, against whom corruption charges were expected to be brought, had committed suicide.

10 June 2000: President Assad died. An emergency session of the Syrian People's Assembly approved a constitutional amendment lowering the minimum age of eligibility for a presidential candidate from 40 years to 34—the age of the late President's second son, Bashar.

1 October 2000: The newspaper *Asara* published an article by a leader of the civil rights movement, Prof. Arif Dalila, which criticized the Government's economic policies.

2 October 2000: President Assad called for an Arab-led campaign to end the international sanctions imposed on Iraq following its invasion of Kuwait.

2 October 2000: Officials admintted that Syria was holding about 50 Lebanese prisoners and described the figure of 250 given by the campaign group Support for Lebanese in Detention and Exile 'exaggerated'.

6 October 2000: The Government announced that it would send an aircraft to Iraq carrying medical aid and a delegation of medical staff led by the health minister, Iyad Shatti.

11 October 2000: The Iranian foreign minister, Kamal Kharrazi, visted the country for discussions regarding the Middle-East peace process.

19 October 2000: At a meeting of the Arab foreign ministers in Cairo, Syria urged an end to the normalization of relations with Israel.

30 October 2000: The German Chancellor, Gerhard Schröder, met President Assad for talks.

4 November 2000: The Lebanese Druze leader, Walid Joumblatt, was declared *persona non grata* in Syria, following his statement that Syria's role in Lebanon should be reviewed; the ban was revoked in January.

20 November 2000: During celebrations of the late President Hafiz al-Assad's seizure of power, President Bashar al-Assad announced that some 600 political prisoners were to be released, among them Communists and members of Islamist organizations.

29 November 2000: The Baath Party issued a statement permitting other political parties to issue their own newspapers. The Communist Party subsequently issued the first non-state controlled newspaper early in 2001.

7 December 2000: Syrian officials announced that all Lebanese prisoners in Syrian gaols would be released. However debate still remained over the numbers held.

11 December 2000: The authorities released 48 Lebanese prisoners who had been detained since the end of the Lebanese civil war in 1990.

13 December 2000: Algeria, Egypt, Iran, Kuwait, Morocco, Saudi Arabia, Syria and Tunisia signed the UN Convention Against Organized Crime, which provided for co-ordination between national crime-fighting bodies, the protection of witnesses, measures to combat money-laundering and the acceleration of extradition proceedings.

29 January 2001: The Minister of Information, Adnan Omran, declared that martial law had been 'frozen'. In response, some 70 lawyers signed a petition demanding a review of the judicial system, including a complete removal of martial law.

8 February 2001: Following the election of Ariel Sharon as the Prime Minister of Israel, who had indicated in his campaign that he would seek to reconcile his country with Syria, Assad emphasized that the Government would only consider peace negotiatons if the Israelis withdrew from the Golan Heights.

3 March 2001: Mero's Government was reported to have tendered its resignation to President Assad, who refused to accept it.

15 April 2001: Israel carried out air raids on a Syrian air base in eastern Lebanon; three Syrian soldiers were killed.

May 2001: Nizar Nayouf, a Syrian journalist and campaigner for democracy, was released after spending nearly a decade in detention.

3 May 2001: President Assad visited Spain for discussions with senior government officials regarding greater European Union participation in the Middle East peace process; it was Assad's first visit to a Western country since taking office.

5–8 May 2001: Pope John Paul II visited Syria. During the visit, he became the first Roman Catholic pontiff to enter a mosque, where he prayed for peace in the Middle East.

6 May 2001: Syria and Turkey agreed to proposals for joint military training excercises.

15 May 2001: The Cuban leader, Dr Fidel Castro Ruz, met President Assad; during the visit Castro spoke about the American embargo on Cuba and the effects of economic globalization.

22 May 2001: Delegations from the Iraqi and Syrian Governments began discussions in Baghdad on ways to improve economic co-operation and trade between the two countries.

22 May 2001: Walid Joumblatt met President Assad in Damascus; despite Syria's earlier proclamation that Joumblatt was unwelcome in the country, owing to his criticism of Syria's presence in Lebanon.

22 May 2001: Iraqi and Syrian officials held talks in Baghdad on improving economic and trade co-operation.

14–18 June 2001: Following public protests over Syrian interference in government affairs, Syria withdrew its remaining troops from Beirut.

15 June 2001: The UN Secretary-General Kofi Annan, met the Minister of Foreign Affairs, ash-Shara', in Damascus; during the meeting they discussed the Israeli-Palestinian conflict, the UN sanctions on Iraq and the situation in Lebanon.

19 June 2001: The Syrian evacuation of Beirut was completed.

22 June 2001: The Syrian authorities denied any involvement in the abduction of Nizar Nayouf, reported the previous day—Nayouf had been preparing to release information on human-rights abuses in Syria before he was abducted.

1 July 2001: Following Hezbollah mortar attacks on Israeli positions, Israel launched air raids on a Syrian military radar station in Lebanon, wounding three people.

16 July 2001: President Assad sent his congratulations to Saddam Hussain on Iraq's National Day; it was the first such communication between Iraq and Syria for 20 years.

Turkey

***c.* 2000 BC:** The Assyrian civilization is believed to have maintained a presence in Anatolia.

1600 BC–1200 BC: Asia Minor was part of the Hittite Empire, towards the end of that period Greeks began to migrate into Anatolia, and the west of the territory was gradually incorporated into the Hellenic world.

546 BC: The Persians conquered Asia Minor.

334 BC: Alexander III ('the Great'), the Macedon King and Greek military leader, defeated the Persians in Asia Minor; Hellenic dominance was restored.

133 BC: Turkey constituted the province of Asia within the Roman Empire.

4th–11th centuries AD: Anatolia remained dominated by the Byzantine Empire and the consequent Greek influence.

330: The Roman Emperor Constantine inaugurated the new city of Constantinople on the site of the Greek trading settlement of Byzantium; the city became the centre of the Eastern Roman Empire (later the Byzantine Empire) upon the Empire's division.

7th century: Chinese annals from this period referred to a Central Asian people known as the *Tu-Kiu*—this is believed to be the first instance of the term 'Turk'.

11th century: Anatolia remained dominated by the Byzantine Empire and the consequent Greek influence.

1071: The battle of Manzikert took place between the Emperor Romanus Diogenes and the Seljuq Sultan, Alp Arslan, who ruled Persia and Central Asia, resulting in an overwhelming defeat for the Byzantine army. Numbers of nomadic Central Asian Turks moved onto the Anatolian plateau and eventually various Turkish principalities emerged.

13th century: The Seljuq Sultanate of Rum became a client state of the Mongol Empire.

1281: Othman I Ghazi created an emirate on the borders of the Byzantine lands in western Anatolia; the Ottomans, as that state's people became known, embarked on expansion throughout Anatolia and into the Balkan peninsula.

6 April 1327: The Ottoman capital was established at Bursa following its capture.

1361: Following conquests in the Balkans, the Ottomans moved their capital across the Bosphorus to Edirne (also known as Adrianople) in Thrace.

28 July 1402: The Battle of Ankara was fought between the Ottoman Sultan Bayezid I and the Central Asian conqueror, Timur 'the lame' (Tamerlane). Bayezid was defeated but the Ottoman state revived.

1453: The city of Constantinople (known by the Turks as İstanbul) was captured by the Ottoman Sultan Mehmet 'the Conqueror' and became the Ottomans' capital.

1475: The Ottomans conquered Kaffa and the Giray Khans of the Tatars became Ottoman vassals.

1517: The Mameluke Sultanate, which ruled the greater part of the Middle East, including Egypt, was captured by Ottoman forces.

1520–66: The reign of Süleyman 'the Magnificent' was the apogee of the Ottoman Empire. Imperial territory was expanded into Arabia and Asia in the ease, and South-Eastern Europe in the west.

15 October 1529: The first siege of Vienna (Austria) ended in the Sultan abandoning the attempt.

1683: The second siege of Vienna marked the furthest extent of Ottoman expansion in Europe.

26 January 1699: The Treaty of Carlowitz was concluded, the first treaty the Ottomans signed as a defeated power.

1768: The Ottomans were at war with Russia regarding the Black Sea territories.

1774: The Treaty of Kücük Kaynarja was signed, ending the war with Russia; under its terms, the Crimea achieved independence. However, the territory was again annexed by Russia in 1783.

1787–92: Wars with Austria and Russia ended in Ottoman defeat.

1792: The Nizam-i Cedid or 'New Order' was promulgated by Sultan Selim III as a first attempt at reform.

1821: A rebellion in support of Greek independence escalated into war. France, Russia and the United Kingdom intervened in support of the concept of a Greek state (and the consequent reduction of Ottoman powers) and the Ottomans were unable to prevent its establishment—they eventually recognized Greece in 1831.

15 June 1826: The Janissaries, the traditional infantry of Ottoman armies, attempted to overthrow the Sultan but instead were themselves eliminated.

1839: Mahmud II died and was succeeded by his son Abdülmecid, who attempted further reforms, most notably of the tax system.

1853: Russia, seeking to gain access to the Christian 'holy land' in Palestine (as the Ottomans had granted to the Latin churches) was rebuffed, and responded by occupying the Ottoman possessions of Moldova and Wallachia. The Ottomans declared war, and derived support from the British and French, who sent fleets to the Black Sea.

1854–56: The allied powers in what became known as the Crimean War eventually forced Russia to withdraw from Crimea and from Moldova and Wallachia (which were occupied by Austria). The war was concluded by the Congress of Paris, which restored the Ottoman territories to their pre-war extents and demilitarized the Black Sea.

1856: The Hatt-i Humayun (Imperial Rescript) was announced, introducing a new phase of legal reforms.

20 June 1861: Sultan Abdülmecid died.

September 1871: Ali Pasha, the last reforming Vezir, died.

July 1875: Insurrection at Ottoman rule in Bosnia and Herzegovina spread to Bulgaria. The Ottoman repression of these revolts drew protests from the European powers.

October 1875: Interest payments on the Ottoman Empire's foreign debt were suspended, an admission of bankruptcy.

27 August 1876: Sultan Murad was deposed owing to ill health—Abd al-Hamid became Sultan.

23 December 1876: The first Ottoman Constitution was promulgated by Midhat Pasha.

5 February 1877: Midhat Pasha was dismissed and then sent into internal exile.

13 February 1877: Abd al-Hamid disbanded the Ottoman parliament and ruled personally, suppressing all attempts at reform.

1908: Power was seized by the Young Turks, a clandestine grouping of military officers, and the Committee of Union and Progress. The new authorities greatly reformed the Ottoman lands, and instituted a Constitution and a parliament.

1911: Italy declared war on the Ottoman Empire, and gained Libya and the Dodecanese.

1912–13: An alliance of Balkan peoples sought to expel the Ottoman forces from their remaining possessions in Europe and made significant territorial gains in the Balkan peninsula.

October 1914: The Ottoman Empire, which had increasingly accepted German influence, entered the First World War on the side of the Central Powers.

October 1914–October 1918: The Ottoman dominance of the Dardanelles prevented effective naval co-operation between the Western Powers and Russia; however, a British attack from positions in Egypt and India was able to expel the Ottomans from Syria, Palestine and much of Iraq. Defeated, the Ottomans were forced to seek peace.

30 October 1918: The Ottomans signed an armistice at Mudros and British, French and Italian occupation forces moved into Turkey.

15 May 1919: A Greek army, under cover of allied warships, landed at İzmir (Smyrna) with the intention of occupying the city and all territory inhabited by Greeks in Anatolia and Thrace. Greek forces subsequently advanced in Anatolia.

23 July 1919: Mustafa Kemal, previously a general in the Ottoman army, convened the Nationalist congress in Erzurum.

September 1919: A second Nationalist congress was held. An Executive Committee, presided over by Mustafa Kemal, was formed and Ankara was declared the centre of the Nationalist movement. The movement subsequently renounced foreign possessions, but demanded a Turkish state within the remaining Ottoman lands.

10 August 1920: The Treaty of Sèvres was signed, dismantling what remained of the Ottoman Empire.

24 August 1921: Turkish forces, commanded by Kemal, defeated the Greeks at the Sakarya river.

9 September 1922: The Nationalist Turks, having driven the Greek forces back to the Aegean, reoccupied İzmir.

11 October 1922: The occupying armies having withdrawn from the region, allowing Kemal's forces to reoccupy eastern Thrace, an armistice was signed.

November 1922: The Sultan abdicated and fled to exile—the Nationalist Government was now in sole authority.

29 October 1923: Turkey was declared a Republic, with Kemal as President.

20 April 1924: A Constitution was enacted, providing for an elected legislature, with executive power vested in a Council of Ministers selected by the President. A single political party, the Cumhuriyet Halk Partisi (CHP—Republican People's Party) gained official status.

24 July 1924: A peace treaty was signed between the allies and the new Turkish Government which recognised complete and undivided Turkish sovereignty.

1925: There was a Kurdish uprising in eastern Turkey in protest against the abrogation of the Treaty of Sèvres, which had included provision for an independent Kurdish state. Kurdish nationalism continued to be repressed throughout Kemal's period in office—the Kurdish language was declared illegal, and the term 'Kurd' was not used, the authorities instead referring to the people as 'Mountain Turks'.

1928: Following a number of actions aimed at reducing the role of Islam in Turkish society, the Constitution was amended to disestablish the religion and specify Turkey as a secular republic; in the same year, a Latin script was adopted, to replace the Arabic one.

1932: In response to the worldwide economic depression, 'statism' (state controlled capitalism) became the basis of the economic policy.

1934: As part of the programme of Westernizing reforms, Turks were required to adopt surnames—Kemal adopted the name Atatürk ('father of the Turks'), conferred by parliament.

1934: The Balkan Pact was signed between Greece, Romania, Turkey and Yugoslavia, amid fear of Bulgarian aggression.

1937: Afghanistan, Iran, Iraq and Turkey agreed to the Sa'dabad Pact, which provided for mutual consultation in all disputes that might affect the common interests of the four states.

November 1938: Mustafa Kemal Atatürk died. Ismet İnönü became President.

19 October 1939: Turkey signed an agreement to support France and the United Kingdom in the Second World War.

18 June 1941: Having observed the fall of France and of many of its neighbouring European countries, Turkey sought to assert its neutrality.

23 February 1945: Turkey, which had reversed its policy and increasingly supported the allies against Germany, formally declared war, as a precondition for participation in the United Nations Conference.

November 1945: The Government ended the one-party system.

1950: The Demokratik Parti (DP—Democratic Party) won Turkey's first free election. The founders of the DP, Celâl Bayar and Adnan Menderes, became President and Prime Minister, respectively.

1952: Turkey joined the North Atlantic Treaty Organization (NATO) as a full member.

February 1955: Iraq and Turkey formed a defence alliance.

November 1955: Turkey joined the Baghdad Pact.

January 1957: An aid programme for Middle Eastern countries, including Turkey, in exchange for a commitment to restrict Communism, was offered by the US President, Dwight D. Eisenhower.

5–11 February 1959: The Greek and Turkish Prime Ministers and Ministers of Foreign Affairs met in Zürich, Switzerland.

5 March 1959: The USA signed bilateral defence agreements in Ankara with each of Iran, Pakistan and Turkey.

13 July 1959: A new NATO base opened at Trebizond, on Turkey's Black Sea coast.

27 May 1960: Amid increasing political unrest, the army intervened in the country's governance and arrested President Bayar and the Prime Minister, Menderes. Administrative power was vested in a Committee of National Union, led Gen. Cemal Gürsel.

25 August 1960: Following the adoption of an interim Constitution, pending the drafting of a final version, 10 of the 18 members of the Council of Ministers were dismissed; their replacemets were chiefly military figures, Gen. Gürsel assuming the roles of President, Prime Minister and Minister of Defence.

13 November 1960: The Committee of National Union was dissolved and replaced by a new, 23-member Committee. The 14 dismissed members were alleged to have been conspiring to seize power.

5 January 1961: A new cabinet was formed in Turkey.

6 January 1961: A new Assembly was convened; its membership comprised the Committee of National Union and 271 elected and appointed members. The new Assembly sought to draft a new constitution.

13 January 1961: The ban on party-political activity was repealed.

11 May 1961: The trial of the deposed leaders of the Menderes regime began on the island of Yassiada, where the legal process against them had begun in October 1960.

9 July 1961: The new Constitution, which had been ratified by the Assembly on 26 May, was approved by national referendum.

15 September 1961: Menderes and two other members of his Government were sentenced to death by the court on Yassiada; 12 other figures from the regime (including the former President, Bayar) also received death sentences, but these were commuted to life imprisonment.

17 September 1961: Menderes and the two other former ministers were executed.

15 October 1961: In elections to the new legislature, the CHP won 173 of the 450 seats in the Turkish Grand National Assembly (TGNA—lower house) and 36 of the 50 seats in the Senate; the Justice Party (JP) secured 158 seats in the National Assembly and 70 in the Senate.

25 October 1961: The first session of the new National Assembly returned Gen. Gürsel unopposed to the post of President.

20 November 1961: Ismet Inönü, leader of the CHP, formed a coalition Government which included members of the JP.

22 February 1962: An attempted military *coup d'état* was suppressed.

25 June 1962: Inönü formed a new coalition Government, without the participation of the JP.

21 May 1963: A further attempted *coup d'état* was suppressed.

23 December 1963: Inönü, who had resigned earlier in the month after the two junior parties left the governing coalition, formed a minority Government, after the JP was unable to form an administration.

21 February 1964: An attempt on the life of the Prime Minister, Inönü, was unsuccessful.

March 1964: Disquiet at the treatment of the Turkish minority on Cyprus escalated into unrest in Turkey, which continued sporadically throughout the year.

June 1964: The JP won 31 of the 51 seats contested in elections to the Senate, thus increasing its majority in the chamber.

3–4 July 1964: The Regional Co-operation for Development, a tripartite arrangement between Iran, Pakistan and Turkey that aimed to promote economic co-operation, was established.

31 November 1964: Turkey commenced its association with the European Economic Community (EEC).

13 February 1965: Following the Government's defeat in a vote on the Budget in the National Assembly, Inönü resigned.

16 February 1965: A coalition Government was formed by the JP, the New Turkish Party (NTP), the Republican Peasants' Party (RP) and the National Party (NP). An independent Senator, Suat Hayri Ürgüplü, was appointed Prime Minister.

11 October 1965: In the legislative elections, the JP secured an absolute majority in the National Assembly, with 240 of the 450 seats. The CHP won 134 seats, the NP 31, the NTP 19, the Turkish Workers' Party 15 and the RP 11. Süleyman Demirel, the leader of the JP, formed a new Government.

28 March 1966: Cevdat Sunay was elected President, in succession to Gürsel, who was relieved of the post owing to illness (he died in September).

June 1966: The JP again performed strongly in elections to the Senate.

19 August 1966: A severe earthquake in eastern Turkey caused over 2,000 deaths.

30 April 1967: A group of disaffected CHP members formed the Reliance Party.

23 May 1967: The Organisation for Economic Co-operation and Development (OECD) granted Turkey US $25m. in credit for three years.

15–30 November 1967: Amid heavy fighting between the Greek and Turkish communities, Turkey prepared to invade Cyprus. However, mediation by the UN and the USA achieved Graeco-Turkish agreement and reduced tension.

15–30 May 1969: By making clear its opposition to a bill to restore political rights to former leaders of the Democratic Party (the precursor of the JP), the army, by the implied threat of a *coup d'état*, effectively overruled a parliamentary majority; the bill was later withdrawn.

12 October 1969: Following the legislative elections, the JP retained its absolute majority, and Demirel's Government remained in office.

26 January 1970: A contract for the construction of a bridge over the Bosphorus was signed in Ankara; the bridge was scheduled for completion in 1973.

11–14 February 1970: The budget was defeated in parliament; Demirel resigned but later formed a new administration.

28 April 1970: Severe earthquakes hit western Turkey, centred on the Gediz area.

15–16 June 1970: In response to serious rioting throughout the country, martial law was declared in several areas, including Istanbul. The rioting continued throughout the year, however, and unrest escalated among the Kurdish community in the east of the country.

9 August 1970: The Turkish currency was devalued by 66.6%.

12 March 1971: Following an army warning that they would take power if the civilian authorities were unable to suppress the increasing disorder, Demirel resigned; Prof. Nihat Erim formed a new administration, composed largely of Ministers without seats in the National Assembly.

October 1971: The withdrawal of the JP's support from the Government caused Erim to resign; however, President Sunay rejected the resignation.

December 1971: Erim again resigned, but was invited to form a new administration.

27 March 1972: Three NATO technicians were abducted by the Turkish Peoples' Liberation Army; they were subsequently found dead.

17 April 1972: Erim submitted his Government's resignation, and announced that he would not seek to form a new administration.

22 May 1972: Ferit Melen formed a new Government, with multi-party support.

6 April 1973: Senator Fahri Korutürk was elected President, in succession to Cevdet Sunay.

12 April 1973: Senator Naim Talu formed a new coalition Government to govern until the legislative elections scheduled for October, comprising members of the JP, Reliance and independents.

14 October 1973: General elections were held.

January 1974: The CHP formed a Government, led by Bülent Ecevit, in alliance with the Milli Selamet Partisi (MSP—National Salvation Party) a conservative, pro-Islamic party.

March 1974: Turkey granted foreign companies petroleum-exploration concessions in the Aegean Sea, resulting in a dispute with Greece over whether the Aegean Islands on the continental shelf can be held to have their own smaller 'shelves'.

July 1974: Turkey claimed the entire eastern Aegean, as far as the median line between the mainlands of Greece and Asia Minor, as its territorial continental shelf.

July 1974: Following the fighting between Turks and Greeks on Cyprus, Turkey sent an armed force to the island, which eventually occupied the northern third (see chapter on Cyprus).

1975–80: Amid increasing political violence, a succession of coalition governments, led by either Ecevit or Demirel, were unable to impose effective governance; instead they added to the country's political instability.

February 1975: The USA imposed an embargo on military aid to Turkey.

July 1975: Turkey reacted to the US embargo by assuming control of US military bases on its territory.

March 1976: After lengthy negotiations a new bilateral defence agreement was reached with the USA (although the USA never ratified the agreement).

6 June 1977: The general elections produced a political *impasse* between the JP and the CHP; the balance of power was again held by the MSP. The prevailing instability thus persisted.

1 March 1978: The Turkish currency was devalued by 23%.

20 March 1978: A general strike was held.

April 1978: A trade pact was signed with the USSR; this was followed, in June, by a 'friendship pact'.

1 August 1978: The USA lifted its arms embargo.

October 1978: The Turkish Government agreed to reopen two US air bases.

22–25 December 1978: Violent disturbances broke out among the Kurdish population in the town of Karamanmarash in the south-east, in which some 100 people were killed. Martial law was declared throughout the 11 south-eastern provinces.

December 1979: Left-wing demonstrations took place in Ankara and İstanbul.

9 December 1979: The 'Hundred Days' development programme was announced by the Government.

January 1980: The Turkish lira was devalued by 33% against the US dollar.

8–16 February 1980: Daily battles took place between workers and police in İzmir.

19 February 1980: Bomb attacks were carried out by left-wing groups in five major cities.

29 March 1980: A five-year defence and economic co-operation agreement was signed with the USA.

31 May–2 June 1980: A total of 37 politically motivated killings took place.

12 September 1980: Amid a further increase in political violence, the armed forces, led by Gen. Kenan Evren, ousted Demirel's Government. A National Security Council (NSC) was formed; the NSC appointed a civilian cabinet, but retained effective power.

April 1981: All former politicians were banned by the NSC from future political activity.

May 1981: A US $1,000m. loan was arranged by the OECD for Turkey.

October 1981: All political parties were disbanded; amid increasing international criticism of the NSC regime, a Consultative Assembly was established to draft a new constitution, in preparation for a return to civilian rule.

November 1982: The Constitution was approved in a referendum—an appendix to the document installed Evren as President, for a seven-year term.

May 1983: The ban on political parties was repealed, although all former political leaders remained banned from seeking office, and pre-1980 parties could not be re-registered.

May 1983: A major offensive was mounted against Kurdish insurgents in eastern Turkey and northern Iraq.

July 1983: There were terrorist attacks on Turkish embassies and other targets abroad.

6 November 1983: Elections were held under the terms of the Constitution drafted in 1982 for a return to civilian rule. Of the three registered parties permitted to contest the elections, Anavatan Partisi (ANAP—Motherland Party) won 211 of the 400 seats in the legislature, defeating the parties with NSC support. The leader of ANAP, Turgut Özal, was appointed Prime Minister in December.

1984: The Partiya Karkeren Kurdistan (PKK—Kurdistan Workers' Party) began a guerrilla war for Kurdish independence.

November 1985: The main opposition parties merged to form the Sosyal Demokrat Halkçı Parti (SHP—Social Democratic Populist Party).

December 1985: A case was brought before the Human Rights Commission of the Council of the Europe alleging that Turkey had violated the European Convention for the Protection of Human Rights. Turkey agreed to rescind all martial law decrees and to introduce an amnesty for all political prisoners.

1987: Turkey formally applied for full membership of the EEC, but was rejected.

September 1987: A national referendum was held, in which the electorate voted to repeal the ban on political activity by some 200 politicians. Ecevit assumed the leadership of the Demokratik Sol Parti (DSP—Democratic Left Party), which appealed to former supporters of the CHP. Demirel, meanwhile, was elected leader of the Dogru Yol Partisi (DYP—True Path Party).

November 1987: Dr Nihat Sargina and Haydar Kutlu, leaders of two proscribed left-wing parties, returned to Turkey after seven years of exile, intending to merge their parties and thereby form a United Communist Party. They were arrested at the airport.

29 November 1987: General elections were held which were contested by seven parties. The ANAP won 36.3% of the votes cast and secured 292 seats in the TGNA. The SHP won 99 seats and the DYP 59. Özal subsequently formed a new Government.

January 1988: The Turkish government signed the UN's and the Council of Europe's agreements denouncing torture.

February 1988: The Sosyalist Parti (Socialist Party), the first overtly socialist political party in Turkey since the 1980 coup, was formally established.

June 1988: The trials of Sargina and Kutlu began. Both alleged they had been tortured.

June 1988: An unsuccessful assassination attempt was made on President Özal by a senior member of the 'Grey Wolves', a neo-fascist organization involved in the violence of the 1970s.

September 1988: Following Iraqi offensives against the Kurds, in which chemical weapons were reportedly used; more than 100,000 Kurdish refugees fled to Turkey.

22 August 1989: Turkey closed its border with Bulgaria.

14–15 October 1989: An international conference on the 'Kurdish question' was held in Paris.

31 October 1989: Turgut Özal was elected President of Turkey in succession to Evren.

9 November 1989: Yıldırım Akbulut was appointed Prime Minister, at the head of a new Government.

18 December 1989: Turkish membership of the EEC was rejected by that organization's Commission until 1993 at the earliest.

20 February 1990: Mesut Yılmaz resigned as Turkish Minister of Foreign Affairs; he was succeeded by Ali Bozer.

October 1990: Bozer resigned as Minister of Foreign Affairs.

3 January 1991: A general strike was widely observed.

2 April 1991: Turkey appealed to the UN for emergency aid for Kurdish refugees who had fled to the country from Iraq.

June 1991: Yılmaz defeated Akbulut in the contest for the leadership of ANAP. Akbulut subsequently resigned the premiership; Yılmaz was invited to form a new administration, which took office on 23 June.

5 July 1991: The National Assembly approved the programme of the new Government.

20–22 July 1991: The US President, George Bush, visited Turkey.

20 October 1991: In the legislative election, the DYP, led by Demirel, obtained 27.3% of the votes cast, compared with 23.9% secured by ANAP and 20.6% by the SHP. The DYP and the SHP subsequently formed a coalition Government, led by Demirel.

3 July 1992: The ban on certain political parties was revoked.

10 July 1992: The ban on the Turkish Socialist Party was reaffirmed by the Constitutional Court.

1–2 December 1992: Some 70 deputies defected from the SHP, undermining the strength of the governing coalition in the National Assembly.

16 May 1993: Demirel was elected President, following the death of Özal.

14 June 1993: Tansu Çiller, who had been elected leader of the DYP in succession to Demirel, was appointed Prime Minister, the first woman to hold the post in Turkey. Çiller's first cabinet contained all the SHP ministers from Demirel's administration; however, all the incumbent DYP ministers were replaced. Çiller subsequently announced her intention to introduce a programme of economic austerity.

28 November 1993: Five DYP ministers were replaced in a cabinet reorganization.

1 December 1993: Iran and Turkey signed a security co-operation agreement.

5 February 1994: The Ministers of Foreign Affairs of Iran, Syria and Turkey met in Istanbul for talks on the implications of events in Iraqi Kurdistan. Turkey urged Iraq to prevent the PKK from maintaining bases on its territory.

16 June 1994: The Democracy Party was proscribed.

18 February 1995: The SHP an the CHP agreed to merge, under the latter's name.

20 March–5 May 1995: The Turkish armed forces conducted an offensive against bases of the PKK in northern Iraq.

27 March 1995: The Cabinet was reshuffled.

23 July 1995: The National Assembly approved constitutional amendments, the provisions of which included the relaxation of restrictions on political activity and the expansion of the National Assembly.

20 September 1995: The Government resigned, following disagreements between the DYP and the CHP; following protracted and unsuccessful coalition negotiations with a number of parties, Çiller recognized that legislative elections were necessary—they were scheduled for December.

31 October 1995: Çiller was appointed interim Prime Minister, leading another DYP-CHP coalition.

13 December 1995: The European Parliament agreed to establish customs union between European Union (EU—the successor to the EEC) member states and Turkey from 1 January 1996.

24 December 1995: In the legislative election the Refah Partisi (Welfare Party, an Islamic party whose support had greatly increased in the 1990s) gained 21.4% of the votes cast and 158 seats. The DYP obtained 19.2% of the ballot and 135 seats, while ANAP received 19.7% of the votes cast and won 132 seats.

January 1996: Both the DYP and ANAP announced tht they would not enter a coalition with Welfare, whose leader, Necmettin Erbakan, had been charged with forming a government. Negotiations between the DYP and ANAP failed; however, the two parties agreed a coalition in late February to prevent the formation of a minority Welfare administration.

6 March 1996: Demirel approved the ANAP-DYP coalition, under a rotating premiership, to be held first, for one year, by the ANAP leader, Yılmaz. A parliamentary vote of confidence was subsequently won.

7 April 1996: Israel and Turkey signed a series of military co-operation agreements.

24 May 1996: The DYP withdrew from the governing coalition, following the failure of a number of ANAP deputies to oppose motions to establish commissions of investigation into alleged corrupt conduct on the part of Çiller.

6 June 1996: The Constitutional Court officially annulled the vote of confidence in the defunct ANAP-DYP administration; Yılmaz resigned as premier.

28 June 1996: Erbakan became Prime Minister, having agreed a Welfare-DYP coalition (a number of DYP deputies resigned from the party in protest at the agreement).

28 August 1996: Israel and Turkey signed a defence agreement.

1 October 1996: The human-rights organization Amnesty International commenced a world-wide campaign against alleged Turkish abuses of human rights.

15 January 1997: The foundation of a new Turkish political party, the Demokrat Türkiye Partisi (Democratic Turkey Party), was reported.

14 May 1997: Turkish forces attacked guerrilla bases of the PKK in northern Iraq.

18 June 1997: Following further defections from the DYP and a series of censure motions against the Government (many centring on Welfare's Islamic sympathies, which contravened the modern state's secular tradition), Erbakan was forced to resign.

20 June 1997: Yılmaz formed a coalition with the DSP and the DTP, which subsequently took office as a minority Government. The DYP protested President Demirel's decision to appoint the administration rather than organize a general election.

16 January 1998: The Constitutional Court ordered the dissolution of the Welfare Party on the grounds that it undermined Turkey's constitutional secularism; the Court banned seven party members, including Erbakan, from political life for five years.

February 1998: Amid increasing popular unrest at the Government's perceived anti-Islamic measures, former deputies of Welfare joined the recently established Fazilet Partisi (FP—Virtue Party); by March the FP was the largest party in the National Assembly.

30 July 1998: The Grand National Assembly approved April 1999 as the date for the forthcoming legislative elections.

1 October 1998: Turkey threatened to invade Syria if its alleged support for the PKK continued and if Syria did not expel the PKK's leader, Abdullah Öcalan; both countries subsequently ordered troop redeployments along their joint border.

21 October 1998: Syria and Turkey signed a bilateral security agreement following two days of negotiations near the southern Turkish city of Adana.

November 1998: Turkey recalled its ambassador from Italy, in protest at that country's refusal to extradite Öcalan, who had applied for asylum there fter leaving Syria.

25 November 1998: The Government collapsed after suffering a vote of 'no confidence' in the TGNA, proposed amid allegations of corruption against Yılmaz.

January 1999: The Italian authorities denied Öcalan's asylum request, and he was reported to have left the country, although his subsequent whereabouts were not known.

12 January 1999: A new Government, led by Ecevit of the DSP, was formed, following protracted negotiations; the DYP had refused to participate in a coalition, but subsequently anounced its support for Ecevit.

17 February 1999: Öcalan was captured by Turkish agents in Kenya, where he had been given refuge in the Greek embassy, and was returned to Turkey for trial on charges of terrorist activity and murder; Kurdish groups in numerous countries protested at Greek and Turkish embassies.

18 April 1999: In the election to the TGNA the DSP won 136 of the 550 seats, the MHP 129, ANAP 111, the FP 86 and the DYP 85.

28 May 1999: A new coalition Government, formed by members of the DSP, MHP and ANAP and led by Ecevit, was announced; the administration won a parliamentary vote of confidence in early June.

29 June 1999: Öcalan was convicted and sentenced to death; the verdict brought international protests.

17 August 1999: An earthquake measuring 7.8 on the Richter scale struck near the north-western city of İzmit; some 17,100 people died, a further 40,000 were injured and an estimated 350,000 were made homeless. A further earthquake, measuring 7.2 on the Richter scale, struck a more remote part of the same region in November, some 800 deaths resulted. The international assistance given to Turkey after the first earthquake was most notable for the participation of Greece, with which relations had begun to improve (Turkey reciprocated when an earthquake struck in Greece in September).

10–11 December 1999: EU heads of state and government, meeting in Helsinki, Finland, agreed to accept Turkey as a candidate for membership of the union.

29 March 2000: The TGNA rejected proposed constitutional amendments providing for the extension of the term of presidential office from five years to seven, the introduction of direct presidential elections and the removal of the constitutional bar on an incumbent President seeking re-election (the aim of this last provision was to permit Demirel to serve a second term of office, there being no agreement among the parties on a candidate to succeed him).

5 April 2000: The proposed constitutional amendments were again rejected; the search for a presidential candidate who would be able to command a majority in the TGNA resumed.

5 May 2000: In a third round of voting, the TGNA elected the Government's nominee, Ahmet Necdet Sezer (hitherto the President of the Constitutional Court), to the presdency.

12 October 2000: Parliament threatened not to renew a US mandate to use Turkish airbases if the US Congress approved a draft resolution, which recognized as genocide the killing of over 1m. Armenians by the Ottoman Turks in 1915. Armenia alleged that 1.5m. of its citizens died in the massacre; Turkey claimed that 300,000 Armenians lost their lives as they revolted against the Ottoman authorities.

24 October 2000: A group of 41 inmates at Aydin regional prison went on hunger strike in protest at government plans to build new prisons, the design of which, they maintained, left them more vulnerable to abuse by staff.

26 October 2000: Greece withdrew from a joint military NATO exercise in the Aegean after accusing Turkey of preventing its aircraft from flying over the disputed islands of Limnos and Ikaria.

1 November 2000: The Russian Prime Minister, Mikhail Kasyanov, met the President, the Prime Minister and other senior government officials for discussions; a number of agreements on co-operation in the areas of energy and defence were made.

2 November 2000: The Minister of State for Justice, Hikmet Sami Turk, announced that five of the new prison buildings were to be completed by the end of 2000. Prisoners protesting against the plan continued their hunger strike and were joined by inmates in several other institutions.

8 November 2000: The upper house of the French parliament recognized the deaths of Armenians in 1915 as genocide. Turkey responded by recalling its ambassador to France and cancelling contracts with French companies.

15 November 2000: The World Commission on Dams reported that the proposed Ilsu Dam on the River Tigris would threaten livelihoods and leave 25,000 Kurds in south-eastern Turkey homeless.

19 November 2000: Öcalan began an appeal at the European Court of Human Rights against the death sentence imposed on him in 1999. Some 15,000 Kurds and 3,000 Turks held peaceful demonstrations outside the court.

20 November 2000: European officials reported that Turkey's accession to the EU would be postponed since the Government had not yet ratified several human rights instruments (such as the Convention on the Elimination of All Forms of Racial Discrimination) or abolished the death penalty. The EU also stipulated that a solution to the conflict in Cyprus had to be found before Turkey could become a member, although this was subsequently amended.

21 November 2000: Following representations made by the EU, the Prime Minister announced that he would consider revoking the ban on Kurdish-language broadcasting.

6 December 2000: Following an overnight increase in interest rates to a high point of 1,700%, the Government received an emergency loan of US $7,500m. from the IMF.

12 December 2000: In the Constitutional Court, the Government began a case seeking the closure of the FP for carrying out anti-secularist activities and continuing the policies of the banned Welfare Party.

15 December 2000: The European Court of Human Rights granted Öcalan leave to appeal against the death sentence imposed on him by a Turkish court.

22 December 2000: The security forces raided 20 prisons in an attempt to end the hunger strikes; some 30 inmates and two soldiers were killed in the violence; over 1,000 other prisoners were transferred to more secure instititions.

22 December 2000: Parliament approved legislation to reduce the sentences of 35,000 prisoners by 10 years; Preident Sezer subsequently ratified the bill, having originally vetoed it on the grounds that it did not serve the cause of justice.

3 January 2001: A suicide-bomb attack occurred at the Security Department in Sisli; a proscribed left-wing organization claimed responsibility for the incident.

10 January 2001: The President received the leader of the Patriotic Union of Kurdistan (PUK) , Jalal Talabani, and pledged to assist the organization in its conflict against the separatist PKK. Later in the month, Turkish troops advanced 160 km into PKK territory in northern Iraq.

30 January 2001: A DYP deputy, Fevzi Sihanlioglu, died after intervening in a fight during a parliamentary debate; two MHP deputies were subsequently charged with involuntary manslaughter.

10 February 2001: Relations with Greece were strained when the Greek Parliament declared 14 September to be 'Genocide Day' in commemoration of an assault by Kemal's forces on a Greek community in Turkey in 1922.

21 February 2001: The Government, with the support of the International Monetary Fund (IMF) abandoned its exchange-rate controls and allowed the lira to float while allowing the central bank to pursue a strict monetary policy to control inflation. The lira subsequently depreciated by approximately 40% against the world's major currencies.

March 2001: The Government announced a programme of political, economic, social and administrative reforms to prepare the country further for membership of the EU.

14 March 2001: The newly appointed finance minister, Kemal Dervis, outlined a structural reform package to bring the Turkish economy out of crisis, including the restructuring of three state-owned banks under one supervisory board.

20 March 2001: The Government announced a programme of political, economic, social and administrative reforms, which would prepare Turkey for membership of the EU.

20 March 2001: Following the deployment of several thousand Turkish troops in northern Iraq, 16 PKK members and three soldiers were killed in confrontations.

2 April 2001: Bulgaria, Georgia, Romania, Russia, Turkey and Ukraine formally established Blackseafor, a multi-national naval unit with a humanitarian and environmental role.

2 April 2001: Salih Izzet Erdis, the leader of the illegal Great Eastern Islamic Raiders' Front, was convicted of seeking to overthrow the secular state and sentenced to death.

10 April 2001: The Israeli foreign minister, Shimon Peres, held talks with senior Government officials regarding the Arab-Israeli conflict and plans for Israel to purchase drinking-water from Turkey.

27 April 2001: The Deputy Prime Minister and Minister of Energy and Natural Resources, Cumhur Ersümer, was dismissed following allegations that he had illegally awarded contracts to favoured companies. The allegations were made by a Government anti-corruption investigation team led by the interior minister, Saadettin Tantan.

27 April 2001: Turkey secured US $10,000m. in IMF and World Bank loans.

6 May 2001: Syria and Turkey agreed to proposals for joint military training excercises.

10 May 2001: The European Court of Human Rights found Turkey guilty of abusing Greek Cypriots' rights to life, liberty and security during its occupation of northern Cyprus; Turkey criticized the ruling.

16 May 2001: The ambassador to France, Sonmez Koksals, returned to the consulate in Paris.

22 May 2001: Mehmet Kutlular, the leader of the Muslim Brotherhood, Nur (Light), was sentenced to two years' imprisonment for attempting to incite anti-secularist unrest; in a speech in 1999, he had proclaimed that an earthquake in that year was God's revenge for the Government's secularist policy.

5 June 2001: The Minister of the Interior, Saadettin Tantan, was dismissed and demoted to a junior post of overseeing customs operations. He had been involved in a public dispute with his party leader, the Deputy Prime Minister, Mesut Yılmaz; two days later he was dismissed from the ANAP and resigned from Government.

7 June 2001: The TGNA approved amendments to the broadcast law, giving the Government greater control over the media—notably, radio and television programmes were prohibited from promoting violence or separatism.

22 June 2001: The Constitutional Court proscribed the FP, for inciting anti-Government religious unrest.

13 July 2001: The IMF and the World Bank agreed to resume a programme of loans following the Government's promise of economic reform.

15 July 2001: The Government announced that it would not build any more prison buildings in the controversial new design; the protesters subsequently ended their hunger-strike, in which 29 prisoners had died.

21 July 2001: A new Islamist party, Saadet (Prosperity), was founded by former members of the FP; its leader, Recai Kutan, claimed that the party would protect religious rights without challenging the secular basis of the Turkish state.

United Arab Emirates

16th century AD: Portuguese merchants came to dominate the Persian (Arabian) Gulf and the settlements on its southern shores. Among these settlements were various centres of sea-faring peoples.

1633: British naval forces assumed control of the Persian (Arabian) Gulf. They came into conflict with the Qawasim, a confederation of sea-faring tribes whom the British accused of piracy.

1793: The Bani Yas, a confederation of Bedouin tribes from the Arabian interior, established a presence at Abu Dhabi.

1800: The Wahhabis, a puritanical Muslim sect based in central Arabia, occupied al-Burayami.

1803–66: The Qawasim Sheikh Sultan bin Saqr ruled Ras al-Khaimah and Sharjah as a maritime power.

1806: A treaty was signed between the Qawasim and the United Kingdom in Bandar 'Abbas (Iran) by which the Arab tribes agreed to desist from their perceived piracy and respect the British East India Company's flag and possessions.

1807–13: The Wahhabi governor of al-Burayami encouraged the Qawasim who had become Wahhabis, to attack Muscat (now Oman).

1809: The British mounted a punitive expedition against the Qawasim.

1818: A British expedition was directed against pirates at their headquarters of Ras al-Khaimah.

1820: A treaty was agreed between Britain and the Arab tribes in the Gulf which dealt with the suppression of piracy and the slave trade. A British squadron was stationed at Ras al-Khaimah to enforce the treaty.

1830: The Bani Yas challenged the Qawasim maritime dominance.

1833: The Al Bu Falasa, a sub-tribe of the Bani Yas, settled in Dubai.

1835: The leaders of the various states and tribes in the region, the sheikhs, agreed a truce forbidding hostilities by sea during the pearling season.

1846: An unofficial agreement was established between the British and the Governor of the Persian province of Fars to act against pirates.

May 1853: A 'treaty of maritime peace in perpetuity' was concluded on the newly named 'Trucial Coast' (also known as Trucial Oman), supervised by the British.

1866: The Qawasim lands were divided after the death of Sultan bin Saqr, resulting in Qawasim decline against the increasing strength of the rulers of Abu Dhabi (whose rule was based on land rather than naval power).

1866: The Chief Sheikh of Sharjah died—his lands were divided among his four sons; thus the number of Trucial states increased from five to nine.

1870s: Dubai became the largest port on the Trucial Coast.

1892: The British entered into a series of exclusive treaties with the Trucial rulers.

1935: The British-controlled Iraq Petroleum Company began petroleum-exploration activities in the Trucial states.

1938: A subsidiary of the Iraq Petroleum Company, Petroleum Development Trucial Coast, obtained concessions from the Sheikhs of Dubai, Kalba, Ras al-Khaimah and Sharjah.

1939: Sheikh Shakhbut bin Sultan an-Nahyan agreed to award a petroleum concession for Abu Dhabi to Petroleum Development Trucial Coast.

1945–48: Abu Dhabi and Dubai were at war, as Sheikh Shakhbut claimed his lands extended as far north as Jabal 'Ali.

1952: Kalba was incorporated into Sharjah and, on British advice, the Trucial States Council was established; the body met at least twice a year under the chairmanship of the British political agent in Dubai.

1952: The Trucial Oman Levies, a force established by the British, expelled the Saudis from the Buryami oasis to which they were laying claim.

1958: Petroleum was discovered offshore in Abu Dhabi's waters.

16 June 1966: Banks in the Persian Gulf and Trucial States, except Abu Dhabi, adopted the Saudi Riyal as the official currency.

6 August 1966: Sheikh Shakhbut of Abu Dhabi was deposed by his family; he was succeeded by Sheikh Zayed bin Sultan, who pledged to use petroleum revenues to develop the country.

21–25 November 1969: A meeting of the Federation of Arab Emirates (formed in 1968 by the Trucial States, Bahrain and Qatar) in Abu Dhabi provisionally chose Sheikh Zayed as President, Sheikh Rashid (Dubai) as Vice-President and Abu Dhabi as the capital.

14 February 1971: A new, five-year agreement was signed by 23 international petroleum companies and the governments of Abu Dhabi, Iran, Iraq, Kuwait, Qatar and Saudi Arabia.

18 July 1971: Six of the seven Trucial States agreed to federate before the British withdrew from the Gulf at the end of the year; Ras al-Khaimah elected to become independent.

29 November 1971: The Sheikh of Sharjah agreed to share the island of Abu Musa with Iran.

1 December 1971: The United Kingdom's treaties with the Trucial States were terminated.

2 December 1971: The United Arab Emirates (UAE) was formed, following the secession of Bahrain and Qatar from the Federation; Ras al-Khaimah confirmed its decision not to join the newly independent state.

29 January 1972: Sheikh Khalid, the Ruler of Sharjah, was killed by rebels; following the apprehension of the insurgents, Sheikh Sultan, Khalid's younger brother, assumed power.

10 February 1972: Ras al-Khaimah joined the UAE.

5 October 1972: Agreement was reached between Abu Dhabi, Iraq, Kuwait, Qatar and Saudi Arabia for one part, and representatives of various petroleum companies for the other, on the eventual 51% participation of the producing countries in the various concessions.

1973: The UAE participated in the petroleum boycotts which were instigated to support the Arab cause in the October War of 1973, including a total ban on exports to the USA (which it was the first of the Arab states to impose).

20 May 1973: The UAE dirham was introduced in the UAE, replacing the Bahraini dinar in Abu Dhabi and the Qatar/Dubai riyal in Dubai and other Emirates.

December 1973: The separate Abu Dhabi Government was disbanded and some of its ministers became federal ministers.

1974: The Buryami between Abu Dhabi and Saudi Arabia was settled.

April 1975: The emirate of Abu Dhabi, Oman and Saudi Arabia signed a demarcation agreement, which ended the territorial dispute over the Al-Burayami oasis.

May 1975: The rulers of the individual Emirates gave their consent to greater centralization of governance.

November 1975: Sharjah merged its National Guard with the Union Defence Force and granted control of its broadcasting station, police and courts to Federal Ministries. Abu Dhabi, Fujairah and Sharjah all discontinued the use of their separate flags, using instead the UAE flag.

1976: The merger was announced of the separate defence forces of Abu Dhabi, Dubai, and Ras al-Khaimah into the United Defence Force or UDF, after Sheikh Zayed bin Sultan had demanded an acceleration of the process of centralization.

January 1977: The Council of Ministers was reorganized on the basis of individual merit rather than equal representation of the emirates.

1 March 1977: The Federal National Council was inaugurated.

February 1979: The Islamic Revolution in Iran provoked a meeting of the Council of Ministers and the Federal National Council. It produced a 10-point memorandum advocating the abolition of internal borders, the unification of defence forces and one unified federal budget.

March 1979: Dubai rejected the memorandum agreed in February and with Ras al-Khaimah boycotted a Supreme Council meeting.

July 1979: Sheikh Rashid of Dubai became federal Prime Minister. A new Council of Ministers was formed, resuming the system of maintaining the balance of representation. Ras al-Khaimah integrated its defence force with the federal forces and Abu Dhabi and Dubai pledged 50% of the petroleum revenues to the federal budget; the new Government pledged to improve the country's social services and communications infrastructure.

May 1981: Bahrain, Kuwait, Oman, Qatar, Saudi Arabia and the United Arab Emirates founded the Co-operation Council for Arab states of the Gulf (Gulf Co-operation Council—GCC) to promote economic and military co-operation in the region.

November 1981: Sheikh Rashid was re-elected federal Prime Minister and Sheikh Zayed was re-elected President.

1982: A bilateral defence agreement was signed with Saudi Arabia.

1984: UAE donations to Iraq were reported to have been discontinued.

March 1985: Sheikh Zayed pledged support for Lebanon against the Israeli occupation forces.

November 1985: Diplomatic relations were established between the UAE and USSR.

October 1986: Sheikh Rashid and Sheikh Zayed were re-elected as Prime Minister and President respectively.

June 1987: There was an attempted *coup d'état* in Sharjah during the absence of the ruler, Shiekh Sultan bin Muhammad al-Qasimi; the ruler's brother, Sheikh Abd al-Aziz, announced Sheikh Sultan's abdication, on the grounds of his mismanagement of the economy. Dubai intervened and the Supreme Council of Rulers endorsed Sheikh Sultan as the legitimate ruler, while granting a seat to his brother on the Supreme Council (as Crown Prince of Sharjah).

July 1987: Sheikh Sultan established an executive council to assist in the administration of the public affairs of the emirate.

August 1987: A Panamanian-registered supertanker struck a mine off the coast of the UAE near Fujairah. The UAE declared the port of Fujairah a danger zone and mine-sweeping operations were carried out.

November 1987: Diplomatic relations between the UAE and Egypt were resumed.

November 1987: At an extraordinary meeting of the Arab League the UAE condemned Iran's continuation of the war against Iraq and recommended the adoption of UN Resolution 598 which called for an immediate cease-fire.

April 1988: The Mubarak petroleum field in Sharjah was closed for two months after an attack on it by forces involved in the war between Iran and Iraq.

7 October 1990: Sheikh Rashid bin Said al-Maktoum, Vice-President and Prime Minister of the UAE and Ruler of Dubai, died.

19 February 1994: The UAE Minister of Petroleum and Mineral Resources resigned.

20 February 1994: Application of Islamic *Shari'a* law in the UAE was extended.

12–13 April 1994: The military committee of the GCC met for the first time in Dubai.

17 May 1995: The UAE Minister of Health resigned.

7 June 1995: The federal Council of Ministers was reorganized.

25 March 1997: The UAE's federal Government was reorganized.

5 October 2000: The first direct flight from the Gulf States to Iraq since the imposition of international sanctions 10 years previously travelled from Sharjah with the UAE's health minister and several heads of government departments on board.

8 October 2000: The first direct flight from Sharjah to the Afghan city of Kandahar took place; the Taliban administration in Afghanistan and the private Emiri Dolfin airline signed an agreement for weekly flights between the two countries.

2 December 2000: The President of the UAE called on Iran to vacate the islands of Abu Musa and the Greater and Lesser Tunbs, which had been in dispute between the two countries.

January 2001: The Minister of Information and Culture ordered a review of current legislation prohibiting the media from debating controversial parliamentary issues or criticizing public institutions.

1 January 2001: A GCC communique expressed support for Abu Dhabi's claims on Abu Musa and the Tunbs islands.

24 February 2001: The Indonesian President, Abdurrahman Wahid, met senior government officials for discussions on developments in the Islamic world and bilateral co-operation.

25 February 2001: At a meeting of the Arab Inter-Parliamentary Union, President an-Nahyan urged the Arab nations to work together to terminate international economic sanctions on Iraq; the President also asked the delegates for assistance in the long-running dispute with Iran over the Persian Gulf islands of Abu Musa, Greater and Lesser Tunb.

25 February 2001: Sheikh Zayed, the President of the UAE, urged Arab countries to work to end international sanctions on Iraq.

31 March 2001: The Iranian Government announced that it had summoned the UAE's ambassador to its foreign ministry to begin discussions regarding the dispute over the disputed islands; however, Iran maintained its claim to the islands, and insisted the Abu Dhabi renounce its ambitions.

9 April 2001: Dubai arrested a number of American missionaries, accusing them of promoting Christianity.

18 April 2001: Following a two-year government investigation, several high-ranking civil servants were convicted of embezzlement. The Director-General of Ports and Customs and chairman of the World Customs Organization, Obaid Saqr bin Busit, was sentenced to 27 years' imprisonment; six other officials were given similar sentences.

4 June 2001: The GCC urged Iran to accept the arbitration of the International Court of Justice (ICJ, which had recently ruled on the subject of the Hawar islands, disputed by Bahrain and Qatar) in the dispute over the Persian Gulf Islands.

7 June 2001: The President pardoned some 6,000 prisoners, who had been convicted of drug-related or financial crimes, on humanitarian grounds.

1 July 2001: A British national, Lee Ashurst, was convicted of seriously damaging the state internet system; he was fined US $2,700.

23 July 2001: The Minister of Foreign Affairs, Sheikh Hamdan bin Zayed an-Nayhan, visited Iran for discussions regarding the Persian Gulf Islands; the Iranian Government reiterated its objection to the involvement of a third party, such as the GCC or the ICJ, in solving the dispute.

24 July 2001: The Palestinian leader, Yasser Arafat, held talks with the President regarding the conflict in Israel.

Yemen

1st century AD: The Himyarite kingdom of the Yemen traded in frankincense and myrrh with the Roman Empire.

4th century: The Himyarites established their capital at San'a.

6th century: Dhu Nuwas, the last Himyarite king, converted to Judaism.

525: Christian invaders from Ethiopia defeated the Himyarites, breaking the great dam at Marib.

575: Persian control was established in Yemen.

628: The Persian governor of Yemen converted to Islam.

819: Muhammad bin Ziyad became the first independent Muslim ruler of Yemen and founded the Ziyadi dynasty, which ruled in Yemen until 1018.

860s: The bin Ya'furids, claiming descent from the ancient kings of Himyar, took San'a as their capital.

893: The first Zaidi Imam, al-Hadi Yahya, arrived in Yemen. The Zaidi form of Shi'a Islam was established and the Zaidi Imans subsequently became the spiritual leaders of the majority of the country.

11th century: The Ma'nids came to power in Aden and Hadramawt. The Ziyadis in the north were ousted by the Najahids, originally their own Abyssinian slave soldiers.

1128–1446: The Rasulid dynasty ruled Yemen.

16th century: In common with the majority of Arabia, Yemen became incorporated into the Ottoman Empire.

1506: A new line of Zaidi Imams was inaugurated by Sharaf al-Din Yahya.

1513: Aden was attacked by the Portuguese naval commander Afonso de Albuquerque.

1635: The Ottomans were expelled from Yemen by the Zaidi Imam al-Mu'ayyad Muhammad.

1839: Aden became a British protectorate.

1849: The Ottomans returned to northern Yemen.

1870s: A Yemeni revolt against the Ottomans escalated into war.

1904: A border commission surveyed the area and established a border between Ottoman and British territories. Imam Mahmud Yahya bin Hamid ad-Din proclaimed *jihad* (holy war) against the Ottoman Empire.

April 1905: An agreement was reached with the Ottoman governor, ceding San'a to the Imamate; however, the Imperial Government sent Ahmad Faidi Pasha to retake San'a.

1911: The Agreement of Da'an was signed which recognised the autonomy of the Imam's territory.

1915: During the First World War, in which the British and Ottomans were in conflict, Aden was surrounded and isolated by Ottoman troops and Yemeni volunteers.

1918: Upon the dissolution of the Ottoman Empire at the end of the First World War, Imperial troops left Yemen and the Zaidi Imam Yahya was in control of the country.

1930s: The Hadramawt was incorporated into the Aden protectorates by the British Governor, Harold Ingrams.

March 1945: Egypt, Iraq, Lebanon, Saudi Arabia, Syria, Transjordan and Yemen founded the League of Arab States (Arab League), which aimed to promote political, cultural, economic and social co-operation between its members and act as mediator in regional disputes.

1948: Imam Yahya was assassinated in a *coup d'état* by forces opposed to feudal rule. He was succeeded by his son Ahmad.

1955: There was an assassination attempt on Imam Ahmad.

2 March 1958: Yemen signed an agreement with the United ARab Republic (UAR—formed by the union of Egypt and Syria) to form a federal union known as the United Arab State.

2 May 1958: A state of emergency was declared in Aden.

11 January 1959: The statute of the Arab Development Bank was signed by Jordan, Lebanon, Libya, Saudi Arabia, the UAR and Yemen.

11 February 1959: The Constitution of the Federation of South Arabia, formed by the six Arab Amirates of the Protectorate of Aden, was proclaimed.

27 March 1961: Imam Ahmad was the subject of a failed assassination attempt.

26 December 1961: The UAR dissolved its union with Yemen.

27 September 1962: A *coup d'état* took place in Yemen, led by Col Abdullah Sallal. The Imam fled to a remote area of the country.

1 March 1963: With British approval, Aden joined the Federation of South Arabia.

14 April 1963: A Republican Constitution was promulgated in Yemen.

24 June 1963: Hassan Ali Bayoumi, Aden's first Chief Minister, died.

10 December 1963: A grenade was thrown at the region's rulers, assembled for a conference at Aden airport; two persons were killed and the conference was postponed.

28 April 1964: A new Republican Constitution was published in Yemen.

13 July 1964: A Joint Co-ordination Council was estblished by the UAR and Yemen.

13 August 1964: The UN Observer Mission was withdrawn from Yemen.

7 December 1964: The British Government proposed the creation of a unified state comprising all the states of South Arabia.

4 March 1965: Abdul Qawi Makkawi formed a new Government in Aden.

24 April 1965: Lt-Gen. Hassan al-Amri, who had taken office as Prime Minister in Yemen in January, resigned; Mohammed Ahmed No'man formed a new cabinet.

2 May 1965: A peace conference commenced at Khamer.

9 May 1965: An interim republican Constitution was announced for Yemen, o replace that enacted the previous year.

21 July 1965: Following the failure of the peace conference, No'man resigned; al-Amri was appointed to lead a new Government.

11–15 August 1965: Further negotiations aimed at ending the war in Yemen were held at Taif (Saudi Arabia).

24 August 1965: A peace agreement for Yemen was signed by the Saudi monarch, King Faisal and President Gamal abd an-Nasser of the UAR.

31 August 1965: The Speaker of Aden's Parliament was assassinated.

25 September 1965: The Constitution in Aden was suspended; the British High Commissioner assumed direct rule. A period of civil unrest, including a general strike, followed.

November–December 1965: The Haradh Conference between Republicans and Royalists in proved inconclusive.

14 February 1966: The Federation of South Arabia submitted new proposals for a United Republic of South Arabia.

4–11 April 1966: Talks were held between representatives of the Federation and of the Front for the Liberation of Occupied South Yemen in Beirut (Lebanon).

25 May 1966: Discussions on the future defence of South Arabia took place between delegations from the Federation and from the United Kingdom; draft British legislation published in February had stated that British forces would withdraw from Aden to Bahrain upon the territory's independence, scheduled for 1968.

9 June 1966: The United Kingdom agreed to contribute to the cost of the defence of South Arabia, but refused to engage in a defence treaty.

18 September 1966: A delegation, led by al-Amri, flew to Cairo to demand that the UAR cease involvement in Yemen and that President Sallal be removed; the delegation was detained by UAR forces and President Sallal assumed the premiership. A purge of anti-UAR elements in the armed forces and administration subsequently took place.

5 January 1967: The UAR air force carried out a raid on Ketaf in Yemen.

6 June 1967: The United Kingdom and the USA were accused by President Nasser of the UAR and King Hussein of Jordan of military collusion with Israel; 10 Arab states imposed an embargo on petroleum supplies to the two countries. Diplomatic relations with the USA were suspended by Algeria, Iraq, Sudan, Syria, the UAR and Yemen; Iraq and Syria terminated relations with the United Kingdom.

29–31 August 1967: At a conference of Arab heads of state at Khartoum (Sudan), King Faisal and President Nasser agreed a further Yemen peace settlement; all UAR troops were to be withdrawn and President Sallal was to lead a transitional administration, pending a referendum on the country's future governance.

5 November 1967: President Sallal, who opposed the Saudi-UAR peace proposals, was overthrown; a new three-man Presidency Council took power.

20–30 November 1967: The Federation of South Arabia and Aden achieved independence as the 'People's Republic of Southern Yemen' (PRSY). The last British troops left, and the National Liberation Front (NLF, a left-wing organization) took over government—Qahtan as-Shaabi was appoined President.

23 December 1967: Gen. al-Amri formed a new cabinet in Yemen.

28–30 July 1968: Extensive fighting with rebel forces was reported in Southern Yemen; the NLF regime sent a delegation to Taiz, Yemen, for the first official talks with the Yemen Republic (YR).

22 June 1969: President as-Shaabi of the PRSY was overthrown and replaced by a five-member Presidential Council.

3 September 1969: A new YR Cabinet was formed by Abdallah Kurshoumi.

25 November–3 December 1969: Armed conflict took place on the border between Saudi Arabia and the YR.

27 November 1969: An extensive programme of nationalization was announced in the PRSY.

5 February 1970: Muhsin al-Aini became Prime Minister of the YR, leading a reshuffled cabinet.

23 May 1970: The YR Government was reorganized and expanded to include former Royalist supporters.

20–24 July 1970: France, Saudi Arabia and the United Kingdom recognized the YR.

30 November 1970: A new Constitution was promulgated in the PRSY, which was thereby renamed the People's Democratic Republic of Yemen (PDRY).

28 December 1970: The first permanent Constitution of the Yemen Arab Republic (YAR, as the YR was renamed) was proclaimed.

5 May 1972: The Omani air force attcked border positions of the PDRY.

3 August 1972: The Government of the PDRY nationalized residential and commercial housing; each family was allowed to retain one dwelling.

26 September 1972: Serious fighting occurred on the border between the PDRY and the YAR.

4–12 October 1972: An Arab League mediation mission in Aden and Sana'a secured a cease-fire between the PDRY and the YAR.

21–28 October 1972: Delegations from the two Yemeni states met in Cairo for peace talks and agreed on the eventual unification of the two countries.

28 November 1972: President Iriani of the YAR and President Rubbayi of the PDRY signed an agreement for eventual unification of their two countries in the presence of Col Muammar al-Qaddafi, in Tripoli, Libya.

13 June 1974: A 10-member Military Command Council seized power in the YAR, led by the pro-Saudi Lt-Col Ibrahim al-Hamadi.

January 1975: Abd al-Aziz Abd al-Ghani replaced Mohsin al-Aini as Prime Minister of the YAR.

October 1977: Hamadi was killed by unknown assassins in San'a. Lt-Col Ahmad bin Hussain al-Ghashmi another member of the Military Command Council (MCC) took over as Chairman and martial law was imposed.

February 1978: The MCC appointed a Constituent People's Assembly.

April 1978: The Assembly elected al-Ghashmi President of the Republic and the MCC was dissolved.

June 1978: President al-Ghashmi was killed by a bomb carried in the suitcase of a PDRY envoy.

July 1978: The Constituent People's Assembly elected a senior military officer, Lt-Col 'Ali Abdullah Saleh, as President of the YAR.

July 1978: President Rubbayi 'Ali of the PDRY was deposed and executed by opponents within the ruling party, the United Political Organization—National Front (UPO—NF).

October 1978: Abd al-Fattah Ismail became Secretary-General of the newly constituted Yemen Socialist Party (YSP) which had been formed from the UPO—NF alliance.

December 1978: Ismail was appointed head of state of the PDRY by a newly elected Supreme People's Council (SPC).

February 1979: A revolt among disaffected YAR politicians won the support of the PDRY; armed confrontations took place.

March 1979: At a meeting in Kuwait, arranged by the Arab League, the two Yemeni states signed an agreement pledging unification.

4–6 March 1979: Iraq, Jordan and Syria attended negotiations in Kuwait to mediate a cease-fire between the People's Democratic Republic of Yemen and the Yemen Arab Republic.

April 1980: In the PDRY, Ali Nasser Muhammad replaced Ismail as Head of State, Chairman of the Presidium of the SPC and Secretary-General of the YSP as well as retaining his post as Prime Minister.

December 1981: The PDRY and the YAR signed a draft constitution for a unified state and established a joint PDRY-YAR Yemen Council to monitor progress towards unification.

May 1983: President Saleh resigned at an extraordinary meeting of the Constituent People's Assembly and declared his intention to seek re-election to the presidency. He was nominated and unanimously re-elected by the Assembly for a further five-year term.

August 1983: The first meeting of the joint PDRY-YAR Yemen Council was held in San'a.

October 1983: President Muhammad was re-elected to the posts of Secretary-General of the YSP and of its Political Bureau for a further term of five years.

March 1984: A joint committee on foreign policy from the YAR and the PDRY met in Aden.

February 1985: President Muhammad resigned the post of Prime Minister but retained his other senior posts in the government of the PDRY. The former President, Abd al-Fattah Ismail, returned from exile and was reappointed to the Secretariat of the YSP's Central Committee.

13 January 1986: Three members of the PDRY's enlarged Political Bureau were killed when President Muhammad's personal guard opened fire on six members who had come to meet with the President. In Aden the situation deteriorated as rival elements of the armed forces fought for control.

24 January 1986: Al-Attas, the Prime Minister of the PDRY (who had been in India at the start of the troubles) was named head of an interim administration after Muhammad was dismissed from all his party and state posts (he, and many of his supporters, later fled to exile, chiefly in the YAR). The USSR formally recognized the new regime.

February 1986: A new government of the PDRY was formed with al-Attas as President and Dr Yasin Said Numan, the former Deputy Prime Minister, as Prime Minister.

March 1986: A general amnesty was announced and Muhammad's supporters were encouraged to return from the YAR where some 10,000 had sought refuge.

July 1986: Presidents Saleh and Al-Attas met for the first time in Tripoli (Libya) at the invitation of Col al-Qaddafi to discuss unification.

December 1986: In the PDRY an election was held to the SPC.

1987: Kuwait acted as mediator between the two Yemeni states in an attempt to facilitate the return of refugees to the PDRY.

July 1987: About half of the refugees from the YAR were reported to have returned to the PDRY.

October 1987: An armed confrontation arose from a long-standing border dispute between the Oman and the PDRY, resulting in 10 deaths.

1988: A preliminary agreement on a formal demarcation of the border between Oman and the PDRY was reached during a visit to Muscat by President al-Attas, the first by a PDRY head of state.

May 1988: The two Yemeni Governments agreed to withdraw troops from their mutual border and create a demilitarized zone between Marib and Shabwah.

July 1988: The first general election took place in the YAR for the new 159-member Consultative Council. A quarter of the seats were won by the Muslim Brotherhood candidates. President Saleh was re-elected later in the same month by the chamber.

July 1988: A programme of reforms was introduced in the PDRY indicating the country's intention to create a free-market economy.

November 1988: An agreement was signed to unify the two Yemeni states.

1 December 1989: A draft constitution for a unified Republic of Yemen was published.

18 February 1990: The border between the two Yemeni states was opened.

22 May 1990: The unified Republic of Yemen was proclaimed; San'a was proclaimed the political capital and Aden the economic centre. The YAR's President Saleh became the new state's President, Ali Salim abd al-Baid, the Secretary-General of the Central Committee of the YSP, became Vice-President, and the President of the PDRY, al-Attas, became Prime Minister.

15–16 May 1991: The new Yemeni Constitution was approved by popular referendum; many groups boycotted the referendum, claiming that the document did not accord sufficient status to Islam.

27 April 1993: In the election to the House of Representatives, the General People's Congress (GPC—a grouping of President Saleh's supporters) secured 123 of the 300 seats, the Yemeni Islah Party (YIP—a new Islamic party) won 62 and the YSP 56.

May 1993: The GPC and YSP announced a merger; a new 31-member Government, with representatives of all three major parties, was announced, al-Attas remaining as Prime Minister.

August 1993: Al-Baid withdrew from the political process and returned to Aden, claiming that the north dominated the new state and that numerous YSP politicians had been assassinated since unification.

October 1993: The House of Representatives elected a new Presidential Council which, in turn, re-elected Saleh as its chairman and thus to a four-year term as President. Al-Baid was re-elected to the vice-presidency in his absence.

November 1993: The armed forces of the PDRY and YAR, which had failed to integrate since unification, reportedly deployed units along the former frontier.

December 1993: Delegations from the GPC and the YSP commenced negotiations aimed at resolving the political crisis; in the same month, President Saleh announced that he would accept proposals made by al-Baid for his return to San'a and reincorporation into the political life of the unified state.

18 January 1994: The principal Yemeni political parties signed a 'Document of Pledge and Agreement', aimed at resolving the political crisis; the President and Vice-President signed the document in February.

27 April 1994: The First Deputy Prime Minister, Hassan Muhammad Makki, was injured in an assassination attempt. Fighting between army units from the two precursor states escalated.

5 May 1994: President Saleh declared a state of emergency and dismissed al-Baid from the vice-presidency. Missile attacks were launched by both sets of forces against cities and military targets in the other's territory.

9 May 1994: President Saleh dismissed al-Attas, replacing him as Prime Minister with the Minister of Industry, Muhammad Said al-Attar; forces of the former YAR attempted to capture Aden.

21 May 1994: Al-Baid declared the independence of the new Democratic Republic of Yemen (DRY), with the same territory as the former PDRY; al-Baid was appointed President of the new state.

23 May 1994: A new coalition Government was formed in Yemen.

1 June 1994: The UN Security Council adopted Resolution 924, urging an immediate cease-fire in the civil war in Yemen; on the same day the House of Representatives etended the state of emergency.

2 June 1994: Al-Baid announced the formation of a Government in the DRY, led by al-Attas.

7 July 1994: Republican forces captured Aden, officially ending the civil war— al-Baid was believed to have fled to Oman and sought political asylum there.

September 1994: President Saleh introduced constitutional amendments providing for the direct election of the President and the redrafting of legislation so that *Shari'a* formed the basis of the country's legal system.

1 October 1994: President Saleh was re-elected.

6 October 1994: A new Council of Ministers, led by Abd al-Aziz al-Ghani and containing members of the GPC, YIP and independents, was announced.

26 February 1995: Yemen and Saudi Arabia signed a memorandum of understanding on their border dispute.

13 June 1995: The Council of Ministers was reshuffled, with all independents being replaced by GPC members.

20 July 1996: The Government published a five-year economic development Plan.

27 April 1997: Legislative elections resulted in an increase in the GPC's strength in the House of Representatives from 123 to 187 seats, compared with 53 won by the YIP and a total of 54 won by independent candidates.

12 May 1997: Al-Ghani submitted his Government's resignation; Faraj Said bin Ghanim was subsequently appointed to lead a new administration.

26 May 1997: The Governments of Oman and Yemen signed maps officially demarcating their joint border.

March 1998: Al-Baid, al-Attas and three other rebel leaders were sentenced to death *in absentia*.

28 April 1998: The Prime Minister, bin Ghanim, resigned following reported differences with President Saleh; the Deputy Prime Minister and Minister of Foreign Affairs, Abd al-Karim al-Iryani, was appointed as his successor.

16 May 1998: A new Government, including three new ministers, was appointed in Yemen.

8 September 1998: The Minister of Religious Endowments and Guidance, Ahmad Muhammad ash-Shami, resigned, citing undue political interference.

23 September 1999: The first direct presidential election was held in Yemen; Saleh was elected with 96.3% of the votes cast.

12 June 2000: The Ministers of Foreign Affairs of Saudi Arabia and Yemen signed an agreement delineating two countries' mutual land and maritime borders.

3 October 2000: The alleged new leader of the illegal Adeb-Abyan Islamic Army, Hatim Muhsin bin Fahrid, was sentenced to seven years' imprisonment.

12 October 2000: A suicide-bomb attack was perpetrated on a US vessel, the USS *Cole*, in Aden harbour; 17 US naval personnel were killed and a further 37 wounded. The following day two Islamic militant groups, the Islamic Deterrence Forces and Muhammad's Army, claimed responsibility for the attacks; the US and Yemeni authorities subsequently began an investigation into the incident.

13 October 2000: A bomb exploded at the British Embassy in Yemen—an Islamic group claimed responsibility.

26 October 2000: The Yemeni authorities reported that they had arrested a number of Islamic miltants in connection with the bombing of the USS *Cole*; among the detainees were several members of Islamic Jihad.

26 October 2000: A number of Islamic militants were arrested in connection with the attack on the USS *Cole*; six people were charged with the attack in December.

20 November 2000: A further six Yemeni nationals were arrested in connection with the bomb attack on the USS *Cole*. The Government and the USA later concluded an anti-terrorism pact, which enabled US Federal Bureau of Investigations (FBI) agents to attend the interrogation of the suspects.

14 December 2000: The Saudi Arabia-Yemeni Co-operation Council convened for the first time since 1990. The Saudi Government agreed to reschedule the debts owed by Yemen and granted US $300m. in new loans for an extensive development programme.

7 January 2001: A bomb exploded at the office of the YSP in the town of Shaab; no casualties were reported.

10 January 2001: Six people were killed and 10 wounded when two gunmen opened fire inside a mosque at Dhibin; the motive of the attackers was unclear.

15 January 2001: It was reported that that the opposition parties had established an Opposition Co-ordination Council to assist them in their campaign against the GPC and the YIP in the imminent municipal elections.

23 January 2001: An aircraft carrying the US ambassador, which was travelling from San'a to Taiz, was the subject of an unsuccessful hijack by a Yemeni national claiming to be a supporter of the Iraqi leader, Saddam Hussain. The aircraft was diverted to Djibouti and the hijacker was detained; he was sentenced to 15 years' imprisonment in February.

29 January 2001: It was reported that the Government had agreed to postpone the trial of the Islamic militants accused of bombing the USS *Cole*; the US FBI agents had requested more time to investigate the statements made by the suspects.

17 February 2001: A further two suspects were arrested in connection with the USS *Cole* incident; the men were Yemeni nationals who had fought against Soviet troops in Afghanistan in the 1980s.

20 February 2001: Municipal elections and a national referendum on constitutional reform took place; the proposed amendments provided for the extension of the presidential term of office from five years to seven and the duration of the House of Representatives from four years to six, the abolition of the right of the

President to issue legislation by decree when the legislature was not in session and the creation of a 111-member Consultative Council. Voting was marred by allegations of electoral malpractice and by violence in several areas; it was reported that some 45 people were killed.

4 March 2001: The results of the municipal elections and the referendum were published, the GPC winning a majority of the the district and provincial council seats; however the results for four constituencies were not announced. It was reported that the constitutional amendments had been approved by 73% of the participating electorate.

24 March 2001: YIP supporters demonstrated outside of the High Electoral Committee's headquarters in San'a, demanding the publication of electoral results for the four remaining constituencies.

31 March 2001: The President dismissed al-Iryani; Abd al-Qadir Bajammal formed a new Government, comprising only GPC members.

24 April 2001: The first issue of a planned monthly human rights publication was banned.

28 April 2001: The new members of the Shura (Consultative Council) were appointed by Presidential decree.

4 May 2001: The British Foreign and Commonwealth Office supported a plea for clemency by five British nationals imprisoned in Yemen for terrorist activities.

16 May 2001: The National Defence Council announced the abolition of compulsory military service.

19 June 2001: Eight men were arrested on the charge of conspiring to attack the US embassy; the men were believed to be associates of the exiled Saudi Arabian dissident, Osama bin Laden.

29 June 2001: Eleven soldiers were killed in a gun battle with tribesmen in the Marib region; the soldiers had been attempting to capture suspects in connection with a bomb attack on an petroleum pipeline the previous day.

8 July 2001: The US embassy was reopened following the attempted bomb attack in June.

22 July 2001: Four Yemeni nationals were sentenced to between four and 15 years' imprisonment for bombing the British embassy in October 2000; the men claimed that the attack had been a display of solidarity with the Palestinians.